ROUTLEDGE LIBRARY EDITIONS: COLONIALISM AND IMPERIALISM

Volume 19

COLONIAL SEQUENCE 1949 TO 1969

COLONIAL SEQUENCE
1949 TO 1969

A Chronological Commentary upon British Colonial Policy in Africa

MARGERY PERHAM

LONDON AND NEW YORK

First published in 1970 by Methuen & Co Ltd

This edition first published in 2023
by Routledge
4 Park Square, Milton Park, Abingdon, Oxon OX14 4RN

and by Routledge
605 Third Avenue, New York, NY 10158

Routledge is an imprint of the Taylor & Francis Group, an informa business

© 1970 Margery Perham

All rights reserved. No part of this book may be reprinted or reproduced or utilised in any form or by any electronic, mechanical, or other means, now known or hereafter invented, including photocopying and recording, or in any information storage or retrieval system, without permission in writing from the publishers.

Trademark notice: Product or corporate names may be trademarks or registered trademarks, and are used only for identification and explanation without intent to infringe.

British Library Cataloguing in Publication Data
A catalogue record for this book is available from the British Library

ISBN: 978-1-032-41054-8 (Set)
ISBN: 978-1-032-45585-3 (Volume 19) (hbk)
ISBN: 978-1-032-45586-0 (Volume 19) (pbk)
ISBN: 978-1-003-37766-5 (Volume 19) (ebk)

DOI: 10.4324/9781003377665

Publisher's Note
The publisher has gone to great lengths to ensure the quality of this reprint but points out that some imperfections in the original copies may be apparent.

Disclaimer
The publisher has made every effort to trace copyright holders and would welcome correspondence from those they have been unable to trace.

Colonial Sequence
1949 to 1969

A CHRONOLOGICAL COMMENTARY UPON
BRITISH COLONIAL POLICY IN AFRICA

MARGERY PERHAM

METHUEN & CO LTD
11 NEW FETTER LANE LONDON EC4

First published in 1970
by Methuen & Co Ltd
11 *New Fetter Lane, London EC*4
© 1970 *by Margery Perham*
Printed in Great Britain by
Butler & Tanner Ltd
Frome and London
416 14930 8

Contents

INTRODUCTION
page xi
NOTES AND ACKNOWLEDGEMENTS
page xxiv
CHRONOLOGICAL TABLE
page xxv

LISTS OF ARTICLES, LETTERS AND WRITINGS

1949 JULY
    The Sudan Emerges into Nationhood   *Foreign Affairs*   *page* 1
  DECEMBER 16
    The High Commission Territories and Apartheid   [Letter] *The Times*   12

1950 FEBRUARY 14
    The Future of the Somalis   [Letter] *The Times*   15
  MARCH 18
    Seretse Khama   [Letter] *The Times*   17
  AUGUST 4
    Divided Policies in Africa   [Letter] *The Times*   20

1951 MAY 29
    The Banishment of Tshekedi   [Letter] *The Times*   23
  JUNE 26
    The Banishment of Tshekedi   [Letter] *The Times*   25
  JULY
    The British Problem in Africa   *Foreign Affairs*   26

1952 JANUARY 21
    The Sudan on the Edge of Independence   [Letter] *The Times*   40
  MARCH 4
    Central Africa: History of Remote Control   [Letter] *The Times*   42

CONTENTS

1952 MARCH 10
Central African Federation: [Letter] *The Times* 44
Lessons from History

APRIL 23
Egyptian Threat to Sudan's [Letter] *The Times* 45
Self-Government

JUNE
Introduction to *The Making of the*   *Faber & Faber* 47
Modern Sudan

OCTOBER 28
A Changing Continent   *The Times* 67

NOVEMBER 17
The Choice before the Sudan [Letter] *The Times* 72

1953 JANUARY 24
The Sudan: the Future of the [Letter] *The Times* 75
South

FEBRUARY 26
The Central African Federa- [Letter] *The Times* 76
tion: Dangers of its Speedy
Enactment

JUNE 9
On the Eve of Central African [Letter] *The Times* 78
Federation

JULY 12
Facilities for African Dissent [Letter] *The Spectator* 81

JULY 28
Central African University [Letter] *The Times* 82

Bringing a Nation to Birth   Draft of article for *The Times* 83

1954 FEBRUARY 10
Difficulties in Buganda [Letter] *The Times* 88

JUNE 16
Delicate Transfer of Rule in   *The Times* 90
the Sudan

DECEMBER 10
Britain's Response to the End of   *The Listener* 93
Colonialism

vi

CONTENTS

DECEMBER 31
Britain's Handling of Mau Mau [Letter] *The Times*   100

1955 MARCH
Nigeria Prepares for Independence   *The Times*   102
   MARCH 17 *The Problem of Unity*
          18 *The Problem of Staff*

APRIL
The Struggle against Mau Mau   *The Times*   108
   APRIL 22 *Bravery of the Kikuyu Christians*
         23 *Seeking the Causes and the Remedies*

JUNE 2
African Pro-Consul   *The Listener*   115

SEPTEMBER 5
Economics Versus Race   *The New Commonwealth*   122

DECEMBER 22
The Sudan after the Southern [Letter] *Manchester Guardian*   128
Rebellion

1956 SEPTEMBER
Foreword to *The Kenya Question: An African Answer*   Fabian Colonial Bureau   130

1957 FEBRUARY 21
A Land of Enormous Contrasts   *London Calling* (B.B.C.)   143

MARCH 18
Kenya after Mau Mau   *The Times*   146

JULY
Out of the Fellowship   *Africa South*   150

DECEMBER 16
The Future of the Somalis   [Letter] *The Times*   154

1958 JANUARY 12
The Motives for Man's Cruelties   [Letter] *The Observer*   156

1959 FEBRUARY 27
Disorders in Nyasaland: Six Questions for Britain   [Letter] *The Times*   158

CONTENTS

APRIL 25
Britain's Pledges in Central Africa   [Letter] *The Times*   159

MAY 6
Divergent Views on Central Africa   [Letter] *The Times*   160

JULY
White Minorities in Africa   *Foreign Affairs*   161
Christianity and Colonialism   *Conference of World Council of Churches* 172

DECEMBER 5
Hazards of Mr Macmillan's 'Wind of Change' Visit to Africa   [Letter] *The Times*   179

1960 JANUARY 5
The Administration of Enfranchisement   [Letter] *Manchester Guardian*   181

MARCH
The Psychology of African Nationalism   *Optima*   182

APRIL 9
Staffing the Transfer of Power   [Letter] *The Times*   198

MAY 12
Kenya: The Decisive Years   *The Listener*   200

JUNE 9
Federation in Central Africa on the Defensive   *The Listener*   206

JULY 4
Problems for the Somali Republic   *The Times*   212

OCTOBER 20
A Prospect of Nigeria   *The Listener*   215

1961 MARCH 15
White Minorities in Africa   [Letter] *The Times*   222

MAY 10
Portuguese Africa: the Achilles Heel   [Letter] *The Times*   223

CONTENTS

	AUGUST 17		
	Northern Rhodesia's Right to Secede	[Letter] *The Times*	225
1962	*Yesterday's Rulers:* Introduction	Oxford University Press	227
1963	Foreword to *Mau Mau Detainee*	Oxford University Press	233
	FEBRUARY 20		
	Kenya Settlers	*The Times*	243
	MARCH 21		
	Kenya in Travail	*The Listener*	247
	APRIL 4		
	Britain and Africa in 1963	*The Listener*	253
1964	Africa—Continent of Disillusion?		260
	SEPTEMBER		
	The African Studies Association of the United Kingdom	*Africa Society Journal*	263
	OCTOBER 28		
	Arthur Creech Jones, 1891–1964	[unpublished]	279
1965	JUNE 3		
	Britain's Role in a World of Racial Challenge	*The Listener*	283
	DECEMBER 20		
	Conservatives' responsibility for Rhodesia	[Letter] *The Times*	292
1966	JANUARY		
	The Rhodesian Crisis: the Background	*International Affairs*	294
	JANUARY 23		
	The Nigerian Crisis and After	*The Listener*	309
	JUNE 16		
	Rhodesia: a Search for Fundamentals	*The Listener*	315
	AUGUST 4		
	Preserving the Records of Empire	[Letter] *The Times*	325

CONTENTS

1966 SEPTEMBER 8
In Defence of the Commonwealth [Letter] *The Times* 326

OCTOBER 18
Conservatives' attitude to Central Africa [Letter] *The Times* 327

OCTOBER 29
Dr Adams and the University of Central Africa [Letter] *The Times* 329

1967 JUNE
Rejected Africans [Reviews] *The Listener* 330

OCTOBER 28
The Many Faces of African Socialism *Forum World Features* 332

1968 SEPTEMBER 7
Broadcast Addressed to Colonel Emeka Ojukwu 337

SEPTEMBER 12
The Nigerian War *The Times* 338

SEPTEMBER 19
War in Nigeria *The Listener* 343
The Nigerian Civil War [Letter] *The Times* 349

1969 JANUARY 23
Britain's Responsibilities for Nigeria's Troubles *Le Monde* 351

JANUARY 31
A Letter to General Gowon *The Spectator* 354

AUGUST 14
Kenya Revisited *BBC Third Programme* 356

Introduction

I must begin by repeating the opening words of the introduction to the first volume of the book which appeared in 1967.

> The publication of these occasional writings needs explanation and, I think, apology. The proposal came from a firm of publishers. I received it with surprise and some hesitation. It was only when I looked through the list of what I had published over thirty-five years that I realized that the collection might have an interest in addition to, or even apart from, any great intrinsic merit in the writings themselves. This interest could be in the serial impression made upon a single mind by the evolution of Britain's colonial policy and government over a long series of years, and these among the most important in our imperial record when the colonial empire at once reached its greatest extent and moved to its end with unforeseen rapidity and completeness. The main concentration in what follows is upon Britain's changing relations with Africa where our power has been at once so extensive, so complete and so brief.

This opening paragraph was obviously prompted by the fear that I had overstepped that boundary of humility at which even writers, all instinctive self-projectors, should draw back, especially in reproducing, as in my case, material which may seem so ephemeral as articles and letters in the daily press. Yet, on second thoughts, I cannot see that it would be so much less presumptuous to scramble all these miscellaneous writings into a new comprehensive form, trying to remember the eventful Africa, that is middle Africa, of the preceding thirty years in the relative tranquillity of 1970, rather than to serve them up in their raw contemporary form.

Before discussing the subject matter of the book there are two comments to make upon its form. Firstly, as with Volume I, the entries are printed with little or no annotation. A full explanatory background might prove to be very much longer than the article itself. But the letters, because of their brevity (how I envy Lugard and his two full columns in *The Times* of the nineties with a promise of more tomorrow) are less self-explanatory than the articles. Some of them are items in a serial

INTRODUCTION

correspondence, and to attempt to summarize other people's letters, even if space allowed, might well give offence to the writers. Articles and letters must therefore be left to speak for themselves in the hope that their interest will be less in their references to the events of the week or the month than in the general trend of current ideas and controversies.

Secondly, these writings are irregular in timing and in distribution because they were incidental to my main academic tasks of lecturing and writing at Oxford, and my travels were often undertaken not to study countries as a whole but to visit universities overseas as a member of the Executive Committee of the Inter-University Council for Higher Education Overseas. Further, it was less practicable for me in these years than in the two earlier decades to travel outside territories under British rule. There is therefore little reference to the French or Belgian colonies although these advanced into independence at much the same time as those of Britain. The omission is less serious because, for neighbouring states in one continent, there was extraordinarily little contact or co-operation between the three groups. In the later years of the period there were meetings between African political personalities both in Europe and in Ghana and the lead given by British dependencies aroused the ambitions of those of France and Belgium. Yet, though the end for all was independence, the three groups went forward by different ways and to somewhat different constitutional destinations.

So much for presentation. Let us turn to look at some of the main political issues raised by the emancipation of 'British' Africa which are the background to these writings.

We must first make allowance for our living now in a mood of reaction from all that the words imperialism and colonialism are held to cover. There seems a widespread temptation in this country first to condemn and then to forget. We want to forget because we know that the worldwide power in which many of our leaders and writers told our grandfathers to glory as the apotheosis of Anglo-Saxon, and especially British, political genius, has melted away in some thirty years. We feel ourselves left with lowered status in the world and in our own eyes. With no very clear vision as yet of any autonomous role in the future, we have become belated applicants for membership of a European group – if they will accept us. Many of the older people who were active in sustaining our former world-wide responsibilities overseas are still alive. But they tend to be silent and perhaps bewildered and distressed that so much which they achieved is either ignored or, if only by implication,

INTRODUCTION

condemned. Although their obituaries in *The Times* may suggest that they were giants in those days, to the younger generation they may seem giants of almost another species engaged like Hercules upon gigantic but unnecessary tasks.

To the young, indeed, these tasks may seem to have been not only unnecessary but injurious. They do not feel any obligation to study the record, even as a whole, still less in its many different chapters. It is enough that our former colonial subjects vigorously condemn their recent tutelage: good relations with them seem to demand agreement with their version of the past. Moreover, the narrower colonial theme has now broadened into the whole issue of race-relationships throughout the world and those who are rightly trying to achieve an ever-increasing equality between the races naturally stamp upon the unequal past in order to gain impetus to reach towards the equality of the future.

It would be more comfortable for those of my generation who have been concerned with Britain's colonial empire to offer the silence of apparent agreement with this natural and perhaps necessary mood. But I feel obliged to pass some comment upon it, carrying further, perhaps, some of the scattered ideas which can be seen developing in this book and, indeed, in both of its volumes.

The first question to ask is whether African civilization before the scramble was of such a quality that the impetus supplied by Britain, at a time, let it be remembered, when no other agency was available, was not only superfluous but injurious. This is the almost universal claim of African leaders today and one they find necessary both to give confidence to their own people and to explain the still surviving political and economic weakness of their new states. It is true that authorities of various academic disciplines have increasingly disclosed the uneven but often high cultures of pre-colonial Africa, while the response of Africans first to the stimulus of the British intrusion, and later to that of independence, has shown up the large miscalculation about inherent negro inferiority which is still maintained as the justification for white supremacy in southern Africa. But mistakes, past and present, can be over-compensated. Leaving aside the more advanced African groups, mainly in western Africa, and even forgetting much 'darkness' which the first explorers reported, to have travelled widely in Africa in the thirties is to have realized the isolation, poverty and disease of many millions of Africans, living in scattered huts of sticks and mud, and divided into some thousands of separate and often mutually hostile groups of various

INTRODUCTION

sizes and kinds. Whatever can be put upon the debit side – and I am considering here only the British colonial enterprise – some sixty-five years of colonial rule, after an inevitably slow start and two distracting world wars, gave African tribes peace and order within wide if arbitrary frontiers, the basic material and administrative structure of a modern state, and the actual or potential mastery of the diseases which preyed upon men, animals and plants. Add to these benefits access to the world and its accumulated knowledge.

At that period no other agency existed which had the resources or the moral and material interest to lay these essential foundations. I have often been surprised to find how Africans often boggle at the fact that Western nations had this material interest in annexing colonies, as if they should have undertaken these often risky and expensive annexations upon motives of the purest altruism. Viewed against history's records of the dealings of men with those they subjugated, the price paid by Africans over the years for our imperial services is small indeed. This is no more than a personal opinion on the morrow of decolonization: it may be many years before the full content of Britain's relationships with her former African dependencies, varying as they do in period and character, will be balanced in the historical ledger. To turn back the other pages of that ledger in order to get a comparative historical view is to find some terrible entries in other accounts, showing what the strong have done to the weak in the past and are even continuing to do today, even within independent Africa.

Another line of criticism against Britain's colonial record, and put as often by British as by African observers, is that though the British administration may have been humane relatively to other colonial systems, it was politically static. At its simplest and most unrealistic this comment can imply that, first among imperial rulers, the British, from the moment of annexation, should have begun to plan urgently for their own supersession. Or it can ask the more reasonable question as to whether at a later stage, in the light of advances in Africa and in the political climate of the world, the British, both at home and abroad, were not too slow to adjust themselves to the changes in the world which were sapping the foundations of colonial rule. I do not want to repeat here what I have said in some of the later entries in this book. But the history through which we have lived continually takes on new colours as it recedes and I think, looking back, that the responsible authorities, politicians, bureaucrats and members of parliament, were too slow to anticipate the changed relations which the Second World War

INTRODUCTION

had brought about in Britain's position and so in our relations with our colonies. The electorate could hardly be expected to make this estimate: the colonies and dependencies, some 43 of them, were too numerous, distant and heterogeneous to be clearly visualized. The colonial governors, few of whom had had political experience, were not always competent to work out the nexus between changes in Britain and in the world situation and changes in the African political mood. But they could at least have reported fully upon the latter. Perhaps, with inadequate response from London, some of them did: the archives of the period are still closed. The colonial service as a whole, though its members were increasingly better trained and brought on their leaves into closer contact with each other and with new ideas and techniques, was not in a position to influence the fundamentals of policy. The very nature of their work, in Africa mostly among tribes far from the colonial capitals, made it difficult for them not to regard native self-government as the disruption of their long-term tasks of betterment as well as the abrupt end of their own careers and of a task to which many felt a deep sense of dedication.

What then, is the charge that we can bring against ourselves in this matter of colonial emancipation? It is not that we made the greatest and most tragic error of failing to grant independence when the moment for it came – though there will be something to be said about this concerning central Africa – but that we did not possess anything like a general staff charged to take wide and prophetic views over the numerous units of lands and peoples which made up the colonial empire and, where appropriate, make preparations for the perceptible approach of self-government. True, the very size and heterogeneity of the dependencies made it difficult to construct any dominant theme of policy. But the alternative was not to be without a policy. It was, for example, nobody's business to apply lessons learnt in Asia to Africa. I think it is true to say that Lord Hailey was the first eminent authority to bestride the continents, but he confined his massive intelligence and almost superhuman energy to observe, record and comment upon the government of Africa. His comment was of course enriched by his long experience of Indian administration and there can be no doubt that within the walls of the Colonial Office he was an influential figure. But I understood from my contacts with him that he very deliberately eschewed the roles of prophet or propagandist that may have been needed to produce rapid and deep adjustments to change in our African policy.

It may be contested here that, allowing for the varieties, complexities and obscurities of the Africa under British rule, we have little need to be ashamed of our record of emancipation. I admit that it is difficult to generalize very confidently about such a large transaction as the enfranchisement of fifteen African dependencies within ten years. But I suggest that we were too slow to realize the effects of the Second World War, both in reducing our own strength and authority in the world and exalting that of two major nations, whose influence was, for different ideological reasons, inimical to our colonial power. These changes demanded rapid and basic adjustments in our relations with our African subjects. It is true that we did not make the grave major mistake of enforcing our rule after it had been seriously challenged. But because each dependency had its own special history and character we made a series of surrenders without sufficiently applying the lessons learned from one to improve the actual process of decolonization for the others.

Let us glance at the acts of enfranchisement serially. The Sudan came first on the list. The articles reproduced in this book will refer to the mistakes which I believe we made in handling the problems of the British service and of the equatorial south. These were fundamental lessons that could have been applied to later enfranchisements though no skill of management could have solved all the deep problems enclosed within arbitrary colonial frontiers. In Ghana independence grew out of long and close association and we had some able governors to handle the process. We could hardly have legislated for the sudden entry of Dr Nkrumah, who proved himself an erratic force which wrenched a relatively mature and united people out of the sober progression we and they might have expected and to which, we may hope, they are now returning. For Nigeria the process of emancipation was carried out over ten or more years in steady co-operative effort between British governors and ministers on one side and the African representatives on the other, and with widespread public consultations in the provinces. The final responsibility for the form of this large federation, now tragically at risk, rests as much, if not more, upon the Nigerian leaders as upon the British.[1] The fault on the British side in both emancipations was the serious one of lack of foresight in failing to train a sufficient number of Africans to take over the senior posts.

It is when we turn to east and central Africa, from Somaliland to the

[1] See the account of the prolonged constitutional discussions and experiments given by the Ibo scholar Dr K. Ezera in *Constitutional Development in Nigeria*, Oxford University Press, 1960.

INTRODUCTION

Rhodesias, that foresight was surely at its minimum. The achievement of independence in the west, which could have been foreseen for many years even if the exact date could not be foretold, should surely have warned the authorities concerned that a chain reaction was inevitable. and that vigorous and imaginative preparations were needed to meet it.

The exposed position of Somaliland, and the planned and dated independence of neighbouring Somalia, should have demanded a 'crash' course of education for political and administrative responsibility. The conflict of Somalia's and Kenya's interests on their frontier was belatedly foreseen but only to the extent of inviting external commissioners to draw up a report upon which Britain did not, and at that very late stage perhaps could not, take any action. The cost was a prolonged, bloody and expensive conflict in this region, and the breaking of relations with Britain by a Somalia which greatly needed our help and could have been a good ally in a highly strategic position. Relations all round have lately been restored and we can only hope they will endure. Shifting our view southward, it is impossible to do more in this brief comment than refer to the different ways in which the East African states achieved independence. Because the British authorities were slow to realize the dynamic effect upon these territories of enfranchisement elsewhere in Africa, in all of them far too little was done to build up African services as successors to our own. Uganda profited from the vigorous liberalism of Sir Andrew Cohen, who pushed on training and development in many directions. But his work was to some extent thwarted by the deep fissure between the component parts of the Protectorate which British authority over the years had done too little to moderate, and which has greatly distorted Uganda's subsequent political development. Kenya figures largely in the pages which follow and it is perhaps unnecessary to dwell here upon the major miscalculation over the physical and political place of white settlement which contributed to the Mau Mau insurrection and corroded our relations with the Africans over so many years of Kenya's history. There is no doubt, as the present position of Kenya shows, that the Africans profited indirectly from the presence of the Europeans and Asians, but they obtained all too little direct and deliberate apprenticeship to their political and administrative responsibilities.

Tanzania, with its international status, was a special case, but it must be confessed that it was launched upon an independence which could easily have been seen as an inevitable and early event, with the minimum of that vigorous education for responsibility which, with its break in

INTRODUCTION

colonial rule and the ravages of the Second World War, it needed more even than other states. It is difficult to comment upon Zanzibar until we learn the full story of our apparently inept handling of its liberation, if such a term can be used, and of the political and human disaster which followed and left it a Communist off-shore island only nominally included within Tanzania.

Upon a general view, then, it could be said that in East Africa the British were slow to recognize how quickly the local colonial situations would respond to the change in the universal environment. Against all our leisurely time-tables for political advance, the handful of educated leaders who were tuned in to the world could inform their people, or at least the more accessible crowds, that they need no longer call the white man master. If, however, the British were slow to foresee the political explosion which would result from this powerful conjunction of external and internal forces, they were quick to recognize its force when it appeared. More than one African leader has told me that he never expected, when he began campaigning, to reach his goal so soon.

Looking further south we find a region where any defence of British policy is very hard to find. I refer to our handling of the three territories of Central Africa. As long ago as 1939, on the occasion of the publication of the Bledisloe Report, in a letter printed in the first volume of this collection,[1] I pointed out the grave possibility that the Southern Rhodesian system of racial domination might be extended to the two northern territories. The story is a sad comment upon the inefficacy of reason in political affairs that in the face of very timely warnings, some of them worked out in a succession of weighty books by serious students of African affairs, the British government, including first senior officials at the Colonial Office, then – for a time – Labour, and finally Conservative ministers surrendered to the pressures exerted by the determined leaders of the small white populations of the two Rhodesias and embarked upon the politically immoral scheme of the Federation. This was at the very time when cleavage between the Afrikaner repression to the south and British liberalism to the north was making utterly impracticable the complicated and illiberal compromise upon which the Central African Federation was founded. The federation met its inevitable demise but the problems it left behind are still embarrassingly present and the whole subject has an importance which justifies my own sustained though abortive interventions in *The Times* and elsewhere, and their reproduction in this book.

[1] See *Colonial Sequence 1930–49*, 1967, pp. 188–9.

INTRODUCTION

A more commonly heard criticism of the British record, and one in my view less supportable, concerns the form rather than the fact of emancipation. It has become almost a cliché to say that Britain forced the wholly unsuitable Westminster model upon a politically inexperienced people. They were certainly as inexperienced in parliamentary practice as in administration. But the model was not forced upon them. It was the form which at the first the colonial people demanded, or at least expected, and this for three reasons. Firstly because they saw that their rulers possessed and valued this model; secondly because their own legislative councils had been conducted as far as possible on the procedures of the House of Commons; and thirdly, and perhaps mainly, because by the simple and certain British processes of winning an election, voting for independence and choosing their own prime minister they could win the political game according to British rules. They were right in their calculations. All that remained for them to do, once independence on these lines was recognized, was to reject the sovereignty of the Crown (towards which we mistakenly believed they had a loyal sentiment), and change over at their leisure to the republican model. This form enabled them to dispense with the rather baffling dualism of governor-general and prime minster and concentrate power in the hands of their chief leader as president.

Even granting these points, it is difficult to believe that the temporary use of the so-called Westminster model has done the Africans much harm, or that the presidential system meant a complete break with much that surely went with the Westminster model, including, above all, the rules of parliamentary procedure. The Kenya House of Commons – note the title – under its respected English Speaker, follows meticulously this procedure and on a recent visit I was impressed by the enthusiasm with which it was cherished as a guarantee of freedom of speech, and this not only by the small opposition party. Much the same could be said of the independence of the judiciary and the British legal procedures, with British judges retained after independence to carry on the tradition. The same could be said of the universities, mostly founded before independence. In spite of some political intervention, the British principles of chartered academic freedom upon which they were founded are valued and have so far been substantially retained. Again, in some new states, the forms and traditions of British local government, mostly established as the British administrations moved away from the indirect rule formula, have been carried over and many Africans have come to Britain to study our methods. How far the whole array of our institutions can be comprehended within the term 'Westminster model' I cannot pronounce. But the impact of our ideas and institutions has been deeper than it is at present politic for us to assert or our former wards to admit. Ghana, though led far astray from the constitutional path by Dr Nkrumah, is probably the African state with the longest and closest association with the British and her leaders are at present engaged in constitutional renovations which are an impressive reflection of this association.

I have ventured to make criticisms of some aspects of Britain's handling of the process of African liberation. Such criticisms, applied to the obscure and distant transactions of colonial policy, may have little effect today even when the cost to the people concerned is heavy, as with Zanzibar and Nyasaland or to those white settlers in Kenya who were told until the last moment by British governments that their future would be fully assured. Responsibility evaporates as these, to the British public, minor happenings pass across the crowded record of events, and the ministers succeed to other ministries and the governors and others who were responsible die or turn to other tasks. There is at the present, however, a continuing tendency, not only in Britain but in other countries (as witness the article included in this volume by M. François Debré), to blame Britain not for any mishandling of the actual processes of enfranchisement but for troubles in the newly enfranchised states which are in fact due to causes deeper than some seven decades of foreign rule could have remedied. We should surely learn from the upsurge of secessionist movements of varying gravity in many parts of the world today, some very close at hand, some threatening centuries-old unities, that the tribal divisions of Africa could hardly be bridged by European governments in their brief colonial tenure. It should be noted that some of Africa's tribal divisions are deeper than any in Europe because the contrasts of climate and terrain, between forests, hills and dry open plains, have made for utterly different ethnic movements and so of ways of life. This is especially true along the line of latitude which divides the dry and the green lands of Africa, the meeting place of Moslem and pagan, nomad and cultivator but divisive contrasts can be found further south, especially in East Africa. Is it yet time to say whether Britain's policy of liberating her territories within wide frontiers, and so enclosing these contrasts within one state, will allow of a better future for the peoples they happened to embrace than the French plan of giving independence to what were, in fact, provinces formerly united within two main groupings?

INTRODUCTION

It rests with the Africans to solve their deep problem of tribal distinction. Their leaders know that it gives them trouble enough and so they cling desperately to their policy of recognizing the admittedly arbitrary frontiers drawn by the colonial powers lest external conflict should be added to internal tribal problems. The tragedies of disunity in the Sudan and in Nigeria may be taken by some critics as a condemnation of Britain's bequest of large-scale states. But the years since independence have been too few in which to judge such deep issues. Certainly in the negotiations preceding independence the effective African leaders, above all the Ibo in Nigeria, were determined to keep their large unities and it was probably out of Britain's power at that stage to have cut up the sizeable entities which had for decades been brought together to make a state, if not a nation. At some future date Africans and other peoples may solve this widespread contemporary problem by finding a new relationship between the demands of cultural identity within small regions and the need for the larger areas necessary for economic prosperity.

There are two final points to raise in this Introduction.

Firstly, it may be asked why some of the contents of a book with this title run on after the virtual end of the colonial era. The answer is that the effects of some seventy years of colonial rule are not brought to an end with the hauling down of an old flag and the running up of a new one. The items which follow 1960, 'Africa's year', a year which did not bring independence to all eastern, southern and western dependencies, deal with the results of colonialism. This is especially true of the tragedy of the Nigerian civil war though I think, as I have already suggested, that Britain would have been more severely criticized if at independence she had used her influence to break up the solid geographical and economic whole which she had put together under her government. The attempt of Colonel Ojukwu to lead the majority of Ibo into secession, with the resultant sufferings of his beleaguered people, aroused widespread concern in Britain and more widely in the Western world. The spectators of this tragedy tended to be sharply divided in their judgement of the issue. In the impassioned but rather unproductive attempt to influence the event I added my own views rather insistently to those of many others, and with a bias, if not to the Ibo case, at least towards negotiations in place of war. One result of my writings was an invitation from the military head of state, General Gowon, to visit Nigeria and see all that was possible which lay outside the small area in which the Biafrans were besieged. The general lent me his own plane and allowed

INTRODUCTION

me to fly in it to whatever point I wished. This visit resulted in reports which are printed in this collection.

It should have been a relief to turn from the sombre and continuing tragedy of Nigeria to conclude this collection with a report on Kenya, so unexpectedly stable under President Kenyatta and so prosperous after years of racial controversy and the cruel struggle of the Mau Mau revolt. The murder of Mr Mboya and the resulting revival of tribal strains remind us that we cannot count any of Africa's new nations happy until tribal, religious and economic separatisms have been overgrown by common citizenship. Recent events, even within the once-named 'British Isles', remind us of the longevity of such separatisms.

The second point is the complete concentration in this volume, as contrasted with the last, upon British territories at a time when nearly all Africa's foreign-ruled territories were advancing *en bloc* to independence. I have already said that for practical reasons my travels in this period had to be concentrated upon British-ruled dependencies. The omission of the others is not so serious a loss historically as the map alone would suggest. It is a feature of the colonial era in Africa that the parts never made anything like a whole even within one empire, still less as between the several empires. Generally speaking it was not until the dramatic fact of British liberation was realized in the 'foreign' colonies that demands for independence were strongly and effectively formulated and as swiftly accepted by France and Belgium, in some cases, and notably the Congo, with less preparation even than in British dependencies. But I think it could be maintained that the influence was all in this direction and that the British-ruled peoples set the example and the pace, and that there was little contact between the leaders of the three groups until the eve of independence. The three groups went forward by different ways, taking the stamp of their European rulers to somewhat different constitutional destinations.

I must add a note about the two Moslem states which figure in this book. I must confess to feeling a personal and unacademic attraction for the drier regions of Africa, and this was especially true of the period when travel in them had to be by horse and camel. I referred in the introduction to the first volume of this book to my exciting earliest experiences of Africa in the then British Somaliland. These stimulated me to write my first book on Africa at a time when I could think of no other way of responding to the inspiration of the continent except in a novel, shortly to be republished in a new series of colonial romances. It is a striking measurement of the pace of African advance that within my

INTRODUCTION

own adult life I was able to see the Somaliland as it was then and also to attend, as the guest of its government, the celebration of its independence, as described in an item in this volume. To this might be added the equally unexpected sequel since that date, that the new Somalia, in spite of its border troubles, can claim to have shown perhaps the purest example of democratic parliamentary government in Africa.[1]

It was many years later that I went to the Sudan and felt in the north the same attraction towards this semi-desert land and its virile tribes. This, too, was horse country – a charm it shared with northern Nigeria and Basutoland – and a country with a dramatic history and a potentially dangerous link with Egypt. But it also had a special interest as a dependency beyond the aegis of the British Colonial Office, responsible to a rather remote Foreign Office. It was thus largely outside the sphere of interest or even knowledge of the British public. For this reason I included a rather large proportion of writings upon this country, which, though never a colony or even protectorate, blazed the independence trail for the rest of British Africa.

I think that the Sudan has a further importance especially for those who pass generalized condemnations upon the record of Britain's dealings with Africa. The British service in the Sudan was separate from the Colonial Service and was, indeed, almost co-opted by the service itself, mainly from Oxford and Cambridge graduates. As prowess in sport was held to be an important qualification the comment was made that the Sudan was a nation of blacks governed by blues. The service would therefore seem to be a legitimate object for current depreciation. But while, like any group of men, the Sudan officials did not possess the whole range of necessary virtues, they showed a devotion to their work and to the people under their administration which reached, I believe, the highest general level in the record of the British empire except perhaps – and here I cannot speak from experience – for the Indian Civil Service in its best days. It is for this reason that I have included the preface I wrote to the book about Sir Douglas Newbold,[2] one of the most distinguished members of the Sudan Service, for I know of no other record which so fully reveals both the character of the British administrators in Africa at their best and also the depth and complexity of the tasks which faced them.

[1] Alas! 1969 saw the President's assassination and a military take-over.
[2] *The Making of the Modern Sudan: the Life and Letters of Sir Douglas Newbold*, K. D. D. Henderson, 1953.

Notes and Acknowledgements

As in the first volume, the items are printed without correction except for some very minor errors of fact or of grammar due to the haste in which some of them had to be written. For reasons given in the introduction the introductory headings have been kept to the minimum.

Grateful acknowledgements must be made to the following for permission to reproduce articles and letters: *Africa South*, Faber and Faber, the Fabian Colonial Bureau, *Forum World Features*, *The Guardian*, *The Listener*, *Le Monde*, *The New Commonwealth*, *The Observer*, *Optima*, *Oxford University Press*, The Royal African Society, The Royal Institute of International Affairs, *The Spectator*, Syracuse University Press, *The Times*.

Chronological Table

Year	Colonial Secretary	General Events	African Events
1949	A. Creech Jones (L)	N. Atlantic Treaty Communist Republic in China Britain devalues pound	Creech Jones visits central Africa: European demand for federation Nominated Africans in Kenya legislature raised from 2 to 4 Widespread constitutional discussions in Nigeria
1950	J. Griffiths (L)	Colombo Plan	Nigeria quasi-federal constitution Racial riots in Johannesburg
1951	*Oct.* O. Lyttleton (C)	Conservatives win October election	Conferences on Central African Federation Egypt abrogates 1936 treaty with Britain
1952			Emergency declared in Kenya Plan for Central Africa Federation published Neguib seizes power in Egypt Federation of Eritrea with Ethiopia
1953		Death of Stalin British troops sent to Br. Guiana	Central African Federation set up Nigerian Constitutional Conference in London and Lagos Deportation of Kabaka of Buganda Kenyatta and five

CHRONOLOGICAL TABLE

Year	Colonial Secretary	General Events	African Events
1953			other leaders sentenced
1954	A. Lennox Boyd (C)	France withdraws from Indo-China	Nkrumah wins general election in Gold Coast France sends 20,000 troops to Algeria
1955		Eden succeeds Churchill Conflict in Cyprus	Buganda agreement: Kabaka returns New constitution for Tanganyika
1956		Russian attack on Hungary	Independence of Sudan, Morocco and Tunisia Revolt in Southern Sudan Nkrumah wins Gold Coast elections U.S. & Britain refuse to finance Aswan Dam Nasser seizes Suez Canal: Suez war Mass arrests for treason in S. Africa
1957		Macmillan succeeds Eden	Ghana becomes independent within Commonwealth Nigerian Constitutional Conference in London U.N. Assembly condemns apartheid
1958		West Indian Federation enacted European Common Market established State of emergency in Aden & Ceylon Racial disturbances in Nottingham and Notting Hill British troops leave Jordan	Whitehead succeeds Garfield Todd in S. Rhodesia European demonstrations in Algiers Army Coup under Abboud in Sudan

CHRONOLOGICAL TABLE

Year	Colonial Secretary	General Events	African Events
1958 (contd.)		De Gaulle elected president	
1959	Oct. I. MacLeod (C)	Federation of Arab States inaugurated in Aden Queen gives Marlborough House as Commonwealth Centre Chinese attack on Tibet Prime Minister assassinated in Ceylon Conservatives win general election	King Baudouin promises Congo independence State of emergency in S. Rhodesia Disorder and deaths in Nyasaland: Banda arrested Hola scandal in Kenya and end of emergency France announces atomic tests in Sahara
1960		Racial troubles in U.S. Independence of Cyprus within Commonwealth J. Kennedy U.S. President U.S.–U.S.S.R. crisis over missiles in Cuba U.S. polaris base in Scotland London conference on future of British Honduras	Macmillan visits West, Central and S. Africa Army revolt in Algeria Africans boycott Kenya constitutional conference Riots in Nyasaland Sharpeville shooting in S. Africa Corfield Report on Mau Mau Congo independence followed by army mutiny, secession of Katanga, despatch of U.N. troops and fighting Mobutu stages army take-over in Sept. Bidhop Reeves deported from S. Africa Monckton Commission report on C. African Federation and conferences on its future

CHRONOLOGICAL TABLE

Year	Colonial Secretary	General Events	African Events
1960 (contd.)			Buganda request to secede refused
Attempted military coup in Ethiopia fails
Nigerian independence within Commonwealth
Independence for Br. Somaliland with Somalia, French Cameroons, Mauritania, Togoland Senegal, Mali, Madagascar, Ivory Coast, Dahomey, Niger, Upper Volta, Congo (Brazzaville) Chad, Central African Republic
Opening of Kariba Dam
Sierra Leone Constitutional Conference
1961	*Oct.* R. Maudling (C) jointly with C.R.O.	Britain sends troops to Kuwait
Fighting and massacres continue in Algeria
Jamaica leaves W.I. federation
24 non-aligned states meet in Belgrade
India occupies Goa
State of emergency in Ceylon
New constitution for Malta
Gagarin circles the earth

U Thant Sec. Gen. U.N. | Afro-Asian 'summit' meeting in Casablanca
Continued fighting in Congo: deaths of Lumumba and Hammarskjöld
Independence for Ruanda and Urundi
N. Cameroons joins Nigeria:
S. Cameroons joins Cameroons Republic
Nobel Peace Prize awarded to Luthuli
S. Africa becomes a republic outside the Commonwealth
Rebellion in Angola
Kenyatta freed |

CHRONOLOGICAL TABLE

Year	Colonial Secretary	General Events	African Events
1961 (contd.)			Tanganyika becomes Independent
New constitution promulgated for S. Rhodesia
Opposition leaders arrested in Ghana:
U.S. loan to build Volta River Project
U.N. recognizes Africa as non-nuclear zone and calls for independence of remaining colonies
1962	D. Sandys (C) from July	W. Samoa independent
Anti-government rioting in Guiana
Army seizes power in Burma
Indonesian troops land in W. New Guinea
50,000 refugees enter Hong Kong
West Indian Federation dissolved
Martial law in Pakistan
Commonwealth Immigration Act passed in Britain
Jamaica & Trinidad become independent within Commonwealth
Chinese frontier attack on India
Guiana conference fails
End of Cuba missile crisis
British troops repress	Continuing bloodshed in Algeria:
France recognizes independence in July
Conference of 'Monrovia' heads of state in Lagos
London constitutional conference on Kenya
R. Butler made head of new Central Africa office
London conference on Zanzibar fails to agree
Coalition ministry in Kenya of KANU and KADU parties
Obote becomes Prime Minister in Uganda
U.N. delegation discusses S. W. Africa with union government
Death penalty for 'sabotage' in S. Africa
Ruanda & Urundi gain independence separately

CHRONOLOGICAL TABLE

Year	Colonial Secretary	General Events	African Events
1962 (contd.)		rebellion in Brunei Kennedy and Macmillan meet in Bahamas	U.N. resolution for more liberal constitution in S. Rhodesia Emergency in W. Nigeria Nkrumah expels Archbishop of W. Africa and Bishop of Accra Disorders in S. Rhodesia: Zimbabwe African Peoples Party banned Uganda becomes independent within Commonwealth U.N. condemns apartheid and recommends members to break relations with S. Africa Nyasaland constitutional conference in London Malcolm Macdonald succeeds Sir P. Renison as governor of Kenya Tanganyika becomes a republic First African dominated government in N. Rhodesia In S. Rhodesia W. Field's Rhodesian Front defeats Whitehead British government accepts Nyasaland's right to secede U.N. troops drive Tshombe out of Katanga

CHRONOLOGICAL TABLE

Year	Colonial Secretary	General Events	African Events
1963		Britain refused entry to European Common Market
Strike and riots in Guiana: failure of London conference
Dutch New Guinea transferred to Indonesia
France withdraws fleet from N.A.T.O.
U.S., U.S.S.R. and U.K. agree on Test Ban Treaty
Malaya, N. Borneo, Sarawak (Saba) and Singapore join in Federation of Malaysia within Commonwealth
Douglas Home succeeds Macmillan
Assassination of President Kennedy
Renewed fighting in Cyprus	Nyasaland self-governing: Banda Prime Minister
U.N. Forces continue fighting in Congo
Deportation of Enaharo from Britain
African Summit in Ethiopia sets up O.A.U.
Britain grants £100,000 to Congo government
Awolowo sentenced to 10 years' imprisonment
Nigeria becomes republic within Commonwealth
Algerian government nationalizes all French-owned land
U.N. Trusteeship Committee asks Britain not to transfer Federal forces to S. Rhodesia
Kabaka becomes first President of Uganda
First executions for sabotage in S. Africa
Security council votes for partial arms ban on S. Africa
Zanzibar an independent state within the Commonwealth
Nkrumah dismisses Chief Justice after acquittals in treason trial
Kenya becomes independent within Commonwealth

CHRONOLOGICAL TABLE

Year	Colonial Secretary	General Events	African Events
1963 (contd.)			African students riot in Red Square State of emergency in north east Kenya Dissolution of Central African Federation
1964	*Oct.* A. Greenwood (L)	United Nations force sent to pacify Cyprus Death of Nehru S. Arabian Conference in London agree on federation State of emergency in Guiana Racial riots in U.S. Indonesian invasion of Malaysia: Commonwealth troops sent Malta G.C. becomes independent within commonwealth Dr Luther King awarded Nobel Peace Prize Chinese explode atomic bomb Labour win general election in U.K. President Johnson elected	Rebels seize power in Zanzibar: Sultan flees Mutinies in forces of Tanganyika, Uganda and Kenya put down by British troops Kaunda first prime minister in N. Rhodesia Riots in Salisbury after trial of Nkomo Zanzibar expels British envoy: Britain recognizes new government Ghana declared a one-party state Ian Smith succeeds W. Field in S. Rhodesia Tanganyika and Zanzibar unite as Tanzania within Commonwealth Kruschev opens Aswan Dam Congo rebels seize Stanleyville: U.N. forces leave: white mercenaries arrive Nyasaland becomes independent within Commonwealth as Malawi Prolonged Lumpa disorders with many

xxxii

CHRONOLOGICAL TABLE

Year	Colonial Secretary	General Events	African Events
1964			deaths in N. Rhodesia Belgian paratroops in U.S. planes recapture Stanleyville and save many Europeans Riots in Khartoum Kenya becomes a republic within Commonwealth with Kenyatta as president
1965	*Dec.* Lord Longford (L)	Amalgamation of Foreign and Commonwealth services Death of Churchill Riots in Algeria: Boumedienne deposes Ben Bella Singapore secedes from Malaysia Indo-Pakistan war	Queen and Prince Philip visit Ethiopia and Sudan Gambia independent as 21st member of Commonwealth I. Smith wins sweeping electoral victory: talks between Smith and Wilson in London and Salisbury: Smith makes declaration of independence which Britain denounces as illegal Disorders in W. Nigeria Mobutu seizes power from Kasavubu Many African States break relations with Britain over Rhodesia
1966	*April* F. Lee (L)	First Negro in U.S. Cabinet General election in Britain: (*March*) Labour retains power Guiana independent within Commonwealth Commonwealth Relations and Colonial	Coup overthrows government of C. African Republic Commonwealth Conference on Rhodesia in Lagos Army mutineers assassinate Nigerian leaders: General Ironsi put in power

CHRONOLOGICAL TABLE

Year	Colonial Secretary	General Events	African Events
1966 (contd.)		Offices merged Barbados independent within Commonwealth	(*Jan.*) and murdered (*July*): Gowon succeeds to power: massacres of Ibo and other southerners in north Obote takes power in Uganda and imprisons five ministers Gen. Ankrah establishes military government in Ghana in Nkrumah's absence U.N. authorizes Britain to stop oilships supplying Rhodesia Kabaka flees after Obote seizes palace: 1,000 deaths reported Malawi a republic within Commonwealth: Dr Banda president Salisbury University closed: 9 white lecturers deported Bechuanaland independent within Commonwealth as Botswana with Seretse Khama president Basutoland becomes independent within Commonwealth as Lesotho U.N. votes to end S. Africa's mandate over S.W. Africa Burundi's king overthrown and republic set up Wilson and Smith

NOTES ON THE CHRONOLOGY

Year	General Events	African Events
1966 (contd.)		meet on H.M.S. *Fearless:* Rhodesian cabinet rejects terms
1967	First Negro government in Bahamas Gibraltar votes to retain British rule Communist violence in Hong Kong Aden rebellion leads to British evacuation Second devaluation of pound Six-day Arab-Israeli war	Nigerian leaders meet at Aburi (*Jan.*): decree for 12 states: Biafra declares independence (*May*): civil war (*July*) Trade agreement between Malawi and S. Africa Army take-overs in Togo and Sierra Leone Twelve states system decreed in Nigeria Tshombe kidnapped and imprisoned in Algeria Mercenaries fighting in eastern Congo

NOTES ON THE CHRONOLOGY

There are four points to notice:

1. The list of events is fuller than in the first volume. The main reason for this is that, as the pace of political advance quickened there were more colonial events to record and more relevant occurrences in the world in general.
2. Although, as suggested in the Introduction, there was little active relationship between the colonies of the three European powers as they advanced to independence, it is appropriate to record this simultaneous enfranchisement.
3. It was also thought useful to include reminders that British authorities had many other colonial problems than those of Africa to engross their attention.
4. The chronology was not carried further than 1967 because, after that date the chronological form becomes unrealistic as there was a

NOTES ON THE CHRONOLOGY

multiplication of activities within independent Africa and in its relations with the outside world. Further, some of the main issues, e.g. in the Southern Sudan and in Rhodesia, were too continuous to be suitable for dating.

1949

The Sudan emerges into Nationhood

Foreign Affairs July 1949

This article was written at the hazardous beginning of self-government for the Sudan. I had been able to make a prolonged visit to the country and study its affairs both at the centre and in the provinces. I had worked in the country between the wars with the intention of writing a book upon its government but the urgent need for a study of Ethiopia as it became a theatre of war cut across this plan.

In August 1947, in the episodic manner of a flash in a news-reel, the affairs of the Sudan were thrown into the glare of world publicity when Egypt accused Britain, among other things, of depriving her of the Sudan. When the case was being discussed at the Security Council there were certain dark and fine-looking men at Lake Success, speaking excellent English and, with one impressive exception, wearing European dress, who claimed to represent the Sudanese nation and to decide its destiny. There was the Umma Party demanding complete independence and other parties demanding various degrees of association with Egypt. Spectators whose attention was not immediately monopolized by the next item on the agenda, Greece or Indonesia, may well have wondered whether a new nation were being born in this obscure part of Africa, and, if so, what was its expectation of success or even of life.

The problem of the Sudan, which baffled the Security Council, can be understood only with some help from geography and history. Between Egypt and Uganda a vast indeterminate region stretches from the desert of the north through a land of precarious rain-grown crops to the green hills and bushlands of the equatorial belt. The three zones are threaded, but not linked, by that astonishing flow of water, the Nile, which goes on to give life to Egypt. Until quite recently this formless region had little common history though on the banks of its river lie traces of ancient Egypt, Greece, Rome and Christendom. When, in the later Middle Ages, Arab tribes entered the Sudan and spread into the harsh immensity of the northern plains, they did not reach the equatorial south. It was only in the early nineteenth century, when a vigorous Albanian, ruling Egypt nominally as the viceroy of the Turkish Sultan, led his restless Turkish and Balkan soldiers to easy victory over the disunited tribes and princedoms of the Sudan, that the region attained a central, if alien, government. The oppression of this government and those of its scattered garrisons, and the raiding of the helpless pagan tribes in the south for slaves, became an international scandal. Just when Egypt, herself in chaos and rebellion, fell under the control of Britain as represented by the able administrator, Lord Cromer, the northern Sudanese, under the fiery religious revivalist, the Mahdi, threw off Egyptian rule. This occurred in 1882–3. To the British it seemed that merely putting Egypt to rights was task enough, and there could be no thought then of a costly reconquest of the misgoverned province. It was in evacuating – or delaying to evacuate – the garrison early in 1885 that General Gordon fell to the Dervish spears, and the suspense and anger of those dramatic days burned the name of the Sudan into the minds of the British people. For the next thirteen years the Sudan suffered the hard and fanatical rule of the Mahdi and his successor, Khalifa Abdullahi.

But by the middle nineties Egypt was in moderate order, while the scramblers for Africa were threatening to break into the great disordered no-man's-land round which Britain, in the name of Egypt, had been drawing purely diplomatic frontiers. Hence Lord Kitchener's expedition of British, Egyptian and Sudanese troops, which worked methodically up the Nile to win the victory of Omdurman in September 1898. It was here that the young subaltern Churchill joined in a rash charge into a gully full of Dervishes and, unlike many of his fellow Lancers, came out alive on the other side.

On the morrow of the battle Britain was faced with a very awkward situation, and the formula she found for meeting it is the one which governs the Sudan problem today. Fact and legal theory were at odds: Britain had decided upon the reconquest of the Sudan and had led the tripartite army, but she had done this as the guardian of Egypt and in Egypt's name. Yet she could not hand back this impoverished country to an Egypt which was under her own control. She was now in an expansive mood and she had, of course, the power to annex the Sudan. But this would have led to jealous protests from the other Powers, especially from France, whose famous Marchand expedition was at this very moment obliged by Lord Kitchener to abandon the Upper Nile. Moreover, British anti-imperialists were by no means silent at home. In characteristic fashion, therefore, the British authorities decided that, having for the moment the substance of power, there was no need to question Egypt's legal rights.

The Agreement of 1899 set up the Sudan as a state separate from Egypt, freed from the foreign capitulations which had been the curse of that country. Egypt's former sovereignty and the rights acquired by Britain through conquest, and not derived from her undefined control of Egypt, were to be combined in a joint rule, or Condominium. The two flags, which can be seen today flying on all public buildings in the Sudan, suggested equal status, but the right to recommend the Governor-General was given to the British Government, and this, coupled with the Governor-General's almost unfettered power, is the keystone of the Agreement. It is one which could work only if one or the other of the two nations, so widely different in character, were unquestionably the dominant partner. So, in 1899, this Agreement was less a partnership between Egypt and Britain than between Lord Cromer in Egypt and Lord Kitchener in the Sudan. It will be observed that the Sudanese did not, and at that time could not, form a third party. Divided, their own militant rulers defeated and killed, they were passive, in desperate need of peace, order and the good government they had never known.

The British came into this stricken and impoverished country with Egyptian troops and Egyptian officials and, for many years, an Egyptian subsidy to pay for the administration of a poor country further impoverished by its misfortunes. They also brought with them Sayed Ali Mirghani, a holy man of a sect opposed to Mahdism. He had fled to Egypt and was now expected to rally orthodox opinion to counter the zealous but unorthodox revivalism which had swept over so many of the great Beggara cattle-owning tribes of the west. Mahdism, though politically defeated, was still regarded as dangerous and was held in horror by the sedentary and urban classes along the rivers who had gained most from Egyptian rule. For this reason the son born posthumously to the Mahdi, who had died at the height of his triumph, was kept under careful watch.

II

From 1900 until the First World War the Sudan Government went quietly about its task of building a firm, effective central and provincial government. Staffed from the products of the public schools and the two ancient universities, it was authoritarian and beneficent. Its officers were chosen as much for their all-round record as for brains, and it was a common gibe that the Sudan was a land of Blacks run by Blues. The confidence of the people, relieved from disorder and uncertainty, was quickly won in so far as this can ever be done in a Moslem country by Western rulers. Departments proliferated and social services were slowly extended; communications developed and with them trade and production. The Government pushed its fingers southward among the shy, ill-treated pagan tribes and took them gradually, but not always quite peacefully, into its administrative grasp. There was no serious difficulty with Egypt, which was still largely under British control and very much the junior partner: she supplied, as reluctant exiles, the trained and educated junior staff not yet available in the Sudan, and her vital irrigation department, under British direction, exercised, in her own literally vital interests an increasingly effective and scientific control of the Nile waters.

The dark Arabs of the north are a virile and dignified people: they accepted the British as agents of a conquering power who did not abuse their position, and they met them upon a basis of admitted difference in which, thanks to the pride of Islam, there was no servility. Looking back today in the present atmosphere of urgency, it must seem that the British service, braced neither by criticism nor by difficult problems such as those presented in some colonies by immigrant communities, conducted their interesting task in too complacent and leisurely a manner. But this wisdom comes after many events.

The First World War broke across this slow, quiet progress. Its effect was indirect, but it disturbed the mechanics of the Condominium which depended upon British predominance. The British, intent upon their war with Germany and her local ally, Turkey, used Egypt as a base and a source of labour and supply with too little attention to the susceptibilities of a people stirred into sudden self-consciousness and political ambition by the war and by the new creed of self-determination. Britain even went so far as to declare a Protectorate over Egypt in 1914, and to denounce the lingering legal suzerainty of Turkey over that country. The end of the war saw the emergence of a nationalist people's party in the Wafd which endeavoured to rouse opinion at home and abroad against Britain; and as Britain felt Egypt slipping out of her control she tightened her grasp upon the Sudan, to protect her own interests, but also because she felt that her task there, well begun, was not even half done. It seemed equally impossible to leave the country to itself, or to hand it over to an Egypt under what Britain regarded as factious, irresponsible and Anglophobe leadership.

In 1922 Britain withdrew the Protectorate and recognized Egypt as a sovereign state, reserving communications and defence, and the Sudan, from her grant of authority. The Egyptian politicians attacked these reservations unceasingly; the next two years saw a rapid worsening of Anglo-Egyptian relations, and Egyptian attempts to foment trouble in the Sudan. The murder of Sir Lee Stack, the Governor-General, in the streets of Cairo in 1924, following a violent anti-British press campaign and mutinies in the Sudan among some of the Egyptian and Sudanese troops, roused the British to severe action. Egyptian troops, not without further incidents, were expelled and Egyptian participation in the administration virtually came to an end. But while Egypt's share in the Condominium was thus in practice almost abolished, Britain did nothing to cancel Egypt's legal rights under the Agreement.

From 1924 to 1936 the British administered the Sudan single-handed. Political instability and excitement in Egypt made it impossible for Britain to come to terms with her, but this period was on the whole one of peace and progress for the Sudan. The new Sudanese political leaders now complain that the progress was too slow, especially in training for self-government and in the closely related matter of education; they accuse the Government of punishing the Sudanese for the sins of the Egyptians by an excess of caution. And it is true that the British moved away from the system of direct rule, under which the Sudanese intelligentsia, who were issuing in increasing numbers and at rising standards from Gordon College, might have hoped to replace their rulers at an early date in a kind of centralized technocracy. But, drawing upon the example of indirect rule initiated by Lord Lugard, the Sudan Government began to develop rural local government upon the long-neglected basis of tribalism.

The reversal may have been too sudden and too sharp. There was, and is, a great contrast in the way of life among the scattered, semi-nomadic peoples in the northern plains and the sophisticated, professional, mercantile and wage-earning groups in the four or five main towns, and especially in the large population of the three towns, Khartoum, Omdurman and Khartoum North, which have grown up at the confluence of the Blue and White Niles. Here men read newspapers, attend cinemas and football matches, listen to the Egyptian wireless and discuss politics ardently in coffee shops. When the writer visited the Sudan in the years before the war and attended meetings with the young intelligentsia, there were fierce denunciations of the 'African colonial policy' by which, the Sudanese said, their progress was being barred and tribal disunion fomented. By that date, however, the Government was already moving toward a broader and more balanced encouragement of a true local government on patterns which varied for large and small towns and for rural areas, and was speeding up the process of Sudanization of the civil service.

Economically, except for the universal slump in the middle of the inter-war period, the country made fair progress in spite of the great difficulties of economic development. Outstanding in boldness and imagination was the so-called Gezira scheme by which the waters of the Blue Nile were dammed at Sennar to irrigate nearly a million acres of land by natural flow. This land is farmed by a partnership among the 20,000 native tenants, the Government and a commercial company – the Sudan Plantations Syndicate – who divide the profits upon a 40-40-20 per centage. The country's revenues have benefited greatly from the export of the cotton thus grown, and the whole country has gained from the production of a large, assured grain crop in a land often afflicted by drought and famine. It is worth noting here that this large scheme is due for nationalization in the near future.

In 1936 a temporary political stability in Egypt under the Wafd and the leadership of Nahas Pasha, in combination with the darkening world situation, at last brought the Condominium Powers together. A Treaty of Alliance was signed which modified the British military concessions in Egypt without abolishing them, and in other ways met Egypt's heightened sense of national self-respect. The Agreement of 1899 in regard to the Sudan was confirmed, but it was agreed that Egyptian as well as British officials could again be appointed when Sudanese were not available. Egyptian troops were to return to the Sudan. (The writer watched the first of these march into Khartoum shortly afterward through silent crowds.) In recognition of the changed political atmosphere, there was a clause in which the parties agreed 'that the primary aim of their administration in the Sudan must be the welfare of the Sudanese'.

III

This treaty led to the first strong, overt expression of Sudanese nationalism, which for years had been developing among the few townsmen who possessed some Western education. The public recognition that, in the absence of any constitutional means of expression, the treaty settled the destiny of the Sudanese without any reference to their views, caused an outburst of protest. Several newspapers sprang into existence, some of them ephemeral and nearly all of them bitter in tone. The 'Graduates General Congress', formed of educated, politically-minded elements, came into being, and, claiming to speak to the Government on behalf of the whole of the Sudan, demanded a legislative assembly, a Sudanese nationality and the right to self-determination. But by this time Britain was at death-grips with the Germans on the borders of Egypt and was in no mood to be patient with this narrowly-based, inexperienced and self-elected body of leaders. Rebuffed, the moderates began to lose control, and membership of the Congress was widened to include Sudanese with any claims to literacy. More ominously, the Congress leaders, informed that they did not represent the people, turned to the two religious figures who divided between them the allegiance of the great majority of the Moslems, and thus infused politics with the sectarianism of the masses and divided their own ranks. One of these holy men was Sayed Sir Ali Mirghani. Pious, aging, delicate and retiring in disposition, he had neither desire nor capacity to lead a political party, but as a rival to the other outstanding religious leader, he became, inevitably, the symbol round which opposition was grouped. On the other side stood Sir Abdel Rahman el Mahdi, the Mahdi's son, who had by this time become a great public figure, winning his way by his moderate and astute political leadership and the great wealth he had amassed from growing irrigated cotton.

So long as the war lasted, the political situation was overshadowed by the country's danger: the Sudanese showed great loyalty to the Government and complete social discipline, while the fighting men lived up to their magnificent reputation. In 1944, in order to meet the pressure of the political groups and obtain an expression of opinion and support from the moderates, the Government set up a nominated representative Advisory Council for the Northern Sudan. By the standards of the British colonies this was a belated and limited gesture, but the difficulties between the Condominium Powers had until then seemed to preclude any important constitutional innovation. Staffed in the main with moderate and experienced professional men and the more intelligent Nazirs (or chiefs) of the major tribes, this Council, which met in the Governor-General's palace, was a dignified, useful but not very lively body. It was, of course, derided by the younger politicians and editors.

These and many other Sudanese waited with impatience for the peace which they hoped would bring political emancipation as a reward for their honorable record in the war. They were, however, obliged to wait with growing excitement and a sense of frustration as, in 1946, their co-rulers entered into prolonged negotiations for the revision of the 1936 treaty, at the request of Egypt. Excitement reached a dangerous height when, after a treaty had been drawn up and initialled by Sidky Pasha and Mr Bevin, the former was credited in the Egyptian press with an interpretation of its Sudan clause to the effect that 'Britain has accepted the unity of Egypt with the Sudan under the Egyptian Crown'. This statement caused an outburst of anger, especially, of course, from the Umma Party. When the treaty consultations had begun the members of this party had tried to co-operate with the parties which had grouped themselves round Sayed Ali Mirghani; these parties used the slogan 'the unity of the Nile Valley', and hoped to gain from Egypt the self-determination which they seemed unable to wrest from the British. The two groups sent a joint delegation to Cairo to represent Sudanese views, but it soon broke up, for the Umma Party rejected Egyptian sovereignty with growing vehemence and, while claiming complete independence, was willing to accept the help of the British in achieving it. The other group, which appeared to comprise most of the urban, educated and trading classes, grew increasingly alarmed at the idea that Britain might relax control in favour of a Mahdist régime; they retained alarming memories of rough tribal tyranny which such a régime had exercised over the riverain groups. It was this fear, rather than any desire to exchange British for Egyptian control, which drove them deeper and deeper into the Egyptian camp. Tribesmen who knew little of politics or constitutional problems responded at once to religious sectarianism, and Mirghanists, claiming to be more orthodox, inevitably took the opposite side from the Mahdists, with their taint of heresy and their bellicose historical associations.

In order to avoid disorder and factional fights, Mr Attlee made a reassuring declaration about continuing the *status quo* in the Sudan; but this still further infuriated the Egyptians, and in July 1947, Egypt took her conflict with Britain to the Security Council. There the question drained away in a waste of arguments and inconclusive resolutions. The central point at issue was whether Egypt would accept Britain's demand, made in conformity with the tradition of the British

Empire, that the Sudanese must be left free, when the time came, to decide for themselves whether to remain under Egyptian sovereignty or to be independent. Egypt refused to grant this demand.

The result was not, however, altogether sterile. The Sudan Government which, through its Governor-General, General Huddleston, had stoutly upheld to the British Foreign Office the Sudan's right to self-determination, decided to take a further step toward the attainment of that objective. It therefore set up an unofficial conference, mainly of experienced Sudanese officials, to discuss the form of a new constitution. This Constitution was put into legal shape and passed unanimously by the Northern Advisory Council, predominantly Umma in composition, in March 1948. The writer attended the debates. Neither the Sudanese nor the senior British officials who led the proceedings were highly experienced in constitution making, but together they hammered out a system on the British parliamentary model in an atmosphere of great good will, the Sudanese requesting and receiving a number of concessions.

In order to keep within the four walls of the 1899 Agreement, the conference retained in the Constitution the large powers of the Governor-General; but these are intended to be kept in reserve. The Constitution departs from the usual British colonial model by setting up a large representative assembly of nearly a hundred members. Ten of these are directly elected in the six major towns, where alone the people were considered ready for the ballot box. Another ten are nominated to represent special interests such as labour, journalism, etc. Fifty-two are elected in rural constituencies in the north by a process of indirect election – a controversial point, since the tribes are still inevitably dominated by their Nazirs and Modas (sub-chiefs), who are still dependent upon government support and draw official salaries. Moreover, the chiefs themselves may stand for the elections which, not surprisingly, they win! The Government decided to include thirteen representatives of the Negro south, as these pagan and newly Christianized people are very much more backward than the Moslem northerners who once raided them for slaves. At present, representatives of these primitive tribes are selected at provincial councils, since any form of election would be meaningless to them.

Finally, there are some twenty members of the Executive Council and the Under-Secretaries. Like the British Cabinet ministers they sit in the chamber and, like them, they are chosen by the Governor-General in consultation with the leader of the Assembly who, in the

Sudan, is elected by that body. In addition to the leader, at present a retired Sudanese army officer, Abdullah Ble Khalil who commands confidence by his fine record and integrity, and who is also the secretary of the Umma Party and Minister for Agriculture, there are three Sudanese Ministers, one for Education, one for Public Health and one Without Portfolio. These four men sit in the new Executive Council with two of the Sudanese Under-Secretaries, those for Irrigation and for Economics and Trade. The British members of the Council are the three senior officials, the Secretaries (Civil, Financial and Legal), and the military commander, all four sitting *ex officio*. The British head of the Sudan Plantation Syndicate, nominated on personal grounds, and the Director of Economics and Trade have been appointed Ministers Without Portfolio. There are thus six British and six Sudanese members, a proportion laid down in the Constitution. The Council meets, like the British Cabinet, in private but it is no secret that its proceedings have been wholly constructive and amicable and that there has been no tendency to division on racial lines.

According to the usual practice in the early stages of British transfer of power, this Constitution gives large functions to the new organs in the full expectation that they will be used constructively. But, in countries where political immaturity, disunion or external interference may cause the new institutions to break down, large and indeed overriding executive and legislative powers are kept in reserve for the Governor so that if a crisis arises he may legally take up again the powers that have been delegated and so preserve law and order. In the Sudan this was made necessary by the continued validity of the 1899 Agreement in which, as we have seen, power is concentrated in the Governor-General's office. In response, however, to both Sudanese and Egyptian criticisms his position has been made less autocratic than in the first drafts of the Constitution. Sudanese criticism has, however, been directed less against these reserve powers, the need for which seems to be widely accepted, than against the methods of election, which are said to bear unfairly against one of the parties.

IV

This brings us back to the main problem of the country. The Constitution has been rejected by the 'Unity with Egypt' parties who boycotted the elections and demonstrated in the main cities against the opening of the Assembly. In this they had the support of Egypt, whose

Government refused all requests to co-operate in the creation or the working of the new Constitution. The 'Unity' parties are mainly represented in the towns and, in Middle-Eastern fashion, in the schools, but they have few able and experienced leaders. The Umma or Independence group, by contrast, although it is based so largely upon the unsophisticated tribes of the western plains, contains some of the ablest Sudanese, men who have literally grown grey in the public service, and who by long and close association with their British colleagues have come to understand the problems and the methods of modern government. Thus the Minister for Education was Assistant Director in that department and has shown himself a most able parliamentarian; the Minister for Health is a senior doctor who comes of a family famous for its public services; the Sudanese Minister Without Portfolio is also Vice-Principal of Gordon College. One of the Under-Secretaries is the son of the Khalifa Abdullahi upon whom fell the mantle of the Mahdi and who was killed by the British troops. These and others now holding senior appointments are men of great integrity and personal charm, well known to the writer and on terms of close friendship with their British colleagues; their wisdom and conservatism are in striking contrast to the intemperance of their opponents and the excitable youths who at intervals parade the streets.

It is still an open question whether the new Constitution will solve the Sudan's problems and become in time a full expression of majority opinion and a centre round which the nascent but still deeply divided nation may form itself. This potential nation has started as well as it could in the difficult circumstances: its simple but dignified buildings, run up in a few months and modelled on the plan of the House of Commons, have been the scene during this spring of debates conducted in English and Arabic in which the Assembly, with its trousered townsmen and its majority of tribal chiefs in the white turbans and flowing white robes, have steadily voted in support of their Ministers and have conscientiously learned, with a Sudanese judge as Speaker, the mysteries of British parliamentary procedure. Most encouraging of all, the black Christian southerners have sent some representatives who have surprised the northern Moslems, not only by their ability but also by their restraint. The writer heard one of them give an excellent speech in English in the course of which he quoted Mr Churchill in favour of a government which was owned by the people rather than one in which the people were owned by the government.

Clearly, much depends upon the attitude of Egypt. There can be no

[1949]   COLONIAL SEQUENCE 1949 TO 1969

doubt that her distraction and failure in Palestine have helped the Sudan to take a quick step toward self-realization and independence. Possible forms of Egyptian participation under the new Constitution were being seriously discussed in Khartoum only a year ago; today it is already difficult to imagine how Egyptians could be introduced into the new Assembly or Council. Contacts between Egypt and the Sudan are very slight; few Egyptians visit the country, and since cotton is the major export of both countries, trade between them is small. The Nile waters are, of course, an indissoluble bond which demand complex and continuous co-operation of a kind Britain has scrupulously fostered. Yet with the large new plans of extending Nile control to Ethiopia and Uganda, in the interests of both countries, Egypt can no longer claim that she must rule the lands from which she draws her water.

If, however, ultimate strife between Egypt and the Sudan, and between the main parties in the Sudan, is to be avoided, Britain must use all her influence to achieve reconciliation between those two interdependent states. The Sudan as it is today has been created in 50 years under British guidance. With dangers within and without, with deep internal divisions, political and physical, with a precarious economy narrowly based on cotton, and now with a venture into parliamentary self-government, there is still much need of protective and educational work by Britain in the Sudan. But if she is to crown the success of her past work she must not only protect the rights of the Sudanese to attain full self-government and make that self-government a constructive and unifying reality, but also endeavour to understand the legitimate interests and natural fears of Egypt. By thus pursuing a policy of harmonization, it may be hoped that Britain can in time transform the now unworkable Condominium into a triple alliance freely accepted by three nations.

The High Commission Territories and Apartheid

Letter to *The Times* 16 December 1949

Looking back from the year 1969 it would seem that the reiterated British defence of the status of the three High Commission territories (see the relevant articles and letters in Vol. I of this book) was justified by their latest history. With the foundation of the United Nations, the independence of

THE HIGH COMMISSION TERRITORIES AND APARTHEID [1949]

most of Africa and, during 1968, of the three territories themselves, their status is as secure as it can be when allowance is made for their small size and economic and political weakness in relation to their giant neighbour.

Sir, – May I take up the question at the end of your leading article today upon apartheid and express the hope, which I believe is generally held in this country, that Dr Malan will not ask for the transfer of the three High Commission territories in the New Year? The question, embarrassingly entangled as it is with that of Union native policy, was fully debated in 1909 and 1934: in 1949, in so far as conditions, internal and external to South Africa, have changed, they unfortunately strengthen the case for refusal.

On the internal side there is no need to repeat the strong historic claims of the tribes upon Britain. But their original unwillingness to enter the Union because of its failure to extend the liberal system of the Cape to the other provinces is stronger now when Dr Malan proposes – and his plans are only postponed – to destroy the last remaining civic rights of the African majority. The consultations to which we are pledged could lead only to the full expression and consolidation of the tribes' rejection of transfer and, at least among the high-spirited mountain people of Basutoland, a British colony and not a protectorate, its enforcement might well lead to prolonged resistance and bloodshed. Even if Britain could conceivably agree to coercion, would South Africans really wish to add an embittered million to their native population just when its affairs are entering a critical stage? Externally, the difficulties would be greater. If both sides shrank from enforced transfer when it would have been a domestic matter, how much more when it would cause a world-wide scandal? Support expressed at the United Nations and offered by Communism would sharpen and prolong the discontent of the transferred. Within the Commonwealth, especially among its newest members, the effects would be most unhappy, while, for herself, Britain would seriously weaken the confidence she is asking from all her colonial peoples during the difficult advance towards self-government.

It is in Africa, however, that the results would be gravest. The states in that continent, taking only those in the Commonwealth, are being developed upon principles utterly opposed to those of South Africa, a position which, history suggests, too often leads ultimately to physical conflict. Britain's wide responsibilities in the continent impose upon her the duty of mediating between these two extremes, while in the east and centre she faces other versions of what is fundamentally the same problem as in South Africa. In dealing with this situation she will need all her moral and political authority, and both will be endangered if, while she treats Africans as men in the Gold Coast and in Kenya, she agrees to treat them as something less south of the Zambesi. Does not the question of these territories, itself a microcosm of the race-relations problem of Africa as a whole, force all those concerned with the continent to face the dangerous drift of its affairs and to look for a way in which, at whatever cost, the security of the white communities and their great contributions to Africa can be preserved without refusing the surrounding Africans any share of the rights inherent in our civilization? So long as South Africans see the transfer of the territories as an isolated, bilateral question they will condemn our lack of understanding for their peculiar difficulties and regard our 'not now' as an officious and unthinking 'never'. If they could see the question in its continental, indeed, in its world perspective, they might realize that Britain has both the right and the power to help in the solution of one of the widest and deepest problems of our century.

The development of larger views and counsels would take time. On the immediate issue the only way to avoid blank irreconcilability and persuade the Union Government not to use the pressures which geography and economics have put into its hands, is to treat this question with the utmost restraint and endeavour to bring moderate opinion on both sides into touch. We know that South Africans are divided both upon native policy and upon the demand for immediate transfer of the territories. Even among the adherents of apartheid there are some who give the word its genuine meaning, and support it, not as a device for hardening the present stratification of society, but as a real and maybe costly opportunity for native development. We upon our side should guard against allowing our wards to crystallize, under our protection, a jealous and archaic tribalism: we should rather deliberately train leaders who, with knowledge wider than their own diminutive nationalisms, may eventually guide their people towards a willing and intelligent acceptance of their South African environment.

Yours faithfully

1950

The Future of the Somalis

Letter to *The Times* 14 February 1950

This letter deals with a problem which gave great difficulties to the United Nations. The friends of the Somalis hoped to see them retain the unity which, by the events of the war and the British victory over Italy, they gained under British administration. The decision in 1950, however, was to place the former Italian Somalia under Italian trusteeship for ten years as a prelude to independence. The hopes expressed in the letter reprinted here were not disappointed: the Italian administration proved, on the whole, a useful preparation for independence, and Somalia was united with British Somaliland in 1960, though the complete unification of all the Somali lands and peoples was denied them. My own relationships with the Somalis, beginning in 1922, had always been close and later in the volume (pp. 212–15) will be found my account of their independence celebrations in 1960.

Sir, – May I make one addition to the suggestions for better relations between Italy and Britain put forward in your leading article of February 4?

Following the decision of both houses of Italy's Parliament, an expedition of troops and officials has now sailed to resume power over her former colony of Somaliland. The British authorities will hand over a people whom they have governed since their conquest of the country early in 1941. Such a transfer of power is not easy to make either practically or psychologically, especially when it is remembered that for most of the years since 1941 neither the British nor the Somalis nor indeed the Italians themselves had reason to expect this retrocession. It is known that British opinion favoured the creation now of that Greater Somalia to which political experience and just principle point as the ultimate end. Britain has, however, accepted the United Nations' decision with dignity and restraint, and has shown her desire to co-operate fully with the new Italy in this matter. This desire will be strengthened by the debates in the Chamber, the reports of which in the Italian papers have now reached this country. In these the humane and enlightened Prime Minister of Italy has shown his determination to distinguish his government absolutely from the regime of Mussolini with its record of ruthlessness and atrocities in East Africa. He said that his suppression of the Ministry of Africa would 'close one cycle for Italy and open another', and he and Count Sforza pledged their country to return to Somaliland in the fullest sense as trustees charged to develop self-government.

This is highly encouraging to the country about to transfer power. In colonial affairs, however, the difficulty is to translate words spoken in Parliament into administrative realities on the frontiers. And there is one question which means a great deal both to the British and the Somalis and which, though it might be taken to be covered by the Ministerial statements, would gain from being explicit. We may be sure that the Prime Minister, remembering that there may be individual Italian colonists and officials who harbour feelings of resentment, has given the strictest orders that the Italian administration is to make a new start and prevent any single act of victimization of Italy's former subjects. The public confirmation of this, as the moment of transfer approaches, would give the deepest satisfaction in this country, and above all to our local authorities to whom the Somalis are not an undifferentiated group, but persons known by name through nine years of association.

The assumption by Italy of her difficult ten-year task gives her a great opportunity to win honour in Africa as a humane and liberal tutor to this high-spirited, individually able, but politically backward and excitable people. Her fulfilment of her trust will be under the elaborately systematized inspection of the United Nations, but she will also hope to gain the more understanding sympathy not only of America, where her work will be keenly observed, but of the other colonial Powers. Nowhere will it be watched with closer interest than in Britain or find warmer appreciation for its success. This is not only for the European reason that we are now trying to repair our old friendship with Italy but for the African reason that we are neighbours and partners in the government of Somalis. This will demand the closest local co-operation between the two countries. It may also be Britain's reconciling part to bring Ethiopia – to which country Count Sforza made a reassuring gesture in the debate – into this partnership and to help her to moderate her sense of past wrong and present fear through working with the representatives of the new Italy.

It is, however, the Somalis themselves who matter most. All their three rulers and the United Nations have declared their interests to be paramount. They are at a difficult moment as they begin to awake from millennia of tribal, nomadic life into consciousness of themselves and their world. In the next ten years their common problems and strivings will demand all that intelligent and liberal administrations, acting both individually and jointly, can give them. When the Italian expedition now at sea reaches their coast it will open another stage in their history: much would be gained if it could begin with Italy and Britain entering upon their new association in close sympathy and understanding.

Yours faithfully

Seretse Khama

Letter to The Times 18 March 1950

On 2 October 1948 Seretse Khama, chief of the Ngwato tribe in the Bechuanaland Protectorate, married the English girl Ruth Williams. On 8 March 1950 the Labour government suspended his chieftainship and banished him for five years from the Protectorate, after which his case would be reviewed. This decision caused a great shock to liberal opinion in Britain and especially to those who knew the Protectorate and the ruling family.

Sir, – The Seretse Khama case has two sides. One is a simple issue of honour and social justice as between white and black, so dramatic and full of that 'human interest' which today makes 'news' that it has swept the world to the grave detriment of Britain's reputation, and inflamed the emotions of those millions, coloured and white, who feel themselves involved on one side or other in a racial conflict. There seems to be an urgent need here to vindicate Britain's good faith by generous action even at the cost of a reversal of policy.

The other aspect of the case is the complex administrative situation in this small tribe on the edge of the Kalahari desert, which has been so inadequately explained by the Government. It seems as though we have been landed in a position in which the first side of the issue demands a political gesture which on the other may be administratively unsound.

On the internal aspect it is ironical to note that the Ngwato tribe, long torn by injurious factions, is one in which banishment, coupled with the destruction of the subject's house, was freely used by the chiefs in dealing with their political opponents, and where the ruling minority held their numerous subject peoples in a state of serfdom and would still regard inter-marriage with them as degrading. By the Christian humanity of the great Khama and the patient – perhaps too patient – influence of the British administration, the caste system, which was based upon the cultural and economic realities of the time, has been gradually modified and some democratic reforms have been introduced. But it is true, as Mr Phillips has so clearly stated, that the future of hereditary chieftainship, and all that is bound up with it, remains one of the chief problems facing Britain here as elsewhere in Africa.

There is little doubt that the highly organized tribal monarchies, which got away to a flying start under the system of 'indirect rule', are now proving the most difficult to democratize and their peoples are torn between the restrictive effects of obsolete powers and a defensive tribal solidarity which finds its only clear focus in the chief. It is probable that in the High Commission territories above all the fear of South Africa has moved tribesmen to rally round their chiefs in spite of influences which pull in the other direction. But this is an issue upon which ruling peoples and subject tribes, aristocrats and commoners, may have different views and interests. The task of British administrators is, therefore, difficult; they feel bound in loyalty to the chiefs who work so closely with them and yet they must try to keep the situation fluid and study the often obscure wishes and interests of the people as they absorb our own democratic ideas.

Is there, then, any way of harmonizing the apparently conflicting demands of the two aspects of this case? It would be rash to answer this question decisively until we have had the full and overdue account of the present situation in the tribe. But it is surely clear that there is no short cut to the deep reforms which the British administration rightly presses but which educational and economic measures alone can bring about, while the reported decision for Seretse of the majority of the official councillors, encouraged no doubt by the very course of the dispute, must be respected.

One thing should be made absolutely clear, and that is Britain's guiding principle in this dangerous world issue of racial relations. It is probable that, although no communication was received from South Africa, it was the potential threat to our relations with the present Union Government, and even to the ultimate future of the Protectorates, which led our representatives into such ambiguous courses. This is a crucial issue. Sooner or later an event was bound to occur which would force us to express our hitherto silent disagreement with the present Union Government upon the fundamentals of African policy. We cannot, without losing our self-respect and our leadership among all the coloured peoples, hope indefinitely to evade this disagreement, and the present issue is one where we stand upon the firmest possible ground. The Bechuanaland Protectorate is under our rule, and so long as this is so we must act there according to the principles of justice and good administration which guide us elsewhere in Africa.

On the question of the inter-racial mixed marriage, it is good to see that the Government's denial of any intention to interfere with this has already had the widest endorsement in the country. Varying private views may be held upon the wisdom of marriages between peoples of widely different cultural backgrounds. But, as science and experience teach us, the difficulties are not inherently racial, and we must recognize that persons have every right to contract inter-racial marriages and to have them treated with public respect. There can be no doubt that as economic and social differences diminish, such unions will increase in number and in general acceptability in the Commonwealth.

The conclusion, then, seems to be that unless the Government can produce very strong justification for its action there will have to be a reversal of policy and a reinstatement of the chief. Britain must shake herself clear of all the muddle and misunderstanding which seem to have dimmed her reputation for good faith and humane administration. It may be hoped that, as in the recoil from the Hoare–Laval agreement, the British people will assert their sense of right and that, in the difficult political conditions of the moment, no party considerations will prevent a clear pronouncement upon a matter that affects the moral foundations of the Commonwealth. When all else fails them, the colonial people fall back upon what they call – in their own expressive way, themselves supplying the capital – British Fairplay. Their faith in this has been damaged in the last ten days and we must set ourselves urgently to repair it.

Yours faithfully

Divided Policies in Africa

Letter to *The Times* 4 August 1950

This letter reports the growing awareness of that fundamental division between South Africa and the rest of the Continent which must be the dominant factor in the Africa of the seventies.

Sir, – The authoritative letter in *The Times* today upon South-West Africa raises two further points.

One is the need that our policies with regard to the rights of dependent peoples, and especially those within the continent of Africa, should not be allowed to go in different directions. Ministers at the Colonial Office make great and, on the whole, justified claims to be moved by the most complete respect for native rights, legal and political. But at the moment it is in southern Africa, in the handling of the South-West African issue by the Foreign Office and of the problem of the High Commission territories by the Commonwealth Relations Office, that the sincerity of our claim is being tested. The questions raised here are indeed difficult, but a policy of evasion or timid expediency must undermine our moral authority in the rest of Africa and in all coloured dependencies and lay us open to just criticism at the United Nations. It is to be hoped that the two departments which are concerned with these closely linked questions will keep in contact with the Colonial Office as to the relationship between their policies.

As today's letter on South-West Africa states, and as your recent excellent series of articles bears out, it is the present racial policy of the Union that exacerbates these problems. White South Africans demand to settle their own intensely difficult and, indeed, tragic racial dilemma without outside interference. But while neither the British nor any other Government has any constitutional right of intervention, can the small white minority in the Union afford to ignore world opinion, which almost universally rejects the principles upon which the policy of the present government is founded?

Two utterly opposed principles are now at work in the African continent and, as things are moving at present, it seems they must ultimately come into collision. In time African, or predominantly African, states will develop in the rest of the continent, and the white minority in the south will find itself holding down with increasing severity its own native majority, which will have the support and sympathy of practically the whole population of the rest of the continent, supported, no doubt, by interested governments and organizations outside it. This may be looking far ahead, but even in the immediate future, as a recent incident in Uganda has shown, the Union may be prevented by the growing fear and hatred of Africans from taking her natural lead in Africa in the fields of science, technical advance, and even – a serious thought at the moment – in defence.

All these dangers are derived ultimately from a conception of inherent African inferiority which a growing number of British people in Africa and in this country know, from their own experience of what those Africans who have been given full education and opportunity can do and can be, is groundless. This is a basic truth that will assert itself in the end. It is one that the British, who are free from the grave national involvement of the Europeans of the Union in its implications, are bound, both by their political traditions and by their colonial commitments to follow. It is therefore to be hoped that in the painful South-West African issue our representatives, in their natural desire not to embarrass our relations with the Union, will not be tempted to compromise upon something even more fundamental.

The conflict of principle, however, cannot, surely, be left to produce mounting tension in the Commonwealth and in Africa, and to make a ruinous psychological breach between Africans and the peoples best placed to assist in the immense task of their development. The time has come for some serious attempt by those who see the great danger into which the continent is drifting to consider ways of bridging the gulf between opposing attitudes and interests, and of making, in as calm and objective a spirit as is possible, an unofficial inquiry into the possibilities of constructive co-operation which should transcend racial divisions.

It may be that the delegation of the World Council of Churches to South Africa, which the Bishop of Chichester announces in a letter which also appears in your columns today, may show the way towards a wider conference, confined at first, perhaps, to southern and south-central Africa, which could consider political and economic questions. It would require for its success both the Christian and the scientific approach. There is a great lack of contact and understanding between those who make or influence policy in the Union and their opposite numbers in British territories, and free and full personal discussion might do much to overcome this. It could bring South Africans, with their deep knowledge and interests, into council with the many others who have experience and responsibilities in Africa in a joint endeavour to turn the continent away from the racial struggle towards which it seems at present to be heading.

                                      Yours faithfully

1951

The Banishment of Tshekedi

Letter to *The Times* 29 May 1951

This was an issue in which I was personally as well as politically concerned, as Chief Tshekedi Khama was a friend who when in England had stayed in my house. I had first met him in Capetown and in his home in Serowe in 1930. Neither at the time nor since have I been able to understand the high-handed and unjust action of a Labour government, in the person of Mr Gordon-Walker, in banishing not only Seretse Khama for marrying a white woman but his uncle, Tshekedi, for no defensible reason. I joined wholeheartedly with Tshekedi's friends, and especially with the Rev. Michael Scott and Miss Mary Benson, who wrote the Chief's life, in working for his reinstatement.

Sir, – Mr Gordon-Walker's decision to renew Tshekedi's banishment does not solve the Bamangwato problem but only adds one more reason for reconsidering it. Nothing less than this will satisfy those who fear that it has not been handled with wisdom or justice.

There may have been a case for suspending Seretse from the chieftainship, though his banishment is much more questionable. But Tshekedi's case is quite different and has suffered from being entangled with that of his nephew. Here is a man innocent of any offence, whose conduct to his nephew, his tribe, and the British Government has been beyond criticism, and who has proved himself in his twenty years of regency to be probably the most intelligent, enlightened and determined chief in Africa.

Is it not advisable to inquire into a system which punishes such a man with banishment? The Government's explanation invites question. He is said to be unpopular with 'many people'. A strong, progressive chief is not likely to be palatable to all his conservative tribesmen. And is it not possible that some of his opponents have been put into power and are undermining his influence and opposing his return? And is unpopularity a penal offence? Is it possible that he is unpopular with some of the officials, used to more subservient chiefs and insensibly influenced, perhaps, by the attitude to 'natives' prevailing in South Africa? Disorder? If any violence has been threatened against Tshekedi, is it not the duty of the administration to ensure his protection? His record and interests both seem to preclude the possibility that he would break the peace.

The question raises wider issues. The Commonwealth Relations Office, with its essentially diplomatic functions – witness yesterday's appointment of an ex-ambassador to deal with these High Commission territories – is not constituted for this one, small, but difficult task of African administration. It should be enabled to draw upon the wide experience and the liberal traditions of the Colonial Office. The problems of these territories are those of a too rapidly changing continent. There is no easy solution for them. The tribal system is everywhere taking a severe strain and Britain must attempt to reshape it upon more democratic lines. But it is an abrupt policy to abolish chieftainship at a stroke, and a timid policy to exclude the ablest and most educated men instead of helping them to lead their people towards democracy by way of a 'constitutional' chieftainship. It is also a despotic policy for a British government to use the old arbitrary power of the chief (or their own version of it) to cast out chieftainship, and it can be a corrupting activity for all concerned in it from Whitehall to Serowe.

Could not Tshekedi, and even Seretse, be trusted to go back, if at first only for a trial period, as private citizens, perhaps with some widely acceptable third man as chief or regent, with every possible measure of public preparation and promise which seems necessary, and under a district commissioner at once firm and liberal? There would be plenty to engage the energies of these men in the councils of their tribe, in the large new development schemes of the region, or in the long overdue legislative council which could pull this row of small tribes together and put them upon a more modern basis. These possibilities are surely worth investigating. They would supersede the elements of timidity and old-fashioned injustice in the present policy and bring it a little more into line with the experiments we are making in other parts of a continent which, as it drifts nearer to racial conflict, calls to Britain for a consistent policy and humane and intelligent administration.

       Yours faithfully

The Banishment of Tshekedi

Letter to *The Times* 26 June 1951

Sir, – The course of the debate over the Bechuanaland issue in the past few weeks reinforces the need for an inquiry.

Tshekedi has stated his case: Mr Gordon-Walker has rejected it. The British Parliament and people clearly wish to come to a just decision between the two. But how can they do so? The issues are intricate; they reach back to the Seretse affair and beyond, and they are not wholly intelligible to those without at least some general knowledge of the African background. In the latest phase the Minister rests his case partly upon a criticism of Tshekedi's character and, in view of the excellent impression the ex-regent has made upon all who have met him, this has only deepened the fear that some injustice may have been done.

The only people who are in a position to supply the essential knowledge are the three or four officials in charge of the area. Yet they are the very people whose handling of the affair is in question. It is they who dealt with the original crisis, who have advised Mr Gordon-Walker upon his policy, and who are now in complete control of this divided, ignorant, and malleable tribe. This arises from no fault of theirs, but from the peculiar position of the territory, and it is no criticism of them to say that, once a serious question has arisen about its administration, this is not a very healthy situation. It means that if, being human, however good their intentions, they made some error in judgement in handling a very difficult situation, both they and their Minister are almost impelled to follow the course to which they committed themselves.

The demand for an inquiry, however, rests upon wider considerations. The whole history of British policy towards subject peoples shows how necessary it is, especially where small native groups and their white administrators are shut away from the direct influence of this country, to open them up from time to time to fresh air and light. Opinion in Britain is not static: it moves towards greater generosity and liberalism, and policy on the frontiers has constantly to be adjusted so as to keep it in harmony with this movement. One of the main methods for securing this adjustment has been the commission of inquiry from this country with the revisions of policy which nearly always follow from it. It is difficult to understand why Mr Gordon-Walker, whose good intentions cannot be questioned, continues to refuse the only means by which British opinion can be helped to understand and to judge an obscure situation and with the help of which the affairs not only of this tribe but of the whole protectorate might be benefited.

The very difficulty of the problems of this region in relationship with South and Central Africa makes it the more necessary that British opinion should be fully informed about it, and greater knowledge, with an administrative stock-taking, would also foster the success of the important development schemes which the British taxpayer is financing in this region. Mr Gordon-Walker's argument that an inquiry will unsettle the tribe is unconvincing, since the tribe is already deeply unsettled and will continue to be so until a really authoritative settlement is achieved. An inquiry will not, of course, be enough. There will be a need for a strong and able administrator, who has not been involved in the events of the past few years, to bring a fresh mind to bear on the problems of a territory which, however small and poor, has yet become a severe test of Britain's capacity for African administration.

Yours faithfully

The British Problem in Africa

Foreign Affairs July 1951

The Gold Coast elections of February 1951 have sent a shock right through Africa, or at least that Africa which lies south of the Sahara. To white men who have made their home in the African continent the shock has come as a perhaps only half-formulated question: 'Is this the beginning of the end for us?' And every African who has heard the news – a number no one can estimate exactly – has felt a thrill of joy, and of the sudden, almost incredulous hope: 'Is this the beginning for us?'

There can be no doubt that the first assumption of ministerial office by elected Negroes in a British colonial territory makes 1951 an important date in the political history of Africa and a very proper date at which to take stock. For this event in the middle of the century means that Britain is committed in act as well as in word to the speedy promotion of self-government in her African colonies. It is just over fifty years, from the occupation of the interior, since British rule over these territories began; and it is not a very bold speculation to believe that they may become fully self-governing nation-states by the end of the century. It almost seems as though future African writers of history books may thus be able very neatly to sum up the first half of the twentieth century as the age of imperialism, and the second as the age of liberation.

When, however, our glance is extended from the Gold Coast to the rest of Africa, or even if it is confined to British territories, the possibility that African self-government will spread surely and smoothly appears much less certain. Developments in Asia, which may give cause for optimism to some who are anxiously looking for reasons for optimism in the stern conditions of the day, are not easily comparable with those of Africa. Even if they were, the great issues in Asia are far from being decided in favour of the West. The two great conflicts of our world – the political issue between the Communist and democratic nations, and the division of race or, less inaccurately, of colour – are in danger of converging. At present, the Chinese excepted, the great majority of the coloured races lie within the orbit of the Western democratic Powers. But in Africa this is because they are still under the political control of these Powers; and in much of Asia it is because they have just emerged from that control and are still linked to the West by many economic ties, and marked – who would confidently assert how deeply? – with the impress of Western civilization.

The task of helping to develop these peoples, and of holding them in partnership, is not the same in Asia as in Africa. In Asia, though the divisions which are called communal are deep and cut across the demands of national solidarity, there are nonetheless great areas of cultural and religious unity, and of common pride based upon the inheritance of ancient civilizations. These peoples have brought their historic cultures through centuries of subjection to Western influence with their deepest elements still inviolate and they are resolved to reassert the validity of their cultures in the modern world. The special offer of the West must therefore be the possibility of a free association of differing cultures, instead of the crushing monolithic system offered by Communism. The meeting of the West with Asia, for all the present disparity of material power, will have to be between equals in status. It will have the nature of alliance rather than assimilation.

The dealings between tropical Africa and the West must be different. Here in place of the large unities of Asia was the multicellular tissue of tribalism: instead of an ancient civilization, the largest area of primitive poverty enduring into the modern age. Until the very recent penetration by Europe the greater part of the continent was without the wheel, the plough or the transport-animal; almost without stone houses or clothes, except for skins; without writing and so without recorded history. Mentally as well as physically the Africans were helpless before a European intrusion all the more speedy and overwhelming because it came at a time when science had given Europe such immense material power. Yet the African peoples on the whole, as slavery proved, are tenacious and adaptable. The revolutionary changes which Europe has imposed upon tropical Africa within fifty years have evoked from them a positive and vigorous reaction which was lacking in some Amerindian and Pacific races. Yet it remains true that in losing their thousandfold tribal past Africans must grow into the general shape of the civilization which has been brought to them, whatever colour they may in time give it from their own character and physical setting. Thus, for the next half-century or so, the relationship between the West and Negro Africa must be assimilative in the broadest sense.

If the West is to win and to hold Africa, the effort needed is thus different from that needed in Asia. But it is no less great. As in Asia, it will be a race with time. The process of enfranchisement from European control has been so hastened by a combination of forcing influences that these least-civilized peoples are likely to have the shortest period of tutelage. They may therefore break prematurely out of a recently imposed framework of unity and order into conditions of chaos or stagnation. If the primitive poverty of this vast area is to be raised there has to be massive application of capital accumulated through the energy and restraint of other peoples; managerial skill will be needed on a vast scale, with large numbers of experts discovering the lessons of science and applying them in campaigns for the betterment of life – human, animal and vegetable – and of the earth which carries this life.

If plans devised in London, Washington and other centres are not to be put through with coercive direction, but are to win the intelligent co-operation of Africans, each must be accompanied by sociological study and patient educational effort. The trained Africans now ready to play any but a subordinate part in these great schemes of betterment are to be numbered in hundreds rather than thousands. Even fewer have the wide knowledge which allows them to recognize their need of European planners, still less to play a part in drawing up the plans. While Africans outgrow the suspicions produced by sheer ignorance, a new political suspicion takes their place and this can be overcome only by political measures aimed at producing a common will between Africans and Europeans.

II

The main political question that we must answer, as we try to look into Africa's next 50 years, is whether the promise of political emancipation which Britain has made on the west coast can be fulfilled and then extended to her eastern and central colonies. The answer will depend largely upon the assessment of the strength of the influences which have prompted this policy of political emancipation. The first is to be found in the character of Britain's parliamentary institutions. By their very nature they could not be confined within her borders and were carried overseas by her own emigrants. The evolution of the white Dominions followed, and their institutions were extended, with hesitation and difficulty, to Asia, and with even more hesitation to Africa. But this does not account for the sudden advance in Africa, during the last ten years, towards an end which, with much justification, was thought to be very distant.

The reason for this acceleration, which has come as a surprise to many people even in Britain, is to be found in a convergence of many different factors just before, during and after the Second World War. Among them was the natural maturing, especially in west Africa, of an educational system which by the thirties had begun to turn out graduates with the training and confidence to occupy responsible positions, and the ability to define and voice their political discontents. The town dwellers and wage earners increased in numbers, and since they were detached from their tribal systems, they became increasingly responsive to the new leaders. Then as the British Labour Party grew in strength it encouraged, by the force of example, the new proletarians who were beginning to develop political consciousness and to call themselves 'underprivileged'; and it encouraged them directly by giving a new urgency and completeness to the promise of self-government. At the same time the uncompromising doctrines of Communism, which damn imperialism and capitalism and exalt the 'toiling masses', began to influence Africans, even though they did not consciously accept the doctrines or even identify them. A further factor which speeded up the process in the years before the Second World War was the effect of the demand of the Germans for the retrocession of their former colonies, since it forced Britain to emphasize the contrast between her own programme for colonial freedom and the doctrine of racial supremacy put forward by the Herrenvolk.

When the war brought a period of extreme danger for Britain, strenuous economic and military services had to be asked from the colonial peoples, upon a basis of willing co-operation. And with the coming of peace, Britain's relatively greater weakness in the world subtly altered her position as a ruler of colonial peoples. Thus the heat of war forced the growth of self-government; and the favourable temperature was kept after the war by pressure from the United Nations in general, and, from their very different points in the political compass, from Russia and the United States in particular. The colonial peoples had behaved with great steadiness and loyalty, and they expected to be rewarded. Their leaders were few in numbers, but they were quick to take advantage of the relaxation of the imperial grasp which had allowed the liberation of India, Ceylon and Burma. Moreover, new and flamboyant leaders emerged. The social and economic life of the colonies had been deeply shaken by five years of war, and, especially in West Africa and the West Indies, Negroes eagerly absorbed those millennial hopes which are born so strangely out of ruinous conflicts. Instinctively seeking to exploit the unifying forces of discontent and of indignation generated by an almost universal inferiority of status of their race, the leaders directed the restlessness of their followers against their foreign rulers. Under the protection of the old British civil liberties, a large part of the immature native press, especially in west Africa, treated every act of the Government, good, bad or indifferent, with unvarying but highly spiced denunciation.

With one of those rapid assessments of a critical situation of which they are capable after a long blind period, the British quickly decided that, since it had become morally impossible for them to answer this agitation by repressive force, there was no alternative to ungrudging and immediate cession of what had so long been promised. Hence the open-handed gestures in Asia were followed by the large instalments of freedom in the West Indies and Africa. In these regions Britain revised almost every constitution between 1944 and 1950, some of them more than once, to introduce or increase native participation in the central colonial governments. Many other measures in the interests of the native people were introduced in the spheres of local government, finance, economics and social services. The recent events in the Gold Coast, the most politically-advanced African territory, by which Africans have drawn up their own constitution, carried out a general election, and put an imprisoned leader and his extreme party in power, are only the most striking results of this policy.

III

If this is the policy, and these the pressures which have produced it, this would seem the line upon which Britain must go forward. But when the situation in all of Africa south of the Sahara is considered, certain factors appear which are not merely unfavourable to the rapid development of African self-government but even hostile to it. The British Commonwealth countries in this vast area fall into three parts: the west coast colonies, South Africa, and the eastern and central territories.

It is not difficult to describe South Africa's place in the political picture, as that country is now and as it apparently intends to be in the future. The Union of South Africa is a stratified society. A minority of 2,500,000 white men are absolutely dominant – politically, economically and socially – over some 8,500,000 Africans and the smaller Indian and coloured communities. No one can judge the policy of the white group who does not try to enter into the tragic dilemma in which their history has placed them. They feel themselves obliged to defend their domination by principles of racial superiority which are an absolute denial of those upon which Britain is acting in her tropical colonies. The Gold Coast election has brought this contradiction into dramatic conflict, and it is not surprising that the fiercest denunciation of the Gold Coast experiment has come from Dr Malan, the Nationalist Prime Minister of the Union. If other native territories followed this example, he said, 'it meant nothing less than the expulsion of white men from practically everywhere between the Union and the Sahara'. What that would mean for Africa was not a matter for conjecture. However, he comforted himself with the assertion that the experiment would undoubtedly fail, since a wrong application of the principle of democracy had made it ridiculous.

Dr Malan was prompted by the very understandable fear that hangs over white South Africa. Even so, he was only putting into extreme terms the doubts about the Gold Coast election, and the promise of an immediate similar experiment in nearby Nigeria, which have been widespread among the white colonists in Africa. Even in England this advance is thought by many to be a leap in the dark. The fact is that the west of Africa, and the south, are moving in opposite directions. Even a partial failure on the west coast will strengthen the determination of the Union to follow its own system, and will deepen the uncertainty that hangs over the large British block of colonies to the east.

These fears about the Gold Coast experiment (which are Dr Malan's hopes) are not groundless. There is no precedent for the sudden grant of the parliamentary franchise to a large, illiterate, tribal population, utterly remote from the political experience of the Western peoples. It is unnecessary to list all the contrasts between the development, setting and character of the British parliamentary system and the conditions in the arbitrarily demarcated region of Africa into which it has been exported. A perilously small fraction of the African people have any knowledge of the arts or sciences by which the modern welfare state they demand is conducted. With an electorate at once so ignorant, so expectant and so racially sensitive, and with none of the conditions present for the development of a party system, the invitation to demagogy seems certain to be accepted. It remains to be seen whether the restraining advice of the colonial government, the powers which it has reserved, and the long-established substructure of local government based in part upon tribal organization, will succeed in containing the full tide of this very new democracy. No hope of easy achievement should be cherished. But it is now in the interests of Britain, as well as of the peoples of these territories, to exert every effort to make the experiment succeed. The direct results of failure would fall first upon the inhabitants who are entirely African, but the results of a breakdown would also discourage and anger the Negro peoples throughout the world. It would harden the caste system of the Union of South Africa and would deeply influence the still undecided future of east and central Africa.

RACIAL POPULATIONS IN EAST AND SOUTH AFRICA

	Africans	Europeans	Indians & Pakistanis[2]	Arabs	Coloured
Union of So. Africa[1]	8,347,000	2,620,000	323,000		1,030,000
Basutoland	540,000	1,700	340		547
Bechuanaland	290,000	2,300			1,700
Swaziland	181,000	3,200			
Southern Rhodesia	1,960,000	129,000			
Northern Rhodesia	1,849,000	36,000			
Nyasaland	2,455,000	3,800	5,250		2,000
Tanganyika	7,332,539	10,648	46,254	11,074	1,335
Uganda	4,914,211	3,448	35,215	1,475	643
Kenya	5,218,232	29,660	97,687	24,174	964

[1] These figures exclude South-West Africa which according to the 1946 census had 259,000 Africans, 10,500 Bushmen, 31,000 Europeans, 44,500 Coloured.
[2] The figures include a small number of other Asians.

Because of the emigration of European and Indian colonists to east and central Africa, and the strains set up by the competition for power among these groups and between them and the native majorities, the situation here is even more sensitive. The tension runs from one territory to the other, affecting even those areas which have no immigrant groups. And it goes down from them to the Union, and then overseas to excite the interest and support of the nations from which the emigrants came. The conflict of power represents in microcosm, in one of its most intractable forms, the world tensions between white and brown, and white and black. The situations vary in the several territories and it may be useful to remind ourselves of the racial distribution in the countries which lie southward from Ethiopia.

To understand the full meaning of the figures shown in the Table opposite it should be remembered that the Union of South Africa is a completely independent Dominion, and that Southern Rhodesia has full, responsible self-government, subject to some formal reservations by Britain over native matters which in practice are never used. All the other territories are administered directly by Britain, though Tanganyika is under United Nations Trusteeship. The penetration of the temperate highlands of these tropical dependencies by white colonists is not the only point of contrast between them and west Africa.

Most of the peoples of eastern Africa were far less advanced in their political organization and in their culture, and were much more sparsely distributed. The chief exception was the fertile and populous region around Lake Victoria, with its large chieftainships. An additional contrast, which still further explains the relative political immaturity of the eastern Africans, is their much later contact with Europeans, and indeed with the outside world. Uganda, which contains the advanced and prosperous kingdom of Buganda, is free from white settlement, but it is closely bound to Kenya through which run its communications to the sea, and its peoples watch the white colony there with deep anxiety.

Individually and as a group, these territories confront Britain with difficult decisions. Here the principles of democracy do not fit the situation: numerically insignificant white minorities have built up the Western economies which are in operation; and they have been the dominant element politically as well. The African tribes as a whole have hitherto shown little sense of solidarity, and little interest in public affairs. Only in the last few years has there been much sign of political vitality, and that has been confined to some of the more advanced tribes, such as the Ganda in Uganda, the Kikuya in Kenya and the Chagga in

Tanganyika. In Northern Rhodesia the copper belt has attracted a mixed and restless African proletariat which is beginning to organize itself effectively in defence of its interests. The Indians are in the main confined to the towns: they are traders, large and small, and they own much of the urban property in the main cities. They are resentful of their political status in Kenya, where they have smaller political representation than the Europeans, though they are more numerous. The present split between Hindu and Moslem, reflected from their homelands, has divided their leadership.

What kind of constitution should Britain try to fit upon this patchwork of races? Partition within mixed territories, the current treatment for irreconcilables, is ruled out. Although there are large tribal areas, the Europeans and Africans outside them are interlocked in a capital–labour, master–servant relationship, while the Indian occupies an uneasy intermediate commercial position. If there were no white settlement Britain would, as in west Africa, concentrate without doubts or distractions upon the all-round development of the Africans. As it is, she faces a problem only less large and embittered than that of South Africa. For more than a century in South Africa she was involved in a painful attempt to regulate the seemingly irreconcilable clash between white colonist and native African; it has left the three High Commission Territories embarrassingly upon her hands. History has shown how difficult it is for a relatively detached imperial government to mediate between its own people and the weaker groups which they have subjected. The United States experienced this difficulty in a special form when it found that victory in a bloody civil war did not enable the Federal Government to enforce its principles of justice and equality fully upon the southern states. Britain's attempt at enforcement in South Africa lasted a century and may be said to have failed. Since the establishment of the Union, and still more since the Afrikaner Nationalists gained power, she has seen the vestiges of her egalitarian policy rooted out one by one until African subordination has been made complete.

The same problem has now presented itself in Kenya and the Rhodesias though in less advanced form. Kenya may be chosen to illustrate the apparent insolubility of the constitutional question. The immediate introduction there of full parliamentary democracy would put control into the hands of some 5,000,000 Africans, of whom not 1 per cent have any knowledge of the working of the modern state or the economy which has been built up over their heads. It would also put them in control of those small groups – British officials, white settlers and Indian traders – who are politically and economically the dominant and dynamic elements in the colony. A few people are led by humanitarian emotion or political doctrines to advocate this as an immediate policy, but even those most confident of the necessity of the new steps in the Gold Coast cannot show that Kenya is at present in a comparable position. Even if it held no immigrant groups Kenya would not be ready for such a policy. African unity and experience would have to grow very much stronger before the Kenya settlers would be ready to relinquish the position they have secured, and the imperial government willing to coerce them and to imperil such a vital strategic area.

With so much to lose it is not surprising that most of the white settlers agree with the South African Government that the racial situation permits no middle course: that if they grant the Africans something, they grant everything. This seems the logical short-term answer; it is also the shortsighted one. The humane and long-term answer is surely that to treat people, whose potential equality has been proved in so many individual instances, as something less than men is to demoralize both those who give and those who suffer this treatment, and to so vitrify society that it cannot grow and must some day break. The alternative course seems to be to continue in the face of all fears and doubts with the present slow and difficult British policy of obliging the impatient white colonists to mark time politically, while actively assisting the advance of the subordinate race and making gradual adjustments to accommodate its advance.

IV

But there is some choice of political direction as well as of pace. The British constitution, with its concentration of sovereignty in one of its legislative chambers, a system developed gradually by one of the most united and mature nations in the world, is obviously unsuited to east Africa. Nor does it seem likely that any superficial adaptations of this system, for example by way of communal voting with racial allotment of seats, will do anything but exacerbate political conflict. The aim should be to distribute rather than to concentrate power. This method runs counter to modern tendencies, but its value in absorbing racial shocks and in widening political education outweighs its easily enumerated defects. The aim might be carried out through a somewhat rigid federal structure for the whole of east Africa, with extensive powers

[1951]   COLONIAL SEQUENCE 1949 TO 1969

resting in large provinces. Their boundaries should be drawn to attain the utmost possible homogeneity, but even so some of their councils would contain representatives of all races, and they would thus allow co-operation at a level where the major political fears need not haunt the proceedings. At the centre there could be a distribution of many social and economic functions to temporary or standing boards. The practical character of their work would be realistic and unifying, while the relative privacy of their proceedings would discourage any playing to the racial gallery. In a government for eastern Africa constructed upon this pattern, with the rights of minorities and the powers of provinces within the federal structure guaranteed by the overall imperial government, it might be possible for the several races to learn to modify their fears of each other, and thus valuable time for the experience of fuller co-operation might be gained.

This result will not be obtained easily. In Kenya, above all, dissensions have been sharp for 30 years, and political attitudes have crystallized. But there are encouraging signs even there, for some Europeans have faced the hard truth that though they built their original privileged position upon African weakness and inferiority, such a foundation is not immutable and preliminary steps must be taken now for its gradual reconstruction. This explains why at least some of the settlers have accepted African and Indian representation in the quasi-federal East African High Commission and in the Kenya legislature, and have even also embarked upon some experiments in interracial social contact. All of this would be impossible in South Africa.

The racial situation in central Africa takes a somewhat different form. There is no Indian population of any importance, and in the Rhodesias the whites are less overwhelmingly outnumbered by the Africans than in the three northern territories. Southern Rhodesia, advancing at breakneck speed today through white immigration and industrial development, is almost a Dominion. Northern Rhodesia, with little more than 1,000,000 Africans, is dominated politically by the white settlers. The copper mines govern the economy of the country. Nyasaland, small and isolated, is a mainly African territory, but is bound by economic ties to the Rhodesias.

There have been many years of vacillation about the relationship of these three territories. In recent years, following a measure of co-operation through a central council, the Europeans of the two Rhodesias have drawn more closely together and demanded some form of federation. The Gold Coast election has now startled them into angry alignment like the crack of a whip. 'The feeling is growing among the European community', declared Mr Welensky, leader of the Northern Rhodesian colonials, commenting on the election, 'that the Government of the United Kingdom is not going to judge self-government for the colonies on the ability of the people to govern themselves: the whole thing will be a matter of political expediency. To the British Socialist Government, the ills of the colonies are dispelled by the provision of the ballot box and a trade union. This is a travesty of development.' The Prime Minister of Southern Rhodesia has said with equal bluntness that sticking to mere numbers in a constitution might turn democracy into mob-rule in Africa.

However, while the leaders condemn Britain in these terms, they also dissociate themselves from the racial policy of South Africa. They claim to be following a middle way between Britain's dangerous surrender to an unready majority and the Union's policy of repression. Britain's reason for refusing hitherto to permit amalgamation of the central African territories has been that the native policy which she has followed in the two northern Colonial Office territories is not compatible with the less liberal system of Southern Rhodesia. Native opinion, just beginning to express itself through a few voices, emphatically endorses this view. Southern Rhodesia hangs unhappily between the Colonial Office territories on the north and the Union on the south. Devotedly British in their allegiance, the white colonists recoil from the increasingly assertive Afrikaner nationalism of the Union. Yet, when they look north, they are repelled, and indeed alarmed, by the native policy Britain is following. At this moment, the delicate problem of their future affiliation has just been discussed in a private official conference which has endeavoured to find some form of closer union which will square all the circles presented by race and politics. If Southern Rhodesia could be attached to the northern colonies without Britain's paying too high a price in concessions at the expense of the African, then a boundary *might* be drawn along the Zambesi against the northward advance of the Union policy.

V

In all these African issues, west, east and central, Britain is obliged to play a leading part as ruler or arbiter. She cannot simply sit back and allow matters to take their course: the forces generated by European intrusion into primitive Africa are too disturbing to be left to work

[1951]

themselves out. Yet, though Britain must play the leading part, and must, if she is true to her principles and professions, take up the Union's challenge with growing boldness, she is not, of course, the only influence even in tropical Africa. Great regions are under Portuguese, Belgian and French rule. But in the development of African self-government, Britain is without doubt the formative influence. Portugal and Belgium have, so far with success, sealed their territories against 'unsettling' ideas. France is deeply engaged in inducing her colonies to fulfil their political ambitions as parts of a great French Union, rather than as autonomous nations. None of these Powers regards British policy with a friendly eye. Britain must reckon also upon the increasing intervention in Africa by America and the United Nations. The relations of each colony are no longer limited to contacts between it and the imperial ruler: many influences are at work to draw Africa together physically and mentally, to link its peoples to the world and to awaken them to the world's growing concern about their affairs. International intervention, which has pushed through plans for the speedy independence of Libya and Somaliland, and which plays chiefly but not exclusively upon the Trust Territories, quickens the political pace by reinforcing colonial nationalism.

Africa is indeed becoming part of the world. This vast raw continent which lies so close to Europe has, apart from that northern strip which has for so long been the southern fringe of Europe, been locked away from the influences of Western civilization. It is now fast being drawn strategically and economically into the Western sphere. Tropical Africa was at first little more to the Western nations than a coast line; then it became a hunting ground for slaves; next, it was parcelled up as the property of Western nations and its people regarded primarily as their supply of labour. And now the West has new and urgent economic and strategic claims upon the continent. In other words, Africa and Africans have been the instruments of other nations. Now, as a result of the civilizing influences brought consciously and unconsciously by the West, Africans are at last demanding the right to state and to follow their own purposes. The difficulties before them, mainly inherent in the physical conditions of the continent and in their own history, or lack of it, are immense. And the West faces equal difficulties in trying to find a way of harmonizing its own interests with those of this awakening Africa. The seeds have been sown for a racial conflict that will weaken, if it does not ruin, the attempt to develop the people and their continent at the speed which the impatience of Africans and the world situation demand. The

West has the desire, the science, the energy and the capital to develop Africa. Africa has a desperate need of all these things. The question is whether Africans will be able to accept them. Their poverty and weakness allowed (it might almost be said to have necessitated) a subjection so complete that when Africans became aware at last of their history and position in the world, the discovery created a deep bitterness. It finds its natural object in the colonial Powers which have brought Africa at once subjection and Western civilization.

The civilization is, however, in its very earliest stage, and it is impossible to foretell whether, Africa being what it is, the process could be carried on if that subjection were suddenly brought to an end. The white colonists say 'no'. But they are deeply interested parties, and the Africans and their supporters reject and resent their opinion just because it is theirs. The very fact of the presence of these white settlers, above all in the form which it takes in South Africa, makes it difficult for many Africans to consider reasonably any proposition about their future relations with the white man. The British policy of a gradual transfer of powers, so logical and defensible as the compromise between two extremes, thus runs against the opposition of black and white in Africa. It is too quick for the whites; it is too slow for the Gold Coast Africans today and will be too slow for those of Kenya tomorrow. Yet, since there is no alternative to this policy, Britain will be obliged to continue with it, and she must not despair if only a fraction of success is achieved. For the stakes are very high. Analogy between peoples and individuals can be misleading, but both do seem to have this in common, that their characteristics are formed very early in their development. The Western nations have grave reason to know what the Romans' failure to impose their civilization over the whole of Europe has meant to that continent: within the next fifty years, or even less, it may be decided whether Negro Africa will be won or lost to the religion and society of the West.

1952

The Sudan on the Edge of Independence

Letter to *The Times* 21 January 1952

The Sudan was the first British dependency in Africa to obtain independence. Being under the Foreign Office and closely linked to Egypt by geography and history, its emancipation was a complex process, and one difficult for British opinion to follow.

Sir, – The Sudan is now upon the edge of independence; but, as your recent articles have shown, the final steps will not be easy.

The Sudanese people, divided internally by race, religion and sectarian politics, are further distracted by having their destinies, and indeed their whole fate, entrammelled with the Egyptian crisis. So far, in all the tension and uncertainty, the great majority of the Sudanese have remained amazingly calm and orderly. This is due partly to their own steadiness of character and partly to their faith in their British administrators who, at a time when the great work of their service, as well as their own future, are in suspense, have shown the utmost devotion and liberal sympathy. Led by their able Civil Secretary, Sir James Robertson, who has to take the chief strain of the crisis, they can be relied upon to carry out loyally the British Government's promise of achieving, within the year, full self-government as a prelude to self-determination.

This will not be enough, however. We know now from sad experience in the last few years what an immensely difficult task it is to withdraw imperial control without this resulting in injury to the ruled and bitterness against the ruler. It is no mere negative process: it requires energy as well as restraint and the generous recognition that this is an adventurous new beginning for the people, and that it need not be merely an end and a retreat for us if we can keep their good will and assist as friends and allies in the new era. It is of vital importance both to the

Sudanese and ourselves to maintain friendly relations, as agreements with them will have to be made and worked with regard to defence and communications, the control of the Nile waters, the future of British officials, the conduct of the Gezira scheme, and any special provisions that may be necessary for the backward areas of the south.

It is, however, on the psychological side that we have shown ourselves gravely lacking in some of the difficult political transactions of the last few years. A few officials, no matter how devoted, cannot alone, least of all when in the very act of abdicating control, create the new relationship. They need full understanding and support from Britain. Unfortunately, owing to its ambiguous constitutional status and the remote and fractional interest of the Foreign Office in its administration, the Sudan has been kept, as far as concerns public knowledge and contact, in an extremely obscure half-light between the clear positions held by foreign territories upon the one side and by the colonies upon the other. In the few months that remain to us to help the Sudan in its birth as a nation, no effort should be spared to widen and deepen our contacts with its peoples, most of whom would welcome more signs of interest and concern from our side. I venture to suggest that a strong Parliamentary delegation should go out, not with any specified task but merely as a visit of good will, to meet Sudanese, to gain a general understanding of their hopes and plans, and to bring this knowledge and sympathy back to Westminster. In view of the suspicion that always corrodes the final period of European control, it might be well if the delegation included one or two men well known for their faith in the policy of self-government.

Such a visit will of course be of value only if our policy towards the Sudan remains steady and just. Here two points must be made. The constitutional problem has now reached a stage, internally and externally, when nothing but self-government can solve it. But before that terminus is reached much in the way of constitutional preparation has still to be done, and in the course of this there are certain to appear half a dozen good reasons, based on the unreadiness and disunity of the Sudanese, for calling a halt. But will they be any more ready in three or four years than in one? And in the interval their trust and goodwill might be dissipated, the present able and moderate leaders outflanked by demagogues, the divisions among the Sudanese further widened, distracting international interventions multiplied, and the external situation worsened. Thus the hope of a reasoned, orderly and friendly transfer of power might be lost.

[1952]

Finally, it is of the utmost importance never to forget, in spite of our present relations with Egypt, that that country, her own worst enemy, has just rights and legitimate fears with regard to the Sudan. We could do no more cruel service to the Sudanese than to leave them on such terms with Egypt than the latter felt the need, as she would have the strength, to destroy the independent nationhood that we have done so much to create in half a century of perhaps the most efficient and humane imperial administration known in history. In our exercise of power along the middle Nile it will be the last steps that will count.

Yours faithfully

Central Africa: History of Remote Control

Letter to *The Times* 4 March 1952

On 4 and 5 March decisive debates on the Central African Federation took place in the House of Commons in which the Conservatives defeated a Labour motion criticizing their handling of the issue and especially their ignoring of the growing African opposition. I had opposed the idea of the Federation from the time of the Bledisloe Commission in 1939 (Vol. I, pp. 187-8) and I continued this vain opposition to the end.

Sir, – In Tuesday's debate in the House of Commons upon federation in central Africa there is one lesson from history which should be remembered. It is the inability of a British Government to retain any effective control over native affairs once the substance of power has been transferred to the white community.

More than once British Ministers, caught painfully between the thrust of white colonists towards independence and the pressure of liberal and humanitarian opinion at home, have sought immediate political relief by claiming to keep the powers of intervention in matters affecting native interests. But so long as only one race can present the title deeds of democracy, this expedient is ineffectual. This could be shown from the history not only of Southern Rhodesia but also from that of New Zealand and South Africa. Mr Churchill will recall, for he was Colonial Under-Secretary at the time, the strong attempt made by his Government in 1906 to intervene in Natal on behalf of some condemned Zulus. The Natal Ministry resigned and returned to power, an argument before which a British Cabinet felt obliged to bow. In South Africa, in addition to British experience before the Union, we have that of the Cape after that event. Britain had engraved her egalitarian principles so deeply into the local traditions that the Cape delegates entered the Union on condition that their liberal practice was given special safeguards in the new constitution.

In recent years we have seen these undermined or destroyed one by one. The British Parliament, distressed in 1909 at being asked to enact a constitution that gave only such localized civic rights to the African majority, comforted itself with the confident hope that liberal principles must, by their very nature, triumph in time over the opposing influences. But when one of these is the fear of a community for its ultimate survival, this calculation is disproved. In South Africa today British principles remain in action, inadequately and precariously it may be, only in the three territories which have been retained under direct British government. The lesson of history would seem to be that Britain cannot escape from her dilemma by provisions on paper for remote controls or vetoes, however ingenious.

Imperial power was driven before into retreat because the majority it was attempting to protect was powerless. That position, in central Africa, is about to change. Africans are just beginning to exert an effective political will and to direct it towards the maintenance of the British connection. This is at a time when the possibility of a great racial struggle hangs over southern Africa, a region where history shows that it is not easy to draw boundaries. It may not be many years before the white colonists of central Africa, if not elsewhere, come in their turn to value the services of an arbitral Power which can command African loyalty and which might help to ensure that their great ability and constructive energy, of which the continent stands in such need, will be preserved not above, or against, but alongside areas of African enfranchisement. Any weakening of British power in southern Africa at this moment might prove to be one more in the long series of tragic mistakes that have been the main theme in the history of this part of the continent.

Yours faithfully

[1952]

Central African Federation: Lessons from History

Letter to *The Times* 10 March 1952

Sir, – Lord Winterton counters my appeal to recent history with one which leads him to the Boston tea-party.

I admit that he is even more relevant than he seems to think, since the part played by Red Indian interests in exacerbating the American colonists is not imaginary. It is to be found in the expensive British plan to control migration and to protect native rights in a hinterland opened up by our victory in the Seven Years War. This ambitious project was swept away at the revolution with all the wreckage of Imperial power, and the Red Indians with it. But are we to base policy in central Africa in the 1950s upon events in North America in the 1770s? Contrast the thousands of unassimilable Red Indians scantily disposed along the frontier of a vast temperate land with the millions of vigorous, adaptable Africans, already the indispensable basis of the new Western economy, and the outposts of large and constitutionally advancing populations in an equatorial north. Contrast, too, the climate of world opinion in the time of Lord North with that of our own day, which has seen the advancement of coloured subject peoples into nations represented upon an international organization which calls the rulers of the remaining colonies to account.

This is not a mere historical exercise. It is a reminder of the changed world which Britain, with her traditions and widespread responsibilities, is naturally quick to recognize, but to which the Europeans in south and central Africa will sooner or later have to adjust themselves. To recognize this is evidence neither of hostility towards them in their tragic dilemma nor of any illusions about the immediate readiness of the African masses to play a full and equal part as citizens. The problem is surely to find the terms upon which European enterprise and wealth can be applied to the development of Africa, with the gradually increasing participation of Africans at all levels, economic and political. The normal precedents of parliamentary democracy do not meet this abnormal situation and bold innovations may be needed. Some members of the Dutch Reformed Church, facing this problem with great intellectual courage, have speculated upon the possibility of a measure not of spurious but of genuine apartheid which would at least diminish the area of friction and help to disperse some of the racial energies, before they gather for wholesale central conflict, into regional expressions.

This and other possibilities for a practical solution lay outside Tuesday's debate in the Commons, which was directed mainly to procedure. Listening, it was disturbing to watch the problem becoming with every speech more and more of a party issue and leading up to a division. Moderation is imperative. While essential principles are maintained, nothing should be said or done to make the position of the white communities in central Africa, as they approach their fateful choice, more difficult, or to give them the impression that in this country their interests are belittled by prejudice or entangled with our deepening party differences. An especially heavy responsibility rests upon those to whom the Africans, in their ignorance and suspicion, turn for guidance. Is there not yet a possibility, even, perhaps, by postponing the April conference, for the leaders of all parties, both in Africa and in this country, to endeavour to draw closer in unofficial or informal discussions that might set the stage for a summer conference with better hope of success than now appears possible? No effort to this end can be too great when it is remembered that the future of central Africa, if not of much more than that, may be decided during the next few months.

Yours faithfully

Egyptian Threat to Sudan's Self-Government

Letter to *The Times* 23 April 1952

The danger to the Sudan arose from the lack of knowledge in Britain about a territory for which the Foreign Office was responsible and from both American and British interest in placating Egypt.

Sir, – It is disturbing that at this critical stage of the Anglo-Egyptian negotiations there should be misunderstanding about the position of the Sudan Government. It may well be asked: 'What is the Sudan Government?' It is one that is undergoing fundamental changes in an atmosphere of great tension with its few British members carrying a heavy and perplexing responsibility. As far as policy and order are concerned, the British element consists of the Governor-General, some 136 members of the administrative branch, and about forty police and military officers. They have to co-operate with a Sudanese executive council; a Sudanese Parliament, police and defence force; a predominantly Sudanese Civil Service and a population of eight millions. They can keep the confidence of the Sudanese only if they can convince them that Britain will support them without deviation in the promises that have been made to establish self-government in 1952. So far the Governor-General has done no more than proceed openly, step by step, in fulfilment of these promises, and there is no justice in the accusation that his Government have imperilled the Cairo talks, by abrupt and unco-ordinated action.

The Egyptian Government, which has done everything possible to prevent this advance and to foment unrest and opposition in the Sudan, demands a concession that would strengthen its internal position. It seems that America is supporting this pressure. The stakes are admittedly high, but if the issues were clearly understood in Britain and America it would be recognized as inconsistent with the rest of the policies of both countries that the attainment of nationhood by the Sudanese should be frustrated even by the highest political expediency. No verbal compromise, however subtly worded, that could satisfy Egypt's immediate needs could fail to embitter the great majority of the Sudanese. They and their British officials would feel themselves betrayed, and bitterness and even disorder would ensue. Britain would lose all moral authority to give the Sudan, so largely her own creation, that further most necessary help which many Sudanese desire. She would have forced upon them a sovereignty – neither Egyptians nor Sudanese understand 'nominal sovereignty' – based upon a conquest and a reconquest achieved in the nineteenth century before the Sudanese were a people capable of expressing their will.

Any British disposition to compromise would make the rest of the negotiations more rather than less difficult and might involve further surrenders. Once Egypt is convinced that the Sudan is not up for bargaining and the Sudanese opt, as seems likely, for independence, the air will be cleared and Britain can then use all her influence to bring about a tripartite agreement that will safeguard Egypt's great and valid interests, especially in the Nile waters. World-wide strategic interests hang upon these negotiations, but Britain has also a world-wide political interest in her reputation for integrity and for the diffusion of freedom, and, in the long run, strategy divorced from politics is seldom successful.

Yours faithfully

Introduction to *The Making of the Modern Sudan*[1]

In this book, published in 1953, Mr K. D. Henderson edited the letters of that most humane of administrators, Sir Douglas Newbold. I wrote the introduction in 1952. This entry is followed by two more on the Sudan which, as the first African state to gain independence, was at the time demanding a great deal of attention.

The inclusion of this book in the series 'Comparative and Colonial Studies' is a new departure. The other books have dealt with constitutional, political, or economic aspects of colonial or formerly colonial countries. This book treats of government through a governor: it is a biographical study of colonial administration. This departure does not, I would claim, demand any editorial apology but it does need an explanation which may help to show the significance of Sir Douglas Newbold's work in relation to those broad questions to which this series was designed to offer some answer.

Before this is attempted the man himself, as I knew him, should be introduced, for what is of general interest in his career arises not only from his happening, through the routine of promotion, to hold a position of exceptional importance at an exceptional time, but also directly from the qualities of his character. This claim must be followed by the immediate admission, both by Mr Henderson (the present Governor of Darfur and a student of Sudanese history and institutions) and by myself, that we were close friends of Douglas Newbold. We do not think, though this is for the reader to decide, that our friendship has affected our judgement of him. Indeed, Newbold's power to feel and inspire affection was, as I shall try to show, no mere delightful accompaniment of his capacity as an administrator but its very essence.

His first claim upon me arose from his own vision of the wider implications of his work. My first visit to the Sudan was in 1936. Coming to this country as a student of colonial government, after travels over many years in other parts of Africa and elsewhere, I found its administration unlike any other and Newbold at the very heart of all that was

[1] K. D. D. Henderson, *The Making of the Modern Sudan*, Faber and Faber, 1953.

most characteristic of its tradition. Not that he was a static figure whom I could select for unobserved study. From the moment I walked into his house in El Obeid he was the aggressor, invading and holding my mind, making immediate demands upon such services as I could offer, and never for the rest of his life releasing me from the bracing claims of his friendship.

How can I describe him? The more individual people are, the less does the much used and abused vocabulary of human description serve to present them. He was sturdy, browned by the harsh sun of the Sudan, and, in spite of his active and, indeed, athletic life, he had the rather awkward movements, more often seen in academic than colonial circles, of a man who is too busily active in his head to bother much about the rest of himself. The immediate impression he gave was of being intensely and happily alive. There might seem something wayward, almost inconsequent about his talk until the general direction in which he was always moving, his pursuit of the interests of the Sudan, was perceived. His conversation made one think of a stream that runs very fast in bright light, tossing from side to side over the impeding stones in its efforts to find its way onwards and almost always breaking into laughter. A little of this flashing, zigzag quality is expressed in his letters. His vitality was not of the kind that represses in the act of impressing: it was always reaching out and trying to meet that of others; to find agreement; to share; to evoke and to fuse, rather than merely to express itself. His dark grey eyes had a perpetual, rather puckish, almost mocking query – but the mockery was mostly gentle and very often for himself – and this was enhanced by the strange upward twist of his thick black eyebrows. He was one of those rare people who have the courage to abandon all defences and whose disarming vulnerability makes others ashamed of their own elaborate system of fortification and rouses in them a desire to help and protect. This was a vain desire since no one could protect Newbold from himself or interpose a shield between him and all the passing beauty or ugliness, happiness or pain which (to borrow his own analogy) his nature, like a super-sensitized photographic film, must register in their sharpest form.

As an administrator it is possible to see Newbold in widening concentric circles of relevance. The widest of them is that of the whole setting of modern imperialism for, strange though it often seemed for a man of his ceaselessly questioning mind, he was an officer in a service which, whatever its name, was essentially colonial. (I do not, of course, use the term with the depreciatory implications which some Egyptian and Sudanese critics of Britain have attached to it.) The attempt, in the

INTRODUCTION TO 'THE MAKING OF THE MODERN SUDAN' [1952]

evaluation of any 'ism', to turn away from theory and see it in the lives and characters of its leading practitioners sometimes gives unexpected results, and when this method is applied to British imperialism, the anti-imperialists are likely to find these results very disconcerting. This is because the relationship between the ruling nation and its dependencies is so broad in its nature and wide in its extension that it contains many diverse and even contradictory purposes and a like variety in the men who carry them out. The relationship also changes its character in time and never more rapidly than during Newbold's term of service. The strongest and most constant, though not the universal, motive for the extension of colonial rule has, admittedly and naturally, been the self-interest of the colonial power. But the humanitarian impulse has often accompanied or even preceded it, especially in Africa. And increasingly for the last hundred and fifty years or more Britain has shown a conscious intention to offer not a cautious selection but all the best of her own version of civilization to the weaker and poorer peoples brought under her rule. She has learned, however, that while military or political domination was easy to impose, and much of the material organization and equipment of an industrial society could be exported, the societies under her rule were often resistant to the penetration of the deeper political and spiritual influences.

The reason for this is not obscure. Colonial administration suffers not only from the infections which are endemic in all modern government but also from maladies which are peculiarly its own. As the modern state multiplies its functions over its millions of citizens and sociologists try to embrace its widening activities within their comments and theories, administration becomes more and more de-personalized both in fact and in theory. Within a nation such as Britain not only is this danger recognized but the wide distribution of education and of equality acts as a corrective while democracy, by giving the ruled their fractional share of ruling, makes for a reasonably healthy circulation of civic rights and duties. But in dependencies the absence of these correctives increases the universal dangers of the powerful and centralized modern state. While it is true that the state, with its inadequate staff, is not so pervasive or efficient as in Europe – there are native villages in Africa which have never seen a District Commissioner – yet the influence of government policy reaches into every hut and wayside market. Even if that government is – the present tense is now not everywhere applicable – in the hands of a minute number of officials, these are armed with even greater and more undefined powers than any in Britain, and they are divided

[1952]   COLONIAL SEQUENCE 1949 TO 1969

from the large populations under their rule not only by function and by power but also by race and culture. The new rulers were generally accepted, perhaps after a first spurt of physical resistance, and they brought with them the incalculable benefits of law and order, prosperity and humane jurisdiction. And yet it was possible, once these advantages were taken for granted, for the policy and the culture of the rulers to lie above the subject society like an insulated stratum that cannot fuse with it. The standards of efficiency, of comprehensiveness, of justice, and even of ultimate beneficence which the British official has inherited from his own contrasting society, may dominate the subordinate human layer without penetrating very fast or far into it. This is especially marked where the dependent society has been crystallized, as in Asian and African Moslem dependencies, by a long-established civilization of its own. Yet, paradoxically, it is the urban and the school-educated people, those whose life has been most changed by British rule, who are the first to challenge it because they have seized, above all other imports from Britain, upon her principles of personal and national freedom. They do not need a conscious majority to support them: the very lack in the provinces of much comprehension of the civilization of the rulers or of positive attachment to them may open the way to their success. The more hostile and disruptive this act of assertion, the less will remain of value from the colonial relationship to either side. The maximum benefits result from a gradual and co-operative process of emancipation. But this will be possible only where the rulers have identified themselves sufficiently with the people to have won their confidence and to have made themselves and what they have brought to the country seem intelligible and even attractive. It is by the application to the imperial system of this searching test that the Sudan Government, and therefore the representative figure of Newbold, attains its greatest general significance.

In colonial government and in the process of 'de-colonialization' there is no standard pattern. The Sudan Government struck me as having a very marked originality. In travelling round the provinces and the districts into which they are divided, it seemed to me there was a more friendly and constructive relationship between officials and people than any I had hitherto encountered. In all colonies the ultimate point of contact between Britain and the people is, or was, the local Commissioner, and it has rested mainly upon him whether colonial rule should stop at law, order and material development or whether some more full and fertile association should be created, which would allow

INTRODUCTION TO 'THE MAKING OF THE MODERN SUDAN' [1952]

him to represent a civilization as well as a government. The need for such a relationship was all the greater in regions like the northern Sudan where there were no groups of British traders, settlers or missionaries, and the government official was almost the sole representative of the ruling nation. The many indefatigable, versatile and humane British officers, in the Sudan and in other dependencies, who grew to the stature of this opportunity, created one of the supreme types of their nation, that of the colonial District Commissioner. But nowhere else in Africa, it seemed to me, was the tradition of these officers so high, or the friendliness and even affection towards them of the people so widespread, as in the Sudan. One of the main reasons why Newbold's career is of general interest is that he can be studied as an outstanding example of this class and one who carried the civilizing qualities of the ideal District Commissioner with him to the headquarters of government. It is important that this should be said early in this book, for while it must concentrate upon Newbold it should be remembered – and the letters in this book should themselves be a reminder – that Newbold was one of a service from which he drew many of his administrative virtues even if he enhanced them from his own qualities. It is a tribute to his service as well as to himself that he could act so freely within it and find promotion to the top of its ranks. That humble, questioning attitude of which I have spoken, so hard to retain in the colonial setting, may have been supreme in him, but it was not unique. I have not forgotten the deep impression made upon me, soon after my arrival in the country, by a talk given by his predecessor as Civil Secretary, Sir Angus Gillan, at the Khartoum Cathedral Supper Club, where some young Sudanese were being welcomed back from a visit to England. It was the first time I had heard a senior British official reveal, quite simply and openly and even with humility, before the people under his government, his sense of the difficulties and possible defects of all he and his service were trying to do.

Newbold was well equipped to represent and communicate the best of his civilization. He was not the highly individualistic type of Englishman, often found among those who have fought a lone way to the top, probably in an urbanized setting, who are unable to understand the deep family and tribal affiliations of simpler societies. Member of a large, cultivated and affectionate family which lived in the country, and was centred round the widowed mother who was also his best friend, he did not regard this intense sense of kinship as his private refuge but brought it into his public life. He not only saw each other person as unique and individual, but he also knew that each was member of a family and he wanted to understand them in this context, to know about their homes, their parents, wives and children, and if possible to know these others himself. From love of family grew love of country, a devotion to England – for he was above all English – both as a nation and as a land, but it was a happy and generous kind of nationalism. With this patriotism for a nation and a liberal nation, with his Christian religion and his love for humane and especially classical studies, he possessed the Western inheritance to the full. He had a gay and passionate curiosity about his world; his mind ranged back in time, finding an early and continuing delight in archaeology while it also urged him outwards in space to find almost his greatest satisfaction in travel and especially in exploring the desert. Everything he was and all he knew he put unreservedly at the service of the Sudan. There was a time when, because of his intense love of his own country, he could hardly bear to be an exile but, because it seemed a necessity with him to love the things and people around him, it was not long before he saw, behind the strange, hard surface of the northern Sudan, so much to excite interest and affection and to demand service, that a new love grew out of the old. Once the bond was made it was complete. He drew no sharp boundary, so common in the colonial environment, between the two sides of his life, between the English life of home and the distant land of his work, or, in the Sudan, between the hours of privacy and leisure with white colleagues on the one side and on the other, the public life of the office and his dealings with the 'natives'. The two spilled over into each other, much to the advantage of both.

Although the humanizing of administration came to him almost unconsciously, he recognized that it should be a conscious purpose of the government and he used all his influence to this end. When working under intolerable pressure upon the central affairs of the country, and even at the end upon the uncongenial and mechanistic problems of war, he was always aware of the figure of the peasant, in all his Sudanese variations, as the ultimate beneficiary of government and of victory. 'It was only', he quotes, underlining his Tolstoy, 'when he felt himself *in alliance with* the peasant that he began to direct him.' As Governor of Kordofan he writes, 'Even here, in the fleshpots and gossip and selfishness of El Obeid, we do get a glimpse of the uplifted faces of the millions of chaps in Kordofan who want our help.' He chafed against life at headquarters because, from the three towns crowded about the junction of the Niles, it was almost impossible to see a man wielding a hoe or to

INTRODUCTION TO 'THE MAKING OF THE MODERN SUDAN' [1952]

hear the creaking of a water-wheel laboriously lifting bucketfuls of the Nile on to the thirsty land.[1]

These pages are full of evidence of this struggle of Newbold against the insulation of bureaucracy from the human beings upon which it works. He was always teaching that the citizen should not be submerged in the species, that to destroy individuality was to destroy ethics, and that reforms should be qualitative and not merely quantitative. The Sudan service already had a great tradition of sympathy and courtesy towards the administered but he intensified this tradition. Incarnated in him, the powerful, alien civilization which had been imposed over the heads of the Sudanese by conquest could in truth become intelligible and even attractive to them. It was as though, to offer it to them, he came outside the walls of alien power, while, at the same time, by trying to understand and appreciate their own culture, he tempted them out of their hard, opposing self-containment and so made a place of meeting in the middle. It is only at great human cost that such reconciliations are achieved as if, to change the metaphor, men had willingly to offer the soft elastic human stuff of which they are made to cushion the shocks of contact between the large, hard group-entities and ideas they are trying to bring into unison, or to be stretched almost beyond endurance between them.

In considering Newbold as an agent of colonial government we may see, however, that there was one mental distress he was spared. He did not question the basis of imperialism or torture himself with doubt about the profession he had entered. One of many of his kind both in the Sudan and in the other dependencies, but more deliberative and effective than most, he accepted the imperial relationship as it had come down to him from history and set to work to shift it nearer to the demands of his own Christian conscience and of his own civilized and personal tastes.

Moving a little closer to the centre of Newbold's work, we can find a second general but more localized significance in the administrative tasks that came to him in the years of his Sudan career and especially during the later years of it. We can see him dealing, in the very special and rather isolated situation of the Sudan, with the same main problems which had confronted Britain in India and were still demanding solution in nearly all the colonies. Following the establishment of law and order and the winning of confidence had come the construction of a system of

[1] There was, however, one such wheel kept outside the house of a religious leader in Khartoum which gave Newbold great satisfaction.

[1952]

local government for both tribal and urban groups; and the juxtaposition, if not the harmonization, of two systems of law and of lawcourts; the delicate tasks of fitting Western education upon societies formed in a wholly different physical and mental environment; and the introduction of Western economic principles into communities of peasant farmers or semi-nomadic pastoralists. Some of these administrative duties demand comment.

Local government was perhaps, for Newbold, the largest of all these tasks. The Sudan authorities had drawn upon the Indirect Rule principle, as exemplified in northern Nigeria, and applied it rather belatedly to their own much less amenable conditions. This was followed by a movement, earlier than in the African colonies, towards a more systematic form of local government. This approximated to the British pattern though Newbold, who played the major part in this reconstruction, searched the world for relevant experience. The importance of this part of Newbold's work hardly needs emphasis and the letters and papers which follow will throw full and comparative light upon this major question for all colonial governments.

With regard to the economic task it was natural that Newbold should feel with peculiar sharpness the usual regret – one could almost say anguish – of the good colonial commissioner who must watch at close quarters the destructive pressure of the modern forces, which he is helping to introduce, upon the vulnerable little societies in his charge. There were two main occasions when Newbold dealt with this painful problem. His first love was for the Beja, the camel-owning tribes near the Red Sea. He was deeply stirred by the impact of commercial cotton-growing upon these ancient, handsome, but agriculturally inefficient nomads, the desert 'Fuzzies' of Kipling's verse, and, as these pages will show, he had the courage to resist and redirect it. He had to deal next with the little groups of manly Nuba pagans, driven by the Arab invasions into the isolated mountain strongholds of Kordofan. He would not have them quickly forced, but rather gently coaxed, into becoming citizens of the new political and economic system that had flowed in like another tide, overrunning the Arab power, and which now surrounded their obstinate rocky hills. In these two matters he took what would be called the sentimental line by those hard-headed men who, with the help of the horrid metaphor about omelettes and broken eggs, justify themselves with the plea of inevitability. And Newbold would have been sentimental if he had simply wrung his hands in ineffective distress. As it was, by harnessing pity to years of patient

INTRODUCTION TO 'THE MAKING OF THE MODERN SUDAN' [1952]

administration, he showed that sentiment could be at least as strong and hard-headed as self-interested fatalism.

In these and many other administrative tasks to which we find a reference in these pages – we shall refer later to education – Newbold, in District and Province, was dealing, though in his own way and in the conditions peculiar to the Sudan, with problems that are almost universal in colonial empires. It is in the later part of his career, with his appointment as Civil Secretary, that we come to his handling of events that have not only a great representative significance as one example of the transfer of imperial power but also a central importance for the Sudan and are also closely intertwined with the Second World War and with Britain's relations with Egypt. These are the events and the years which fill the largest part of this book and where, because we enter here the innermost circle of our study, we must, if we are to assess its meaning, look more closely into Sudanese circumstances which Newbold had to try to master. It is a story with four concurrent themes; relations with Egypt; the second world war; the educational measures which were complementary to the advance in self-government; and lastly, and most important for a book in this series, the constitutional advance and the handling of the Congress movement.

Comment upon the first three subjects must be brief.

First, Egypt. It must be remembered that Newbold and his colleagues had to conduct all their administration under the bitter scrutiny and the opposing influence of their northern neighbour. Egypt was denied any real share in the government of a country over which, by conquest, by re-conquest jointly with Britain, and by the Condominium Agreement, she could claim co-sovereignty, and whose green flag all British officers, with almost provocative official propriety, flew beside their own Union Jack. This is a difficult question to discuss, especially at a moment when Anglo-Egyptian relations have reached a climax of irreconcilability over the Sudan.[1] The connection between the two countries, which began with Britain's intervention in 1882, has been one of enforced partnership between two unequal and incompatible countries with tension growing as, with each advance by Egypt in strength and self-consciousness, she strained against bonds that were drawn about her in the days of her weakness and poverty. Her unhappy inheritance of oppression and corruption from the past and her deep social and political divisions would have made her a difficult partner in any case, but in their anger

[1] This was drafted before king Farouk's abdication. Upon revising it in September 1952 the hope may at least be entertained that the climax has passed.

55

[1952]

at what they felt to be the humiliations imposed by Britain, Egyptian political leaders tried, from time to time, to injure Britain through the Sudan. The murder of the Governor-General of the Sudan, Sir Lee Stack, in Cairo and the mutinies fomented by Egypt in the Sudan in 1924 turned the distaste of the British officials for administrative co-operation with Egypt into a settled determination, while scrupulously safeguarding Egypt's rights in the Nile waters, to allow no further interference with their wards in the Sudan.

With his character, standards of administration, and devotion to the Sudanese, it was natural that Newbold should hold this view at its strongest. Egypt's reply to a virtual exclusion, which the Treaty of 1936 did little to modify, from any share in administration was to intensify her efforts to make trouble and to buy adherents in the Sudan. Had her leaders been wise and moderate enough to make more legitimate use of their treaty position, and especially to send efficient and co-operative men to represent her, the British would hardly have persisted in their rigidly exclusive policy. Unfortunately, in the intemperance of Egypt's political life, moderation towards Britain became treachery punishable even by assassination. Nothing is easier than to condemn Egypt as her own worst enemy, and yet might not something more have been done to save her from herself? The British are not always apt in dealing with the neuroses of other nations, even where they have a strong interest in alleviating them. And the Sudanese, though long unconscious of it, had an overriding interest in the moderation of Egyptian bitterness. I sometimes presumed to argue with Newbold as to whether the Sudan Government had not too easily yielded to the temptation to turn their eyes away from the north and from the unwelcome facts that Egypt had, by treaty, at least equal rights with Britain in the Sudan, and that some difficult day she would assert these with the accumulated bitterness of her long exclusion. Psychological rather than political concessions might have been made with more attempts to meet and inform such reasonable Egyptian opinion as existed, in order to preserve some links, however slender, across the gulf of diverse purpose and action. It was a difficult case to plead and Newbold, feeling that every British instinct and Sudanese interest supported him, was unmoved by it. The condition and conduct of Egypt in 1952 and the contrasting soundness of the Sudan seem to endorse his view. Yet a satisfactory relationship with Egypt is vital to the Sudan and Egypt's bitterness and ignorance with regard to her southern neighbour remain the chief obstacles to its attainment.

INTRODUCTION TO 'THE MAKING OF THE MODERN SUDAN' [1952]

Both Egyptian relations and the constitutional reconstruction were intertwined with the theme of war. The chapters in this book which deal with this have much to show. We can see the effects of war upon government and how forty years of good administration was rewarded by the steadiness and loyalty of the Sudanese when their rulers were in danger. We are shown the importance of the Sudan as a centre of communication not only from north to south, with Cecil Rhodes's Cape to Cairo route fulfilling through air transport the hopes it had disappointed for road and rail, but also with the transverse route from west to east cutting across it at Khartoum. There is much to be learned here of the strategic meaning of Africa and these chapters will throw new light upon the politico-military history of the war in this region. But these pages are, above all, an unconscious record of courage. As in Britain, so in the Sudan only a few men at the top knew the full extent of the danger in the months of deepest crisis and they took the strain for the people under their care. By all rational calculation, when Italy entered the war in 1940, the position of the Sudan was hopeless. Caught almost defenceless between two fronts and with the relatively huge, well-equipped forces of the Italians ready to descend from their Ethiopian stronghold upon its open plains, it seemed a doomed outpost of a doomed Britain. Newbold and his Governor-General, almost overwhelmed with new and urgent responsibilities for which they had neither the staff, the equipment, nor the experience, and nightly expecting the bombers to destroy their unprotected capital, maintained that confidence at headquarters which wins battles at the front or ensures that they shall never be fought. Newbold would allow no talk of the Sudan being undefended, still less of having no intention to defend itself. The handful of Sudanese troops, appearing and disappearing along the invaded south-eastern frontier like a stage army, bluffed and thwarted the hosts of Italians, and the Sudan, seemingly by a miracle, was not overrun.

As the files dealing with war and external relations, ever increasing in number and size, piled up on his desk, how welcome must have been the appearance of one dealing with education! Newbold was a born teacher, and the most congenial of the many parts he must play as a colonial administrator was when he could think of the Sudan as a school and of himself, with the mingled eagerness and humility of a good master, trying to expound the best lessons he knew from the history and experience of his own country. Enough has been said to make it clear that Newbold would hold with great strength the belief that to give the Sudanese the Western institutions they were desiring and receiving

[1952]

divorced from Western education and cultural influence would be of little more use than to give a motor-car without the petrol upon which to run it. The extension of the school system among both Moslems and pagans; the Cultural Centre in Khartoum; the promotion of Gordon College towards university status; the dispatch of young Sudanese upon visits to Britain – these were among the happiest and most fruitful activities of Newbold's period as Civil Secretary. The spirit of them is well represented in the papers in Part II, some of them addresses given in all the strain of his war-time administration when he had hardly an hour to steal from his office in order to think out what he should say. It was part of his liberalism and courage that, while as an administrator, he foresaw all the hazardous ferment that the teaching of Western history and politics must bring, he wanted to have more not less of such stimulus and to give the educationists an absolutely free hand in its provision.

Yet, when we come to the largest of Newbold's four main tasks as Civil Secretary, that of the constitutional advance, he seems to have been caught almost unprepared by the Congress movement. But before we can discuss the part he played here we must take a backward glance over the subject.

The British service in the Sudan administered a people who were politically acquiescent for nearly forty years. There had been a single sputter of trouble, inspired from Egypt, in 1924, but it was not until the Anglo-Egyptian Treaty of 1936 referred to the interests of the Sudanese without their having been consulted over its terms that the small Western-educated minority began to stir into political consciousness and mutual co-operation. As I was in the Sudan at the time and met groups of these young men in their clubs, I was able to see something of this groping towards the twin ideas of nationalism and freedom. It certainly was surprising, upon coming to the Sudan at that date, to find that nothing had been done to dilute the pure autocracy of its Government which still had no formal method of consulting the Sudanese and seemed to have no plans for any advance in this direction. It was impossible not to remark that even the oppressive Egyptian government of the Sudan in the nineteenth century had made some attempt at a council of notables. The exceptionally good personal relations between the British and the Sudanese of all ranks and the use of unofficial consultations seemed no excuse for not initiating formal conciliar institutions. Only in these could the Sudanese learn the business of central government and begin to build a real national unity into the artificial unity of

INTRODUCTION TO 'THE MAKING OF THE MODERN SUDAN' [1952]

the boundaries which foreign power had demarcated. Otherwise, it was clear that a political movement, which seemed, in view of the sophistication of the urban and riverain people, to be overdue, must assert itself outside the constitution. I frequently raised this question with Newbold and he discussed it with his usual readiness to welcome and to test criticism. If, as appears in the letters which follow, I pressed for Province Councils it was not as an end in themselves, since Provinces were often very unreal units, but as half-way houses between tribal administrations and a central council or as electoral colleges for such an institution.

There is no need to anticipate here the story that is told in this book by Mr Henderson and by the papers themselves. But, since almost the only criticism brought by the Sudanese against Newbold refers to his handling of this issue, some comment must be made.[1] He found himself, as Civil Secretary, confronted, early in 1942, with a list of constitutional 'demands' by the self-appointed Congress of 'graduates', the school-educated *effendia* of the towns. The Sudanese criticism is that by the uncompromising tone of his replies to the committee of Congress in the spring and early summer of 1942 he split the Congress into a moderate section and an extreme section which turned to Egypt for support.[2] Moreover, by questioning the credentials of Congress to speak for the country he drove the two groups of educated political leaders, looking for the easiest means of creating a mass movement, to call upon the support of the two great sectarian groupings into which the Moslems of the northern Sudan were divided. This was a turning-point in the young nationalist movement and it was, the critics say, a wrong turning. It led to division, extremism and the demoralizing confusion of sectarian and political purposes.

I would not presume to pass a final judgement upon this difficult question but only to offer some comments upon it. Readers may think that the letters sent by Newbold to Congress in the spring and summer of 1942 were severe in tone and seem to contrast with the liberal spirit of his private discussions with the leaders and with his remarkable note to Council of 10 September.[3] We might ask, indeed, how many colonial governments could afford to publish, and to publish so soon, a confidential report upon the first outbreak of nationalist agitation.

[1] See especially, in this series, Mekki Abbas in *The Sudan Question*, 1952, pp. 107 ff.
[2] Actually Congress had split spontaneously earlier than this. See below, p. 176.
[3] See below, pp. 553–8.

59

[1952]   COLONIAL SEQUENCE 1949 TO 1969

Several reasons may be given for the apparent discrepancy between Newbold's views and the action he took. Firstly, whatever his views, his formal acts had to be confirmed by the Governor-General and the whole of the official Executive Council. Secondly, both he and they had to deal with the situation as bequeathed by past, indeed long-past, administration, with its lack of foresight in this matter. Thirdly, Newbold and his government were acting in an extraordinarily isolated position. Cut off from direct and open responsibility to the British Parliament and people by the ambiguous status of the Sudan, and denied the support enjoyed by the colonies of an experienced Whitehall department, the few senior officials had to improvise policy almost wholly out of their own ideas and initiative. Fourthly, it should be remembered that the main challenge came when they and the Sudan were involved in the strain and anxiety of a war that was a struggle for existence and that it came at the most desperate crisis of that war and drew from Newbold the exclamation that they must beat Rommel first.

To all these special considerations may be added one that is more general. Newbold was facing the most exacting moral and political test of imperial government. The first protest against its authority is, in the nature of things, bound to come from some small, inexperienced, self-constituted group. Such a movement may be constitutionalized but it will not be smothered by finding expression through some form of representative council. The group will almost certainly be unrepresentative, inexperienced and wholly unready to provide not only an alternative government but even leaders able to share in the central responsibilities of government. The gap between the actual and the potential efficacy of the movement has to be bridged and the emotional situation is such that this can hardly be achieved in an atmosphere of sweet reasonableness. Nor are the emotions all upon one side. A service of British officials who have built up a tradition of benevolent paternal and authoritarian government which for fifty years or so has met the real situation, is bound to react almost automatically against the first challenge which seems to threaten at once the policy of their nation, the work and the ideals of their service and their professional interests.

The documents published in this book seem to show Newbold caught in the recurrent struggle of our nation to resolve the dilemma of being democratic at home and autocratic abroad. To the question 'Did he succeed?' must be added 'What is success?' in such an issue, and this would drive us back to a discussion, upon which we cannot enter now, of the fundamentals of British policy. There are, moreover, few deep

INTRODUCTION TO 'THE MAKING OF THE MODERN SUDAN' [1952]

political adjustments that can be made anywhere with perfect smoothness and general agreement, and least of all in the colonial environment. It may be that it was the presence in the Civil Secretary's office of Newbold, so little the autocrat, so sympathetic towards the young and the ideas of youth, and so anxious to keep in friendly personal touch with the Congress leaders, that prevented still greater bitterness. He kept his mind and those of his colleagues at headquarters open to the play of external ideas and experiences and he passed these on as best he could to a scattered service, which might find it hard to assess the meaning of events in the capital against a commonwealth and, indeed, a world background.

Even if a fuller examination of all the evidence should show that Newbold's handling of the matter was not faultless, especially as regards the delay in setting up a representative council, this would not prove the justice of Sudanese critics in their search for an explanation for their loss of unity and their divergence from the straight path of political leadership. It is the usual fate of pioneer reformers to fall into moderate and extreme groups: the appeal to Egypt, or rather from Egypt, must have been an irresistible temptation for historical and less respectable reasons. And it may be that no policy at that time could have saved the first trickle of political nationalism from being engulfed in the much larger and older streams of religious sectarianism. In the event, whatever the degree of delay or rigidity, the Sudan Government had sufficient accumulated credit of Sudanese confidence – a balance to which Newbold had very substantially contributed – to enable it to go forward under his friend and very able successor, Sir James Robertson, in an atmosphere of co-operation almost unprecedented for such transfers of power.

Before we leave this very contemporary subject it should be remembered that the creation of a legislature is only one part of the process of developing self-government, though it is the one that generally steals all the historical limelight. There were at least three other parts in Newbold's programme and each had to be kept more or less level with the others. Of the aspects of education and of local government something has been said, though we should remark that the democratization of the latter, especially in the towns, was being pushed forward by Newbold right up to the end and proved, when the first real transfer of power was made, to have given an excellent training for some of the leading Sudanese politicians and officials. The fourth task was the Sudanization of the civil service. This may not have been spectacular but it was quite as important as the legislative side and it was a ceaseless, arduous and embarrassing task. On the one side was a service being asked to co-operate in a task that must lead through dilution to its own eventual disappearance. Upon the other side were the educated Sudanese, eager for promotion, jealous of all inequalities, confident in their own capacities and sometimes achieving, sometimes ignoring and sometimes rejecting the standards which a very proud service was trying to retain. Parallel with the development of Gordon College and with courses of training in administration, the Sudan Government drew up elaborate schedules for the gradual substitution of Sudanese for British staff at progressively higher levels. But no schedules could prevent anomalies, or allow for changes in the political climate. The process was always coming up for reconsideration and Newbold was constantly urging upon the Provinces the need for sincere efforts to accept the policy and to make it a success. Sudanization continues today at an accelerating pace and it will not come to an end until the last British officer vacates his post, bequeathing, we may hope, traditions that will continue to make the Sudan Civil Service an example of integrity and devotion to surrounding countries.

Before leaving the constitutional question it should be remarked that the documents printed in Part II of this book should make it an important source for the future history of the Sudan. They will show how and why the Sudan Government, always original, struck out in this matter of self-governing institutions upon a rather different line from the colonial governments. We can trace here, alongside the letters of the chief actor in the event, the genesis of Sudanese independence, while the book published this year in this series by Mekki Effendi Abbas supplies a commentary by a Sudanese who was himself also involved in the events.

Mr Henderson takes Newbold's story to the end, and the end was wholly in character. After the first crisis of the Italian entry into hostilities Newbold settled down to the long strain of the war, with the ever-increasing work it imposed on him, while the whole task of internal administration remained and, indeed, grew in complexity. He had escaped death in the field in the first world war to be killed at his desk by the second. It was not only that, deaf to all entreaties, he refused to take home leave, always finding that others, and especially married men, had a better claim to each one of the limited seats in the planes, and protesting that public men in Britain carried a heavier burden than his. It was also that he could not or would not learn to protect himself, even

INTRODUCTION TO 'THE MAKING OF THE MODERN SUDAN' [1952]

by the most justifiable defences of senior officialdom, from his own sympathy and generosity. While emperors, kings, generals and prime ministers, many of the famous characters of the grand alliance, were descending upon Khartoum from the skies, and demanding entertainment and information on their way, his house was still open to his humbler friends, new and old, while far into the night he would write those long, intensely personal letters in the clear, round handwriting that were always so exciting and cheering to receive and which did much to keep up the morale of an overworked and harassed service.

One of his heaviest burdens was the grief he felt at the deaths of his junior colleagues who had gone into the army or of young officers, like my own nephew, whom he had taken to his heart and house while they were stationed in Khartoum. He never failed to write long letters to their mothers expressing not a generalized sympathy but his sense of the individual, irreplaceable worth of each young man and of the full meaning of his loss to his own family. There are some people who slip through life easily by preserving a smooth surface to which nothing can stick. But Newbold could not move a yard amongst people without getting stuck, accumulating ever new obligations of friendship. To stay in his house was to realize that this intense but discriminating affection embraced not only his friends and colleagues but also his servants and their children, and went out to the very animals who lived in his household. One of my own most happy memories of Newbold was to come out in the early morning for the daily scurry over the jumps at El Obeid and to find him in almost human converse with his beloved old horse, Dood. So we find that when, at the very end, he went down to Uganda it was not to rest, nor was it only to absorb all that was new and useful to the Sudan in that country, but also to make such friends with the young African students at Makerere College that he must needs write long letters to them and even remember that they might be short of money to stamp their replies. One of the last two letters he wrote just before his death was to the young Kikuyu student, Gecaga. In this letter he said – and for how many could these words be the simple truth – 'I never forget a friend', but Gecaga could not know what, by that time, was the cost of such remembering.

Readers of this book who did not know Newbold may, if they read this introduction, do so with a very natural measure of scepticism. The verbal commendation of a good man's character is seldom effective, above all to a generation still in recoil from the constant and heavy-handed use by their grandfathers of the example of the great and good as an instrument of uplift. It may be hoped that the closer knowledge of the subject of this book through his letters and papers will allow those who read to share in imagination the pleasure of his friendship as well as to appraise the significance of his place as an agent of British rule. But there are few claims for a man more unconvincing and even repellent than one for perfection, and both as editor and friend I feel, if I have one more duty, it is to make clear that this claim is not being made or even implied.

What claim, then, is being made? For myself I must make it clear that, in a good many years of travel and study devoted to the subject of colonial government, Newbold showed to me the highest standards I had ever seen in colonial administration. Certainly such standards must be individual and friendship, while a key to understanding, is also a temptation to a loyalty improper to the student. But, if the picture of Newbold I have given seems to some too indulgent, it should be remembered that it is not only my affection that would make it hard to criticize in print the record of a friend within the few years following his death: it is also because both the man and the events are too close for conclusive judgement. Nor, I repeat, is any claim being made that Newbold was faultless. I have ventured in this introduction to raise two questions with regard to Newbold's policy towards Egypt and towards the Congress, which time will help others to answer. There are doubtless more that could be raised and a third doubt may be added now. It is that, especially in later years, his colleagues sometimes found in him a tendency to procrastinate which made it difficult for them to obtain from him a clear and prompt decision. This was, undoubtedly, a defect in an administrator. It was, however, the obverse side of a virtue, his sense of the complexity of the issues with which he had to deal and of their ultimate significance for the Sudanese. He knew, moreover, that the answers to his problems were not all to be found in his own head, his own Secretariat, or even in the Sudan. He kept all the windows of his mind open – to the Middle East, to Africa, to Britain, the Commonwealth, and the world, to the past as well as the present. Drawing upon ideas and experience from all these sources, he distilled them in his own mind to make a twentieth-century policy for the Sudan. Some of his British colleagues might well have preferred a brisk, confident chief, ready with all the answers. But there is only one Newbold for a score of such competent secretariat officials and there can be little doubt which sort of administrator the administered prefer and whom they will longest remember.

INTRODUCTION TO 'THE MAKING OF THE MODERN SUDAN' [1952]

If, as I hope, this book becomes authoritative material for Sudanese students and historians of the future, I would ask them, in considering the possible imperfections of their former rulers, to open their minds to the same possibilities in themselves. Young nations need myths and legends about their origins to give themselves pride and confidence. But though in former days these generally told of the successful struggles of their own heroes against their wicked enemies, this simple contrast is surely not needed to interpret the birth of a nation under British tutelage in the mid-twentieth century: the wrong and the right of the story are far too complex in distribution for that. As for the right, if Newbold loved the Sudanese it was because they deserved his affection and returned it. It was a Sudanese, and a nationalist critic of the Government, Mekki Effendi Abbas, who said of him after his death, 'We know that it was of exhaustion that he died. And we know that his motive, when he worked himself to death, was not just the discharging of a debt but he had a more sublime motive for working so hard. That was his love for the Sudan. Whenever he was tired of working in the office, he would, to use his own terms, go out to see some children and some cattle and some "eish" [grain] because the sight of these would give him refreshment more than anything else.'[1]

Mekki Abbas, whose friendship Newbold had kept for all their political disagreement, was not the only Sudanese who showed his appreciation of the Civil Secretary. After his sudden death the young press of Khartoum and Omdurman, journals of all parties, showed the same intense and perceptive appreciation. The President of the Graduates' Congress himself laid a wreath upon his coffin and expressed on behalf of the Congress 'profound sorrow for the death of Sir Douglas. His death was grievously felt by all Sudanese circles which fully appreciated the valuable services he so devotedly rendered to the people of this country.'[2] 'He knew the Sudan perfectly, loved it, was sincere to it, and realized that in adopting this attitude he was showing love and sincerity to his own country,'[3] wrote another Sudanese newspaper. In yet another we read, 'Newbold closely acquainted himself with the shepherd in his wilderness, the cultivator in his farm, the merchant in his shop and the Effendi in his office. ... He believed that the Sudanese were capable of administering their own affairs and his strenuous efforts towards this end exhausted his strength.'[4] A Sudanese

[1] *Arabic and English Newsletter*, Khartoum, 28 March 1945.
[2] *Sawt El-Sudan*, 24 March 1945.   [3] *El-Rai El-Amm*, 24 March 1945.
[4] *El-Sudan El-Gedid*, 30 March 1945.

poet, Sheikh Abdulla Banna, wrote a verse which declared, to give a translation which hardly conveys the style of the Arabic:

> He was a martyr of his love to the Sudan in which he spent the flower of his life and in which he remained until he was confined to the grave.
> And when he passed away grief overcame the whole community,
> Who lamented the loss of their benefactor.
> They have mourned his death with roses, and they
> Were right: for roses are fit to commemorate a rose-like character such as his.

It should be remembered, when these quotations are read, that they are not from a press remotely resembling that of Britain but from young journalists of the fiery Middle East in the full flush of nationalist intemperance and eagerness, whose nearest model has been the violent press of Egypt. To those who know the atmosphere of Moslem countries in this region, these quotations about a senior British representative of 'Colonialism' will be almost unbelievable. We may read them not as a tribute to Newbold only but to Newbold and the Sudanese together in their sense of mutual appreciation and of shared purpose. Newbold achieved this because he was working not so much *over* as increasingly *with* a people who had many fine qualities, traditions of clean fighting, good humour, and a respect for their own religion which allowed them to respect his. The making of the modern Sudan, to which Newbold as the head of a service gave his great gifts and, indeed, his life, was thus a joint creation to which British and Sudanese may look back with a common pride. The kind of devotion and of giving which in different ways the Sudan claimed from both Gordon and Newbold, and which led to both of them leaving their tired bodies in the sandy soil of the country, had the character of adoption, and the Sudanese might justly claim such men as belonging as much or more to their own country and history as to that of Britain.

One last word. To those unfamiliar with the Sudan or with the professional abbreviations and elliptical talk of men of action writing in a hurry, some of the allusions in his letters may appear a little obscure. It seemed better to the author and the editor to risk this result than to load these pages with explanatory notes. May I endorse Mr Henderson's advice to the reader that he may safely pass on, knowing that he will not miss the heart of the matter which is, after all, that of the man. And if he finds the record bewilderingly various and episodic, that is of the very nature of colonial government. It is, or at least it was up to yesterday, a sphere in which British officials had to handle at speed in the provinces the heterogeneous affairs of up to a million people with the aid of good intentions and a classical education, while those in the central secretariat did much the same upon a five- or ten-fold scale. That day has gone but what is new is being built upon foundations laid in this way. It may therefore be of value that the record of one of these creative administrators, struck off day by day without thought of posterity, should be compiled by one of his colleagues and edited by one of his friends. It appears only a few years after his death and at the very time when the implications of his policy, which are being worked out by another friend who now holds his office, appear to be reaching their fulfilment in the peaceful emergence of an independent Sudan.

A Changing Continent

The Times 28 October 1952

With news from Africa assuming even more prominence in the world's newspapers, this seems a suitable time to consider whether there are any deep conditions, common to the whole of Africa, of which the present disturbing events are symptoms.

The answer is not reassuring. It becomes clear that among many recent changes none is more pregnant than the sudden exertion, in a continent which has long lain passive under European control, of a political will which, in parts of British and Commonwealth territories, and beyond, looks like developing into an ill-will towards white men or at least towards their system of rule; and this is happening at a time when Western Europe, which has lost political and economic control of the other continents, is beginning to take up seriously the immense task of civilizing and developing this vast neighbouring backward region. With Britain, whose political initiative has done much to evoke African ambitions, and whose government and influence are so widespread through the continent, lies the almost impossible task of trying to ensure that her African peoples, while demanding European civilization, do not make it impossible for Europeans to help them to obtain it.

Africans in the British dependencies are not suffering from oppression or from such extreme poverty and congestion as is seen in India.

[1952]

The problem is, above all, one of political psychology. Success in handling it, with which success in all urgent practical plans is bound up, therefore depends much upon the mental approach of British people to it. The British have made large adjustments to the changing Africa, but many old-established attitudes of mind still seem to hinder acceptance of some of its more unexpected and unwelcome developments. One is the familiar claim that only a small minority is disaffected and that the rural millions are friendly and loyal. True, perhaps, but are they an effective or permanent majority? The fact, easily verified in London, is that nearly every young African who rises above this unconscious mass and becomes aware, through education and travel, of the world beyond Africa, and the place in it of himself, his colony, and his race, is tempted to project all his resultant bitterness at the one obvious target, the colonial power. His influence, seeping down, gives the same 'seditious' colour to the vague discontents of a disintegrating society, especially in and around the problem-ridden towns.

Another response is to emphasize the humanitarian record and the undoubted benefits of British rule, forgetting that even beneficence can have a crushing effect upon those whose greatest needs are for self-expression and self-respect. The natural result, as the West African Press so clearly illustrates, is that Africans seek out and exaggerate examples of imperial selfishness and build up myths of a former golden age.

Is there not, also, too much reiteration of the case, all too easy to make, against African ignorance and incapacity, disparagement which falls with deadly effect upon the minds of people needing every encouragement in their upward struggle. Gloom or regret, for example, about West African constitutional advance will not stop, but may well embitter, its progress. It is too often forgotten that events in Africa are the result of the sudden, belated penetration of primitive tropical Africa by modern Europe, which began effectively only in the time of men still alive today. The unprecedented social strains thus set up among the tribes cannot be eased by blaming Africans and justifying British rights and intentions but only by daring and imaginative remedies. A further illusion is that the relationship between governments and their African subjects is still wholly bilateral. But the winds of egalitarian ideas are now blowing uncontrollably upon Africa from all quarters, some doubtless poisoned with hostile intention, but all giving Africans external support for their new internal assertions.

The conclusion must be that Britain and her colonists have not only a duty but an overwhelming interest in working with and not against the awakening African desire to catch up quickly with the rest of the world. If, in the psychological situation which threatens in Africa, this growing desire is opposed, or even too grudgingly met, Britain and the other colonial powers may find one day that they have nothing less than a delinquent continent upon their hands. It is against this background that we must set the changing position of the white settlers. Their fathers, when such pioneering was an undisputed virtue, built their societies, and above all their economies, upon the reality of African inferiority which they found. African advance, freely encouraged and accommodated elsewhere, now demands in settled areas the most hazardous reconstruction of the foundations of society. Hence, within British and, still more, within Commonwealth Africa, arise deep conflicts of principle and practice.

This exacerbating issue tends to throw the wider African picture out of perspective. The colonists, our kinsmen, have achieved great things and their established regional and minority rights claim Britain's utmost recognition. But, with imperial, international and American action developing alongside it, colonization cannot claim to be the only civilizing agency for Africa. It is highly localized, and in British dependencies (including Southern Rhodesia) colonists number only some 200,000 in an African population of more than 66,000,000. Beyond the immediate question of white settlement there looms the immensely larger problem of civilizing Africa's vast areas and populations, and it would be ultimately fatal, above all for themselves, if, by too great a reliance upon their present individual superiority and economic contribution, this European minority should find themselves in a position which seemed to lie across the main road of African advance.

Britain is being asked to work out a political theorem in which the two elements of numbers and civic competence are at once incommensurable and variable. To this the Central African federation proposals offer no certain contribution. Constitutions for multi-racial and uneven societies should not follow Britain, a mature and solid democracy, in concentrating parliamentary sovereignty. They should rather disperse power as far as possible between black and mixed areas in order to provide political education, to divert the oppositions between races, and give both of them the security of a rigid, written, imperially guaranteed framework. If the racial-constitutional puzzle could be solved, a developing Africa could absorb vast numbers of Europeans, though these are not likely to attain a majority in any territory north of the Zambezi. If

[1952] COLONIAL SEQUENCE 1949 TO 1969

it cannot be solved, the modern world's unhappy and impoverishing method of meeting irreconcilability with complete partition may be the only remedy.

Looking at the continent from the outside, it may be asked whether the Commonwealth and Britain are adapting their central institutions to accommodate the new Africa. African colonies aspiring to full self-government will probably make equality of status a *sine qua non* of remaining in the Commonwealth, and a rebuff on the doorstep of this august club would be deeply humiliating. Have the member nations been asked to put this question upon their agenda? The Asian affirmative response can be expected. So can the negative of South Africa's present government, though time may suggest to them both the unwisdom of alienating almost the whole of the population with which they have to share the continent, and also the future mediatory value to Africa of British influence and of the Commonwealth link. Australia and New Zealand, for their part, might weigh the future significance of the continent, whose massive bulk lies between them and Europe, as it stirs into autonomous life.

Secondly, Britain's own response in government would seem to be the re-marriage of the Commonwealth Relations (formerly Dominions) and Colonial Offices, divorced in 1925. African dependencies, unlike the Asian, are likely to attain self-government with all too brief a preparation for it. With the present separation of departments this would cause the abrupt transport of their files from the region of Victoria Street to Downing Street, which would suddenly cut off these still underdeveloped ex-colonies from needful scientific and other services. It would also harm the morale of the Colonial Office as it saw the major colonies one by one exultantly renouncing its authority, while those smaller ones remaining would, with each departure, more deeply resent their continuing public tutelage. If the departments were reunited, then, within the four walls of a single great Commonwealth ministry, each member, irrespective of status, could maintain its appropriate relationships with Britain. The African territories, which have many common interests and also prospects of increasingly close mutual association, would not be divided up between two departments according to their size and their uneven and changing political status.

Such a reorganization, which might require a single co-ordinating Cabinet Minister, might seem at first to ask too much of the foundation members of the Commonwealth. Yet it need make no difference to their independent diplomatic relationship with Britain while, on the credit side it might not only allow them to enter into a fuller economic and military partnership with Britain in the affairs of a developing Commonwealth, but might also prevent the African and other colonies from breaking out of this great association. If this kind of reorganization should prove impossible, a second best would be a new Ministry serving the African territories.

Thirdly, the Colonial Service urgently needs reshaping for its changing task. In politically advancing territories it is being put to a very severe strain, professional and personal, that may impair its ability to carry through the final exacting process of creating succession governments. Men entrusted with this supremely important duty should have the dignity and security of belonging to an imperial service of experts and advisers from which they could be posted as need arose.

The greatest contribution Britain could make to a potentially grave predicament would be to train competent African leaders and professional experts and to work with them as partners. This will not be easy in view of the great gap between the tribal mass and the Western-educated Africans, nearly every one of whom is on an intellectual rack stretched between Africa and Europe, a position not conducive to moderation. Yet, unless these are accepted and, indeed, generously assisted in their difficult leadership, they may be outflanked by impatient, xenophobic forces. These could break up lawlessly from below, led by small organized urban and industrial groups, who might teach the masses to look for a more speedy millenium than that offered by the gradualist West.

The effort of winning African co-operation will be great, above all for the European communities. New and horrible possibilities of violence are opening up. The proper line between maintenance of order and repression will be hard to draw. But those who are offering Christianity or higher education to Africans know very well that these can be fully shared only in a relationship of equality. This equality, already happily possible at the highest level, is surely the ideal, however distant, to be openly and urgently pursued, in every sphere. It is the only one for which Africans will work wholeheartedly with Britons. If the cost is high, so is the prize, the winning of Africa, which lies so close to Europe, by filling her vast cultural vacuum with the best we have to give.

British Africa, divided and malleable until a few years ago, is now over large areas quickly hardening into self-realization. Its new and scattered leaders may very soon draw together in the hope, which may not stop at British frontiers, that Africa, so long the slave, servant or beneficiary of other continents, shall, like them, become a continent in its own right, its peoples free to choose for themselves to which side of the world they will belong. If the present division in the world continues, with its balance of peoples, resources and strategic space, the choice of the last uncommitted continent may be decisive for the future of our civilization.

The Choice before the Sudan

Letter to *The Times* 17 November 1952

This letter brings out the dangers and complexities which accompanied the first British emancipation of an African state. Looking back from a later date it is difficult to accept that Britain successfully solved the problems stated here.

Sir, – General Neguib, by the refreshing contrast between his personality and methods and those of his predecessors, seems to have so captured the good opinion of the British Press and public that neither seems in the mood to scrutinize his recent memorandum on the Sudan with the care that our responsibilities for that country require.

Yet it contains some proposals which might imperil the plans for the orderly and effective attainment of self-government which have been so carefully worked out between the British staff and the Sudanese Ministers and Assembly, and postpone to an uncertain date the long promised elections which were about to begin.

It is not possible here to work through the document in detail. But there are four points that surely must be questioned. First, the erection of a new seven-member 'neutral' commission under Indian or Pakistani chairmanship, itself subject to an Egyptian Government veto, would reduce the Governor-General's position to one of paralysis at the most hazardous moments of constitutional suspense and transfer. The removal of all British along with Egyptian troops one year before the election of the constitutional assembly would complete the security vacuum. Secondly, the Sudanization committee is so designed as to hold out the threat of an omnibus dismissal of all British staff within three years, in conditions which might lead to their still earlier voluntary disappearance. Thirdly, while the constituent assembly is specifically free to vote for unity with Egypt, it is to be denied in advance the freedom to choose any form of association with Britain or the Commonwealth. Fourthly, the safeguards under which the Southern Sudanese agreed to accept a unified constitution have been deleted.

Admittedly General Neguib, for his part, has abandoned Egypt's claim to sovereignty, and offered the Sudan his friendship. For the Sudanese these gains are great. But so is the price to be paid for them, and it may be that this has not yet been fully calculated by them. It may prove no less than the elimination or emasculation of that executive power which has guided their development for 55 years at the very moment when full nationhood is within their grasp, but divided from them by two or three years which may be the most difficult and fateful of their history. For the processes of the transfer of power a framework of order and an atmosphere of confidence are necessary, with a rational and gradual withdrawal of British staff which will do justice to both sides and guard the country's administration and economy from sudden dislocation or decline.

The implied reason for these very questionable proposals is, of course, that the Governor-General and his staff cannot be trusted to carry out the British Government's promises with impartiality and honesty. I doubt whether any of those Sudanese who have been working in daily partnership with their British colleagues during the last few years of rapid constitutional development really feel this doubt. Let them remember that Britain has a strong – from the point of view of the Sudan, perhaps, almost too strong – interest in achieving a harmonious military settlement with Egypt. Let them also remember that there is in Britain a warm appreciation of their character and of their aspirations for independence. But we are also hopeful, in view of the many strands of co-operation and friendship that have been woven between our two countries during the last half century, that we may keep intact all of these which are compatible with the independence of the Sudan.

The decision rests with the Sudanese: and it is imperative that they should realize that the initiative in this matter now lies with them and not with us. It would be tragic if through the silence of our Government, mute in an excess of official correctitude, the Sudanese leaders failed in the next decisive weeks not only to detect the real administrative significance of some of the proposals before them but also the desire of the British, based both on interest and sentiment, for neither of which there is any reason to apologize, to retain the many links which bind us. Once these are cut, it may be impossible ever to restore them.

Yours faithfully

1953

The Sudan: the Future of the South

Letter to *The Times* 24 January 1953

This letter draws attention to the dangers of a situation which led to the massacre of northerners in the Sudan and to prolonged insurgency and repression in the south which still continues as this book goes to press.

Sir, – I agree with Mr Scott in his letter in your issue of January 17 that in the difficult question of the southern Sudan, the last outstanding issue between Britain, Egypt and the northern leaders, Britain should do nothing to widen or exacerbate the division between the two regions. Above all, remembering some tragic mistakes we have made in not dissimilar situations in the past, the southern attitude should not be stiffened by hopes of lasting measures of British protection which later we may not have the will or the power to fulfil. But a policy of restraint and reconciliation does not demand that we should entirely abdicate our responsibility to ensure that a fair and open settlement is reached.

In view of the abrupt Egyptian assault upon a constitution which had been carefully worked out in the Sudan Legislative Assembly and accepted by the southern representatives, there are some things about the southern Sudan which need to be restated. It is sometimes said that the division between the two regions is largely due to British influence. It is true that the Sudan Government did meet their striking contrasts by a measure of administrative differentiation and that for many years, while the idea of a self-governing Sudan lay outside the imagination of any party, the ultimate affiliation of this equatorial region, so lately and so oppressively grasped by Egypt, seemed to be an open question.

True also, that British administrators, while they showed an absolute respect for the deep Moslem conviction of the north, had a faith in their own religion without which they could not have so well served the Sudan, and they allowed missionaries to offer their self-sacrificing and inexpensive educational services to the pagan tribesmen with the result that many of them are now Christian. But when the prospect of self-government suddenly appeared and the decision was taken, largely upon good economic and financial grounds, to bring north and south into one legislature, British officials honourably supported this policy, which endeavoured to bridge a deep cultural and historical division which existed long before the advent of Britain.

Even under their present experienced and humane political and economic administration, the southern provinces are still a financial liability to the north. If they were to sink into anything like their former disorder or stagnation, they might become a fatal drag upon the prosperity and reputation of the new state, and make more difficult those future works for the better regulation of the Nile waters which flow through them and which are so vital for both Egypt and the Sudan. There are many able and enlightened northern Sudanese, some of whom have themselves aided in the administration of the south, who know this and will understand that the future of their relationship with these isolated and still politically immature peoples depends very largely upon the provisions made today to meet their needs and their fears.

The northern leaders would add to their already existing reputation for dignity and moderation, and win the respect of all truly democratic peoples if, in writing the first all-important chapter of their history as an independent nation, they could win over their southern neighbours by showing them the respect, toleration and political understanding they are claiming for themselves.

Yours faithfully

The Central African Federation: Dangers of its Speedy Enactment

Letter to *The Times* 26 February 1953

This letter drew attention to the political awakening of the Central Africans as they suddenly found themselves in an exposed position between the racial pressures of Southern Africa and the awakening peoples to the north.

Sir, – Sufficient arguments have surely been advanced in your columns to make the Government hesitate to impose the present federal scheme for Central Africa against the wish of the Africans, supported, as they are, by strong sections of opinion in Britain and especially in Scotland which has a historic religious connection with Nyasaland.

It is said in defence of such imposition that Africans are incapable of understanding the question. This may well be true of the actual federation proposals, but, like other subject peoples in our own and other empires, they can distinguish clearly between the relatively disinterested rule of a distant imperial Government and that of the local white community whose position in some vital matters conflicts with their present interests and their future hopes. Africans know that the whole drive of the white element for many years has been against the authority of this country and its native policy.

Long and profound experience teaches Africans to distrust the proposed safeguards, both the African Affairs Board and the delusive promise of unchanged Protectorate status. Mr Welensky himself, the probable future federal Prime Minister, has referred in a recent article (*Optima*, December 1952) to imperial restrictions as 'museum pieces' of 'little moment'. If the African Affairs Board were ever to act as an obstacle in some matter deemed vital by the Europeans, their leaders, reinforced perhaps by an appeal to their electorate, would probably raise a storm in which the safeguards would be declared intolerable and unworkable. Can we be confident – and upon this the whole scheme depends – that our Government would stand out against such pressure, especially if it were acting through a Commonwealth Relations Minister trained in the long tradition of acquiescence to Dominion wishes? The hopes and promises affirmed today would be likely to pass into history with those put forward on other occasions to silence humanitarian protests.

Realists consider it sufficient to show that the Africans will benefit from the economic advance. But, upon the evidence of our contemporary world, people who feel their human dignity injured cannot be soothed by material palliatives. The Union shows that even a booming economy, if built upon the basis of black, colour-barred labour and a disintegrated peasantry, cracks at the foundations. If realists also urge that it is hopeless to attempt to contain the dynamism of the local Europeans, it should be recognized that other powerful counter-influences are now at work and playing upon the Africans from within Africa and from the outside world. The risk of disorder is one that no one can estimate, but violence is unfortunately at work in parts of Africa and it would be tragic indeed if our British forces had to be used to punish Africans for asserting too vigorously their loyal desire to remain, as at present, under the unimpaired authority of our own Government. It is not inconceivable that something very like the Ulster dilemma might emerge in Central Africa.

Those who resist the imposition of federation do not claim, as is so often asserted, either that the Africans are now ready to play their full part in a democratic Government or that the Europeans are morally inferior to themselves. It is just because the Africans are politically unready that power over them should not be transferred to a group of people who, however high their individual merit, together represent a small racial minority of employers and large landowners. The situation still requires the arbitral power of the Imperial Government, in spite of its admitted limitations.

The dangerous political psychology of Africa today makes the retention of the encouraging, liberal and adjustable power of the British Government all the more essential. Public opinion should therefore resist the shock tactics by which, in some quarters, this far-reaching scheme is being pressed, and should challenge the coercive statement in the last White Paper that 'if this scheme should be rejected the Government would see no prospect of re-opening the subject within any foreseeable period of time.' On the contrary, rejection of this scheme should be followed by a patient attempt to secure some at least of its undoubted economic advantages by more gradual means, worked out alongside those measures of higher and technical education and those first instalments of equality by which alone the confidence and co-operation of the Africans will be won.

Yours faithfully

On the Eve of Central African Federation

Letter to *The Times* 9 June 1953

This letter expresses the fears of many in Britain about the federal experiment in Central Africa, which, unheeded, were proved to be only too well-founded.

Sir, – A recent visit to Kenya and Uganda has confirmed my fears that by the form of Central African Federation and by the way in which it has been handled we risk losing the greatest asset we have in the continent – the confidence of Africans. Some eleventh-hour pledges and concessions in tomorrow's debate might at least lessen this risk.

First, with regard to the imperial connection, the Government have made the almost unbelievable assertion that the erection of a strong federal legislature over the Territorial Governments in no way impairs their protectorate status. They must prove this by word and act, since it is only by making the utmost use of the powers left to her that Britain can keep the promises the Government are now making to the British electorate and to the Africans. I venture to disagree with a statement of your Colonial Correspondent in the recent articles 'Africa Emergent', and still more with the interpretation put upon it in the last debate on Central Africa, that policies directed from Britain must have a decreasing function. On the contrary, I believe that British authority and influence, in the high democratic spirit reaffirmed at the Coronation, were never more needed in Central Africa or more desired by the Africans. There are especially three ways in which the Government should pledge their exercise:

(1) There should be no impairment of the position of the Colonial Office, the expulsion of which is stated as a chief aim by the European leaders – a point which the Government have not answered – or of the Colonial Service. The liberal purposes of the imperial Government can be exercised in province and district only through a trained and impartial administration. Upon this subject the hurried report of the Civil Service Commission was highly equivocal.

(2) The British civil liberties must be carefully safeguarded to allow Africans to organize themselves politically in order to make full use of the limited representation allowed to them. Admittedly, this is a difficult matter amidst the tensions of a racially mixed society. But nothing could be more fatal than, by a severe treatment of fancied sedition, to foster real sedition and to drive the strong leaders Africans must try to throw up, or their European friends and advisers, into courses which lead to deportation or gaol. This comment has no reference to current cases about which I have insufficient evidence: it is based on unhappy experience elsewhere, and the imperative need to foster constitutional African leadership.

(3) With regard to the promised economic development which seems, mistakenly, as I believe, to have led many of the otherwise unconvinced to accept federation, the Government should be asked to show that they have the power and the policy that will enable them to shelter the

peoples of the Protectorates from such truly horrifying schemes as Mr Welensky has proclaimed. The pressure of such rapid and extensive development upon a scanty population, already strained to the utmost, and based on the present destructive system of migrant labour, could so undermine the natural morale and economy of African society that all the revenues produced will be needed to buttress it artificially by expensive social services, including additional police forces and prisons.

If Africans are to be given an increasing share in the legislative and executive branches of the constitution there must be active measures to train them. One of the greatest causes of African bitterness is the belief that tardy and inadequate help is given to raise them from the ignorance and inexperience which is so frequently emphasized. Even if the problems – and they are many – which beset the proposed inter-racial university are quickly settled, it will take at least five or six years before the first fully qualified Africans pass out of it. Nothing could do more to overcome that deep suspicion of the white man's intentions which blights co-operation in Africa than the announcement by the Government of a generous and immediate provision of scholarships and grants for travel and study to cover the interval and to expedite the training of Africans for political leadership, for the Civil Service, and for industry.

May we also hope that in this debate some of the oft-repeated clichés will not be used again? It is no defamation of our 'kith and kin' in the Rhodesias to believe that no small, local minority should be given such wide powers over a subordinate race and class without Britain retaining the fullest possible rights to influence and revise. As for rejecting either 'white or black domination', it may be asked whether power can be indefinitely suspended between the two. This Bill legislates for white domination now but, unless the experience of history and all British policy and principles are to be reversed, there must one day be black domination in the sense that power must pass to the immense African majority.

Whether it passes peacefully, without destroying the influence of the European minority and the great contributions they and their nations have brought to Africa, may depend upon the deliberation of Parliament tomorrow and the spirit in which this hazardous constitution is instituted.

Yours faithfully

Facilities for African Dissent

Letter to *The Spectator* 12 July 1953

On 12 May 1953 Chief Gomani of Nyasaland initiated a movement of civil disobedience directed against the imposition of the Federation. The Rev. Michael Scott supported him at a public demonstration. Police were sent to carry out arrests and Michael Scott was deported and the film he took of the incident confiscated. Upon his return to England he defended himself against the criticisms of Mr (now Lord) Alport and others in letters to the press.

Sir, – Michael Scott has written with such strength and fullness in answer to Mr Alport that he stands in no need of reinforcement. But the controversy raises at least one issue which needs further consideration. It is clear that Mr Alport does not understand the depth of conviction with which some people hold the view that in putting the Nyasaland people under the southern settlers – for that is what the present federal constitution amounts to – Britain is committing a wrong.

This in turn raises a problem of political action which needs to be faced. The citizen in this country, when his representatives are defeated in Parliament, has well-defined methods open to him by which he may try to obtain amendment or reversal of the decision. But what are the Nyasaland people to do? They have no parliamentary representation through which to express opinion and register dissent. And when a constitution, which destroys the *status quo* of their cherished imperial connection, is imposed upon them against their will, how can they try to change the decision? And what course is open to the very large number of people in Britain who agree wholeheartedly with them and, while unable to advise them to oppose, since all the penalties will fall upon the Africans, must hope that their opposition will lead to the reversal or radical amendment of the constitution? It would seem hard that all this effort and the risks of opposition should now fall upon the Africans, weak and inexperienced as they are.

As I understand it, Michael Scott solved this problem for himself by going out to Nyasaland and mastering his serious ill-health, not only to show his sympathy and agreement with the Africans, but also to turn their angry opposition into peaceful channels. But for those who lack his speed of decision, his logic and his courage, the problem of their relationship with the African opposition, left to struggle alone for their rights against a government which they believe has betrayed their future, this problem remains and it may become increasingly difficult with the years. Shall we all risk deportation or being declared prohibited immigrants if we try to go to Central Africa or will British civil liberties be maintained under the new federation? The problem could only be solved if the new rulers of Central Africa showed from the first that not only in economic development, but in education and political advancement, they meant to provide all, and more, that the people of Nyasaland could have hoped for at the hands of the Imperial Government.

Yours faithfully

Central African University

Letter to *The Times* 28 July 1953

Sir Alexander Carr-Saunders presented a report on a Rhodesian university to the Inter-University Council for Higher Education overseas. On the Council we saw the proposed inter-racial university as a promise not only for African advancement but as the most effective medium for promoting understanding between white and black. The University was established but has had to struggle as a non-racial institution within an area of intense racial controversy and the break-up of the Federation it was meant to serve. The secession of Rhodesia from the Commonwealth must radically affect its position.

Sir, – In the deep controversy about Central African federation which reaches its final parliamentary stages here tomorrow and Tuesday, there is one matter upon which there is general agreement. That is upon the urgent need to found a university which will be open to all races. If such an institution were established upon the basis of full academic freedom, so well tested in this country, and developed as one of the great fraternity of Commonwealth or, indeed, Western universities, it could do more than anything else to diminish the profound doubts held by so many in this country about the federation, the future success of which must be shadowed if these doubts should be retained or increased.

The establishment of a new university gives rise to many problems, some of them highly technical, others demanding long experience. This is especially true of the first years when one false step may start the young institution off in the wrong direction from which it may be difficult, or even impossible, to retreat. There can be no doubt that the universities of this country would be most eager to help in the many ways open to them, not in a spirit of patronage, but of equality and friendship. So far we have been offered no more than warm but vague promises of good intentions. It would take too long, and it would, perhaps, be unwise, to discuss in this letter the several points now at issue, most of which are fully treated in the Carr-Saunders Report. It can only be hoped that they will be handled during the next few months – for this is an urgent question – with the greatest possible wisdom and discretion upon both sides.

Nothing should be allowed to prevent the energy and ambition of a young community, longing to express itself in action, from entering into a fruitful partnership with the great reserve of academic experience and good will in this country, to which must be added the realistic help of imperial finance. The university could grow in the centuries to come into the place where the races, which now seem so far apart, could meet at the highest level of common thought and understanding, sharing the inheritance of other civilizations and finding expression for their own unique contribution as Central Africans.

Yours faithfully

Bringing a Nation to Birth

I wrote this article when I was travelling in the Sudan during 1953, at a time when the British officials were distressed by the prospect of their abrupt removal, the uncertainty of the conditions of this termination, and their anxiety about the future of a people they had served so well. The article is the only unpublished entry in this book. I surmise that the editor felt that the issue of the future of the British staff, being still undecided, was too delicate a matter to discuss in public at this stage.

The excitement caused by the Agreement between Britain and Egypt and by the great public celebrations that followed it has died down. The

[1953]

Sudan now faces a period, which can last as long as three years, during which the complex and rigid provisions for self-government and self-determination will be enacted. In the three cities which sprawl round the junction of the Niles everything seems much the same upon the surface. In Omdurman, its low skyline dominated by the new silver dome of the Mahdi's tomb, the tall, white-robed and turbanned Sudanese move about the streets with their usual dignity. In Khartoum, in their solid office buildings along the Blue Nile front, and in their provincial and district headquarters all over this vast country, British officials carry on their long-perfected routine with what appears to be the old, splendid confidence.

But beneath the surface the strains of the coming fundamental changes are at work. British officials, amidst all the jubilation about the Agreement, never had any illusions about what it must mean for the country and for themselves. And now the Sudanese are facing its full implications. It is not, of course, that they value any less the great gains they have made, the removal of the historic threat of Egypt's claim to sovereignty and the consequent unity between their own long and deeply divided parties. It is that they are confronting for the first time the great psychological and practical difficulties involved in the passing of power from an imperial to a national government. These problems, encountered in Asia, should be studied again by the British under their Sudanese manifestation, for they are inherent in that act of abdication which must, from time to time, be repeated elsewhere. True, many of the Sudanese are embarrassing in their gratitude and appreciation, the reward for fifty-five years of just and efficient administration by generations of British officials. Yet all these conversations lead up to the questions round which fears and suspicions gather and which might lead to the loss of much, if not all, of this fine harvest of goodwill.

The first question is that of unity. Countries that pass so easily under foreign rule, mainly because of their lack of unity, do not automatically acquire it at the deeper level just because an administrative unity has been imposed from above. The very prospect of the removal of the foreign control, which has held the diverse parts together within its own steel framework, at once creates intense fears and ambitions as the groups contemplate having to find their own balance of power without the restraints and supports of that framework. The policy of the Sudan Government in maintaining for many years a somewhat separatist administration for the pagan Negro south, and the introduction there of Christian missions, has left a legacy of suspicion even though that policy has been clearly abandoned in deed and in word since the south was brought into the Legislative Assembly. Northerners flinch from accepting that the old historic, southern fears have been rekindled by the very idea of losing British protection and also by their own neglect of the south in the recent negotiations with Egypt. They therefore assume that the whole blame lies with the anti-northern bias of British administrators in the south. Suspicion is confirmed by the difficulty of finding, among these primitive tribes, leaders who can represent and express opinion upon the complex constitutional issue. And in an excited and lightly administered region, it is no easy task for officials to protect wandering delegations from Egypt or the north in search of the evidence they want to find. Nothing less than a large and laborious conference of northern and southern leaders, held in the south, is now needed if this potentially dangerous situation is to be remedied. It is too late for Britain to go back unilaterally upon the accepted policy. The future security of the southerners rests in part upon their being helped to take with both hands the not inconsiderable opportunities and safeguards offered to them by the draft constitution. It also depends upon the goodwill of the northerners, which might be drained away in a prolonged period of unhappy incidents. The election which can provide a Sudanese Parliament and Government is therefore a most urgent necessity. In the meantime, the greatest test of the northerners will be the generosity of their approach to the south, even going so far, perhaps, as to allow appeal against themselves to some international body.

The second main problem concerns the position of the administration during the transfer of power. There is no harder task to set an administration than that of liquidating itself. This is certainly not understood by those Sudanese who implore the British to go on helping them now as before and do not see how difficult this has been made by the terms of the rapid Sudanization arrangement. But is this difficulty fully understood even in Britain? The will to govern, and the co-ordination of all the many branches of administration, resided in the 140 or so like-minded British political officers, held together as they were by the very strong and high tradition of their service. These men are now trying to carry out the hardest task of all, one requiring great intellectual steadiness and sympathy with the nationalist movement, whose impetus must be controlled and harnessed to an orderly constitutional process. Yet at this supreme moment, this service faces dissolution. It is inevitable that its members must be prepared to see all they have worked for thrown into the melting pot of a new national government.

[1953]

But is it an essential part of this process that they should be asked to carry through their final task, upon which the future relations of the two countries largely depend, while racked with complete uncertainty about their own position and rights? The British taxpayer would lose some hundreds of thousands of pounds, perhaps a million or so, if the successor government should refuse to honour its obligations. Even though a default on the part of such an honourable people as the Sudanese may be difficult to imagine, yet British officials have to perform their last, all-important duties under a load or anxiety not untinged with bitterness. An imperial power should surely find ways of allowing its agents to abdicate its powers with a dignity and goodwill that are difficult to achieve so long as their own interests are so painfully and uncertainly involved against such abdication. Nothing should so become the life of a great colonial service as the leaving of it.

The third necessity for retaining the goodwill of the Sudanese depends upon Britain taking a firm line with any Egyptian infringements of the Agreement, and not even seeming to subordinate the Sudan's interests to those of the Egyptian negotiations. Sudanese fear the pressure of an America which may give little weight to their needs against the importance of the state which is a hinge of world strategy and communications. The independence leaders promise Britain solid, if modest advantages – commercial reciprocities; a field for investment; acceptance of a military mission; basis for defence. Their country straddles the Arab world and Negro Africa and could reinforce British influence in either sphere. Certainly, to a power hoping to hold a rapidly maturing Africa to the Western alliance, the warm friendship of the Sudan must have its political attractions. Nor need it be regarded as a threat by Egypt, which has more to gain by alliance with a strong, self-respecting Sudan, through which the Nile waters can flow under perfect regulation, than from one torn to pieces by the intrigues and sectarian conflicts which it is now so easy for her to foment.

We in Britain must adjust ourselves quickly to the need to build up a new empire of influence as our empire of power falls away. This influence, which menaces no one, must, of course, depend ultimately upon the political, economic and moral strength of Britain herself. But, immediately, we must show energy and imagination in responding to demands such as those the Sudanese are now making. Fortunately, in Khartoum, one of the universities Britain has helped to found, securely placed, we must hope, in its chartered independence of government, will remain to deepen our fruitful intellectual partnership with the

Sudanese. But many other responses are now asked of us, in terms of such deep appreciation of what Britain has done and could still legitimately do, that no one who listens to such moving appeals could doubt that here too, if the dangerous transactions of the coming months can be wisely and firmly handled, in losing a dependency Britain may gain a loyal friend and ally.

1954

Difficulties in Buganda

Letter to *The Times* 10 February 1954

Sir, – British opinion is distressed and confused that a constitutional crisis should have developed in Buganda, a country where Britain has a long accumulated balance of trust and affection, and where, as those who have seen him at work can testify, there is a Governor whose great gifts are wholly devoted to African advancement. The explanation is that recent events have touched off a series of political mines which were laid long before the Governor and the contemporary Buganda leaders came upon the scene.

Of the four main difficulties, two are internal to Buganda and two of wider import. Internal is the need to face the long evaded question of the constitution of Buganda. The circumstances of Buganda's entry into British protection had a crystallizing effect. Britain has since built up the Uganda Protectorate around and above Buganda, making of it a heart that could never, without fatal results, be torn from the larger body politic and economic.

Today, while in terms of modern administration Buganda is merely a disproportionately large and wealthy province, to its people, as a student of its history can well understand, it is a proud and ancient African kingdom. Clearly, an acceptable constitutional compromise between these opposing ideas has still to be worked out within the four walls of the original Agreement, in such a way that it can be fully accepted and understood by the Baganda. The second internal problem centres upon the powers of the Kabaka, still the essential mediator between the Governor and the people, but at present suspended bewilderingly between the old absolutism and the new status of constitutional ruler with a rapidly awakening representative assembly.

The Governor's own well-devised plan to ameliorate the constitutional situation was hardly launched when it was struck by a gust of fear about federation. This long-standing fear, the first of the two external factors, explains much. Last year in Uganda, even before Mr Lyttelton's speech, the question was put to me by one of the most experienced Baganda: 'Why, if the British Government could force Nyasaland against African wishes into federation dominated by Southern Rhodesian colonists, could not the same happen here?' This fear explained the refusal to elect members to the new Legislative Council lest, against its Buganda minority, it should vote Uganda into a federation.

The people's second external fear is that a new economic empire, complete with copper mines, and manned by increasing numbers of immigrants, is being constructed above their reach and outside their understanding. The new Legislative Council, and the recent bold educational plans, should help to bring the people into the developing industry and commerce at gradually rising levels of understanding and co-operation. But this, also, is not yet understood.

I would urgently suggest that a small and expert constitutional commission should be sent out to Buganda to discuss fully and informally with the Governor and the Lukiko what measures are needed to amend the internal defects of the constitution and define the meaning of 'an African state'. This step would relax tension and allow for calm and rational consideration of very complex problems. It would be a visible sign of the deep interest and sympathy felt in this county towards Buganda, and a response to a delegation which, even if all their demands and statements cannot obtain acceptance, have made a very good impression here, as have their leaders in Buganda, by their restraint and dignity. Such discussions could, as Mr Lyttelton's recent happy experience at more formal conferences will have proved to him, hasten the political education of an already advanced African people eager for more political opportunity.

The position of the present Kabaka, upon which it is difficult for opinion in this country to pronounce, might then be considered in the calmer and clearer light of an agreed constitutional settlement. The relations of Buganda with Britain have been almost uniformly happy, deepened as they have been by the bond of Christianity which is much older than the political tie. Under Sir Andrew Cohen's liberal inspiration the present difficulties could, once reason had mastered suspicion, be turned into a new constitutional start for Buganda with happy results for the Protectorate and, indeed, for East Africa as a whole.

Yours faithfully

[1954]

Delicate Transfer of Rule in the Sudan

The Times 16 June 1954

The visitor returning to Khartoum after a year's absence sees few apparent signs of change. The Governor-General still lives in his fine white palace by the Nile; British officials work at their desks under the whirring fans, dine at night in the theatrical setting of their gardens, and go to bed on their roofs under the crowded stars.

Even those who probe more deeply, and are aware that under this calm exterior a hazardous transfer of power is being made, may not realize that anything threatens the delicate transaction. The British, having given to this vast, dry block of north-east Africa some fifty odd years of unity and order, have lately helped to endow it with a complete set of Western democratic institutions – an elective two-chamber legislature, a Cabinet system, Westminster parliamentary procedure, and an independent judiciary and Civil Service.

But a great change has come over the minds of these British officials as they go with such apparent calm about their final duties. A year ago they were bringing themselves, not without some mental anguish, to accept the hard truth that there was soon to be an abrupt end to all their devoted labours. Today the mood has changed. There is a conviction that the moment of suspended power is intolerable to the erstwhile rulers and unhealthy for their Sudanese successors, and that the sooner the last official link is cut the better for both. But it must be cut in such a way as to save the new Sudan, if this be possible, from sinking into the dangers which threaten it.

The first danger is that these excellent institutions which the Sudanese have accepted will not survive the shocks of transfer. The new constitution was not imposed upon the Sudanese: it was desired by them and its forms were hammered out over several years in Sudanese committees and assemblies. But it so happens that the Umma Party, which provided the Ministers—mostly experienced Civil Servants – who for some five years have worked closely with their British colleagues, lost the recent election and power has passed into the hands of men most of whom are without political or administrative experience and whose principal qualification is their former hostility towards 'the colonizers'.

Thanks both to British correctitude and to Sudanese courtesy, personal relations have not quite broken down under the strain. The dignity of parliamentary ritual has been maintained: Ministers are learning the realities of power and have made reassuring statements about such matters as their attitude to foreign merchants and the independence of the all-important University College. But it would be too much to expect that the restraints and the respect for legitimate freedoms by which a mature democracy works can be learned in a few months. Moreover, good administration is as necessary as good politics. In these new, poor countries where almost everything, material as well as constitutional, has to be created rapidly by governments of little experience, much – too much – depends upon the civil service. The Sudan has a sadly small number of trained men to fill the chairs of the departing British. There are some fine, well tried administrators, and a small cadre of excellent doctors, but every one of the many departments needed by a modern State is short of trained senior Sudanese.

Unfortunately the new Sudanese Ministry has not yet succeeded in providing an atmosphere which would make it easy for British staff to remain. Under the terms of the agreement of February 1953, which the Foreign Office made with Egypt in the vain hope of easing the Suez Canal dispute, the British in the administration, the Defence Force and the police are to leave *before* the date set for self-determination. The police in fact have already been Sudanized. The terms of the agreement are unfortunate: they leave men tied to posts which are becoming difficult to hold, and entrust the initiative to discharge and the arrangements for cancellation and compensation to a Sudanese Ministry which has hitherto shown more complaisance towards Egypt than towards Britain.

The men carrying out this difficult task of abdication have deserved well of their own country, and Treasury considerations of finance and of precedents should not prevent a consummation of their work. And what happens to the services designated for automatic Sudanization will influence the far larger number of so-called 'technicians', who are anxiously watching to see what sort of treatment they may expect. Many of these, so Ministers assured the writer, the Sudanese Government is most anxious to retain. Any large exodus of British staff would certainly bring some of the departments of Government to a standstill and ruin the hard-won administrative achievements of half a century. This would be a bitter conclusion to our partnership with a fine people. It would be especially ruinous to the Gezira scheme, which requires the framework of modern services. And it would spell misery to the primitive south, where the tribes need expert and sympathetic handling.

[1954]

The second threat is to the independence of the country. It comes from Egypt. Even while the supreme power there was being tossed from hand to hand like a Rugby football, Egypt's policy towards the Sudan and Britain retained, as if by instinct, its energy and continuity. Egypt has every reason to grasp the Sudan: it holds the life-stream of the Nile; it is an immense contiguous area, full of still unexplored possibilities; it is a breeding-ground of strong soldiers; it is a former conquest where pride demands reassertion; and it is the place where the prestige and influence of Britain may be most easily injured, and Egypt's long exclusion from the realities of the Condominium revenged. It now rests with the British Government, whether through unilateral or international action, to meet Egypt's legitimate fears and to check her improper interferences. Such prevention is no longer possible for the British element in the Sudan. Even the Governor-General is now fettered in his remaining powers by a supervisory commission with a pro-Egyptian majority.

The shadow of a third and even graver danger hangs over the Sudan. If the National Unity Party at present in power leans upon Egypt, as Britain prepares to retire, it is because it is haunted by the memory of the Mahdia and the long tyranny of the western tribes over the commercial and riverain peoples who mostly adhere to the rival religious sect of the Khatmia. The unfortunate, and almost accidental, flare-up of violence on 1 March, when the Mahdist demonstrators and the police had a brief but bloody tussle, has fanned the ancient fear. The Umma, the Mahdist party, made an unexpectedly poor showing at the last elections, in which it failed to co-operate with other groups, and an election map would reveal clearly how local memories of the Mahdia affected the voting.

For the next all-important election for the constituent assembly, although Egyptian troops will be withdrawn along with British, the Umma Party will have against it all the force of Egyptian money, so powerful to buy men in a poor country, and also the strength of the government in power, which, from fear of its rivals, may still feel tempted to lean heavily upon Egyptian support. This in turn might tempt the extremist section of the Mahdist party to abandon what to them are the uncongenial and disappointing techniques of democracy and to return to their former methods of ousting Egyptian power. Nothing could be more fatal for their country and also for themselves, for the Government today commands weapons a hundred times stronger than were wielded against brave fanatics in the 1880s. It would also have the right to call for rapid reinforcements from the Condominium Powers for the restoration of order.

In the interests of the Sudanese, as well as in her own, Britain should use without delay all her remaining power and influence to prevent a situation developing which might evoke such a tragic repetition of past history. But the chief responsibility rests with the present Sudanese Government. It is urgent that it should create within the country that atmosphere of unity and reconciliation in which the old internal feuds may die away and the Umma Party and the great western tribes make their proper contribution to the new nation. In external affairs – though these are really indivisible from the internal – it should try at least to limit corrupting interventions and to strive for that true independence in the face of which the long unhappy rivalry of the Condominium Powers would become irrelevant.

Britain's Response to the End of Colonialism

The Listener 10 December 1954

There can be no dispute about the general nature of Britain's colonial purpose: to develop self-government in the colonies, and to do it in such a way that their peoples remain voluntarily within the Commonwealth. And we do not forget the economic side of self-government. It has come increasingly to the front since Lord Hailey began to enquire what would happen if the colonies asked from us bread and we gave them the vote. The more I study the question, meet colonial nationalists, and travel in their countries, the more I become convinced that three-quarters of our problems today are psychological. So I want to begin with that side. I want to ask two questions: first, how far are we towards understanding the colonies in their present restless condition? In other words, are we dealing with the causes as well as the symptoms? Secondly how far are we making the necessary adjustments of our institutions here, in Britain? We must not be complacent. We should remember that we have shown ourselves capable of making great mistakes as rulers of other peoples. We should remember Ireland and Palestine, and the Mau Mau in Kenya, to go no further.

Have we adjusted our minds to the psychology of the colonial situation? In our dealings with colonial nationalism we are – let us admit it – finding ourselves obliged to make concessions we never meant to make so soon. We yield to pressures without fully understanding what they are and where they come from. We claim – but it is only a half-truth – that what is happening is merely the fulfilment of our own policy and promises. We preside with a fair measure of dignity and goodwill over these uncomfortable processes of de-colonization. So far, except perhaps in one instance, none of these difficult situations has got quite out of hand. All this is greatly to the credit of our adaptability and also the high quality of our harassed agents in the colonies. But could we not do still better? If we could attain to a greater understanding of the common causes underlying these scattered assertions which so often take us half by surprise, could we not manage to guide and contain them? Our response might then be less negative, less abrupt, less of a retreat and more of a planned manœuvre. Clearly, if we could understand the colonial peoples better we could help them to understand us. And perhaps, as a result, when the moment comes for the decisive delegation of power, we might not need to be so anxious about what these new nations are going to do with their freedom.

In nearly all our colonies we are now in one or other of two critical phases. The first is the period immediately leading up to self-government. The second is the initial period of that self-government. Both phases present grave hazards to us and to the peoples concerned, even in territories where the major problems of multi-racialism do not exist. Consider the first phase: the conditions in which we try to transfer power today seem calculated to bedevil this delicate transaction. It is as though a surgeon were asked to operate upon a vigorous patient without an anaesthetic and with a critical, and indeed a largely hostile crowd, shouting and pushing round the operating table. The analogy is not exact because, ideally, the colonial people should be actively co-operative rather than passive. Unfortunately their activity is too often shown in distrust, impatience, hostility, sometimes even disorder. It is useless for us to marvel that this damaging distrust can persist in spite of those many precedents in our history of our abdications in the face of nationalism. Rather we have to find the cause of distrust and deal with it.

It lies, surely, in the truth that independence is something that cannot be given but must be taken. And first it has to be demanded, and demanded by more than the first half-dozen lawyers and journalists who have learned to direct against us the civil liberties we wrested from the Stuarts: by more than the first handful of 'nationalists' who have created a miniature copy of the Indian Congress. Before their demand can be taken seriously, before there can be any successor to whom we can hand over our power, these first self-constituted leaders have to create at least the appearance of a nation. To do this it seems to be inevitable that they first set about breaking the crust of habitual subservience to the colonial government: their weapons are invective and ridicule. They try to rouse the desire for freedom by playing upon every possible cause of discontent. Any concessions by the government, short of the final one, are ignored or condemned. They merely spoil the leaders' plans. A high emotional temperature is needed in which they can fuse their diverse human material and hammer it into the rough shape of a nation. And how painfully natural it is that the readiest emotional element from which to draw the required heat, is hatred. There is always a small but responsible group of people, the first generation of 'nationalists', who struggle bravely for moderation, but they are often thrust contemptuously aside as imperialist stooges.

This, then, is the scene on the stage of almost any colonial territory, but if it were the whole play we might agree with those who still exhort us to deal firmly with the few 'agitators' and who assert that the loyal masses would then long remain content under our beneficent rule. But while it would be accepting what I consider the heresy of determinism to regard colonial leaders as mere puppets jerked about on the strings of fate, it is true that they are acting under the influence of a powerful world force which at once inspires their demands and makes them almost irresistible.

This force is the desire for equality, for self-expression, for freedom from any kind of external mastery and its stigma of inferiority. From Russia to Haiti, and from China to Peru, it is the great motive force in the world today, acting in different ways upon nearly all states, both in their internal affairs and in their foreign policy. Is it not also the impulsion behind the peaceful revolution taking place today in our own country? Through most of history men have for the most part accepted subjection, whether imposed by empire, nation, tribe, class, or caste, as if it were in the natural order of things, like storms and droughts. Only in our own day has the rule of one people by another come widely to be regarded as morally wrong and injurious. What an opportunity, what an invitation for the expression of discontent! And what an audience our one world, with its public platform in New York, provides for that expression! An audience, be it noted, largely made up of peoples who have themselves been ruled, or at least dominated – as China was – by the strenuous Western nations.

[1954]

The emancipated Asian peoples are obsessed by the memory of their subjection, and it might be said that behind each colonial movement there is now the heave of the great shoulder of Asia; and these colonies are also open to the pervasive indoctrination of communism. And so, when education wakes the sleeping African to the world outside his own, after fifty years or more of apparent contentment with colonial rule, he hears at once the view that his status is shameful and also that nearly all this newly realized world is urging him to throw it off. The quality of the rule seems to make no difference to the violence of the new rejection. In the Anglo-Egyptian Sudan, colonial administration was surely seen at its most disinterested and sympathetic. Yet we hear the new Sudanese leaders speak of those fifty years, in which they were given the shape and the equipment of a potential nation, as years of misery and slavery.

This, then, is the force with which, when it reaches a colony, we have to reckon, knowing that we cannot conduct its government against the organized opposition of the small élite we have educated. Unless, that is, we are prepared to shoot against purely political demonstrations – which we are not, or certainly not more than once. This is why, one by one we throw all our leisurely administrative and constitutional programmes into the waste-paper basket.

Knowing all this, as we now do, we should surely set to work, wherever the chance still remains, to prepare a colony by every means in our power for the premature self-government which, in this second half of our century, it must attain. At present our minds are divided. Our colonial officials still find it hard to believe that they should begin to stop administering and start to teach how to administer. In most cases we refuse even to consider the constitutional timetables which the peoples so ardently desire. The pioneers in nationalism still too often feel themselves forced into the wilderness of sedition. We do not everywhere seek out and urgently train native talent as we should, especially in countries like Northern Rhodesia, Nyasaland, and the High Commission territories, where there is a dangerous dearth of educated and experienced leaders. By dramatic schemes of education and training for self-government, openly planned and with the drive we freely devote to military operations, we could at once pacify and prolong the period of approach, and ensure a promising start for the next stage.

That stage is the beginning of independence. There is no escape, it seems to me, from a period of enormous risks, as we withdraw our steel framework of order and unity. Inexperienced politicians take power who are 'responsible' – if we can use the word – to even more inexperienced 'electorates', another rather flattering term. The superficial unity, racial rather than national, which springs up in support of self-government, tends to melt away with its attainment. Tribalism re-emerges. The new leaders have to try to work a new and difficult model of parliamentary democracy, unrestrained by tradition or by public opinion. They are tempted to entrench their power by showy gestures which may be bad administration, bad finance, or bad economics; or by trying to score off their departing rulers. Yet this is the all-important time which we must approach, not as a mere exit, an abandonment, but as the building up of a wholly new and active relationship. The newly independent people will need practical help: capital, expert advice, the loan of technicians. Even more they will need the non-material things: respect for their new status, appreciation for their successes, understanding for their failures, and recognition of their cultural identity.

The relationships to be built up will vary. Those people who, as in Asia, possess their own ancient civilizations, will be more culturally detached: the contact will be more with governments than with peoples. The West Indians are, through slavery and enfranchisement, the foster-children of our civilization; they already have an intimacy with us which they are clearly determined to develop to the fullest and friendliest extent. But it is tropical Africa that will present our greatest difficulty – and our greatest opportunity. The destiny of this vast, long-isolated continent, so near to Europe, is still uncertain. We cannot be sure that after what may prove so brief a hold over so raw a continent, Africa will take from the West all she needs to replace her own crumbling tribal past. Already, at the very possibility of such a large vacuum of power, economic and political competitors are converging upon Africa. And indeed we can no longer hope for an exclusive relationship. An immense and prolonged effort, especially on the economic side, will be needed from Britain, in co-operation with her friends, if Africa is not to drift away into chaos or chronic opposition.

So much for the assessment of our psychological difficulties and the spirit in which we should meet them. Shall we have to adjust our institutions as well as our minds? Or can we assume that the old empirical ways which served well enough when the white, and then the brown, dependencies graduated into equality, will somehow do for Malaya, the West Indies, the Gold Coast and Nigeria? I fear the answer is 'No'. There is the extremely delicate question, which cropped up recently in the House of Commons, of invitation to membership of the Commonwealth Conference. The privilege of full membership is now not wholly ours to give. But we can and we must give a lead to our fellow-members in the Commonwealth or risk the secession of young and sensitive states if they should be black-balled – appropriate term! – after reaching a qualifying degree of stability in self-government, itself a difficult test to define. We know the contradictory responses to this appeal that we are likely to get from South Africa on the one side and the Asian members on the other. But has the issue yet been seriously put to Canada, Australia, New Zealand? The Prime Minister's recent answer in the Commons did not suggest to me much forethought on this urgent question. Even if this hurdle of the entrance formula could be settled, there would loom up the difficult question of numbers, and then the consequential problem of where to draw the invidious line.

What of the Colonial Office? It has certainly adapted itself, especially in the last fifteen years, to meet the changing character of the colonies. Among other things, it has drawn into its committee rooms hundreds of experts from public life, bringing their knowledge to bear upon colonial questions and carrying away with them knowledge of the colonies to spread in their institutions and cities. But these, and other valuable reforms, cannot touch the main question: that is whether the Colonial Office as it exists at present should continue at all. Some of us have been asking questions about this for two or three years and so far no satisfactory answer has been given. What happens when the Gold Coast or Nigeria reaches the full status of self-government? Are all the files dealing with its affairs burned or sent to the Record Office? Or does a van call at the Colonial Office and drive at least a selection of them from Great Smith Street to the Commonwealth Relations Office in Downing Street, followed by one or two taxi-loads of the necessary officials? Clearly the African territories' achievement of independence cannot be of quite the same character as that of India or Ceylon. Their status will almost certainly run a little ahead of administrative realities and they will probably be ready to receive some continuing services – if these are offered in a spirit in which they can be accepted. Could a colony, newly graduated to independence and super-sensitive about its position, continue dealing with the Colonial Office? Yet could the Commonwealth Relations Office, a diplomatic clearing house, offer young African states or Caribbean islands such services as they might still need?

Is the solution, perhaps, one great Commonwealth Office, behind whose solid walls members of the Commonwealth could all establish their proper relationship with the proper department, whether they are large or small, whether independent, approaching independence, or too small ever to aspire to it? One objection to such a scheme is that as one Minister could hardly manage so large a department without subordinate Ministers, there would have to be an overlord in the cabinet – and overlords are out of fashion. Much more serious is the objection that the older Commonwealth members would resent departmental as much as conciliar propinquity with young 'black' states. The answer to that can only be that, if racial discrimination is to rule at the highest level, there is an end of all our hopes of the new Commonwealth, one in which the coloured peoples will be in the majority.

Here, then, are the demands, psychological and practical, which colonial nationalism is making upon our country. I have dwelt on the difficulties. This does not mean that we have not, as a nation, done an immense amount to meet them. But our problem is one of time. There is so little of it. Nor would I leave the impression that the kind of acceptance, of integration, to which I have referred will be easy, demanding only a little goodwill. Colonial leaders, educated, eager, amazingly adaptable, spring into equality in a generation. But the millions behind them move slowly. A gulf still separates them from us – a gulf of culture, of language, of poverty, of distance. Colour is only one of our barriers. But nothing, I believe, but recognition and sympathy will win the leaders. And nothing but that leadership will bring their people to nationhood and to friendship with ourselves. What is happening now in the colonies is not only, as some see it, the tragic and humiliating end of a great and beneficent imperial system. It is, or can be, the beginning of something new. As a nation we have great experience as a reconciling agency – there is plenty of it to be done, within the disunited colonies, between them, between the unequal members of the Commonwealth, between their several races; and also between these young colonies and the world as they enter this dangerous place for the first time as free nations.

Britain's Handling of Mau Mau

Letter to *The Times* 31 December 1954

This letter, written during Kenya's so-called 'Emergency' reveals the deep disquiet which some of us felt about the Kenya Government's handling of the crisis.

Sir, – May I comment upon two points in your leading article of 22 December upon Kenya? First, you deplore European disunity as a threat to multi-racial government. But surely it is the prerequisite of its success. So long as each race acts through a united party, so long is it likely to be dominated by its implacable extremists and pursue a rigid irrational policy of racial interest instead of co-operating with other races in devising measures of common interest for the new Kenya. The courage of Mr Blundell and his colleagues is thus a most heartening portent.

Secondly, you refer to the possibility of 'a return to Colonial Office rule which would be welcomed by none'. But what is that Office but the agency through which the British Government exercise an authority which is likely to be required for a long time to come? British troops and funds are needed now. But the Government's powers and the trained Overseas Service officers at headquarters and in the districts will be long needed to steady the Government during the difficult period of the multi-racial experiment. The non-European leaders insist that they would welcome the prolongation of British authority. Only the European element, hoping to be its successor, has denied it. With the end of that hope and the prospect of minority status, some far-sighted Europeans see that authority as the only safeguard making it possible for them to launch out into the uncharted and hazardous depths of multi-racial government.

The Mau Mau movement has, indeed, made close British association essential. The terrible strains it imposes makes the supporting and restraining control from Britain necessary for the local authorities. In the eyes of the world Britain remains responsible. The Kenya Government made history by commissioning a psychological inquiry into an active rebellion. But too little has since been heard of Dr Carothers's penetrating report. Yet it supports the historical evidence that, from the widest viewpoint – one which the atrocities of the rebels make it hard to sustain – there is a sense in which the Kikuyu are innocent, being what we have made them in the sixty-five years since we found them an untouched tribe. Then the first authoritative observer, Lugard, declared them to be the finest tribe he had met in Africa, and praised especially their welcome to himself, their helpfulness, and astonishing agricultural skill and industry.

In Britain there is deep sympathy for the losses and strains endured by all races, and appreciation of the many constructive efforts being made. But some of us, when we read of executions at over fifty a month, mostly for 'consorting' with terrorists, and also that the War Council sees 'no early end of the emergency', while you, Sir, state that the bulk of the Kikuyu are still sitting on the Mau Mau side of the fence, must ask whether every possible effort has been made to deal not only with the symptoms of disorder but with the deep psychological causes for the delinquency of this able tribe.

Yours faithfully

1955

Nigeria Prepares for Independence

The Times 17 and 18 March 1955

1. *The Problem of Unity*

African affairs are well reported today compared with some five years ago, and Nigeria has been much in the news. But some of its problems are hard to interpret without breathing the political air of its main centres and interviewing its leaders against the background of their own regions. For Britain's largest dependency stands, like the Gold Coast, poised perplexed on the edge of independence. The last conference emasculated the centre in favour of the regions, and the country is now awaiting the conference of 1956, which should terminate a ten-year process of constitution-making. What are the prospects of success for this large and hazardous experiment in self-government? And what remains for Britain to do in order to promote this success?

The first question raises another – 'What kind of success?' British policy, as Mr Lennox-Boyd said recently, aims first at preserving a proper measure of unity. Yet today in Nigeria the will to unity seems weak. Political leaders in the past found it easy to rouse the educated minority into united opposition to British tutelage. But with the removal of this useful overhanging surface against which to generate pressure, and with the introduction of almost universal suffrage, the leaders have had to look inwards and downwards, and to create support out of such material as they could find. The most promising was tribal separatism. For just over half a century the British state system lightly boarded over the divisions between the many independent groups embraced within the haphazard lines of annexation, divisions surely deeper than those the Romans failed to erase in Britain in some three centuries. Now they reappear. The tribes, as in the Gold Coast and Uganda, are beginning to assert their identity again, and they are encouraged by chiefs who feel their position endangered by modern forces. We therefore have an ironic situation in which Britain strives to unite and rule while the Africans try to divide and rule.

But 'tribe' is an inexact word, and the disunities of Nigeria are neither simple nor uniform. The regions represent groups of tribes. Three of these, the Western, Eastern and the Southern Cameroons, cut the great southern coastal belt into three, while along them stretches the vast block of the Northern Region. British rule provided a framework in which these disparate elements could exist together in mutual security. The prospect of its removal is now throwing them together and forcing them to work out their true balance of power. The result is a counting of heads and of assets, and a hardening of cultural self-consciousness in self-defence or aggression. No rearrangement of Nigerian boundaries or peoples is likely to produce an orgy of massacre on the Indian scale, but the Kano riots of 1953, when northerners and immigrant southerners murdered each other and looted, showed that inflammable feelings do exist.

The constitutional aims of the regions correspond with their character and their interests. The Yoruba of the West share their language, their old tradition of chieftainship and city life, their long history, and their prosperous self-containment founded upon cocoa and craftsmanship. They are a sophisticated people, long in contact with the outside world. Their women have commerce in their blood. In their great city of Ibadan, with its half a million people, their booths and tables and trays of wares almost spill over on to the highways, and are lit far into the night by little palm-oil lamps. Economic initiative flourishes in the streets: hundreds of notice boards proclaim barbers ('European style'), tailors ('High-life'), photographers (in significant excess), printers, solicitors, barristers, produce merchants, building contractors (including some large firms), cabinet makers (visibly constructing beds and tables by the road) and moneylenders. There is the Paradise Hotel, the Parisiana Cocktail Bar, and even the 'Agitation for Freedom Bureau'. Their Action Group Ministry, under the able and austere lawyer, Mr Awolowo, is busy building up a strong region, fit for almost independent life and inclined to turn its back on the rest of Nigeria.

There was an early tendency to do everything at once and at high speeds, like the motor buses which hurtle about Yorubaland, placarded with the surprising destination 'All Roads'. As roads are narrow, and flanked by deep and dangerous trenches, the analogy is close. It can be extended to the ferocious nature of party warfare, since these vehicles try to drive an oncoming competitor off the narrow crown of the road, to the peril of the streams of pedestrians on each side. For even the Western Region is not solid. It is divided by both party strife and tribal separatism, the latter threatening from the so-called Middle West, where the Benin and Delta provinces are playing with the idea of fission. The Action Group would not be sorry to shed them since they could then hope to consolidate their party control over the truly Yoruba provinces. In this sanctuary Mr Awolowo, whose Ministry has just launched a costly and partly effective system of free universal elementary education, would like to create a model state. All he asks is security, above all from intruding forces of unity. He would like to see the constitution buttressed against them by imperial or other sanctions. He would also like to exclude 'foreigners' who man the federal police and vote in elections.

These 'foreigners' do not come from very far away. They come from the Eastern Region, within which the famous 'Zik', Dr Azikiwe, now its Premier, first built up his nationalist party, the National Council of Nigeria and the Cameroons. This party aims at a more unitary constitution. This is the natural ambition for a people mainly Ibo, crowded upon poor soil, with much the same numbers as the Western Region, and only about half its revenue. A forest people, remote in their little clans from influences which developed their neighbours, they knew nothing of chiefs, large states, cities, and the pride of having a history. Their gaze is, therefore, wholly on the future. Ambitious individualists, yet capable of mass-co-operation, they swarm out of their insufficient homeland into those of their neighbours, taking their politics with them. Their party has won Yoruba members. It disputes with the Action Group the largely Yoruba city council of Ibadan, regional capital of the west. Their party defeated the Action Group in the west in the last federal elections, and it co-operates with the Northern Peoples' Congress in a political *mariage de convenance* to form a federal Ministry. Dr Azikiwe, a fierce nationalist turned constructive premier, wants a more fragmented Nigeria with a stronger centre. The north, he urged strenuously upon the writer, with over half the population, is too large for a federation.

Such views spread outside the Eastern Region in spite of the unpopularity of the Ibo who carry them. Will they penetrate to the north itself? The Northern Peoples' Congress, which stands for the maintenance of a solid, separate north based upon its ancient traditions, had an overwhelming majority in the federal election. It was helped, perhaps, by an indirect form of selection. The Emirs still rule their states from their crenellated palaces of red earth, but the challenge from the south has penetrated to the innermost courts of these labyrinthine buildings. Reform, and especially democratization, is the order of the day. And is the north so solid? Will its hierarchical traditions stand the test of reform? What of its so-called Middle Belt, which was only partially won for Islam and princely rule, and where fissures may open to southern influence? And though the northern rulers may deeply resent the infiltration of the southerners, and especially of the Ibo, their own tardy acceptance of western ideas and techniques has left them in humiliating dependence upon those intruders. The north, under its imposing premier, the Sardauna, significantly of the royal and sacred line of Sokoto, has, like the west, a great history and great qualities. Yet the long-robed Hausa and Yoruba may be thrown upon the defensive by the Ibo, as, naked only yesterday, they stream out of their forests in their shirts and shorts, energetic, ambitious, modern-minded, democratic and heading for a fully united Nigeria.

11. *The Problem of Staff*

If we attempt to sum up the favourable and unfavourable factors which govern Nigeria's great experiment in democracy, we start with one immense advantage. All the chief political leaders aim at remaining within the Commonwealth and adapting, so far as the federal form permits, the British system of social democracy. This shows astonishing faith in us and our constitution.

The desire to stay within the Commonwealth can be appreciated only by those who have studied the nationalist movement during its 20 years of bitter striving. Nothing, it seems, short of the first act of substantial delegation, can convince a colonial people of Britain's sincerity in promising self-government. But with that act comes an almost incredulous gratitude. There is in Nigeria today, as in the Gold Coast, profound goodwill towards Britain. The feverish grasping for full power has ceased and the leaders seem to be pausing on the edge of independence. The senior British officials, to whom so much of this confidence is due, are the last people to stop paying out the rope because the pull on it has slackened. As experienced agents of an experienced nation, they know too well that power cannot for long be held in suspense or in division. So, though the goodwill has come like sunshine after a protracted tropical storm, the time we have for making use of it is likely to be very short.

[1955] COLONIAL SEQUENCE 1949 TO 1969

What of the desire to adopt the British constitutional model? The process has gone so far that it is already rather academic to discuss alternatives. But we should remember that it means applying to a sudden and many-sided revolutionary change the experience of a nation which has had less to do with revolution than almost any other. Professor Toynbee has warned nations which try to select only the apparently desirable items of another's culture that they will find themselves forced to absorb the whole. The northern Moslems may well have to learn the truth of this warning; the rest of Nigeria seems quite ready to absorb the whole.

Is it possible yet to judge the experiment? Everywhere the outward forms are being adopted. House of Commons procedure is being carefully followed in the central and regional parliaments, and since most Nigerians have a genius for ritual, the use of the procedure may well with time communicate its inner spirit. Some ministers are rising to their responsibilities, and tribesmen are learning what it means to be an electorate. Mr Awolowo, for example, has courageously realized that large promises mean large taxation, and the rates, regional and local, were put up to pay for his schools. Taxpayers inclined to repudiate the acts of their representatives had to be sternly brought to order. The experiment was therefore highly educational for ministers and citizens, as well as for schoolchildren.

Local government is being pushed forward on democratic lines in all regions. At a meeting of the urban district council in Enugu, for instance, the members were too industrious to accept the reports of their committees and, in spite of the protests of the British-trained clerk and city engineer, went out in a body to investigate a minor contravention of the building regulations. At a district council in the remote steppe of Sokoto, elected members – farmers and nomad pastoralists, teachers and clerks, Moslems and pagans – debated the control of gleaning cattle and the provision of Rhode Island breeding stock for poultry. They conspired together as cunningly as their most experienced counterparts in Britain to push on to regional revenues as much as possible of the cost of rebuilding a public meat store.

There are, of course, some unfavourable symptoms, such as costly excursions in the southern regions into state enterprises for production and finance; reckless bids and counterbids with wage rates for party advantage; and shocking lack of restraint in political controversy. As new ministries, looking rather like magnified pigeon-holes, are rushed up in all regional capitals, and new ministers roll up to them from their new houses in their new cars, it is natural that they should relish their first taste of the sweets of office. Corruption flourishes at all levels. Fortunately this is frankly recognized and condemned. Public inquiries are demanded (Dr Azikwe has just ordered a region-wide investigation), reports of municipal misdoings are published, leagues of 'bribe-scorners' are formed, and printed official estimates list the post of 'anti-corruption agent'.

Before condemning this too severely one must remember that the country is only just beginning to drag itself out of acute poverty, and that social obligations have not until recently extended much beyond the family. Furthermore, the problem of running a modern welfare state has come very suddenly and the shortage of trained staff is very acute. The leaders have immense plans under way for training their own people, but until these mature they are utterly dependent on the present British staff, and need many more. In the north their need is so great – there is not yet one qualified northern doctor among the population of 17 million – that they dread independence, for it will leave them open to 'colonization' from the south. They plead passionately for more British staff, but there are simply not enough available.

Why is this so? The problem must be approached from the point of view of the individual British asked to take the strain of the new relationship. Money is one element, but perhaps the least problematical. Security is another, and is more difficult because the politicians who so sincerely offer it may not be in a position to fulfil their promises. But the most difficult is the psychological element. The new relationship demands that men who have been masters should become servants. This is especially difficult because the new masters, though often of character and ability, are necessarily inexperienced and may often be working more for personal or party ends than for the public good. The more optimistic and sympathetic of the British staff can accept this, and find the new task even more exciting and constructive than the old. Others, with different temperaments, become embittered and unhelpful. They suffer from the sense of having been too successful in the past.

We have here a most urgent problem, upon the solution of which in the next five or ten years may depend the whole future of Nigeria and of Britain's long and not unprofitable association with it. There is abundant goodwill on the Nigerian side and an almost crushing sense of need, which extends, of course, beyond the sphere of government to the deeper and more enduring levels of the Christian churches and the new university. There is goodwill in Britain, too, and much of that adventurous and missionary spirit which can inspire a service. But special if not desperate measures are needed. Some imaginative director of recruitment might be appointed and the Colonial Office and the Treasury might abandon caution, routine, and a false economy and find ways, administrative and financial, which might lead men and women confidently to Nigeria – or keep them there.

There are no stereotyped patterns in the Commonwealth. If Britain can help to satisfy the urgent needs of the Nigerians, while still respecting their new independence, she may find that she can build a more intimate relationship with this immense African country than anyone could ever have envisaged.

The Struggle against Mau Mau

The Times 22 and 23 April 1955

1. *Bravery of the Kikuyu Christians*

The Mau Mau country includes the three Kikuyu districts which stretch over some 2,000 square miles from the foothills of Kenya mountain almost to Nairobi. It extends its influence into that largely Kikuyu city and covers the heavy overspill of the tribe into the European farming districts to the west. Rather, it *did* cover these until, following an expulsion of some Kikuyu squatters from the most endangered area, almost the whole of their fellows, moved by an impulse as common, sudden, and almost as reckless as a migration of lemmings, flung themselves in tens of thousands back into the overcrowded reserves. Since last autumn this area, holding nearly one million Kikuyu, has been darkened by a murderous hate and it is necessary to go into it and breathe, for however short a time, the atmosphere in which its inhabitants live, especially after sunset, in order to understand a little what has happened to Kenya.

Kikuyu country is rich and beautiful. Almost every inch is cultivated like some vast allotment. But it has none of the ugliness associated with that word. It is a place of low hills running in linear or horseshoe ridges. No cultivation lines run straight and there is a lush miscellany of banana groves, wattle plantations, plots of maize, sweet potatoes or beans, a dozen different greens interspersed with red or purple earth stripped for planting. In the valleys children herd goats or cattle by the streams. The huts, with a soft bloom on their round, mushroom-coloured thatch, are grouped half-way up the hills on grassy clearings and from the air testify as clearly as a population chart to the heavy load of humanity carried by the land. An African arcadia, the visitor might exclaim. Then he might remark that it is one in which there are few young men, in which no one smiles or greets him, not even the children, who in most of Africa respond overwhelmingly as if by reflex action.

I have stood on a mission station on a hill-top looking over this glorious country, striped with sun and blue cloud-shadows stretching away northwards between the long ridge of the Aberdares and Mount Kenya. It was hard to believe that, as the sun went down, gangs in the forest, and even apparently innocent farmers in those huts, were preparing to set out not only to murder Europeans but to burn alive or hack to death their own neighbours, with, perhaps, their wives and children. And whereas European farms are now, so far as possible, armed, barricaded, and patrolled, and less than a dozen Europeans murdered, the Africans, scattered in their huts, which are perfect traps and funeral pyres, can hardly be defended and have fallen in hundreds to the assassins. Most of them died, moreover, not by accidental fate but because they chose ostracism, hatred, and the ever-present fear of a horrible death by a deliberate refusal to take the Mau Mau oath.

Why do they do this? I saw one reason when, as darkness fell, I went into the mission house. Here were some of the African clergy and teachers who had come with many other Christian refugees – for this was one of the worst of all Mau Mau areas – to a place which offers some measure of protection. It is little enough, as they have forsworn the use of arms and go out to their churches or schools each day on their bicycles, marked men, to carry out their work. There were empty chairs in the room for their casualties have been heavy. The priest on my right had been seized and slashed repeatedly – this by well-dressed young men talking English – and asked at each cut to deny his faith and say that Christ was a European. Six others were killed nearby, and he was left for dead, one terrible gash still visible on his head. Opposite sat another man, weak and limping from torture. Yet all looked calm, confident, even happy.

It was almost startling to look at Kikuyu faces lit with friendly and intelligent response after the visible shadow of suspicion and hate that I had seen upon faces in Nairobi and along the road. The senior African, the Rural Dean of the area, led us in prayers for the country, for all races, for the growth of fellowship among them, and not least for their Mau Mau enemies. In the morning they were all at prayer again with others, including many women, people who had been shot at, beaten, threatened, bereaved of their families, but who seemed to have found confidence in their inner victory over fear.

The same conquest could have been found upon other mission stations. But the wrong conclusions should not be drawn. It would mislead Government and injure the faith if any attempt were made, as is so often attempted in the struggle with Communism, to try to use Christianity as a political asset. What seemed once to be an advantage to Christianity, that it was the faith of the rulers, has now become a handicap from which St Paul and his first successors did not suffer. And these Christians are not the less good Kikuyu, or less critical of Government, because they are ready to die rather than stoop to the foul *mystique* of Mau Mau. It is spiritually, not politically, that the small remnant of the faithful, some five per cent perhaps, may be the rock upon which the tribe may be rebuilt. There are others, chiefs and African home guards, who also risk their lives by opposition of a more active kind, often older men roused by atrocities such as the Lari massacre, or the perversion of tribal custom. But many of these, too, are more anti-Mau Mau than pro-Government.

One outstanding chief I visited, Muhoya, often threatened, lives on the very edge of the forest from which gangs emerge to leave the mutilated bodies of their opponents. At any moment a shot from the forest may reach this brave man. His home guard were posted thinly among the trees near his farm, ragged men, some of them of middle age or more, with spears or bows, standing rather pathetically at soldierly attention as we passed.

It is difficult to suppress pervasive and secretive guerilla movements without a margin of inhumanity. Here the sudden need to improvise an increase of military and police forces, white and black, the initial lack of co-ordination, the difficulty of control, and the deep anger roused by Mau Mau bestialities, have combined to make that margin all too wide. Africans, doubtless exaggerating in unconscious self-justification, pour out stories of looting and beating. Sweeps by the police, perhaps unavoidably, net thousands of the innocent. Efforts are being made and more are still urgently needed, to cut down the undoubted degree of abuse. However, criticism should be made only by those who have some understanding of the conditions in which the forces of order work.

One of the little police posts newly set up in the reserves, for example, I found in charge of two young settlers, recruits to the police reserve, mere boys, just in from the exciting and dangerous job of hunting men. Not far away a patrol of King's African Rifles, rough tribesmen from northern Uganda, were scouring the bush. Their officer, a fine-looking young settler seconded from the white Kenya Regiment, frankly told me there had been irregularities with prisoners, now remedied, but that he still found it hard to control his men in action against secret enemies dedicated to those hideous methods which have so depressed the friends of this tribe. Yet strictly impartial justice and discipline, openly demonstrated, could do much to rally the wavering majority, torn between their fears of Mau Mau and of its repressors.

How long will it take to restore order? That is the universal question of the weary men and women who take the brunt of the insurrection. No one yet seems to have the answer. I gathered some material for it by going with an air patrol. The black, snow-dusted cone of Mount Kenya swung up and down at every angle as we came down to circle the tree-tops and collect the faint wireless reports at each post on the isolated farms on the edge of the forest which clothes the immense base of the mountain. In one clearing we could see a herd of buffalo, in another the white cross of yesterday's plane which had crash-landed, happily without casualties. Above this began the impenetrable green wall of the bamboo. The flat land between the two mountain ranges was veined with stream-courses choked with bush, perfect cover leading down to the reserves and settled areas.

Squatters on the forest edge, now being concentrated in stockaded villages, Malaya-fashion, had been forced to choose between being victuallers or victims of the gangs. Across the lion-coloured plains, dotted with herds of European cattle, rose the Aberdares to provide equally spacious headquarters for murder. But are even the forests so effective a mask as the faces of men who go about the streets of Nairobi like ordinary citizens, yet hold, perhaps, in their hands some of the threads of a conspiracy that dooms men and women of all races to death? The answer is still uncertain. So is the still larger question of how, when rebellion is mastered, its deeper causes can be understood and remedied.

[1955]

II. *Seeking the Causes and the Remedies*

The Mau Mau movement, and the active or passive acceptance of it by – perhaps? – 90 per cent of the Kikuyu, has come as a profound shock to Kenya and to all connected with the colony. On nearly every side the inquirer finds astonishment, deep depression, and frank admissions of inability to discover the deeper causes of the movement. This may be because they are, in the main, the unavoidable consequences of imposing modern Europe upon primitive Africa, especially in the world context of the last 15 years. The intricate but fragile social structure which contained this tribe has melted imperceptibly away at the contact of a new and powerful system which could destroy, but could not reintegrate into itself, the human units set adrift by its action. The Kikuyu suffered most because their region pivoted upon Nairobi and was almost surrounded by European settlement while they became the great purveyors of labour.

The system of migrant labour, so long regarded as Africa's great convenience, may come to be seen as its curse. Certainly for this tribe the perpetual drifting to and fro between an unskilled labouring and a free farming life has added to the sense of social homelessness. Family life has been undermined and an impossible burden placed upon the women, while the men have failed to become settled and competent either as farmers or wage labourers. The grievances of Nairobi, with its admitted inadequacies of wages and housing, have been carried back into the reserves, and those of the reserves, above all the passionate grievance about the land-shortage, have haunted the Nairobi locations.

The stabilization and betterment of African life in both town and country are deep, long and very expensive processes. They are already under serious examination, in part by the Royal Commission which could devise the largest remedy for the present discontents. But there are other troubles, more open to immediate treatment. The first concerns administration. Because there was never a system of chieftainship, the Government never attempted indirect rule, but it may have been sufficiently influenced by it, as well as by arguments of economy, to think that it could run a district containing two or three hundred thousand disintegrating Africans through three administrative officers and a few Government-made chiefs. As the social services grew in complexity and paper-work expanded the administrator became imprisoned in his office by the tasks of co-ordinating and reporting. The dangers of this, as of discontinuity of posting and of the official motor-car tearing along the ever-improving roads, have been the commonplace of all discussions of African administration for 20 years. Yet the overt effects were not sufficiently alarming to provide a motive power strong enough to compel reform.

This crisis has been needed to reveal how remote administration had become; how few officers speak the tribal language and how little the political will of the Africans has flowed into the theoretically excellent institutions of local government provided for them. Between the confident discipline of the old days and the county council millennium of the future lies a vacuum. Today a picked team of young administrative officers, stripped for action, are trying to fill it with close administration, evoking the initiative of Kikuyu in their own defence today with a view to continuing it for their own development tomorrow.

However, the key to the Kikuyu problem lies in the psychological sphere, in the mental effects of the disintegration caused by European contact. The Kikuyu have been intimately confronted with a new and exciting civilization, with its big houses, motor-cars, hotels, and shops full of luxuries. The first eager interest and hope has been followed by disappointment as it was realized that these desirable things were in the possession of another race, indeed, with the Asians, of two other races. The Africans, cut off by ignorance and poverty, began to feel they were doomed to serve but never fully to share.

Other primitive tribes followed earlier a cycle of physical resistance, more or less, to European domination which was followed by a period of acceptance. This was followed in turn by an attempt, when the new paradise seemed obstinately locked against them and all responsibility over their own destinies lost, to satisfy their need for confidence and self-assertion by violence and a return to their own old gods. Something like this happened among the Maoris, the Cape Kaffirs, and some north American tribes. The grievances of the Kikuyu, individual and tribal, real and imaginary, have been accumulating over the years as in a great reservoir, and it only needed dramatic leadership from within, responding to stimulus from outside, to release this in a flood of conscious antagonism.

The crisis lights up not only the alienation of the Kikuyu but the unsoundness of the entire political situation. The several groups are enclosed within their own customs, languages and interests, with little mutual contact except those of economic necessity. The British colonists form the only group upon the loyalty and civic competence of which the Government can firmly rely, especially in a crisis, and the price of their support is a measure of sectional influence which only increases the suspicions of the other groups and their sense of detachment.

At the moment the British colonists are experiencing a profound crisis. Conscious of the relative moderation of their own policies, and their sense of responsibility, and often of affection, towards their African employees, they have seen with almost incredulous horror some of the most altruistic of their fellows atrociously butchered by their own trusted house-servants. They have had to sit up night after night, never knowing if the blow would fall upon them and their families. Yet moderate leadership has asserted itself strongly and it seems possible that a split may occur between those clinging to the old idea of domination, and those with the courage to face the grim realities of the present and to seek co-operation with the moderates of other groups.

This will not be easy to achieve. As regards the Asians, the Pakistan element, as a minority in Kenya and in its homeland, tends to be co-operative. But many of the Hindus have been stimulated by the independence of India and the influence of its agents in Kenya, and impressed by the anti-colonial propaganda of its leaders. They are anxious to make terms with a potential African nationalism while there is time, and some may even be speculating, as the commercial sections in the Sudan have done, that they may need another and more kindred protecting Power if British control should begin to weaken. There are Asian leaders who, in spite of their long struggle for greater equality, still believe in inter-racial co-operation, but, like the other moderates, they are in danger of deposition.

What are the political possibilities in a situation revealed but not created by Mau Mau? One, the best, an inter-racial constitutional conference, is on the programme but might now end in stalemate. Another would be a strong assertion of imperial power, exercised in clear detachment from any sectional interest, introducing a more egalitarian system based on the needs of Kenya and its vulnerable land, with protection, but no privilege, for minorities. Such a policy, if they were convinced of the will to maintain it, might win the support of moderates of all races. In a Kenya no longer the battleground of insulated groups governed by mutual fear, the Europeans, as in the West Indies, might well maintain their position by their own high competence. But can Westminster and Whitehall provide the firm and continuous policy needed? Britain has long governed Kenya with a divided conscience: hence the series of commissions and committees groping for a policy.

Perhaps only another committee of both Houses, sitting in Britain and, if possible, in Kenya also, could produce, alongside the economic advice of the Royal Commission, a political resettlement that would satisfy all British parties and Kenya races and provide, perhaps for a decade, the strong framework within which co-operation could be born. The alternative would be to balkanize Kenya, sacrificing administrative efficiency and introducing an elaboration of tiers and gears, in order, as far as possible, to regionalize political pressures.

Whatever constitutional line is followed, Britain's main task is to win the struggle for the body and soul of the Kikuyu, and not only of the Kikuyu. The Government must encourage, almost create, a constructive African leadership which can lead away from a tribal nationalism impossible of fulfilment. A combination is needed of strength and of a sympathy which reaches down in friendship to the individual level and tries to remedy the pathological sense of inferiority and the tragic inner conflicts of the educated. Great Britain has the almost impossible task, in the face of strong interferences and paralysing suspicions, of proving to the Africans that she has both the will and the power to complete for them the task of civilization begun some fifty years ago.

African Pro-Consul

The Listener 2 June 1955

A new word has come to the surface lately in international affairs: 'colonialism'. It is a word of abuse, but it is one which is used very inexactly to describe not only true colonization but almost any kind of domination, so long as it is wielded by Western powers who are – or perhaps we should say were until the Bandung Conference – always the villains in this historical play. This word of condemnation is certainly meant to apply to Britain's position in Africa. It thus reinforces, though much more vaguely, the Marxist analysis of economic imperialism. It is used by Britain's critics at the United Nations: it is taken up by colonial leaders and repeated by a great many of our own people. Altogether, 'the colonizers' have a pretty bad press today. A few of the critics may admit that they are now making some amends for their past sins. But what sinners – it surely follows – those nineteenth-century 'colonizers' must have been who broke in upon great virgin tracts of Africa,

[1955] COLONIAL SEQUENCE 1949 TO 1969

appropriated them for their own nations, and built up an alien system of government over them.

I happened to know one such man. I knew him intimately. He was Frederick Lugard, Lord Lugard in later life when I knew him and worked with him. We lived a few miles from each other, and I used to motor over or ride along the Surrey escarpment to his house. It was on the side of Leith Hill, among pines, beeches and azaleas. I would find him in his study, crammed with books and files. A worn gazelle skin before the fire; a record elephant tusk over the door; an affectionately signed photograph from Joseph Chamberlain on the wall. He would spring – yes, even at eighty, he would spring – to his feet from his crowded desk, glowing with welcoming courtesy. He was a man rather below average height, taut, lean, with very right-angled shoulders. He made the cliché 'every inch a soldier' come instantly to life. He died in 1945, and I am now writing his biography at his own request. It is a long one, for his was a very long life. It spanned a great distance, too, in the history of imperialism from the period of African acquisition, through the period of paternal rule, and right into the beginnings of what might be called de-imperialization.

I think that for those who are not wholly given over to a mechanistic interpretation of history, some evidence is to be gained by taking, as it were, a prime sample of an imperialist from the classic age of expansion, and asking what he thought he was doing and why he did it. But before I can begin to talk about Lugard's character and ideas, I must give you his career in briefest chronology. For there are no modern historical figures so misty as the lately dead.

He was born in India in 1857, the year of the great mutiny. His parents' families had bred soldiers and clergy. They themselves were earnest missionaries of intense evangelical piety. They bequeathed to him their own strenuous ideals of public service, also the confidence of being a gentleman (a pride men then acknowledged), and poverty. This was a combination which made a stimulating tonic for youth. The late seventies and early eighties saw him as a young infantry officer. He was rushed hither and thither about the Far and Middle East – India, Afghanistan, Burma, the Sudan. He was always on the edge of waves of British policy: ebbing and flowing with the advances of Disraeli or the retreats of Gladstone. Lugard, in fact, was soon well on the way to being a conventionally successful soldier. Then this straight road forward was suddenly broken by an emotional earthquake. Lugard had appeared to be no more than a first-rate, pig-sticking, pony-racing subaltern, dead keen on his work, slaving at his language exams and efficiency tests, certainly a *pukka sahib*, and yet one who scorned the tiffin-parties and the fishing fleet handled by Mrs Hauksbee and those other ladies of the station, who have been caught for ever by Kipling in his *Plain Tales*. Lugard had loved and lost all too early a splendid mother. His childhood and boyhood had not been wholly happy, and had left him with a thirst for affection which was as strong as everything else about him. It so happened that just as he was thoroughly undermined by the strain and fever of the Burma war, he experienced a desperately unhappy love-affair. The result was important not only for Lugard but for Africa. In a mood of despair, he sailed off, as a deck passenger in a small steamer going down the east coast of Africa. He knew almost nothing about the continent. He chose it as a wild place far away from anything connected with his past. He wanted to die in such a place but he could at least expend his life usefully in some great enterprise, such as the struggle against the slave trade.

In this way began ten years of adventures between 1888 and 1898 in an Africa, the great central inner block of which was still, in the late eighties, largely unmapped and unoccupied. First, Lugard found his way by native canoe up the Zambesi and Shire rivers and attacked an Arab slaver's stockade on Lake Nyasa, and was terribly wounded in the attack. Next he went up through what is now Kenya – but was then largely uninhabited wilderness – to Buganda, as the servant of the new Imperial British East Africa Company. He went to try to win that remote, fascinating country for Britain before Britain was ready for an official policy of expansion. That, his friends believed, was his finest hour. With a handful of porters and soldiers from the coast he lived through all the threats and alarms which surrounded his little camp, on a hill called Kampala, 800 miles from the sea.

A few weeks ago I stood on the site of his camp – it is still preserved as a little grassy knoll – and looked round me at the large city of Kampala sprawling all round it. It is a view which gives plenty of scope for retrospective thought. In Uganda he survived a civil war, he pacified the country, he made a treaty with the Kabaka, and went upon a great march out to the western lakes and mountains – perhaps the most glorious scenes in Africa – to beat the bounds of his new annexation. He endured hardship, exposure, fever, war, ambush, swamps and charging elephants, and hurried back to England to fight another campaign of a very different kind. This was a battle of words. He fought it in newspapers and journals and political drawing-rooms and Westminster lobbies and on the lecture platforms of all the great cities of England – all this to prevent Gladstone's ministry from abandoning the new colony which Lugard had done so much to win. It was said that Gladstone's election agent telegraphed to his chief: 'If you evacuate Uganda you will evacuate Downing Street.'

After this metropolitan interlude, Lugard went across to the opposite side of Africa, to the bend of the great Niger, to work for the Royal Niger Company, with orders to outwit and out-march the French in unexplored and dangerous country. The next assignment was in the Kalahari desert, trying to find gold and diamonds for another company, round the disappearing Lake Ngami. By bad luck he struck the year when the great rinderpest killed all the transport oxen needed to take him over the desert and came very near to death by thirst. He was suddenly and rather dramatically recalled from the interior of this country by a runner sent by Joseph Chamberlain to fetch him back to organize the West African Frontier Force, and hold the Middle Niger against the French. He did this successfully up to the very edge of war.

The first day of the new century saw him at last with his heart's desire, an imperial appointment to administer the vast region of northern Nigeria, most of which had still to be won from the great Moslem emirs. Lugard won it in quick, almost bloodless, little campaigns. Then from the Niger to the Far East to govern Hong Kong. He left it in 1912 the richer for a university which he founded, and which he willed to be the bridge between the ancient civilization of China and the culture of the Western world. Finally, he went back to Nigeria commissioned to bring the whole of its divided administrations together under one government. He then spread over the new whole the principles of administration he had created earlier in the northern part and carried the country through the strains of the first world war.

I said 'finally', but the word was inaccurate. For Lugard was a man who never retired. For the next twenty-seven years, until a few days before his death in 1945, he worked with hardly a day's holiday. He served on the Mandates Commission and other international bodies. For he combined being a nationalist with being an internationalist. He wrote his classic on colonial government, *The Dual Mandate in Tropical Africa*. He encouraged research into African customs and languages; he took part in debates in the House of Lords – an ordeal he found far more alarming than any he had endured in Africa. He kept up a vast correspondence, and he entertained at his Surrey home students, governors, politicians and diplomats, African chiefs and emirs, always trying to spread knowledge of Africa and its problems, and to promote what he regarded as the right policy in dealing with them.

'The right policy'! What was that? This surely is the main question. Lugard's actions have been listed but his purposes have still to be defined. The first in time, if not in importance, was his desire to win new lands for the Empire. He grew up when opinion was beginning to run against the so-called Little Englanders. Their millennium of free trade and world peace which seemed to make of empire an expensive superfluity had not come; instead Britain saw great conscript armies marching about across the Channel, protective barriers piling up against her trade, and a scramble beginning for Africa. So the alternative was no longer between Britain taking control over Africans or leaving them to their old freedom – it was between Britain or Germany annexing them, or Britain or Portugal, or Britain or France. And could any Englishman, above all in the nineties, have any hesitation over *that* issue! But annexation seemed a beneficence as well as a necessity. Lugard saw the poverty and ignorance of Africa, something almost unbelievable when suddenly seen from that other world of the Victorian industrial state. Worse than that: like Livingstone before him, he saw what might have appeared only a rather stagnant black Arcadia being horribly ravaged by the Arab and the internal African slave-trade, and by the wars and raids this trade promoted. Without help, Africa was utterly unable to throw off this new cancer which had succeeded and outlived the old European slave trade with the west coast. Lugard never had to argue with himself whether annexation to Britain was a 'good thing': it was to him the only possible good – imperative, urgent. Good for British trade, and indeed for world trade, but equally good for the Africans, that the riches of Africa should be reached and developed. This was his theory of the 'dual mandate'. And that mandate could only be fulfilled amongst the thousands of little warring tribes if they were brought together under civilized government.

But not any sort of government: preferably British. Not that even the British were perfect. Lugard was no blind patriot. Here came the second strand of his policy – government must be humane and just. Africa was a fierce test for a civilized man; moral restraint often weakened or snapped when men were alone, weary, sick, or in danger. They would resort to the quick and easy argument of violence to persuade or to punish. Here Lugard's training in the nursery and in the army kept him steady. Admittedly, on the march, when the long file of loaded porters wound through the endless bush, and camped in danger at night,

Lugard kept an iron discipline, for that often meant the difference between life and death for all of them. This he explained to Harcourt when the old Liberal looked at him with a sort of doctrinaire horror. But Lugard's men were always men to him, never things or pack animals. So that when they set off at dawn on their endless perilous safari into the unknown country, they would start off singing '*Mwaka, mwaka*', which meant 'Years, years' – meaning we will follow you for as long as you like to lead. While Lugard believed in the superiority of his own race, he knew a *man* when he saw one, whether black or white. He saw the greatness of the chief Khama, Tshekedi Khama's father, at a glance and made friends with him. He was a 'gentleman', was his comment in his diary, and he could say nothing higher than that.

Lugard's third great characteristic was his demand for knowledge. He knew how difficult it was to understand Africa, its customs and languages. He had a surprising humility for such a positive man. When he was a governor he set his staff to learn African ways and respect their customs, above all their religion. When he retired, he presided over societies which were studying anthropology, language, or history. He had a great respect for the expert – the student. Too much sometimes. How often, indeed, have I been humbled by his deferring to *me*, making me talk to people who had come to hear him, helping me in my work instead of getting on with his own!

His name will always be linked with that special system of administration which was called 'indirect rule'; one in which expediency and principle were fused together. When in 1900 he took over the vast, almost unexplored block of northern Nigeria, his lack of staff, of roads, and money made it impossible for him to impose close administration. Not that he wished to do this. These Moslem Hausa people had their city states, with their castellated red mud palaces, their hierarchy of robed courtiers, their settled revenues, their law-courts, and the rest. He accepted these and used them. He was much too masterful and logical not to insist that the rulers must surrender their sovereignty – but, having taken, he gave back all he could of responsibility and dignity. He erected his higher, larger structure of government above and round the existing societies; he gave his officers clear and voluminous instructions – telling them to mould these old institutions into better shape, gradually, courteously, to prune away waste, cruelty, corruption, to strengthen order and justice, but never – this was basic – never to undermine the sense of responsibility. That was the theory.

The practice at first seemed brilliantly successful. A skeleton service of a few dozen British officials supervised millions of Africans all going about their ancient lawful occasions under rulers astonished and delighted to find their conquerors so considerate. What began in part as a necessary expedient by Lugard the governor became in time a philosophy in the hands of Lugard the elder statesman. The idea spread, partly in print, partly by example, and partly by Lugard's own school of administrators going out on promotion to govern other parts of Africa. But his 'indirect rule' was too successful, with the result that lesser men used it as a ready-made system, not as a principle for flexible application. And we, looking back, can see that it had at least one inherent defect. It was, like so much the British carry abroad with them, an almost wholly political concept. The colonial governors, still following *laissez-faire* in economics, let loose large economic forces which weakened, or even destroyed, the tribal structures upon which the new system had to be built. Then – something which Lugard could not have foreseen – the time factor was upset by two world wars, and all the hurricane of new ideas and conditions released by them and especially, of course, by the second. Indirect rule demanded several quiet generations for the tribal parts to grow slowly towards a national whole and without an intelligentsia suddenly breaking out on a short cut to nationhood, and parliamentary self-government, both of which were beyond Lugard's first horizons. But no system could have wholly obviated the effects of the dislocating shock caused by the sudden intrusion of modern Europe into tribal Africa. It may be that Lugard's policy prevented this dislocation being too destructive – that it did cushion the shock for a useful twenty to thirty years. And by doing this it may have given time for the growth of mutual knowledge and confidence between the two sides which – dare we still hope today? – will save us from an absolute breach with our African colonies as they hasten towards independence.

Economics Versus Race

New Commonwealth 5 September 1955

A discussion of the main themes in the Report of the Royal Commission on East Africa.

The Report of the East African Royal Commission should be widely read far beyond the circles of those interested in East Africa or, indeed, in Africa. For it deals with what we begin to see as the great problem of our age, the creation of a world economy in which the standard of living should be levelled up to that of the more advanced and wealthy nations. It is as though the great gap between the wealthy and the poorer classes *within* the Western nations, which we have done so much to narrow during the last fifty years, has been reproduced as *between* nations. And the international, like the domestic issue, is not only economic: it has its political and, in addition, its racial aspects. The Western nations, and especially Britain, are trying to apply to this wider field the ideas and methods learned in the internal setting. Russia and the Communist States compete by offering their newer, more revolutionary method of economic advance. The future balance of world power, which will be based upon what prove to be the winning ideas of human society, may be decided by the choice the poorer nations make between the two methods and the two philosophies which are now being put before them. Even the grave current problem of the use or abuse of nuclear power is linked with the possibility of its greatest potential use for fostering peace, that of speeding up the development of the retarded peoples.

This may seem rather too cosmic an introduction to a Report on the economic advancement of East Africa. But this Report represents a most thorough attempt, on the part of a group of British experts, to apply to part of the largest and poorest region still under Britain's control the long accumulated experience of their own country. And it is clear that the authors of the Report were very conscious of the national and international significance of their work, though it is for others to point out its widest meanings.

It is therefore most regrettable that the length of the Report, nearly 500 pages, and its combination of wide range with massive detail, makes its mastery a formidable task. Yet it must be read as a whole: it offers the readers no short-cuts and it is not surprising that, after the first round of journalistic expositions and exclamations, not all of them well grounded, there has been something like a period of silence while all those concerned with East Africa get down to the serious study this document demands.

It is clearly impossible, in a single article, to embrace even in outline the whole of this Report. But it would be useful, at the outset, if only as ground-bait to attract the hesitant reader, to summarize its purpose, to consider the qualifications of its authors, and at least indicate the scope of its contents.

The terms of reference required the Commission to examine the measures needed to raise the standard of African life in view of the increase of population and its local congestions, paying special regard to the problems of peasant farming, land tenure and settlement, to the introduction of industries, and the social problems arising from the growth of towns. This is a large brief and the Commission took the liberty of enlarging it further. The Report covers almost all aspects of the economy of these territories and opens up large racial and political questions. As East Africa, and above all Kenya, are countries of controversy it may well be imagined that the Commission's proposals, which are uncompromising, are likely to run into a great deal of criticism. It is therefore necessary to consider the quality of this Commission in order to decide what weight must be given to their opinions. The eight members were carefully chosen to combine rich and varied knowledge in their task. The chairman, Sir Hugh Dow, was a distinguished member of the Indian Civil Service, who had carried large financial, commercial and administrative responsibilities. Sir Frederick Seaford has had long commercial and political experience in the troubled colony of British Guiana. Professor Frankel holds the chair of Colonial Economic Affairs at Oxford and has made a life-long study of African problems. Mr Gaitskell, the brother of the Labour Chancellor of the Exchequer, was managing director of that unique and successful Gezira scheme of irrigated agriculture in the Sudan. Mr Hudson represented official knowledge and administrative experience at all levels, from the bush in Northern Rhodesia up to direction of the African Studies branch of the Colonial Office. Professor Jack was another Professor of Economics, who had already extended his wide English knowledge of labour and industry to Africa. Chief Kidaha Makwaia is a man still young, who conducted successfully an important chieftainship in Tanganyika and who won our respect and affection when he studied at Oxford. Mr Frank Sykes is a highly successful English farmer in Wiltshire: he assists in the management of the Queen's farms and advises on colonial agriculture and mechanization. Both he and Professor Frankel went out to report upon the Groundnut Scheme of unhappy memory, which must have had some valuable negative lessons for their East African task. Finally, Dr Audrey Richards, the experienced Director of the East African Institute of Social Research, was asked to be anthropological consultant. It would be hard to imagine a more well-chosen and well-balanced team. And they did not spare themselves. They worked for two and a half years, in England and in East Africa, making two long tours round the territories – with Kenya in the throes of Mau Mau – drawing their information from no less than 1,300 groups and persons. Clearly, their final conclusions have to be taken very seriously.

The report contains a reasoned description of the basic conditions of the three East African territories, Kenya, Uganda and Tanganyika; of their 19,000,000 Africans, quarter of a million Asiatics and 70,000 Europeans; of the patchy distribution of these over a physical surface as large as Western Europe. It scrutinizes the new economy which Western governments and immigrants have built up above the primitive tribal economies. It points out both the achievements and the errors of this process of development in all its aspects – trade, investment, mining, transport, water development, immigration, social services. It examines both rural and urban conditions; proceeds to a number of recommendations of reform, and concludes with a section on race-relations and adds a number of most enlightening tables and four maps. These illustrate dramatically the unkindness of nature in providing, over vast areas dominated by drought or the tsetse-fly, such inadequate rainfall and so little fertile land where agriculture can rise above the low and precarious level at which most of the Africans exist.

Throughout most of this Report there runs one main theme. I propose to concentrate upon this, though well aware of the danger of disentangling it from its complex setting of supporting facts and figures. It is that the population of East Africa, faced by an exceptionally difficult task of development because of the poverty of the region and the isolation and backwardness of the Africans, have tried to meet it with restriction rather than freedom, with division rather than co-operation, with a policy of conserving tribalism rather than of fostering individualism. The character of the Report, long, detailed and closely reasoned, does not easily lend itself to single representative quotation – it cannot claim to be a piece of brilliant writing – but perhaps the following paragraph best gathers together its central idea.

> East Africa cannot afford to permit that the customs or vested interests of the past should continue to lead to the waste of resources through ill-used land or useless cattle, through conspicuous consumption based on privilege or status, through ill-trained and badly directed labour, through restrictions on employment of members of particular races, through agricultural production protected by anti-social devices, or through outworn restrictions on the use of land for agricultural and urban purposes. (p. 196)

Anyone who knows East Africa, and especially Kenya, which is selected all through as the Commission's main problem, and who reads this passage carefully will note that it censures every racial and functional group in the region. It is, indeed, coagulation in groups which the Commission dissects and deplores. As a result, although this is an economic report, nearly all the conditions it mentions are shown as resulting, either directly or indirectly, from the racial factor.

The Report does not minimize the difficulties of the situation. It pictures vividly the two basic strata, physical and human, upon which Western government and economic influences had to work when, a mere half century ago, they penetrated East Africa. The human element, scattered over the unpromising physical basis, consisted mostly of very primitive tribes, cut off from contact with the world, divided into small groups, living at an extremely low level by semi-nomadic cattle-keeping or by shifting cultivation. Population was mostly clustered upon the lands of better rainfall, especially round Lake Victoria and on hilly or mountainous places. Survival was only possible for these small groups in their difficult and dangerous environment, if they followed rigidly the social and economic pattern they had developed through centuries, if not millenia, of this hard existence. The Commission believe that the new European government should have tried to dissolve the tribal barriers behind which the groups clung to their land and to a way of life no longer applicable to their new twentieth-century conditions. They should have been helped to behave as individual members of a wider, new, exchange economy. Instead, the Government played down to tribal fears and isolationism. Each tribe was administered within gazetted boundaries, behind which it rigidly conserved much of its old farming methods and land-tenure. These were now wholly unsuitable

[1955]

for the growing numbers: people and stock were no longer free, as of old, to wander on to new land, or to leave long fallows, and the results were soil exhaustion and soil erosion, diminishing returns, fragmentation of holdings, the sense of overcrowding, and resultant bitterness.

This unproductive, conservative group-attitude to land was immensely strengthened by the occupation, in Kenya, of a considerable block of the small amount of really favoured land by white colonists. This was not because there was much African eviction: for various reasons most of this land had been almost unpopulated. And the Commission admit that the skill and energy of the settlers have been vital to Kenya and their products are at once valuable exports and a guarantee against the danger of food shortage, which always hangs over the millions of ineffective African subsistence farmers. But, by demanding what is, in effect, a tribal boundary round the 'white highlands', the Kenya settlers intensified the African's attitude to land as the possession of his clan or his tribe. His sense of insecurity in a bewildering new world led him to resolve that not another square foot of his land must be given up for public purposes, or to another clan or tribe, still less, of course, to another race. This attitude frustrated government intervention in matters of land-holding and usage, which tended to become crystallized. Fears for land and distrust of Kenya with its dominant white settlers, spread to the other territories. Racial suspicion was also directed towards the Asiatic immigrants, who outnumber the Europeans, and who are by custom and law almost wholly denied access to land in Kenya and Uganda and segregated as urban communities of traders, contractors and higher artisans.

Racial sectionalism and suspicion, the Commission believes, prevents the economy, above all of Kenya, from being regarded or treated as a whole. Resort is had to a number of measures, which would be economically or socially unthinkable in Britain and which perpetuate divisions by protecting one race or tribe against another. The economies of new countries, struggling against great physical odds should be free, mobile, energetic and – a much used word – 'co-operant'. Hence the major recommendation is for the abolition of tribal or racial restrictions on ownership. All land should be registered in ownership, either by individuals or corporations and made available to all races. This will allow its full economic usage through applying to it the energies of individualism plus security for the capitalization of farming. The Commission, however, are realistic enough to recognize that for the present this freedom must be subject to careful safeguards to meet the fears and difficulties which this great change will cause, especially to Africans and Europeans. Economic farming must be matched by economic wage-earning and the ending of the now wasteful system of migrant labour in favour of a stabilized and well-trained industrial and urban population.

These recommendations will be questioned both in detail and in their underlying conception. To take the latter, the Commission reject a major premise upon which British colonial policy was largely based until a very few years ago and which still underlies much that is being done. It has been called the differential policy. It recognized that in their isolated and backward stage, and their division within long-matured tribal societies, Africans needed special measures to help them forward; to preserve their group confidence and social energy and to protect them from the full blast of new and Western influences. This conception underlay the whole edifice of indirect rule. It is true that, under modern pressures, in some ways both the Government and the people are lately showing a readiness to depart from this principle, for instance in re-modelling 'native administration' upon English local government and adopting direct election to central bodies. But these currents have set up in several parts of Africa a counter current in favour of tribalism as a sort of lesser nationalism. Wrongly handled, the ready African suspicion could easily turn this, as with the Kikuyu, into a fanatical rejection of new influences. Certainly, when the Commission touch such an exposed nerve as tribal land-tenure, they would need all the co-operation of the patient if it is to be remedied.

But the Commission are attacking an even more strongly entrenched interest than tribalism. If British governments have treated Africans as 'different', white colonists have treated them as inferior. The present South African leaders, with whom the Kenya settlers are in distant contact, might reply to the Commission that racial domination, and indeed survival, are more important to them than further economic advancement. Have they not ignored a long series of South African commissions pointing out, less overtly perhaps than this East African report, that economic principles know nothing of racialism, except as an expensive luxury? The East African Commission might reply 'We were asked to show how African standards could be advanced. We answer by applying what we believe to be the most valid economic principles of our day to territories where the people are 99 per cent African. They can advance only in equality and freedom as part of the world with the help of the world. If the British or East African governments decide, upon racial and political grounds, that our economic advice is unacceptable, the decision, of course, lies with them.'

What, then, are the prospects of their policy? That is another story which will soon begin to unfold itself. I would only suggest in conclusion that the Kenya settlers are not in a position to obstruct the main proposals of this Report if British opinion is converted by it. Nor, I believe, would all of them today desire to do so. The policy is more likely to run upon the rocks of opposition from Africans, unwilling to co-operate with others in carrying through such great economic and social changes while their energies are directed towards the political task of building up self-government. This is a large question which we cannot discuss here. But we need not wait fatalistically for the answer. It will depend upon the resources and ability which we in Britain can contribute to the prosperity and the unity of East Africans, and in helping them to release their own energies for the task. Whether or not we accept all items of this fine Report, we owe a great deal to the men who gave so much of their time and knowledge to its contruction, and have faced us so squarely with the distortions in Africa of our own economic principles.

The Sudan after the Southern Rebellion

Letter to the *Manchester Guardian* 22 December 1955

This year saw a serious rebellion in the southern Sudan in which the Equatorial Battalions of the Sudan Defence Force revolted and there was a general massacre of northerners, including many officials.

Sir, – The Sudan has declared its independence, and the next few months may be decisive for shaping the future of the nation-to-be and for their credit in the eyes of the world. The British, above all, must earnestly wish them well and those who know the country must be heartened by the moderation and wisdom of the Prime Minister and the religious leaders and by the conduct of the young Parliament, as shown in the daily record of their proceedings. It is regrettable that not all that has been said and written in this country about the southern crisis has shown understanding of the difficulty of the problem or of the restraint of the Government in the face of an appalling personal and professional loss, or of those measures which show a desire to act correctly and prevent reprisals. We must hope that, after the minimum of punishment needed to restore order, the Government will continue to grace their new independence with magnanimity towards primitive tribesmen whose outbreak was due more to fear than to malignancy.

The Sudanese Government faces a larger and longer problem than the immediate restoration of order, the future relationship of an Arab and Moslem north with a Negro and pagan south. Two ways are open.

The first would be to use education, language, finance, preferment, and all other instruments of the State to enforce a 'northern' uniformity. The pledge to give equal consideration to the southerners' demand for a federal status is, therefore, a very hopeful sign. Yet there must be a great temptation, especially when dealing with a people so unorganized and politically immature as these Southern tribes, to take a repressive course. The removal of southern schools to the north and certain other measures must cause anxiety. For this policy could hardly win more than brief and partial success. Its cost would be to alienate now friendly nations, and also to deepen the southerners' historic antagonism and stimulate migration over their wide borders. And one day, when there emerges a self-governing Negro and part-Christian, part-pagan Uganda, this new State might exercise an irresistible attraction over its kindred neighbours.

The other policy would be to recognize that the tribal pride and the Christian element in the south should be allowed to develop freely from their present roots so that their strength would be expressed in loyalty and unity towards the Sudan State instead of in disruption. This policy would represent the extension to the south, which for a period must be in something very like a colonial relationship with Khartoum, of the absolute respect for a people's religion and culture which the north itself received from Britain.

This would greatly enrich the nation by diversifying it and it would make the Sudan a real bridge between Moslem-Arab Africa and pagan-and-Christian Africa. It would fulfil the high promise of religious toleration and democratic rights which the Sudanese wrote into their Constitution. And it would retain for the Sudan the friendship and confidence of an important part of the world, including that of the governments which lie upon three sides of the southern provinces.

Yours faithfully

1956

Foreword to *The Kenya Question: an African Answer*

Mr Tom Mboya came to Oxford in 1956 to study at Ruskin College. We became friends and I was deeply impressed by the clarity of his mind and the strength of his will. In his pamphlet, published in September 1956 by The Fabian Colonial Bureau, while disavowing the atrocities committed by Africans in the Mau Mau movement, he condemned the government response as unconstructive repression, and defined the African goal as straight majority rule with no privileges for race or wealth. While agreeing with him about this I still hoped at that date, seven years before independence was to come, that there might be a period of British rule vigorously employed to prepare the Africans to take over the government. As it turned out, the dethronement of the local Europeans from their political and economic supremacy was only achieved by a series of hard-fought struggles and, though the British officials did what they could to set the stage for the final handover in December 1963, Africans succeeded to power with the minimum of political and administrative experience. It will be seen in The Times *article of 18 March 1957 that I felt it necessary to stress the need for more urgent preparation for the coming transfer of power. Readers will hardly need reminding about the outstanding part Mr Mboya played after he wrote this pamphlet, both before independence and as a leading cabinet minister.*

I

I must begin with two explanations. The first may sound a little ungracious to the publisher as it is really an apology for writing in a political production. This is against the rule which, as an academic worker, I have set myself. The breach is due to my having very much wished to introduce this pamphlet to readers and to my finding that the writer was already committed to publication through the Fabians. For

FOREWORD TO 'THE KENYA QUESTION' [1956]

myself the Kenya problem is not a party matter and I am convinced that we shall be unable to help Africa in the next difficult twenty years unless we can maintain, at least in large measure, an agreed policy.

My second explanation is that my desire to write an introduction to this pamphlet does not mean that I endorse the whole of it. Mr Mboya and I agreed upon the same terms under which I had the opportunity to introduce Mr Awolowo's book, *The Path to Nigerian Freedom*.[1] These are that I would not ask the writer to revise his views in order to satisfy me but that he on his side must be prepared to let me write whatever I wished, even in disagreement. My motive in both instances was the same, the desire that the views of Africa's potential leaders should be widely read and, if possible, sympathetically understood.

I commend this pamphlet to the serious study of all those concerned with the affairs of Kenya. The peoples of that country have just suffered terribly in life and wealth from an outbreak of ferocity. The important psychological study of the Mau Mau rebellion by Dr Carothers,[2] to which not nearly enough attention and publicity has been given, shows that the movement was a sudden ignition from the discontents which had accumulated their intensest heat among the Kikuyu but which, from the same deep cause, may exist in greater or lesser degree among the other tribes. In brief, this cause is the almost intolerable sense of frustration suffered by an isolated tribal people when suddenly dominated by a superior civilization because this at once destroys the basis of their old society and at the same time seems to forbid entry into the new. The stern and necessary repression of disorder by heavy military action has stamped down the forest-fire of Kikuyu violence; and it is probable that for a time there may be a period of quiescence. But the embers are still there and unless Africans can find an outlet in public and organized definition of their inchoate fears and needs the spark may rekindle again and this time over a wider area.

In this pamphlet we have the attempt of an African who, incidentally, is not a Kikuyu, to explain the attitude of men of his race in Kenya and to put forward clear-cut proposals for reform and political advance. A man such as this should be given a serious hearing and a full opportunity to contribute his ideas to the intense political discussion by the other races which has been evoked by the coming elections. If this is denied, others, less rational and experienced than he, may be driven back to the underground method and blow up the hidden fires of discontent.

[1] Published by Faber, 1947. See *Colonial Sequence 1930–1949*, pp. 306 ff.
[2] J. C. Carothers, *The Psychology of Mau Mau* (Nairobi, 1954).

[1956]

'A man such as this?' But what sort of man is he? He is a Luo from South Nyanza. For three years he has held the post of general secretary of the Kenya Federation of Labour, a body which, like its constituent unions, is still young and inexperienced but is drawing upon expert help and advice from outside Kenya. In 1954 he visited India and Pakistan. In 1955 he was a delegate to the Inter-African Labour Conference at Beira of the Committee for Technical Co-operation in Africa South of the Sahara. In Kenya he has been a member of the Labour and Wages Advisory Board and the Rural Wages Committee, and has been the local representative of the International Confederation of Free Trade Unions. From 1951-53 he worked as Health Inspector for the City Council of Nairobi and in 1953 founded the Kenya Local Government Workers' Union. In 1955 he mediated, very effectively I understand, in the Mombasa dock strike and helped the dockers to put their case to the tribunal. His work has naturally brought him into contact with many parts and peoples of Kenya. With the help of the Workers' Travel Association he has just spent the academic year 1955-56 studying at Ruskin College, Oxford. He is spending the summer partly in Belgium at the headquarters of the I.C.F.T.U. and partly in the United States before returning to Kenya in the early autumn.

I have given Mr Mboya's record in order to show that he is a travelled man with much practical and administrative experience and with a down-to-earth knowledge of labour conditions in Kenya. He has also the advantage of youth: he is still only twenty-six. In Britain he has made many friends. He has met a number of political leaders and members of Parliament. He has been frequently in London and he listened to the recent important debate on Kenya in the House of Commons on June 6th. In Oxford he has taken part in discussions and seminars with postgraduates upon subjects connected with his own field, and has held his own. He has a clear head and a quiet restrained manner. He is a fluent speaker but as far as my experience goes, avoids emotion and maintains a very rational manner. When I heard him at a recent conference in London I was surprised at the end of his speech to see that he had spoken without notes for 80 minutes; so completely had he held my attention that I had not been aware of the time. I should judge that he has a steadiness of character and a very strong will, but time alone can prove this.

I expect that some of those who read this, especially in Kenya, will deplore this published appraisal of a young man on the grounds that it will turn his head. I do not think it will. In any case he has had the

FOREWORD TO 'THE KENYA QUESTION' [1956]

compliment of serious attention in so many quarters, British and foreign, where people are eager to make contact with the mind of young Africa – especially hitherto almost silent East Africa – that these few additional words of mine are unlikely to affect him. And it is very important that these words should be said. The possibility that Mr Mboya will become conceited is far less dangerous than that he, and other responsible African leaders, should be faced with prejudice and refused a fair hearing.

This statement is not a piece of political blackmail, as it might be in a normal country. For Kenya is not a normal country. It is highly abnormal and is at this moment, with the non-African and the first African elections imminent, moving into a gravely testing period. Africans stand desperately in need of intelligent leaders who know something of the world beyond East Africa. Many of the older chiefs who showed such courage and loyalty during the emergency are not, unfortunately, qualified to take part in central political affairs. It is the educated men who are likely to be elected. There are few enough of these and they are unavoidably young and inexperienced. They need, not necessarily agreement, but an understanding of their views and of their difficulties.

II

In this foreword I have no intention of plunging into the middle of Kenya's problems and volunteering detailed remedies. I want rather to speak of the *approach* to these problems and the need to understand their nature and their setting in the world of today.

Seen close up from the farms and the lovely downs and forests of the White Highlands or the villas and clubs of Nairobi, the Kenya problem seems, to judge by much that is being said there today, to be an African problem – the threat of the Africans to the established political and economic position achieved over some fifty years by the European minority. Hence arises a siege mentality, with all its deep fears, its defiance, its isolation, its vow of white blood-brotherhood between the defenders to show total solidarity and the highest courage to the end. But, from the wider outside view of most of the rest of the world, Kenya presents less an African problem than a settler problem.

The settlers' position certainly appears one of great danger, even of siege, but it is a siege of the high citadel of privilege and domination which they occupied easily in circumstances which are rapidly passing

[1956]

away, a process which cannot be reversed and can hardly be delayed in the world of 1956. Courage and defiance from behind the walls of this citadel shut out realities more effectively than dangers and are not appropriate to the situation. Constitutions which embody the domination of an immigrant racial minority over millions of the indigenous peoples have been thrown on the defensive even in South Africa, are in the melting pot in Central Africa, and are being bloodily attacked in Algeria. Such a system of minority rule is certainly untenable by a few thousand whites in the very heart of Negro Africa. Most of the subject peoples, including those of eastern Africa, with the approval or support of nine-tenths of the rest of the world, are beginning to move towards self-government with majority rule. Is it likely that any native population will for long continue to accept the accident of white settlement as a reason why the rights given to their brothers, sometimes literally their tribal brothers just across a border, should be denied to them? The courage that is needed in Kenya today is the courage not to make a last stand but to take the first steps towards a new stand.

The people in Britain who, by and large, accept this last view, are almost certainly a large majority of those who have any knowledge of Kenya. With few exceptions, they are not, I am sure, moved by any prejudice or hostility towards the settlers. It is important to repeat this because many Europeans in Kenya seem to be lashed into an unreasoning anger by a sense that they are the victims of some kind of plot or deliberate animosity. Those who make an unpromising assessment about the future of the settlers' privileged position are neither responsible for the factors they assess nor necessarily pleased by them.

Speaking for myself, from my first visit to Kenya twenty-five years ago I believed, and said, that the special position of the settlers was unjust to other races and in the long run untenable. But I have been inclined to blame, not so much the individual settlers who have made their beautiful and productive farms on these highlands, but British governments and governors who allowed them to build up also a political position which contravened British ideas of justice and democracy. A desperate eleventh-hour attempt by the settlers, or a large section of them, to hold this position against all the forces which are ranged against them in Kenya, in East Africa, in Africa, in Britain and in the world, can end only in failure, but in a failure which may destroy any hope of maintaining white settlement or even the British connection.

It is not difficult to see that to many Europeans who have spent a lifetime or the best part of it in Kenya, the demand of the Africans to advance towards majority rule – for that is the main sense of this pamphlet – must seem a dangerous madness. They see the ignorance of the African servants and labourers, the inefficiency of their agriculture, their unpunctuality and unreliability in the setting of modern conditions. Their minds are still full of the bestialities of Mau Mau committed on their doorstep, threatening all, and destroying some, of their own number. They regard with horror the possibility of passing under the control of the Africans.

Of course, these fears are not without much reason. Students of history or sociology, indeed any thoughtful onlookers, would possibly agree that it would have been much better if Negro Africa could have had another century at least of British rule, of order, education, unification, economic development, at the hands of beneficent and expert trustees. But – and this is where the approach is all-important – we cannot have these desirable conditions. We have to make terms with things as they are, however unpleasant or even dangerous. People undergoing Africa's deep social changes, which will accelerate with each acceleration of economic development, cannot be kept psychologically static. This means that they cannot be kept in a state of arrested political development.

As a people we British are lacking in foresight. Let us then close our eyes and try to imagine the position in Kenya ten or twenty years ahead. For one educated and travelled Mboya there will be a hundred or more and scores of highly educated graduates from Makerere and elsewhere, many of whom will, I hope, have rounded off their education in Britain. These men and women will be increasingly in touch with all those centres in the world, in Europe, Asia, the Middle East and America, from which they can draw help and political encouragement. Unless they can be convinced that they can completely fulfil their natural hopes for greater dignity and welfare for themselves and their people within a parliamentary constitution and within the British association, they will set to work not to make Kenya as most of us wish to see it but to break it.

The mistake made by many of those who refuse to face these possibilities is to think that we who try to do so are wholly deluded about African capacities and the ease of the courses we recommend. This is not so. No honest observer can be blind to the grave problems and dangers of disunity, corruption and the rest, which threaten the newly emancipated countries in Africa. But we must ask whether British governments, once ambitions for self-government had been aroused, could have averted these dangers and solved these problems. We are trying to deal with situations which, because of the backwardness of Africa, have no precedent. But it seems that there comes a moment when Britain can no longer effectively govern a subject people against the will of the educated minority. Once that position is reached we find we have to go with and not against their ambitions. There should, therefore, come first a period of vigorous preparation for self-government and then another period, the longer the better for them, though difficult enough for us, when we begin transferring power while still supplying trained staff and retaining ultimate powers of security. Perilous work indeed! But let us remember that, even if we consider the date for emancipation is premature, the goal itself is in line both with our own principles and our declared colonial policy.

It may be countered that there *are* ruling minorities in Africa and elsewhere who, by uncompromising repression of their subjects or by insulating them from outside influences, appear to be able to avert the political changes we have been discussing. But here again we must accept the environment within which we have to work. Part of that is the British policy of colonial emancipation, the freedom of our politics and press with all their repercussions upon Africa. The British, in other words, are by character and constitution incompetent repressors and had therefore better try something else in good time.

If this is true, the things which many Kenya settlers are today denouncing as dangers are really their safeguards. The experienced and educated African leaders, such as the author of this pamphlet, stand in as much danger from violent African extremism as do the Europeans or the Indians. The tragedy is that with the late and all-too rapid opening up of Africa to the west – the abnormality which underlies all others and which should never be forgotten – these leaders are still so few. They are trying to be rational, having made the great struggle against poverty, language and the rest, to master knowledge of their world; they have to stand at the head of the African masses, and try to canalize their often blind and dangerous discontents into legitimate political action, and to turn the almost indefinable revolt against inferiority into a practicable party programme.

The position of these leaders will be made almost hopeless if they are confronted with personal contempt and utter political negation by the leaders of other races in Kenya. If they should be treated thus the only thing that might still help them to keep to the narrow and difficult path of constitutional action is the knowledge that in Britain, if not in

FOREWORD TO 'THE KENYA QUESTION'   [1956]

Kenya, there are politicians who will support them and friends who have faith in them. I have known African leaders from west and central as well as eastern Africa. *So far*, I believe that all of them would prefer to take what they need – and they will acknowledge the extent of their need if it is not forced upon them as a means of humiliation – from Britain rather than from anywhere else. But they are in a hurry, not necessarily from sheer ambition – though why should personal ambition be regarded as a crime in African politicians? – but because the tide of nationalism is rising behind them and though they may guide it their power to delay it may be limited.

Believing this, I must regard some of the speeches that are being made this summer of 1956 by some of the settler leaders as extremely unwise. They do not, as Mr Mboya says, reveal much change of ambition from the old purpose of minority rule: they seem to conceive that strange amalgam 'multi-racial government' as a very limited, almost delusive advance upon the old regime, with Mr Blundell facing the first waves of the tide of African political consciousness in the posture of King Canute. If the settlers challenge the Africans to a political duel *à l'outrance* the Africans are now in a position to take up the challenge with every hope of an ultimate victory not on 'multi-racial' or any reasonable terms but on those prompted by their own unreasoning anger. Can the white colony afford to invite open conflict? To drive Asians and Africans into alliance? To alienate British public opinion? Is the alternative so unthinkable, that of abandoning group solidarity and privilege and accepting as a final goal a system in which, as in the West Indies, they will play their part as individual citizens, for a long time the most wealthy and able members of society?

III

I know well that these arguments will be labelled defeatism. But private and personal courage and public political courage should never be confused. History teaches that the greater political courage lies more often in the fearless acceptance of change than in blind defiance of it. As for courage of convictions, surely in Kenya there are higher convictions demanding our support even than the defence of 'the interests of our countrymen' – as they define those interests. There is faith in the human nature of the other races and of their capacity to enjoy the freedoms that are part of our heritage of convictions.

To return to our pamphlet.

[1956]

Mr Mboya suggests stages of advance towards this democratic situation. He is too optimistic, of course, when he says 'There is nothing to fear'. There is much to fear, but less, surely, than will result from piling up racial hatred by the claim to racial dictatorship. It is necessary to look, in a practical manner, at the results which settlers naturally fear and see how far they can be avoided.

This brings me to the main point I wish to make. *The end of settler domination need not and must not be followed immediately by African domination.* Of course the Africans are quite unready to take over the government of the country. Experienced African chiefs, civil servants and members of the Legislative Council all know it and admit it. They are prepared to accept safeguards for the minorities retained in the hands of the British Government. But do not let us presume upon the 'loyalty' shown in the emergency. It is probable that even the loyalists ask, like this pamphlet, for a hope, a promise that they are not to be treated differently from other peoples in the Commonwealth and the world. They ask that their poverty and inexperience should not be used to justify their being kept indefinitely in a subordinate position, but attacked vigorously by all the most modern methods of education and betterment in order to qualify them as soon as possible for self-government.

They now have the authority of the Royal Commission[1] behind them both to justify many of their complaints and to give expert definition to many of their requirements.

But they know as well as we do that they are very far from being able even to supply full political control still less to carry out executively all the functions of the modern state. These are the more difficult in Kenya because its physical conditions need the fullest application of scientific method and the acceptance by a peasant population of often uncomprehended measures urgently applied to safeguard their basic resources. Politically the tribes of Kenya are far behind those of West Africa: they have still to start their progress towards nationhood, an end which the government, far from obstructing as it is at present, could accelerate with all its powers, once the goal were openly acknowledged.

At this point I might be reminded of the safeguard that is actually being applied to the first African elections, that of the limited franchise. I should like to believe with the Capricorn Society, the sincerity of whose members I greatly respect, that this measure, if applied to all races,

[1] East African Royal Commission 1953-5 Report, Cmd. 9475 (1955). See above, pp. 122-8.

might prove a workable, if only an interim solution of Kenya's hard constitutional problem. But I feel forced to share Mr Mboya's doubts of this expedient because of the administrative difficulties it presents and the invidiousness of the tests applied to the voters. Furthermore, the fact that this system has been rejected by almost every democracy in the world must put the rejected candidates in a position to make a powerful appeal to the unenfranchised over the heads of their elected rivals.

There must, therefore, it seems, be an interval during which government by racial minority having been renounced and government by majority still being impracticable, the only possible course will be for the British government to strengthen its relaxing control over the country. This was the main theme of what will have struck many people as the surprisingly moderate and statesmanlike speech of Mr Bevan in the Commons debate on 6 June. The government has all the apparatus for this in its Colonial Office and Overseas Service. Of course there are defects in the system, but a defective system is better than an advance towards catastrophe. And defects can be remedied. The Colonial Office cannot continue much longer unchanged in a changing Commonwealth. New forms of organization may be needed. It will be necessary for example, to link closely the trained staff needed in Kenya to carry out the recommendations of the Royal Commission with those associations and agencies in Britain which could stimulate both the science and the administration of these new measures.

In other words, during this interval, some selected and modified elements of the new concept of 'integration' should be applied. The traditional links between metropolis and colony were forged in a period when Kenya was not within twenty-four hours' flying time from London, and when the rapid economic and cultural advancement of a tribal people was not the first item of policy. A strong Secretary of State, relieved of some of his present impossible burden, and a strong governor who could win the trust of all races in his sense of justice, would be essential to the success of this regime of arbitral imperialism.

It seems certain that the Africans would agree to this strengthening of British control and even welcome it. I believe that Mr Mathu, so long the chief African spokesman in Legislative Council, would be in favour. Mr Mboya has said as much though he does not show here the emphasis which I believe represents his views. There is, of course, one condition for African assent. It is that in this interval, which in Kenya's condition must be long, the British government, while it retains the overriding control in Kenya should set to work with all its energy to advance African education and especially to help Africans, not only in schools and universities, but by training on the job, to undertake increasing responsibilities of all kinds.

This will cost money. The emergency has been very costly to the British taxpayer. A further considerable sum has been granted from Britain for African agriculture. Another sum of three or four million pounds should be given for African education, in the sense described, and especially for still greater facilities for higher education both in East Africa and Britain. The Royal Technical College is not enough. It is more than time to begin making plans for the foundation of a full university in Nairobi which could be the focus of study and research for all races and a source of common pride. I believe that it is impossible to over-estimate the healing effect all this would have upon the minds of Africans who, once reassured about their ultimate political future, and relieved of their fear of settler rule, would respond both in co-operation with the government and in happier personal relations with the other races. It would also avert the dangers hanging over East African co-operation. It is the fear of association with a settler-dominated Kenya which has always governed African opinion in Uganda and Tanganyika.

There would be another side to Britian's responsibility in this interim period. It would be to guarantee the racial minorities in all their legitimate rights. Certainly much depends upon the definition of the adjective. On the burning question of the highlands the proposal of the Royal Commission, to which Mr Mboya refers, of opening up unused land to buyers irrespective of race, but under very stringent conditions of good farming, seems reasonable and has been recognized as such by some settlers. It is, of course, only part of a policy of gradually freeing economic life from tribalism, black, brown and white. But not only the settlers but all the immigrant peoples of Kenya, including the oldest immigrants of all, the coastal Arabs, would need to be reassured that their rights and interests would be the special care of Britain during the long period before the country passed over to majority rule. And though, of course, the old feverish counting of heads in Legislative Council would lose its exacerbating significance, adequate representation of all groups and interests would be one of the main safeguards Britain would guarantee.

IV

To return to Mr Mboya's pamphlet, the possibilities I have sketched would seem to be in line with his own ideas. But, as I said at the beginning, I have not used this foreword to discuss Mr Mboya's specific proposals but have endeavoured to suggest a general approach to the problem of Kenya. If I have dealt in generalizations it is not because I think that the detailed working out of such a programme would be easy.

Let me say again that my introducing this pamphlet does not mean that I endorse all its proposals. I think the writer underestimates the difficulties which Africa's long isolation has bequeathed to us in his people's poverty, ignorance and disunity. But let us remember that this backwardness is so continuously reiterated by white settlers in Africa as a justification for permanent domination that African leaders may regard it as unnecessary to intone in unison with this depressing chorus. They know the meaning of backwardness all too well but they know also that what their people most need to overcome it is hope and not a dangerous despair with its temptation to a revival, such as Mau Mau exhibited, of a corrupted savagery.

Even allowing for this I think that Mr Mboya might have shown more realization of the difficulty of his proposals. There is also too little of the sense of history which reveals to us that domination of the weak by the strong has been the almost universal practice of the human race and that, insofar as Britain has failed in Kenya, it has been in not applying those high standards of imperial altruism which the world owes mainly to her initiative. And though there have been mistakes in Kenya made by both settlers and government – a government for which we in Britain are ultimately responsible – there has been also a wealth of energetic and practical goodwill towards the African shown on many sides, certainly by large numbers of settlers. These services have been greatly increased both in range and in vigour during the last few years and if, as he rightly says, this has been largely due to the emergency, at least government and settlers had the wisdom to learn much from that experience. Probably never in the history of colonial empires has such a wealth of intelligent concern and dedicated service been given to the needs of a native people as is being given today in Kenya. This must be set on one side of our picture to balance the figures on the other, the murdered and massacred, the thousand and more sent to the hangman and the 50,000 behind barbed wire.

As for the handling of that emergency, it is salutary that the writer should help us to realize how repressive measures are seen and felt from the African side and should remind us of the many injustices or even atrocities committed in the name of law and order. But we may question whether he has fully weighed, as a people with long experience of government must do, the absolute necessity of that same law and order, the gravity of the threat to it and the perilous inadequacy of the government's powers and personnel in the earlier days of the Mau Mau movement. But these are the kind of lessons which can be learned only by the exercise of responsibility. And the dangers of sharing that responsibility with African leaders, especially when they can act with the authority they will draw next year from election, are far less, I would urge, than the dangers of shutting them outside the circle within which are taken the decisions which govern their lives.

As I write, the speeches being made at Salima at the Capricorn Society conference are urging the peoples of East Africa to think of themselves as fellow-citizens rather than as competing races. The conference itself is a noble venture in racial association and many of us who are not members will agree that the future welfare of East Africa depends upon the measure in which thousands of personal inter-racial relationships can be infused with unselfishness and mutual understanding. We must hope, indeed, that not only European but African and Indian leaders, in the testing situation which now faces them in Kenya, will ignore the insults of extremists and show the utmost restraint and understanding of the difficulties of the other side.

But I venture to disagree with the Capricorn Society upon two important points. One is that, like Mr Mboya, I believe that the races are more likely to understand each other and to work together if the fact that Kenya is primarily an African country and must work towards a constitution founded squarely upon the fact, is not veiled in concepts of 'multi-racialism' or qualitative citizenship. The second disagreement is that though ultimately, of course, the future of Kenya will be decided in Kenya, there must first be a period of graduation towards self-government. During this period I believe that the races will best make the deep adjustments demanded from them if they are relieved from their mutual fears and given a sense of security. There is only one source from which Kenya could draw a security in which all the races could trust, and that is Britain.

1957

A Land of Enormous Contrasts

Broadcast in 'Calling West Africa', published in *London Calling* 21 February 1957

People often ask me when I am travelling in Africa, or in England: 'What led you to take up work on Africa?' I have to go right back to my childhood to find the answer. Almost the very first books I read were about Africa. One was *King Solomon's Mines*; fiction, of course, but how alluring! It made me long to make a great journey over unknown mountains, on and on, seeking new lands and mysterious peoples. Fiction – yet Haggard knew his Africa: he gives the real romance of discovery, the real adventure of a continent that was then little known. My other book was quite different, Fitzpatrick's *Jock of the Bushveld*, the story of a brave dog which went big-game hunting with its master. So when people asked me, in the rather patronizing grown-up way, 'And what are you going to be when you grow up?' I would answer: 'A big-game hunter in Africa.'

Things did not turn out exactly like that: true I did hunt big game, buffalo in Tanganyika and lion in Somaliland. But I quickly loathed the idea of killing or, worse, wounding these magnificent beasts, and came to think that people who go on finding joy in such killing are indeed like children who never grow up. Our energies should rather be given to preserving the world's last great treasure of such animals. The game reserves might be one of the glories of Africa.

To go back to my own story. I did go to Africa, if not to hunt, to travel over many parts, south, north, east, west and centre, trying to understand and write about its peoples and problems. I never made the anthropologist's detailed study of one part or tribe. I wanted to see Africa (mainly British equatorial Africa) as a whole, especially its government, and try to learn what Britain was doing with the peoples

[1957] COLONIAL SEQUENCE 1949 TO 1969

whom she had taken under her rule. I do not want to talk now of these serious matters but to sit down before the map of Africa and share with you, as if you were looking over my shoulder at the map, some of the pictures and memories which come as I look back over nearly thirty-five years of intermittent travelling over this great block of land.

My first thought is of the enormous contrasts of the physical scene of Africa. When you go about Britain you will find hills here and plains there; here woods, there open land. But it is all very much the same, green land, much the same trees, crops, cattle, way of life. This is true of a great deal of Europe. Compare Africa! At one extreme you have the desert. I saw Africa first in Somaliland, trekking on camels up to and over the Ethiopian border: sand and rocks, a few thorn trees, water the colour of cocoa scooped out of deep wells, no crops, men living on their wandering animals. Later I saw the semi-desert of Bechuanaland, and saw in Eritrea and the Sudan even emptier desert. What a wonderful shock, going south from Khartoum over the glaring sand, when I suddenly saw a line of green, rich dark-green, straight as a ruler – cotton; the edge of the irrigated area where Nile water had been channelled over the desert. This was what water could do with Africa's sand and heat.

My eye runs down the map to where nature pours rain-water lavishly, and great forests tower up in response. In Nigeria you have forests in the south where giant trees soar 200 feet in height. I remember a forest in the French Cameroons where a cutting had just been made for a railway: it stood like a vast green cliff, solid with leaves and creepers, almost terrifying in its height and thickness. Between the extremes of desert and rain-forest lie all the intermediate types of forest and bush.

Sometimes the contrasts lie close together. I camped once on the cedar line of Kilimanjaro, with its dome of snow just above me; I bathed among the tree ferns in an icy waterfall coming down from a glacier. Yet I could see below me the burning level plains where the Masai drove their thirsty cattle in search of water-holes. As for the dramatic in scenery – stand on the height of the forested Cameroon mountain and gaze across the warm sea at the sister mountain on the island of Fernando Po.

Yes, indeed, Africa, and especially East Africa, is full of glorious sights and contrasts. We from Europe gaze and admire. But sometimes Africa seems almost hostile and menacing to us, so out of scale, out of character, with all we know. It will need to be tamed and loved for centuries, given permanent farms and villages, with real village churches, I hope, and freed from all that is dangerous in nature. Once I took two

A LAND OF ENORMOUS CONTRASTS [1957]

African friends to Exmoor. As we lay flat on the grass and heather, relaxed and secure, they said: 'We could not do this at home.' And we thought of the ants, the snakes and scorpions, and all the cruel reptiles and insects which guard their kingdom against man. True, in spite of this, tropical Africa seems a happy place: almost wherever I go, along roads and in villages, people laugh and wave and dance – how many scores of dances have I seen! But think how much happier it will be when the hopes brought by Western science are fulfilled, and the dangers and diseases hidden in Africa's beauty and fertility have been conquered.

Then, looking at the pictures called up by the map, I think of equatorial Africa as the stage for a play, the play of history. And what a play! So rapid in action, so brief! We should remember, for it explains so much, that over most of middle Africa written history began only in the lifetime of old men still alive. Much of West Africa, of course, has a longer history. The Moslem states reach back many centuries in the pages of Arab chroniclers, and some of the western pagan kingdoms made their contacts with the outside world, especially with Europeans coming by sea. And everywhere there are tribal traditions, lists of chiefs, and other scattered evidence which archaeologists and anthropologists are still sorting out. Yet, even in the West, the great event which changed the old Africa so utterly – the coming of European rule – happened over large areas within the past sixty years.

I walked about the battlefield of Omdurman and saw exactly the place where in 1898 the young Churchill charged on horseback in the action which brought the Sudan under British rule. In Uganda I sat on a little hill on which in 1891 Lugard (a friend whose life I have written) made his first camp and decided the future of Uganda. And though Lugard died in 1945 his *elder* sister is still alive. Last year I revisited Nigeria, and at Sokoto an old man reconstructed the coming of Lugard's little force in 1903 and the brief fight outside the town which confirmed British rule over the Hausa states. I was at Lugard's English home when emirs and chiefs from Nigeria – Kano, Katsina, Abeokuta, too – visited the man who first governed Northern Nigeria and later made all Nigeria one. They talked with him as friend and partner in their common task of making a nation out of a great block of African plains, hills and forests, and its separate kingdoms and tribes.

This is not a political talk. But I will venture to say that Africans should study their Africa, not only its politics but its beauties, its contrasts, its still untamed, undeveloped nature, and, above all, its history.

[1957]   COLONIAL SEQUENCE 1949 TO 1969

We must never forget how lately, how suddenly, this vast equatorial region, most of which through all historical time had been locked away from the world, was pierced through and through by the power of that world – with what deep, disturbing, yet exciting effects! It was no fault of the Africans they were so long isolated; it was no fault of Europe either.

Do not let us seek escape from this great historical fact, with all its resulting problems, by blaming each other or even ourselves. If some mistakes were made, yet the contact had to come, and it was bound to have these shattering effects. The Africa of King Solomon's mines called to me as a place of romance. But, in truth, the old lonely Africa, for all its beauty and the vigorous life of its kingdoms and tribes, was no paradise. As the brief tide of British mastery turns and begins to run back, leaving a changed country behind it, we see that paradise has still to be created – and created by Africans with all the help that we are still able to offer and they are willing to take.

Kenya after Mau Mau

The Times 18 March 1957

This article rightly had for its sub-title 'Many Uncertainties in the Path Ahead'. In the Lyttelton constitution the British Government had for the first time allowed Africans to be elected to the Legislative Council, but only six in number and on a restricted 'fancy franchise'. The six, led by Mr Mboya, at once rejected the constitution and, inspired by the Gold Coast's achievement of self-government, demanded an immediate advance. The Lennox-Boyd constitution was the answer which again failed to meet their demands.

Flying to Nairobi from Lake Victoria the scenic drama of Kenya is gloriously visible. Hills and mountains stand about in their inconsquent Kenya way. To the north one sees Mount Elgon and the Nandi escarpment; below is the ant-like congestion of the Kavirondo plain; south lies the Masai wilderness. Then comes the chain of lakes and the rectilinear designs of European farming; the farmhouses, so lately in deadly peril, standing among the violet mists of jacaranda trees. Then, to the north, beclouded Mount Kenya; south, the dun Athi plains alive with protected game; and below, the mouse-coloured huts of the Kikuyu, followed by the growing suburban and industrial sprawl of the young capital. Half a dozen different sets of weather chase each other across the scene, black storms lanced with silver, muffling brown rain, then clear blue and gold. Before the earth rushes up at the traveller he has felt the impact of Kenya, vital, full of contrasts, physical and political, of conflicts, and wonderful possibilities.

Mau Mau, it seems, is finished. But that terrible assertion of discontent which, in its tenacity and beastliness, still seems to defy our understanding, has left a changed Kenya. The Africans can never again be seen as they were before this event, while the settlers have proved their own tenacity. Yet, surprisingly, today no absolute alienation divides the races. The danger was too grave to be met merely with hatred, and the Kikuyu reputation was saved by the amazing courage of the Christians and the loyalists without whose help Mau Mau could not have been beaten. Also – a strong practical reason – the Kikuyu are the most versatile workers, and the settlers whom they lately threatened to slash to death are now urgently calling them back to their farms.

The economy has withstood the storm surprisingly well. Production was affected only locally. The country found £9 million of extra taxation to meet Britain's contribution of some £25 millions. Nairobi continued to extend outwards and upwards, even when it was headquarters for murder. Now its huge new blocks, light in tone and texture, with coloured panels brilliant in the sun, and the broad new avenues flanked with trees and gorgeous bougainvillaea, flaunt civic pride and faith in the future.

Socially there are now ten points of racial contact and co-operation for every one before Mau Mau, and with them the first small signs of racial equality. The Royal Technical College has opened its lecture rooms and hostels to all races. With only a very little tact Indians and Africans can be entertained at some of the best Nairobi hotels. In racially mixed districts joint committees of African and European farmers are being formed. The sportsmanship of all races was fused in excitement over their common Olympic team. The representatives of the four races share all the amenities of the parliament building, a light-hearted architectural fantasy which seems designed to banish the gloom of intolerance.

In the administrative sphere what most strikes observers is the avalanche of reforms – a mere list would fill this column – poured out both to regenerate the shattered Kikuyu and to satisfy the loyal tribes. First, due partly to the Red Cross workers who refused to regard Africans as 'different', come the services directed to the hitherto largely inaccessible women and children. A British contribution of £5 million, co-ordinated through the Swynnerton plan, has stimulated better and more diversified farming. Africans in Mau Mau areas are today producing the best coffee in all Kenya and are starting to grow tea. The detainees now streaming in thousands out of the 'pipeline' – an intricate system of release by stages, based equally upon humanity and security – should find their green hills and valleys cleansed from the stains of murder and obscene sacrifice, and promising to become what they appear to be, an equatorial Arcadia.

These advances depend upon two revolutionary measures which are changing the face of the Mau Mau country – 'villagization', and the consolidation of scattered holdings into family farms, surveyed, listed, terraced and fenced. The errant tribes are thus being coaxed to accept the best of western European experience – the pride of ownership and the amenities of village life centred round school, church, and village hall.

In Africa deep changes mean deep problems. What measure of control is to be retained? The new reforms had been the hopeless dreams of generations of administrators. Now the iron discipline, backed by the overwhelming military force needed for security, has been turned to social betterment and closer administration. Where two or three commissioners struggled to manage a district of up to half a million tribesmen, there are now several sub-stations under assistant commissioners, each in turn sub-divided into locations with chiefs and councils. The D.C. who lately stood back helplessly while Kenyatta or his agents openly flouted his schemes for betterment is now back in something like his pre-war supremacy, the paternal head of a team of specialists. How can this regimented march to a millenium – one of our own devising – become a spontaneous advance? Progress has depended upon the gold of Britain's subsidy as well as the iron of her discipline. What will happen when both of these diminish together?

Turning to politics, we see that paternalism may be actively threatened. The recent African elections will send to the legislature men with the first chrism of democracy on their brows. They will almost certainly claim to by-pass the established structure of 'native administration' and to act directly for, and upon, their constituents. They will inject a new and incalculable factor into the central executive and legislature. Their coming, indeed, is likely to prove a startling reminder of the great racial question-mark which, for a Kenya which seems very successfully busy upon the plans of this year and next, haunts the further future.

The Lyttelton constitution has a precariously balanced racial representation in the legislature, and a ministry of men belonging to six categories, each responsible to a different source of power. Like a house of cards which stands so long as no one breathes, it works only because, in the face of crisis, practical men of all races want to make it work. But while all concerned, including Africans, know that the majority race cannot predominate tomorrow, almost everyone knows that, at some unknown date, this succession must occur. How, for how long, and by whom, can the interval be held?

The answers to these three questions lately given for Central Africa by Sir Roy Welensky are no longer possible in Kenya. British governments, uncertain how to apply the ineradicable lesson of the Boston tea party to multi-racial Africa, prefer to give no answer, other than year-to-year adjustments to changing realities. Is this traditional empiricism any longer appropriate? It demands from all races an absolute trust in Britain's power and wisdom; the first is diminishing, the second is too often shrunken by parliamentary inattention or marred by party conflict. Has not certainty become Kenya's greatest need? Even the settlers, their long hope of domination waning, now need the certainty of protection. Still more do the Asians need it. Africans, whose Mau Mau was a symptom of their insecurity between two worlds, begin to scan their future. Many still desire British control but, with Britain silent, they lie open to distracting influences emanating from U.N.O., Egypt, India, Ghana, Somalia, and elsewhere. Their administrators exclaim: 'If only we knew what we were working *for*!' With a clear policy, as bipartisan as possible, the race with time for the development of African responsibility might be won. Only Britain can hold the dangerous interval, and only if she can clear the future from an obscurity as thick as the clouds which at midday hide Kenya mountain.

Out of the Fellowship

Africa South July–September 1957

A comment on the South African government's plan for Bantu universities.

The extension of apartheid to the universities by the South African government has deeply disturbed academic circles in Britain. The universities of the world, except those which have retired behind the intellectual ramparts of communism, are, in some aspects, a community. The higher human minds attain in their search for truth the more they can reach out to meet other minds across the barriers, which are all too high in our world of today, of language, nationality and race. If any member of the community of universities becomes weak or diseased or, worse still, inflicts injury upon itself, it falls out of the community and both the community and its lost member are impoverished.

These statements are truisms which are so well understood that they seldom need to be said. The South African policy of university apartheid demands their repetition. They are, moreover, especially real to me because of two special experiences which I have been able to add to my own university work. I have for many years, indeed from the beginning of the enterprise, been concerned as a member of the Executive of the Inter-University Council for Higher Education Overseas. During the last fifteen years this body has, in partnership with local energies, created university colleges in the West Indies, the Gold Coast, Nigeria, the Sudan, East Africa and Malaya and has assisted in the founding of the Central African College. I have referred to this partly to explain my personal approach and, more importantly, to show the large and energetic part which British universities have been playing in the extension of higher education amongst colonial and especially African peoples. Thus South Africa is moving backwards in the very sphere in which we have been trying to advance and in which we have gained some experience.

A Nationalist might retort that, in fostering colleges for Africans, Britain has been doing no more than the Union Government intends to do. It is, of course, true that, in West Africa especially, the future universities will be mainly for Africans. But in East Africa, Makerere College is open to all races and some Europeans have already entered it. In Rhodesia, British influence, associating with liberal elements in

Central Africa, has helped to make the new college fully inter-racial. In Nairobi, the new Royal Technical College, brought into being with the help of an organization in Britain parallel to the Inter-University Council, is fully inter-racial. The beautifully sited University College of the West Indies in Jamaica, which is residential, is one of the happiest expressions of inter-racial co-operation upon a basis of absolute equality that can be found in the Commonwealth. More than this, the Asquith Commission, which laid down the policy, insisted that the new colleges should in every way be modelled upon the best which Britain had to offer in traditions, in standards and in staff, and that they should be chartered bodies, independent of state control. Staff and students mix freely socially as well as professionally and as local members of staff increase, they are fully integrated with their white colleagues.

Our Nationalist critic might still contend that it is all very well for Britain to be liberal at a distance, but that those with close experience of dealing with Africans know that they are fundamentally different and are denied by nature from entering into the heritage of Western civilization. It is upon the basis of this belief which is, of course, to label the African as inherently inferior, that attempts are being made to revive what is called Bantu culture and to piece together the shell of tribalism which the white man, in pursuit of his own economic interests, has so completely shattered. My reply to this is based upon the second experience I have had. For some twenty-five years I have been able to number Africans among my students. In recent years, as Fellow of a graduate college, these have been postgraduates. There can be few closer associations of mind with mind than this between teacher and pupil, sometimes extending over two or even three years, carried on through the medium of the weekly individual tutorial, and often supplemented by close social contact outside the study. No doctrinaire illusions about racial equality could survive this process, even if it did not have to culminate in the stern test of an examination of exacting standard.

What then has been the lesson of this experience? It is neither less nor more than the teaching of all reputable scientists, that there is no inherent difference between the intellectual capacity of the Negro and the European. It is not at all difficult in the intimate academic relationship of the tutorial system to distinguish the differences of nurture from those of nature; to recognize the struggle of the intellect to overcome the series of obstacles which history and geography have set between the African pupil and the proof of his equality. He has come out of one cultural world in order to assimilate another. His early environment and even his earlier education may have done little to help him to jump the chasm. He works in a foreign language in a foreign land. He may be short of money, cold and lonely; his health is often poor. His life is one long effort of adjustment in small things and great. His arrival at this level of education is often partly the result of accident; he is not, as for Western students, the product carefully sifted out of a whole population through the grid of an all-embracing educational system. Is it not remarkable that so many African students reach the middle standards of our own relatively favoured youth and that some even reach the upper classes of the examination list? This result reveals character as well as intellect, perseverance, self-control and great powers of adaptation. And if our critic intervenes to say that the result is often a lack of balance, even a distortion of character, the answer is that of course members of the first and second generations of pioneers in this severe test do sometimes warp under the psychological and physical strain and that they need every help and encouragement during the period. The conclusion from this is very relevant. It is that in a university with small residential colleges such as Oxford, the non-European students are greatly helped, both socially and intellectually, by mixing fully and freely in a community with their European fellow-students.

It follows from this experience, which many Europeans in South Africa who have taught Africans must share, that separation in higher education is an indefensible evil. We cannot accept the Nationalist plea that the Africans will be given equality of education in separation. It is not so much that we cannot believe that a government which in every way treats Africans as both different and inferior will find the staff and the money to provide colleges of equal standards with those of the Europeans. The separation is in itself a betrayal of the knowledge and the values we have inherited and by which, not so long ago in the historical record, we were ourselves lifted out of tribalism and enabled to develop our present wealth and culture. It is of the nature of this inheritance that it must be kept in movement, in the full light and air of the international forum, tested by criticism and enriched by exchange. It goes bad if it is locked up in a national strong-room, above all in that of a small and isolated nation. And it will be only a small portion of this endangered culture that the Nationalist government will break off and give to the poor and hungry African majority, telling them to go off and nourish themselves upon it in isolation, an isolation, moreover, which close state control will turn into something like an intellectual prison.

It is the more tragic that many members of the Dutch Reformed

Church – there are important exceptions – should be ready to twist and darken the central, golden strand in our bundle of civilized values, that of our religion. Text is bandied against text in the effort to force Christianity into a confirmation of the doctrine of racial superiority. The whole spirit of Christ's teaching and its extension by St Paul and St John is utterly contrary to such a terrible judgement upon our fellow-men and such a Pharasaic claim for ourselves as that enshrined in apartheid. This truth must apply at all levels of human life but few can be so conscious of its meaning as Christian university teachers who are trying to share with others the most difficult enterprises of the human mind and spirit. The Christian respect for the individual personality has been grafted upon the philosophic claim for the liberty of the intellect: to deny both of these is to contract out of the fellowship of Western civilization.

In a recent discussion I had with a leading Nationalist, I was told that no nation which is not endangered by a black majority has any understanding of South Africa's problem or any right to pronounce upon it. True, national policies and trends cannot be judged by blemishes and mistakes but upon the policies of governments and the more dominant national ideas upon which they are based. There is, I believe, among informed people in Britain today a very sincere attempt to understand the unique colour problem of South Africa. But, however great the difficulties, in this closely integrated world it is impossible for any nation to be wholly a law unto itself. We in Britain are concerned with the affairs of the Union through the political bond of the Commonwealth, the links of neighbourhood on the African continent, Britain's connection with the High Commission Territories and the embarrassing votes that have to be taken at U.N.O. There is also this issue of our many-sided relationships with a group of universities which may be forced into a position of outlawry from the academic citizenship. And the cause of it would be a matter of such fundamental principle that no appreciation of South Africa's special difficulties should allow any compromise. We know from our experience in Kenya and elsewhere that, for a period that may be long, it would be unreasonable to expect a premature fusion of education between tribal and ex-tribal Negroes and Europeans at the lower or even, for a time, at the middle grades of education. But these adjustments of convenience and timing and language fall away at the highest level, and nothing remains but to face the issues of principle which have been stated.

This principle is being magnificently maintained by many of our

[1957] COLONIAL SEQUENCE 1949 TO 1969

colleagues in South Africa. For them it is a matter of professional life and death and they are staking everything upon the issue while we can only watch and applaud. It will not be easy for us to decide what we can do to help and it will not be easy for them to advise us. At this eleventh hour we can still hope that the South African government will not take those final steps backwards from the position from which almost all the rest of the world is still advancing, and divorce the races at the one point where they could now meet in full equality and understanding and so perhaps save the Union from a division which may one day destroy it.

There are wider interests at stake even than those of South Africa. The very need of the Africans is their chief claim upon us. It was through no fault of theirs that their inner continent was left out of the world until this latest age. Their own past has moulded them and some of its traditions and habits may long stay with them. But for the most part they must find a new culture, and a new form of society. At present, they are asking for a share in ours, but they will only take it if it is given without reserve and with faith in their capacity to take and develop it. This refused, or even grudged, they will turn elsewhere, and there are other offers. There is hardly time in South Africa to permit this turning away. The issue is a test of the Western peoples' faith in their own civilization and in the values which prompt them to give and to take risks. The rejection of opportunity in South Africa may well affect the whole continent, with results that will reach Europe and further weaken our imperilled civilization.

The Future of the Somalis

Letter to *The Times* 16 December 1957

Sir, – Have the Government prepared their policy for the Horn of Africa? All the ingredients for an international witches' cauldron are being collected in this region and may come to the boil when Somalia is given its promised independence in 1960.

Here are some of the ingredients: (1) The political and financial unreadiness of Somalia for its new status. (2) The effects of its promotion upon the neighbouring and equally immature British Somaliland. (3) The historic imperialism of Ethiopia, which, *pace* Bandung, was the fourth colonial Power to partition Somaliland and which now, armed by the United States, has lately resumed possession of the Somalis' essential Haud grazing area. (4) The possible repercussions of any trouble in this region upon Aden. (5) The probable intervention of Egypt, already bitterly vocal on the air, in a region which she once partially and briefly occupied. (6) The still unspecified but certainly generous contribution which we can expect Russia to make to this promising brew.

Even the approach to any rational solution is beset with difficulties. In Britain the problem may appear so small and remote, so far from public comprehension, that it may become a casualty of our concentration upon our major dangers. It may suffer, as did Palestine, from a division of purpose, and responsibility between the Colonial Office, with its tradition of trusteeship, and the Foreign Office with its principle – its duty? – of *real politik*. The Somalis themselves, individually spirited and intelligent, are so divided between numerous and often mutually hostile tribes that they are unlikely to offer much constructive co-operation to their friends.

A united Somalia under international control would be the ideal settlement. It would be based on the surrender of their portions by all four colonial Powers; would help to solve the problems of finance, of grazing, and nomadism, and allow of the gradual development of the Somalis towards a viable and neutralized state. But Russia, as in 1946 with the plan put forward by Mr Bevin, is almost certain again to use her veto. The second best is for Britain, Italy and France to win American support for a plan of co-ordinated development, aimed at eventual unity and self-government, for the three maritime portions and to try to win Ethiopia to bring her indispensable interior slice into the project. This would be not only generous on her part but wise. The Somalis as a whole will always be bad neighbours to a Christian nation which, as all who have trekked in this region know, lives on her green ramparts high above one of the most dramatic natural frontiers in the world and yet claims to incorporate the bleached plains at her feet where the pastoral, Moslem Somalis from British and Italian territory must seek their grazing for several months of the year. Much light has been thrown upon the unhappy situation there by articles in your columns upon this difficult region.

1960 is not far away, and it is more than time for informed opinion in this country to urge the Government to enter into diplomatic preparations for that year. The worst of all procedures would be for Britain, which has twice been forced to evacuate her own Somaliland, to betray the still surviving trust of this people by a policy of fumbling expediency or by making isolated and irredeemable promises.

Yours faithfully

1958

The Motives for Man's Cruelties

Letter to *The Observer* 12 January 1958

This letter was part of a correspondence about man's inhumanities arising out of an article by the Rev. Michael Scott.

Sir, – The Editor of the *Islamic Review* claims that Moslems have never indulged in racial prejudice or bred a Malan or a Strijdom. It is certainly an impressive sight to see Moslems of several races and nations going in together to some cosmopolitan mosque, as, for instance, in Nairobi. But let us not indulge in a competition, historical or contemporary, in self-righteousness. It happens that I have just been re-reading about the conquest of Ethiopia by Mohammed Gran, acting in the name of God 'the most merciful'. His historian, recording the plundering and massacre of 'the idolaters', adds, 'May God have no pity upon them,' and goes on to describe the slaughter of 500 monks in a church so that 'the blood ran out of the door'.

Why do I drag in this horrid story of the sixteenth century? Not in a mere spirit of *tu quoque* or to try to take an opponent's trick with a moral trump. Mr Majid could probably over-trump with some equally pious 'crowning mercy' by our own or another nation. My purpose is to direct attention to the deeds of cruelty. They have a sickening similarity all through human history and in our newspapers: the reasons given for them are less substantial.

When any people believes it has an interest in oppressing or destroying another, it has always justified its action by whatever principle seemed appropriate at the time. There were historical reasons why Moslems did not emphasize race. But on what grounds did they deal with Armenians, Chaldeans, Assyrians, and the rest? Race, as an isolated factor, seems seldom to have been a real reason for repression, and, even as an excuse it has been going out of favour for good scientific reasons during the last half-century.

Even religion is giving ground today, to ideological justifications. In much of our world it is meritorious to destroy or proscribe capitalists, counter-revolutionaries, deviationists, imperialists, or colonizers. For Western nations, whose power over other peoples is being challenged, the objects of repression are no longer called by the almost respectable name of 'rebels', but have become 'terrorists', a name not always wholly justified by any change of methods.

It seems that we need to probe beneath the reasons men give for their actions to the basic reason which prompts them all – the ruthless self-interest of the group, whether it appears to be predominantly racial, national, religious, economic or ideological in character. Viewed in this way, the test is at the point of action, in the lack, in Schweitzer's teaching, of reverence for human life. By this criterion we need all to go down on our knees and confess the sins committed by our fathers, by ourselves or in our name and leave it to God to calculate the exact proportion of national guilt.

The evidence suggests, however, that God is more interested in individual than in communal sin. I think it was implicit in Michael Scott's article that since the Founder of the faith of Christendom preached universal love and self-sacrifice, died to demonstrate His teaching, and lives to help men to follow Him, those who bear His name and dishonour it are under the greatest condemnation.

Yours faithfully

1959

Disorders in Nyasaland: Six Questions for Britain

Letter to The Times 27 February 1959

Sir, – The disorders in Nyasaland allow those of us who questioned the imposition of federation upon that Protectorate to repeat our questions – I have six to put.

(1) What moral right had we, after ruling a people for some 60 years, to force them against their will into a federation controlled by Rhodesian Europeans?

(2) Was it not mainly in the interests of economy that the British Government insisted upon this inclusion?

(3) Is it sedition for a people to desire to remain under the British Colonial Office?

(4) How much of their remaining goodwill must be lost, how much disorder and, perhaps, bloodshed must there be, before they convince us, as the Basuto did in 1880–84, of the strength of this desire?

(5) Does the British Government intend to honour its promise, already weakened by certain concessions, written in the preamble of the federal Act that the Protectorates 'should continue, under the special protection of Her Majesty, to enjoy separate governments so long as their respective peoples so desire'?

(6) Upon what principle do we offer to lead towards full self-government the unready Somalis and the somewhat less unready Tanganyikans and deny this hope to the much more mature people of Nyasaland?

I put these questions with full sympathy for the difficult position of the Europeans of Central Africa. I believe that, at least north of the Zambesi and east of the Luangwa, it is too late to impose a political Kariba dam upon the flood of African nationalism and that it will be better in all our interests to consider these questions in 1959 rather than in 1960.

Yours faithfully

Britain's Pledges in Central Africa

Letter to *The Times* 25 April 1959

In view of the continuing problems of Central Africa, even after the dissolution of the Federation, it may be worth remembering the pledges we made to the African peoples, now broken in Rhodesia.

Sir, – We must not allow the Federal leaders either to intimidate or alienate us by threats of secession and rebellion. If the Federation is to continue – and there are strong reasons for detaching Nyasaland at least – then we must coolly judge our responsibilities.

First, our constitutional obligations. We cannot too often re-read their definition in the Federal constitution. The two protectorates 'should continue under the special protection of her Majesty, to enjoy separate governments *for so long as their respective peoples so desire*, those governments remaining responsible (subject to the ultimate authority of her Majesty's Government in the United Kingdom), for, in particular, the control of land in those territories, and for the *local and territorial political advancement of the peoples thereof*'. And the Federation should advance to 'full membership of the Commonwealth' only *'when those inhabitants so desire'*. (My italics.)

Mr Lennox-Boyd had confirmed that this makes a federal declaration of independence impossible. But too often we have seen a façade of constitutional rectitude maintained while its foundations were quietly removed from behind. Unfortunately such a process has begun here. In Central Africa last year I found that in face of challenging assertions from Salisbury, unanswered by Britain except by disturbing concessions, there was fear and doubt not only among Africans but among our overseas service. Their independent position, essential if protectorate status is not to be a sham, was being condemned even by cabinet ministers in Salisbury.

Secondly, Britain's political responsibilities. The dangers which threaten Central Africa arise from the Africans' lethal sense of humiliation as they become aware of their own poverty and political immaturity. This cannot be remedied by an immediate grant of majority rule, but only by some 10 to 20 years of whole-hearted and overt measures to hasten their advance towards a proclaimed goal of political

[1959] COLONIAL SEQUENCE 1949 TO 1969

equality. There is still a chance that the protectorate Africans might accept this training, essential for the ultimate success of the Federation, from Britain. They will certainly not accept it from Salisbury.

Yours faithfully

Divergent Views on Central Africa

Letter to The Times 6 May 1959

My continuing comment upon the handling of the Federation had provoked authoritative criticisms of my views in letters to The Times, *notably by Lord Salisbury. The main issue was the need to trust the white Federal leaders, a point emphasized by him in a reply, printed 13 May, to my letter.*

Sir, – I must reply to those points in Lord Salisbury's courteous rebuke in his letter on 29 April, and Professor Macmillan's criticism, in his letter on 28 April, which others have not answered.

First, both deprecate my whole approach. Psychology is certainly important. Rhodesian Europeans are embittered if extremist critics here play a party game in which, over there, the counters may be lives, African and European. But I disclaim anti-settler bias. Members of my family have long lived in Kenya and I gratefully remember kind hospitality in the Rhodesias. Most Europeans settled in good faith in Africa's primitive and passive highlands and I feel deeply for their anxiety in discovering that these lands are politically volcanic. Accused of over-estimating African character I reply that to have passed nights in Kikuyu country during the Mau Mau rebellion induces a realization of the savagery inherent in African discontent. But Africa's backwardness and too abrupt awakening make our inescapable problem and, being human, too much encouragement and responsibility will make them less dangerous than too much denunciation and distrust.

Secondly, Lord Salisbury accuses me of undermining confidence. But whose confidence? Africans' confidence may be restored by knowing they need not resort to violence to assert their interests. And some federal leaders may be over-confident in demanding what Africans have the constitutional right to veto. It is dangerous to agree with the violent but our history shows the greater dangers of ignoring their power or neglecting, early in the conflict, a dispassionate study of their reasons. And it is not only 'intellectuals' who are expressing doubts. Surely a

Cecil should have considered the views of many Churchmen here and also of missionaries whose great work is so tragically affected by the conflict. And there are outstanding liberals within Central Africa who also criticize federal policy.

Finally, this question of Britain's authority, generally attacked under the pejorative term 'the Colonial Office'. The department, like the people it serves, is sometimes lethargic or short-sighted. In certain practical services for Africans, Southern Rhodesia has surpassed the Protectorates, and Britain's position creates a division of authority against which young European nationalism chafes. But, in the Federal context, the division may be healthy. Southern Rhodesia's ethos and experience are peculiar to herself and cannot be stretched to cover the mainly African lands to the north. No censorships, deportations, or exclusions can insulate the Federation from Africa and the world, and the British presence can be a linking and stabilizing factor. Federal leaders should cease to divide opinion here by abusing the Colonial Office and use its indispensable authority to build up the primarily African States of the north into more equal and so more willing partners.

Yours faithfully

White Minorities in Africa

Foreign Affairs July 1959

We are becoming used to the acceleration of political movement in our world. But surely all records of the pace of change have been broken in the continent of Africa during the last few years with the sudden emergence of one state after another from colonial control, or the promise of such emergence in the near future. Whereas the period of 'colonialism' for Britain's major white and Asian dependencies could be measured in one or two centuries, her black ones, immeasurably more backward in every aspect, have run the course from annexation to independence or its threshold in little more than half a century.

As the tide of independence rises until it covers almost the whole of Africa, with some parts clearly on the edge of submergence, certain islands of European control catch the eye. The great majority of the 5,500,000 Europeans who live among the 220,000,000 'native' peoples of Africa are in the two temperate extremities, Algeria in the north,

[1959] COLONIAL SEQUENCE 1949 TO 1969

South Africa in the south. Here are long-established European populations which are determined not to allow the indigenous population to take control. Algeria is still under metropolitan rule and there the political settlement waits upon a military decision and upon the mind of General de Gaulle. In South Africa the Nationalist government seems to be sternly entrenched against the ideas and experience of nearly all the rest of the world, defying economics as it digs itself in, and is apparently bound for disaster. But not yet. The unwavering resolution of a small and lonely nation, which can see no alternative between domination and disaster, may long hold down a black majority which so far shows few signs of being competent at revolution.

The patches of African political landscape which seem to be in the most immediately equivocal position lie in the British territories between South Africa and Ethiopia. Here are small areas of white settlement, containing some 300,000 people, by no means all true settlers, scattered amongst an African population of more than 20,000,000. Will this small minority be able to control the rate of the rising flood of Africanism? Will they float buoyantly, still a secure and influential minority, even if the tide should flow over their present position? Will they be submerged? Or will they be swept back to Europe? These are not academic or distant questions. During the last few years and, especially during the last few weeks, as this is being written, we have seen conflict, both physical and political, in this region.

The purpose of this article is to endeavour, not, indeed, to offer confident answers to these difficult questions, but to put together some of the material out of which these answers must be constructed. The region is too vast and disparate for any detailed description and only generalizations and impressions can be offered. But we must at least chart its main features.

This part of Africa is no monolithic slab of the continent. It is all in the British Commonwealth, but that inclusion seems to encourage diversity rather than uniformity. The area contains six states: Kenya, Tanganyika and Uganda, Southern and Northern Rhodesia and Nyasaland, all, of course, entirely the creation of European pioneers and diplomats who pegged them out on the obscure and plastic surface of tribal Africa about 70 years ago. Each differs from the other in size and in the natural physical and human character it possessed before demarcation, while European government and economic development and, above all, European settlement have subsequently imposed new layers of difference.

Constitutionally, the territories are confusing. The first three in the list, the northern three, have each a different status. Kenya is a Colony, Uganda a Protectorate, and ex-German Tanganyika a Trust Territory. In spite of these distinctions they are administered by British governors, responsible to the Colonial Office. All three have Legislative Councils upon which local representatives of all races, elected and nominated, play an increasing part, though the official control is maintained. The three territories co-operate, mainly for purposes of administrative convenience and technical services, under a High Commission. Fears of the Kenya settler influence shown by the Africans of the two other states have thwarted attempts at any closer union.

The three territories of Central Africa also differ, perhaps even more confusingly, in constitutional status. Since 1953 they have been bound together in a Federation of a very peculiar kind. It has brought together a Colony, Southern Rhodesia, which was all but self-governing long before 1953, and two Protectorates which remain under the Colonial Office.

The distribution of land, population, immigration and wealth are shown in the statistics on the following page.

The table tells us something about the poverty of these countries; the scantiness of population but not its patchy distribution; it shows where immigrant groups are most numerous but not the historical and other factors which determine their political strength. A comparable table for West Africa would show populations of greater weight and density and also the absence of white settlement. But it would not reveal the contrast which explains the great problem of the eastern side – the much greater advancement of the West Africans due both to the higher indigenous cultural level of most of their people before European contact and the much longer span of that contact.

The political difficulties in East and Central Africa spring ultimately from the attitudes of mind of the three parties concerned: the settlers, the Africans and the British Government. True, there is an Asian element in East Africa, much larger than the European, but it has not yet acted as a major political influence.

First, the Europeans. They have been the subject of so much humanitarian or doctrinaire criticism that it is important to remember that they did not go to Africa, like the missionaries, for religious motives or, like the officials, for professional, romantic or patriotic reasons. And, unlike these groups, they committed themselves wholly to the unknown country, investing their lifelong energies, perhaps their whole capital,

[1959]

	AREA IN SQ. MILES	POPULATION 1958 EST.		REVENUE AND EXPENDITURE 1958–9 EST. (in pounds sterling)	VOLUME OF EXTERNAL TRADE 1958 (in pounds sterling)
Kenya	224,960	Eur.	64,700	R. 40,091,705	94,093,380
		African	6,080,000	E. 40,426,725	
		Asian	165,000		
		Arab	35,000		
		Other	5,700		
			6,351,000		
Uganda	93,981	Eur.	9,600	R. 21,857,216	73,391,317
		African	5,695,000	E. 26,739,677	
		Asian	58,000		
		Arab	2,100		
		Other	1,400		
			5,767,000		
Tanganyika	362,688	Eur.	21,200	R. 19,787,095	77,373,062
		African	8,788,000	E. 20,975,844	
		Asian	80,900		
		Arab	21,400		
		Other	4,100		
			8,916,000		
N. Rhodesia	288,130	Eur.	72,000	R. 15,100,772	
		African	2,250,000	E. 15,000,266	
		Other	8,400		
			2,330,400		
S. Rhodesia	150,333	Eur.	211,000	R. 19,127,000	(Total for the three territories given below)
		African	2,590,900	E. 19,663,612	
		Other	14,900		
			2,815,900		
Nyasaland	49,177	Eur.	8,600	R. 5,331,802	
		African	2,720,000	E. 5,072,278	
		Other	11,500		
			2,740,100		
Total: Central African Federation	487,640	Eur.	292,000	R. 51,441,000	293,431,397
		African	7,560,000	E. 51,300,552	
		Other	35,000		
			7,887,000		

perhaps their families, in what was often a very speculative venture. The land seemed untamed and unloved. The Africans were encountered almost entirely as very unskilled labour. Language and custom were barriers. To the urgent white employer, uninstructed in anthropology, perhaps unimaginative, the Africans seemed almost sub-human in their non-comprehension – dirty, lazy and utterly unreliable. He could see, superficially, their way of life, their pathetic agricultural scratchings, perhaps their drunkenness and witchcraft. The farmer might suffer severe loss, perhaps of valuable animals, through what would seem an African's incredible neglect or stupidity or even his stock theft.

Was it surprising that many settlers developed two convictions, one of the almost irremediable inferiority of the Africans and the other of their own mission to bring civilization into the millenial ignorance and savagery of Africa? Americans, who confront Negroes who have had two centuries or more of acculturation, and who need have no fear of submergence under a vast black majority, should understand the settlers' political and social attitudes. With time these attitudes changed as the labourers became somewhat more efficient and the employers more understanding. But only in part. Settler leaders in Kenya, for instance, in the 1920s and early 1930s, would talk of the 2,000 years it had taken for Britain to graduate in civilization. In the political sphere the settlers' very understandable sense of superiority was expressed in the demand for a monopoly of elected representation, an authoritative influence over the imperial power and then the right to succeed it. The historical precedent was close at hand in South Africa.

The second party is that of the Africans. When first annexed, the tribes could not, of course, understand what had happened to them. After the initial resistance to conquest put up by some, but by no means all the tribes, the great majority accepted their new rulers and responded actively to the deep changes imposed upon their lives. There was, after all, much that could be welcomed as good: the new peace and security; the new freedom to move over large areas; the new skills they were taught; above all, perhaps, the wonderful new goods, clothes, lamps, bicycles, tin roofs and the rest. Shut away from the outside world within a bilateral relationship between rulers and ruled, the fact of subjection to the white man was accepted as an inescapable new order.

But during the 1930s in West Africa and rather later on the eastern side, a sizable generation of Western-educated youth was coming of age. Africans had eaten of the tree of Western knowledge: the receptivity of ignorance was shattered. They now knew that in the ruling country

[1959]

there was often a difference of opinion about the rights and wrongs of their treatment. They began to read about law, history and politics. They began to find words – English words – to define the strains and pressures they had hitherto taken for granted. With the Second World War the external influences making for conscious discontent with the colonial status multiplied, while the schools in Africa turned out an increasing number who were aware of the world in which they, and indeed the Negro race as a whole, seemed to be kept in subjection and treated with indignity. This knowledge seems to act like a poison in the blood, more or less inflammatory according to temperament and circumstances. In order to find alleviation, those who suffer from it struggle for equality with other races and especially, of course, with the people who rule them. Equality of every kind – social, economic and political – is demanded and generally demanded at once.

The third participant is the British Government, that long projection of power and influence which originates in the British electorate and finds its ultimate agency in the colonial governor and his civil service. Critics of 'colonialism' tend to simplify what they condemn. They forget, firstly, that the British Government often followed up its pioneering nationals in order to control them in the interests of the indigenous peoples and, secondly, that it sometimes found it impossible to assert this control. During the 1930s British governments, extending some of the lessons learned in the increasing plans for social betterment at home, began to direct vigorous and expert services – medical, educational and agricultural – amongst the African tribes and fostered their local government. But though the Gold Coast and Southern Nigerian politicians were beginning to reveal the dimension and urgency of African hopes, the authorities generally failed to anticipate that full self-government would be demanded and promised before the half-century was over. In East and Central Africa the British Government showed that it could do little more than influence the varied situations, intensifying the African character of Uganda and Tanganyika, partially retreating before European pressure in the Rhodesias, and unable, in spite of a long series of commissions, committees and white papers, to discover a policy to solve the Kenya problem.

Here, then, were the factors of the Central and East African situation up to some ten years ago: confident and dominant British minorities in the Rhodesias and Kenya; divided and quiescent African majorities just awakening to both discontents and hopes; and a controlling British government – increasingly humane, liberal and active in African interests, but lacking in foresight and by no means in control of all the factors.

II

The present decade has seen this situation roughly shaken. The rapid evolution of the Gold Coast into Ghana, the first British Negro colony to gain independence, accompanied by quick steps towards independence by non-African colonies, has given the native leaders in East and Central Africa an intoxicating draught of confidence. They have learned in these years to reinforce their weak position by drawing upon the practical or the psychological support they have found in the outside world – the United Nations; the International Confederation of Free Trade Unions; the Bandung, Cairo and Accra Conferences; the sympathetic influences in the United States, India and elsewhere; and in the very existence of the Communist world with its military and ideological threat to their rulers, and its alternative system. What has been the impact of this upsurge upon the countries we are considering?

Let us look first at East Africa. In Tanganyika, Britain has quickly made large constitutional concessions this year to meet the pressure generated by the able African leader, Julius Nyerere. Further steps towards majority rule are being planned. The Africans had, of course, the support of the Trusteeship status, while the immigrant community was small and was much divided in race and nationality. After a vain attempt to claim parity of representation, they quickly came to terms with the Africans. There will be no racial conflict here. But the British Government must have acted with secret misgivings. Tanganyika has far fewer of the qualifications for nationhood than Ghana. It is a large and poor country, with an ill-distributed population and inadequate communications, while its brief period of existence as a state under European tutelage has been divided between two nations and interrupted by a destructive war in the territory. Its leaders must bring themselves to accept much help if they are to make an ordered and prosperous unity, still more a democracy, of such a country.

In Uganda, the dynamic and liberal governorship of Sir Andrew Cohen showed British rule in its most positive response to the new forces at work in Africa. But even he came up hard against Uganda's main obstacle to the advance of the Protectorate towards full self-government: the great pride, wealth and self-sufficiency of the Kingdom of Buganda. Its Kabaka and chiefs, tenacious of their ancient and highly developed kingdom, unique in East Africa, refuse to join in the largely elected Legislative Council through which the British Government is trying to foster unity and political experience among tribes of very diverse culture and advancement. But the policy is clear. Britain has declared Uganda to be 'primarily an African State' on the road to self-government and no European settler interest complicates the future or need alarm the Africans of this compact, well-watered country. The Asians, the commercial community, are, however, being threatened by African antagonism, shown this year in an attempted boycott of 'foreign' goods, and they have grave fears for their future.

In Kenya there is the same story of recent and rapid African advance. The European settlers have lately accepted, some of them with fear and reluctance, the increase of African members, and *elected* members, in the legislature. Equal opportunities have been opened in the Civil Service; and equal access to hotels and a host of other measures for African betterment in town and country have marked the years since the end of the Mau Mau movement. But the African members, under the uncompromising leadership of Tom Mboya, have lately been refusing any collaboration so long as European settlers still retain what the Africans regard as a numerically disproportionate position in the Legislative and Executive Councils. Mr Mboya has drawn heavily upon external sources for support. By his activities in Accra, in the United States, and as a labour leader in close touch with Transport House in Britain and the I.C.F.T.U. headquarters in Brussels, as well as by his wide travels, he has built for himself an international status.

In April of this year the European leader, Mr Michael Blundell, resigned from his position as Minister for Agriculture, a government nomination, and has thrown himself into the storms and cross-currents of party politics in order to try to lead his own community towards participation in a truly multi-racial government. He has advocated a number of liberal measures, including a movement away from tribal exclusiveness, African or European, in the holding of land – hitherto the 'White Highlands' have been sacrosanct – and even an experiment in multi-racial secondary education. These proposals mark the abandonment of the old aims of complete white social and political superiority. Inevitably his own right wing is indignant.

Will the African leaders respond or will they reject all compromise and demand at once the absolute control which the 'undiluted democracy' they claim must give to their numbers? A few days after Mr Blundell's dramatic action the Colonial Secretary made the statement, long demanded by the Africans, that in Kenya, as in other dependencies, Britain aimed 'to build a nation based on parliamentary institutions'. With this ultimate prospect at last recognized, it is possible that the Africans will recognize their need, at least for a period, of cooperation with those Europeans and Asians whose stake in the life of the Colony and whose civic and economic capacity are so much greater than their numbers. But the psychology of the Africans makes it difficult for them to achieve patience or agree to any compromise based on such a claim. The answer may soon be known.

The Africans have reason to pause. They are still deeply divided by differences of tribe and of way of life. The two main groups are concentrated in two areas distant from each other. Pastoral and partly Nilotic tribes are scattered thinly in the northern and southern fringes. The coast, divided by a dry area from the more populated highlands, has known a long Arab settlement. The larger commercial centres, especially Mombasa and Kisumu, are more Asian than European or African. While it is true that African agriculture has made great strides in the last five to ten years, largely through a campaign of betterment financed by Britain and by a policy of consolidating scattered African holdings, yet the skilled farming of the European highlands is still an all-important element in the economy. The needs of the country have far outrun its revenues. Without large financial as well as military aid from Britain the Mau Mau rebellion would have utterly ruined the country. In other words, Kenya, as a state and an economy, is a precarious structure. It is difficult to imagine the Africans in control in the near future. Even if they could supply enough competent individuals at the top, they could hardly create sufficient unity and party organization to give them the necessary steady democratic support from below. And though each year sees more Kenya-born Europeans and even more Asians who either would not or could not leave the country, there are many others who would not remain under an unstable and inefficient government but who, at great cost to themselves and to the colony, would take their skill and their capital elsewhere.

The greatest hope for the interval between the renunciation of settler ambitions and the capacity of Africans to take over the major share of power may rest with the British Government. The African leaders have always distinguished clearly between imperial power and settler power and have admitted their need of sustained help at the first. This Mr Lennox-Boyd has now promised. By the sincerity and energy of its actions in advancing both African opportunities, and also the education

[1959] COLONIAL SEQUENCE 1949 TO 1969

to use them, the Government might retain their confidence and at the same time safeguard the interests of the minorities. Both sides might in this period learn to cease putting race before any other consideration – an achievement well established in the West Indies.

III

The future of Kenya is cloudy enough, especially for the immigrant races. But at least there are not the materials there for bitter and enduring racial conflict. In Central Africa the Europeans are in a much stronger position to struggle for their supremacy. Their headquarters are really, as the statistics show, in Southern Rhodesia. Their community is not isolated in the heart of Negro tropical Africa, as are the Kenya settlers. They are the extension of the strongest and most deeply-rooted block of European settlement in Africa. Penetrating northwards from South Africa in the last years of the nineteenth century under the stimulus of Cecil Rhodes and his British South Africa Company, and heavily defeating the powerful Matabele tribe, they were from the first in a much stronger position, towards both the local Africans and the British Government, than the Kenya settlers. With the later development of copper still further north, thousands of Europeans, many of them Afrikaners, were drawn to the string of mines running up to the Belgian Congo. In 1923 the Company's control ended; the Rhodesians voted in a referendum against joining South Africa and obtained from Britain virtually complete internal 'self-government' as a white minority. Northern Rhodesia, with its fewer whites, remained a Protectorate under the Colonial Office.

These few thousand white men scattered about the immense areas north and south of the Zambesi felt anxious from time to time about their status and their future. Shut off from the sea by Portuguese East Africa, their economies narrowly based upon a few primary products, they considered intermittently whether unity would strengthen them.

Passing over the years of uncertainty, let us examine the motives which led to the formation of the present Federation in 1953. First, the Rhodesians, being mainly of British stock, were increasingly alienated by the Union of South Africa because of the anti-British bias of its Nationalist Party government and its repressive native policy. Second, they hoped, with wider unity, to rationalize and advance their economy and attract more settlers and capital. Third, they felt a nationalist urge to create a new, large self-governing nation. Fourth, watching uneasily the political stirrings in Africa, and suspicious of Britain's tendency to what they regarded as premature surrenders to African nationalism, they wanted full control over their own African policy. Britain, upon her side, saw that a weak and isolated Southern Rhodesia must one day be absorbed by South Africa. Northern Rhodesia could not long escape the influence, and there might then be an extension of Afrikaner nationalism and apartheid almost to the equator. The alternative was to build up a large dominion, loyal to Britain and the Commonwealth, in which Britain would retain sufficient control to support the liberal elements in the Rhodesias and promote a great new experiment in racial partnership. Mainly upon British initiative, the isolated little Protectorate of Nyasaland, where, with a few European settlers, 2,400,000 Africans live poor and crowded in glorious mountain and lacustrine scenery, was added to the two Rhodesias.

The Federation was built upon an insecure foundation of compromise and conflict. The compromise was between Rhodesian ideas of partnership and those of Britain, between a distant and inconstant liberalism and the clear-cut determination of the colonists (in spite of the concessions they were obliged to make in order to get British agreement to the Federation) to maintain white supremacy for as far ahead as they could see. There was compromise, too, in retaining the status of Northern Rhodesia and Nyasaland as Protectorates linked with an all-but-independent Colony in an all-but-independent Federation. But there was conflict enshrined in the very wording of the Federal Act which held out to Europeans the prospect of going forward to full self-government and yet made any changes dependent upon the will of all the inhabitants.

The Federal constitution is, indeed, an elaborate structure designed to give the African educated élite a limited representation in the Federal Parliament and the right to an 'ordinary' vote alongside Europeans. At present this group consists of a relatively small enfranchised minority, while the great mass of the poorer and more backward Africans are checked, by the grant of a 'special' vote of less representative value, from swamping the polls. The northern Africans, and especially those of Nyasaland, are fearful of permanent subordination to the European minority, while the advances of fellow Africans, and especially of Ghana, have reinforced their desire for independence. The recent disorders in Nyasaland have tragically revealed the tensions which underlie the Federation and have aroused anxious debates in Central Africa and Britain.

[1959] COLONIAL SEQUENCE 1949 TO 1969

At the moment the problems seem grave and all but insoluble. The Europeans of the Rhodesias cannot hand themselves and the governments and the economies they have built up to an African majority that is wholly unready for such a different responsibility. Can they succeed in their plan of at once encouraging and yet controlling the flow of educated Africans to the ranks of responsible citizenship upon Rhodes's oft-quoted dictum of 'Equal rights for all *civilized* men'? Impatient African leaders, resenting any gradualism imposed upon their advance, and knowing their strength lies mainly in numbers, claim 'full democracy' and encourage the intimidation of moderates who collaborate individually with the four governments. One hope lies in the remaining faith the northern Africans have in their direct contact with Britain as a distant and impartial power which has encouraged African political advance elsewhere. Although this means the continuation of a difficult division of authority within the Federation, with British public and party opinion playing upon a delicate situation, this may still be the best way of gaining a period of perhaps ten years in which the Protectorate Africans may be helped to advance in political experience, while profiting from the economic development of the Federation. But no distant observers should underrate the grave difficulties which, whether in the 'all black' or the 'mixed' territories of East and Central Africa, lie between them and their ordered and prosperous advance into nationhood.

Christianity and Colonialism

Address given at Thessalonica in July 1959 to the Conference of The World Council of Churches on Rapid Social Change

Our discussions in this Conference have been so full that when I was asked to deal at the end of our proceedings with any point that had been left out, it seemed that we had covered every imaginable aspect of our subject. Yet there is, perhaps, one factor which has been assumed rather than defined, or even mentioned. It is the obstacle you see to most of the reforms you have proposed, and the target of most of your criticisms, or, at the least, the inert mass that you see lying across the path we want our fellow-men to take. This X factor is government, the colonial government. This subject is most directly relevant, of course, to the remaining dependent areas, but 'colonialism' still influences the thoughts and often the policies of the newly independent. Since, however, Africa is the region in which there are still the larger number of the remaining colonies, that is the part of the world of which I will speak. And, mainly, of British Africa.

I shall be accused in what I am going to say of being an apologist for imperialism. I run the risk of being stuck as full of the arrows of your criticism as that unfortunate Saint Sebastian whom the old masters painted so often – too often for my taste. What I want to try to do is to 'place' government in the perspective of our subject, that of countries experiencing 'rapid social change'. After all, if we are deciding to reform something we should try to understand its nature. Even if we only want to remove it we will still need to measure its size and weight. It so happens that in this Conference there are, I think, only two of us whose experience has been in the sphere of government, certainly of colonial government. Not that I am in the *service* of any government! I have often been a victim of the mistakes and faults of my own, but in my work I have had opportunities of seeing colonial government from the inside as well as the outside.

It is not easy today to get a balanced view of colonial government. There are three reasons for this. The first is that in this 'one world' in which we live, with all its pressing dangers, with new nations coming into existence almost monthly and the need to understand a vast range of problems and regions, it is difficult enough for citizens to master even their contemporary settings. Yet full understanding of any national or international question requires knowledge of its historical background. This is certainly true of Africa. The key to the African situation lies in the amazing historical fact that although Africa lies so close to Europe, and though its northern margin was part of the ancient world, the great solid block of tropical, middle Africa lay almost completely shut away from the rest of the world until some sixty to seventy years ago. It was then that modern Europe, with all the power of its new science and equipment, penetrated this lonely Africa with great power and speed. This trick played by geography and history has thrown a strain upon poor human nature almost greater than it could bear. It had a literally shattering effect upon the societies most directly exposed to the new influence, but all of them have suffered from the process of disintegration which Professor de Vries analysed so realistically in his opening address – a disintegration on one face of the coin, a release on the other. On the European side the helplessness of Africa was a great temptation. We must face the fact of the immense gap between the cultures which were brought so suddenly into intimate relationship. This does not mean, I need hardly say, that we accept any *inherent* differences between races. I think that Christians, at least *some* Christians, with our Lord and St Paul to teach them, were led by their faith to believe in the potential equality of all men before the scientists decided to confirm this belief. That Christendom as a whole was slow to act upon this belief was explained, though not justified, by the poverty of most of middle Africa and the unintelligibility to the outsider of its thousand tribal societies. Since that first contact an ever-increasing number of Africans have entered through education and experience into the world community and external influences, political, religious, scientific and economic, are hastening the transformation of the continent. But in view of this long isolation and of the scanty and uneven distribution of people and resources, especially in Eastern and Central Africa, it must be a long time before these regions can draw level with the other continents. The pace of advance will depend, of course, upon the alliance between internal energy and order with external investment both of capital and of skilled service.

These hard facts of history have been emphasized because there is a tendency on the part both of Africans and Europeans to blame the other side not for some, but for *all*, the strains and disharmonies of their contact. It should surely be a reconciling thought that perhaps the greater part of these can be ascribed to harsh circumstances and not to wilful human error. Admittedly by annexing large areas when they could not have the knowledge or the resources to carry the burden successfully, and sometimes by grave mistakes or sins, the colonial powers added an extra margin of responsibility to those which were inherent in the unequal contact.

Annexation was, however, difficult to avoid. Once modern Europe had opened the locked doors into the interior, a return to the tribal *status quo* was no longer possible, and, in the absence at that time of any effective international agencies, the issue lay between the controlled impact of government and the uncontrolled impact of external forces. The period of colonial rule in Africa has been brief in comparison with that in Asia. Development, depending upon full administrative control, had hardly begun before the outbreak of the First World War. This was followed by a serious slump and a second World War. This should be remembered when the achievements of colonial governments are judged by the new standards of the urgent welfare state with little allowance for past handicaps of time, concepts and resources.

A second difficulty in gaining a balanced view of colonial government is harder to define though it springs out of the first. It affects us especially in such a gathering as this. Our sympathy is with the governed – we want to understand their problems, to enter, belatedly it may be, into their minds. And they are mostly in that phase of their history when the very dynamic of their assertion and rejection almost forces them into an attitude of wholesale condemnation towards their governments. Their political leaders especially, because Africa offers them so little positive material out of which to create the needed spirit of unity and nationalism, seem forced to rely almost wholly on the use of negative factors. The pace of events in our world affects Africa: there is no waiting for the slow, natural maturing of a national movement and in the methods of haste are sometimes those of intimidation, mental as well as physical. In this full swing of the reaction against 'colonialism', in which most of the nations of the world, for various reasons, support the African view, there is little room for discrimination. The balance of the good and bad, of the useful and the destructive, both as between periods and territories, is too easily ignored. Today in the tragedy of Algeria and the grave mistakes, as I see them, of British policy in Central Africa, the relatively peaceful and successful progress of other regions towards national fulfilment tends to be forgotten. And now that Africans have left the age of tribal innocence and eaten of the world's tree of knowledge, though the balance of responsibility may still rest with the colonial powers, are there not standards of conduct, of veracity, of wisdom and forbearance that we must long to see displayed on the African side of the movement for emancipation as well as upon the colonial? We in our desire to understand and to help those who suffer from a sense of frustration or indignity are tempted to agree with their views, *all* their views, or at least to refrain from dissent or criticism at any point lest it cost us their confidence. I know the temptation so well myself. Yet is it not a subtle form of mental superiority not to be wholly frank, not to risk disagreement or offence by stating where necessary what we believe to be true whether about historical causes or contemporary situations?

I spoke of *both* sides in the colonial situation. But is not this dualism already beginning to pass? The end of the colonial power is in sight. The three major colonial powers in Africa have declared their objective. All French colonies except Algeria are free to choose independence or membership of the French Community. The Belgian government has declared the aim of freedom for the Congo, though in that vast region

[1959] COLONIAL SEQUENCE 1949 TO 1969

the fulfilment of the promise may be slow. Britain has already recognized the independence of the huge territory of the Sudan and the small one of Ghana. Nigeria will take her freedom in 1960 and become Africa's most populous state. Uganda is being coaxed unto unity in the face of African divisions. Tanganyika has started on the road to freedom. In Kenya, as a white-settled country, the way forward is complicated but the corner has surely been turned in the last few months. Only in Central Africa does the future seem to be in doubt, and I believe that the present troubles in Nyasaland will lead to a series of steps, difficult and slow though the way may be, towards African self-government in the two northern territories.

These tendencies must be estimated for they affect our studies here. Among members of this Conference there has been general agreement that the growth of nationalism in countries of rapid social change is to be welcomed as an expression of freedom and of individual and group personality. We assume that colonial power is something to be liquidated in the briefest possible time. But even if we believe that in this progress the interests of the governed are alone to be considered, these must be affected by the way in which emancipation is carried through. The peoples have much to gain from an orderly transfer of power in which the constitution and the economy are taken over in such a way as to preserve their structure from damage and to ensure their unbroken development. Those skilled services, technical and educational, built up over decades, must not be torn up by the roots: the new agencies must be carefully grafted upon them.

These operations are not easy. The transfer of government is a most hazardous process. The states, their economies and the boundaries within which they have been built have been the recent creation of the colonial power. Although Africans in the British east and central territories of which we are mainly thinking have been entering the lower ranks of the civil services and of industry, there is still an inadequate number of trained, and still more, of experienced, persons to conduct all the affairs of a modern state. We are not now considering whether their apprenticeship could have been begun earlier but what can best be done during the next few years. Each of these years, if good use is made of them, will see an extension of responsibility and also a new and larger generation of men and women coming out of the universities or other educational institutions. It would be a difficult but valuable achievement if nationalist leaders could see that they have even more to gain from an ordered programme of advance to independence than have their rulers. Nigeria is a valuable example. Large and composite, it will be no easy ship of state to launch into independence. But the two or three years of careful and co-operative preparation which has been achieved by government and people should provide the best possible conditions for the great event next year.

How can such useful co-operation be more widely achieved? We have never forgotten in this Conference that the young nations are made up of individuals. We should equally remember that governments, even colonial governments, are composed of human beings. And during the period of the transfer of power they are human beings working under very great strain. They have to bring their work, both as a national task and as that of their individual careers, to an unexpectedly early end. They have to cling to their goodwill and high standards of integrity while perhaps they are being criticized, even maligned, both by the people amongst whom they are working and by the world in general. They have to try to guide and also to control the turbulent forces of nationalism. They may have to make grave and instant decisions to preserve law and order. They need encouragement for good acts as well as criticism for bad ones. The agents of reconciliation above all should be hard at work making it possible for all the staff needed to carry on the conduct of the state to remain and serve the new government for so long as they are needed. This is one of the hardest changes an official can experience and only those with a great sense of vocation will undertake it. There are leading Sudanese today who know how much their country lost by allowing the sudden exodus of their British officials.

Christians could do much to help towards an ordered and amicable act of emancipation. By so doing they would help not only the new nation but also their churches. These suffer greatly when nationalism becomes embittered or distorted. Those who suffer most of all are the thoughtful, educated and often Christian Africans who are torn between the standards of conduct laid down by their faith and their desire to be at one both in mind and in act with their own people at their moment of crisis. And since it is the presence of white colonists which mainly causes the government to delay that surrender of power which it makes more readily where these hostages to the future are not present, it may also be a Christian duty to understand *their* fears and consider their interests and to act as a reconciling influence, interpreting the one side to the other. They might thus make it possible for some of these colonists to remain as citizens and to incorporate their wealth both of experience and of capital in the new state.

[1959]

I may be wrong – it is difficult to generalize even about Britain's remaining African colonies – but I have the impression that British governments are a little bewildered by the support – in some instances the very new support – which the Churches are now giving to the forces of nationalism. Only yesterday it seemed that in the sphere of education at least there was a close co-operation with governments in the interests of the peoples. It may well be, especially in some regions, that an increasing disagreement between Church and State is inevitable, and is healthy. It is certainly not new as I thought Dr Kiano suggested, in his speech the other night. In Uganda and in Nyasaland, for instance, the churches, whose missionaries went out in the service of the people long before the European state arrived, have certainly not always accepted government views in the political sphere. In Kenya from the early 1920s, it was Dr Oldham, that great but most self-effacing Christian statesman, and the Archbishop of Canterbury, in alliance with Lord Lugard and others in England, and with the churches in the Colony, who protested long and effectively against injustice to Africans in matters of labour and land.

In this Conference, perhaps the latest representative evidence of Christian opinion, we are declaring ourselves wholeheartedly, shall I say urgently, in favour of the independence of Colonial peoples. Where members of British governments, and especially, perhaps, senior members – and these are the men who have the power to apply the brake excessively, even dangerously – are out of sympathy with this urgency, is it not partly our fault? Are not these men of authority somewhat cut off from the influences which move us and the ideas we generate? Power, especially power held over another people, tends to isolate its holders. Some officials live in remote and lonely districts. Do visiting Christians, especially the non-British, call upon governors and their staffs as well as upon their own opposite numbers? Do the churches abroad direct their pastoral care sufficiently to members of governments, and discuss their ideas with them? If it is better for all concerned that colonial rulers should hand over their power under the pressure of ideas rather than of agitation and virulence then it is important that the kind of ideas we have generated here with the help of Africans and of those who have graduated out of the colonial status should be shared as widely as possible. I would therefore venture to suggest that, not only in the colonies but also in the home country, more contact could be made with officials and also with those who represent industry and settlement. Except as regards the position of European and Asian minorities and the need for bases, I do not believe that Britain has now any important interest which inhibits her from emancipating her colonies except fears for the economic and political liability of the potential nation itself. Fears and misunderstandings exist, especially a failure on the part of rulers to recognize the psychological and, indeed, spiritual elements in new nationalism and on the part of the ruled to understand the genuine doubts and difficulties of the governments. These are the factors which further complicate the already dangerous process of emancipation. Would it not be possible for the World Council of Churches, as a further stage in the project which has brought us here from all over the world, to plan a further conference, perhaps in Britain, which should bring together Christians from these other groups of which I have spoken. These are at least as deeply concerned as ourselves in building constructive relationships at the deepest level of understanding, not only on the eve but also on the morrow of independence.

Hazards of Mr Macmillan's 'Wind of Change' Visit to Africa

Letter to *The Times* 5 December 1959

Mr Macmillan's programme allowed just over a week in Salisbury.

Sir, – The Prime Minister's visit to Central Africa is a tribute to the importance of the problem he goes to study. But the very novelty of his expedition must raise questions. In general a Prime Minister does not attempt to master the intricacies of his colleagues' tasks, especially the numerous and exotic responsibilities of the Colonial Office.

Central Africa faces us with one of the most involved and morally perplexing decisions the colonial empire has ever presented and the heart of the difficulty is to assess the strength and nature of African opposition to federation, especially in Nyasaland.

All the more determined opponents are, and have long been, in prison or detention, untried, divided from each other, cut off, as now appears, even from their British friends and advisers, and their party proscribed. How then will Mr Macmillan be able to measure for himself the strength of the indignation and sense of betrayal which impels their party, and weigh it against the many opposing estimates which will be offered to him, some of them by those who have an interest, conscious or unconscious, political or professional, in minimizing its significance?

The Africans' greatest difficulty at this stage is in communicating, perhaps even in defining, the deep conflict of fears and hopes which inflames them. It is often their despair of conveying their side of an issue, which they feel is weighted against them by the clever and powerful Europeans, which tempts them to violence as the only means of demonstrating the strength of their opinions.

At this critical moment the Colonial Secretary (Mr Maudling), though known to be a man of strong and open mind, is new to his office and is not himself visiting the region at present. The Monckton Commission has been so composed that it is unlikely to win the confidence and co-operation of the African leaders, especially as it has failed to win the membership of the party they regard at this moment as their better friends. The Africans will fear that the Prime Minister, who is regarded as a friend of Sir Roy Welensky, will return to Britain from his first brief visit to their country believing himself to understand what they may feel they have been unable to express. If so, their doubts may thus turn to despair.

Let us not forget how often, and at such cost of time, money, goodwill, dignity, and even life, in the face of our long historical experience, and because of our temperamental distaste for emotion in politics, we have failed to measure the force of young nationalisms. Or how blind we may be, as citizens of a welfare state in which the standard of living seems to be the prime object of our political parties, to recognize that other people may put non-economic purposes first.

We may be sure that Mr Macmillan is aware of the difficulties which confront him. But his journey is not a private enterprise, and it is justifiable to emphasize in advance some of its public hazards.

Yours faithfully

1960

The Administration of Enfranchisement

Letter to the *Manchester Guardian* 5 January 1960

My colleague, the late Professor Vincent Harlow, was my co-signatory for this letter.

Sir, – The acceleration of the movement towards colonial independence has shown up a serious defect in Britain's equipment to handle the problems of transition. Anyone who is closely connected with problems of staffing and providing services to territories emerging into independence knows that at this heady moment of transition they are offered an extremely rickety bridge between the Colonial Office and the Commonwealth Relations Office.

All planning has to be done under the impending stroke of the Treasury axe. This will fall roughly at a given, or even a speculative date, and perhaps present the new nation, not a wealthy unit, with a bill for its share of any continuing expenses, an experience which may well prompt it to prefer to look elsewhere for any further help. Certainly, for the acute sensitivity of young independence perfect discretion is needed. But so is expert knowledge of its needs and how best, on a basis of formal equality, to meet them.

How wasteful therefore to allow the long-accumulated experience of the Colonial Office, with its historic tradition of service, to be abruptly cut off just at the same time as far too many officers of the Colonial Service are packing their bags for the voyage home! Is it beyond the capacity of a nation which prides itself upon its empirical genius for administration (though it has not always succeeded in curing departmental separatism) to remedy this damaging process before it is too late – and that means very soon?

The Commonwealth will continue to need three things from Britain. First, a centre – not necessarily and for all time *the* centre – for intra-Commonwealth consultation and co-operation. Secondly, the continuing administration of the remaining smaller dependencies. Thirdly – and this is the new need – the provision of aid and services which the recently independent territories cannot and would not accept from the Colonial Office as it is at present constituted, and which may be as much needed as a contribution to international as to national plans of assistance.

The inclusion of these three kinds of service within the walls of one department would not only avoid the embarrassments and dislocations of a sudden transfer from one office to another but would, for the first time, enable the wealthier nations of the Commonwealth to join easily and effectively with Britain in assisting the still dependent territories. Above all, following the strong recommendation of the Public Accounts Committee, this inclusion would allow the retention of the best brains and experience of the Colonial Office. This is vital not only for the future but for the present for, as it is, an almost impossible burden is being thrown upon this department, that of bringing its long task to a series of critical fulfilments while at the same time it is in a state of gradual dissolution.

Yours faithfully

The Psychology of African Nationalism

Optima March 1960

The political shape of Africa has been changing so rapidly in the last five years, with the pace accelerating during the last two, that Africa has at last caught the attention even of our distracted and endangered world. Interest is naturally concentrated upon the explosive force that is changing the political scenery as dramatically as the natural forces that produced the great rifts, mountains and lakes of this continent of extremes. But at this early stage in its appearance, African nationalism is still in a molten, plastic stage, and any opinions upon it must be offered as very provisional.

Nationalism is a protean word into which each of us reads his own historical or contemporary ideas. Some writers, despairing of an exact definition, conclude that, where a number of people make or accept a state within a given area, that is a nation. A variety of forces are seen to assist in welding the people together for this purpose and giving strength and durability to their association. Chief amongst these are common history, customs, language, religion and, at least in large measure, environment and way of life. While nations exist which lack at least one of these ingredients, the older nations have, in the course of centuries, enormously strengthened and enriched the common elements of their life, and, especially when seen from the outside, are judged to have developed something like a national character.

By re-stating these obvious truths we realize that most of the potential African Negro nations lack every one of these components of nationalism except common land, and even this factor shows exceptional features. In British colonial Africa – to which this article will be mainly confined – the population was divided into hundreds, by some calculation of units into thousands, of independent tribes. The colonial frontiers within which, for the most part, Africans are aspiring to create nations, generally enclose large numbers of these tribes of varying size and character. Some of the larger of these so-called tribes lack any political unity, though their peoples may be very close to each other in customs and language, but most territories enclose groups which are sharply distinct in both, and may have a long history of conflict with each other. There may be the deep ethnic and linguistic distinctions which divide Bantu from Nilotic. Upon the earlier religious distinctions found almost everywhere within these territories between Islam and the manifold pagan religions there will have come the further addition of Christianity. Common history, as distinct from misty tribal legend, is rare. Where it exists, as in parts of West Africa, it is very seldom a record of sustained unity for any group that could be classified as a nation.

The Asian dependencies showed large contrasts with the African. They had their divisions, their political weakness and, relatively to the modern West, their poverty. But they had populations which possessed large cultural and linguistic unity, even though they were often intermingled with other groups. These peoples had the pride that comes from a long history, a highly developed art, an ancient literature and famous and widespread religions of the book. It may be said that the origin of most nations could be traced back to congeries of tribes which were welded into unity through the centuries by conquest, external pressures and other forces. The difference between these older nations and those coming into being in middle Africa lies in the time factor. In Africa, the step from tribe to nation and from foreign rule to democratic independence is being taken within a very few years with conscious intention.

[1960]

Denied so many of the things which have given birth and nourishment to nationalism elsewhere, Africans, it seems, are obliged to draw upon one main source. This is their sense of humiliation upon realizing their own retarded position among the peoples of the world. The political weakness resulting from their isolation implies, as the scientists now agree, no inherent inferiority but it allowed them to become the world's main source of slaves and, in modern times, brought them into quick subjection to European nations. Asians share in the Africans' sense of humiliation in some measure – was it not Mr Nehru who added the fourth freedom 'from contempt'? – but their sources of pride and their materials for unity assuage the hurt. African nationalism – we must use the word for convenience if not with exactitude – should be seen in its earlier stages as the sum of the sense of indignity felt by individuals. The humiliation has not been felt, with one or two possible small exceptions, in the context of anything that could be called a nation. It has been experienced by Negro Africans not only separately but also as members of a race, a situation underlined because that race, in colour and form, had such very distinctive features. We may contrast the long subjected Greeks or Poles who could feel as a nation the shame of their status but who, as individuals, could feel the equals or the superiors of their rulers while they had no sense of racial inferiority or, indeed, of race. This contrast needs emphasis because some African propagandists, and those who have accepted their view, often talk as though the movements for independence in Africa were those of nations demanding no more than a return to a status of which they had been deprived.

It was, indeed, just because Africa was encountered in its tribal stage by the powerful nations of modern Europe that, for the most part, its annexation was so easy; and, it might be said, so unavoidable. Here and there a strong tribe, which like the Ashanti, the Zulu, or the Basuto, possessed in microcosm some of the elements of a nation, would put up a stiff resistance. But most of the tribes quickly accepted European rule as part of an irresistible order, one which brought many benefits, above all peace, and exciting novelties, railways and roads, lamps, bicycles, ploughs, new foods and crops and all that could be acquired and experienced in town and city. For the ruling classes, traditional or created, it brought a new strength and security of status and new forms of wealth and power. For many years after annexation, though there was much bewilderment, revolts were very few, and there does not *appear* to have been much sense of indignity at being ruled. It was not until a small minority, through their attainment of the higher levels of Western education, and above all through travel, came to understand something of the world at large and of their own place in it that the spell of acceptance began to be broken. Intoxicated by the wine of these new ideas, and smarting, perhaps, from some experiences of the colour bar in Europe, and especially in Britain, the young African would return after some years to his own country. He would see its poverty and subjection with new eyes, and he was now ready to believe and to preach the idea that only by self-government could Africans escape from personal humiliation and win equality of status in a world of which they were at last becoming aware. This purpose had its adherents much earlier in West than in East Africa. The writer, in studying African affairs and visiting Africa in the ten years before the Second World War, could mark its rapid growth in the minds of Gold Coast and Nigerian students in Britain, and in the towns of the West Coast and the Sudan. Observations in the thirties showed that the numbers of those whose education had reached the stage of world consciousness was still small, and the masses outside the few towns on or near the coast seemed to be unaware that their status was, as the young Press was beginning to declare, a humiliating slavery. But the next ten war and post-war years saw a concentration of events and influences that spread the consciousness of 'colonialism' as an evil, and raised hopes, especially along the West Coast and in the Sudan, that its supersession in Asia would be followed soon in Africa.

The view that African political consciousness is bred mainly from an individual reaction against an inferiority of status as a member of a race and not of a nation seems to explain some of the characteristics of African movements for self-government, especially in their early stages.

First, most basic and most obvious, comes the question of the area within which each of these young nationalisms has so far operated. The annexing powers marked out their boundaries upon the map of Africa in arbitrary fashion, very often in the chancelleries of Europe, before most of the regions concerned had been fully explored, still less demarcated on the ground. Yet, after not much more than half a century of European rule which, until very recent years, had done little to develop unity amongst the tribes thus enclosed, most of the African leaders find themselves obliged to begin the building of their nations within these boundaries. Doubtless, in time, the attempt will be made to re-draw frontiers more in accordance with the character and wishes of the peoples – the French colonies and Ghana are already experimenting in this way – but the point being made here is that there was a lack of any larger proto-national groups which could at once, at the very prospect of freedom, draw attention to their sense of unity.

This basic lack leads on to the second feature of African nationalism, and largely helps to explain it. This is the character of the leadership. In Africa, the general quiescence and passivity of the tribally divided masses under foreign rule has meant that leaders have arisen to create a movement rather than that a movement has thrown up a leader. The question arises at once as to why almost no traditional authorities have come forward as nationalists. It might have been expected that the almost universal and deep-rooted institution of chieftainship would have supplied, as it were, ready-made leaders. But the chiefs were chiefs of tribes, or of something even smaller than those more sizeable groups which that rather indeterminate word is generally used to describe. In most British territories, under the principles of indirect rule, chieftainship had been deliberately accepted, strengthened and developed in the sphere of local government. Where the chief was powerful and the group was large and coherent, and especially where it faced special dangers, there has been some tendency for an embryonic tribal nationalism to look to the chief for leadership. Part, at least, of the Ashanti people for a brief period hoped to build up their old kingdom under their Asantehene as a federal unit in order to preserve its distinction within the new Ghana. The three High Commission territories, dominated by fear of the overshadowing Union of South Africa, have naturally clung to their chiefs as symbols of continuity and identity. The Baganda, for all their small number, had perhaps more of the features of nationhood than most tribes of British Africa – a long history, a strong monarchical tradition, a ruling class, something very like a civil service, a great tribal unity and pride and, relatively to African standards, a prosperous economy. Here the new spirit of assertion tended to find a centre in the chief, the Kabaka, with resultant complications.

In most parts of Africa, however, chieftainship is tending to wither at the first breath of a national movement. Against most British expectations the impressive Indian princely states, expressive of autonomy and rooted in separatism, melted away before the nationalist movement. The African chieftainships are rooted in tribalism, and represent the principle of division; the nationalist must, therefore, set to work to destroy at least their political content. African chiefs were mostly much less autocratic and elevated than most of the Indian princes, but they suffered even more than these from being not only associated with, but even integrated within, the ruling power. As its agents in day-to-day administration they merged their own traditional authority with the new, irresistible colonial government. This partnership, which has to its credit some forty years or more of economical and fairly effective local government, tends to be automatically dissolved by the onset of self-government, leaving the chiefs, in the eyes of the new leaders, more or less tainted by the association. In the Sudan, in Ghana and in Nigeria, there has been perplexed debate about the positions of chiefs in the new situation, and a debate on 19 March last year in Nigeria's Western Region House of Assembly showed minds torn between their lingering respect for the social and customary status of the chiefs and doubts as to whether they could, or should, play any part in politics and administration in the new democratic order. Where chiefs were no more than agents appointed by the government, as in Kenya, they have not even the aura of tradition to protect them from the bitter antagonism of the new leaders, who see in these authoritative types the projection of colonial power, competing with their own new bid for influence right down to the level of sub-district and village.

Who, then, are these new leaders? It follows from what has been said that they must be entirely self-constituted. The first few educated men nominated by governments to sit in the legislature or in other advisory positions are generally disqualified as would-be democratic leaders by their dependence upon government or by moderation either of nature or as the fruit of experience. With tribalism and chieftainship seen as barriers, there is no wider community than the tribe with ready-made precedents or traditions that can be utilized. The masses, except perhaps in the towns, or in regions most exposed to Western influence, are probably unawakened in any effective political sense. The new leader must, therefore, by his own initiative build his own platform and jump upon it. He must build it, in the main, of imported materials which he has most probably begun to collect during his travels abroad in Britain or the United States or both. His response to the political vacuum in which he must operate is naturally to build himself up as a striking personality, and this not only in the metaphorical sense, since he must keep up the interest and emotion of the masses by combatant acts and attitudes against the rulers. He cannot afford to be moderate lest he be outflanked by some more dramatically belligerent figure. Sociologists have applied the word 'charismatic' to this new type of leadership, which emphasizes itself with new ceremonies, slogans and symbols.

These necessities of the leader become clearer when we look more closely at the other side of the partnership, the people to whom he is appealing. Since, in most contexts, he dare not make use of the only existing solidarity, that of the tribe, he must make a direct appeal to the individuals. The appeal is first of all to their sense of grievance. Causes of discontent, tangible, psychological and imaginary, are many. The apparent acceptance of colonial rule tends to wear thin, in proportion to the varying intensity of that rule in time and place, after some forty years. The older generation, which was overwhelmed, whether in a military or a psychological sense, by the first impact of the European, dies out. Familiarity has eroded awe and admiration. The growing disharmonies in tribal, family and economic life become identified with the disintegrating effects of the White man's rule and are rightly charged to it. Towns, large and small, draw peasant men and women into a difficult and often an impoverished and demoralizing life. An increasing number of children educated in European schools are coming to maturity with high expectations, based upon their new qualifications, which, in many cases, are doomed to a disappointment that can now be vocal. Government policy, through ignorance or inefficiency, may strike harshly. Even essential sanitary or agricultural controls necessitated by the new order may seem oppressive. The social colour bar, of which the African in the first few decades of annexation is hardly aware, begins to strike the rising and competing African and to infect its sufferers with an almost unappeasable hunger for equality.

In general it might be said – and this is especially true of the areas of white settlement – that the European appears to Africans to be guilty of turning them out of their lowly hut of contentment, or at least of unconsciousness, erecting at its doors the glittering house of his own civilization, and then forbidding him entry except to the kitchen and the workshop.

Discrimination was felt first and most bitterly by those who had reached to the very top of the Europeans' own educational ladder and had found themselves denied the same status and pay for which the arduous achievement seemed to entitle them. They saw no way of gaining it except by taking over, as Asians and Arabs had done, the government of their own country. To produce a potentially revolutionary situation in a very few years they had only to appeal to the half-conscious discontents and resentments felt in varying degree by the clerk, the wage-labourer and the peasant, with the assertion that all their ills were due to the colonial government, and that all their hopes could be met by

THE PSYCHOLOGY OF AFRICAN NATIONALISM [1960]

freedom. '*All* their ills' because, though the historian must make the difficult attempt to judge between those due to the mistakes and even the crimes of the 'colonialists' and those inherent in the sudden and belated penetration of industrial Europe into primitive Africa, the political leader need make no such distinction. His attitude is generally 100 per cent negative; he dare not admit one merit to the colonial régime.

But a sense of restlessness and inferiority, even when thus organized, and even when shared a millionfold or more, is not always enough out of which to make an immediately effective movement for self-government and to induce the colonial authorities to make the desired concessions. This is especially true of the more recent nationalisms. The leaders need to look outside the purely bilateral relationship within the colony and find extraneous support. This has come to hand in increasing quantity during the last thirty years or so.

The first external aid can be found in the political principles of the colonial powers themselves, especially, perhaps, of Britain. The contradiction between democracy at home and imperialism overseas had troubled the British since at least the time of Burke. The Indians, West Indians and West Africans, led or instructed by those who had reached the Inns of Court, quickly learned to borrow for their own use the liberties the British had so slowly and painfully acquired for themselves, and to employ them with powerful rhetoric and noble quotations. As Britain herself became more fully democratic so the possibilities in this field increased. The acquisition by Britain's own labouring class, first of powerful representation and then of majority power, was an immense encouragement to colonial aspirants for freedom. In major acts of policy it may not be easy to draw sharp contrasts between the records of Labour and Conservative cabinets, but there can be little doubt that the pronouncements of the Labour Party, whether in or out of office, and the personal encouragement, and even the tuition, given to colonial leaders by individuals in the party greatly hastened an already moving current of liberalism in colonial policy.

A decisive point was the extension to the colonial dependencies of the general adult franchise so lately won in Britain. Acquired in Asia, extended to the West Indies, it could not, it seemed, be denied in Africa. Its sequence, by the irresistible logic of Britain's own democracy, was for leaders to organize the new electorate into parties, or a party, that would vote the colonial government out of the country. Furthermore, in countries of settlement, by the principle of 'undiluted democracy', it could be hoped that dominant European and Asian minorities might, in the few days it takes to count the votes and summon the legislature, be swept out of the seats of political and economic power.

If at the onset of the first waves of a freedom movement the colonial bastion remained unshaken by the weakness of its own inner contradictions, the new leaders could bring in from outside a second battering ram, perhaps the most powerful engine of all. This was the force of world opinion against colonialism. Changing components have made up this force. America's share in it was very strong before, during and for a few years after the war. Today, for reasons both of greater knowledge and more instructed self-interest, while by no means dead, this force has declined in power. The Communist states offer a challenge of constant strength, but one in which the ingredients change. In the twenties and thirties the attack was mainly theoretical, aimed directly and also indirectly through the writings of left-wing socialists. This period was followed by one in which it seemed that the Communist system had achieved in Russia for a recently servile peasantry the exact results, both in character and in speed, which the Africans desired for themselves. Russia had even drawn strength from the same motive force as theirs, the desire to catch up rapidly with the West and escape the weakness of poverty and the stigma of inferiority. A new phase of Communist influence has now developed, one in which Russia and China are entering into direct relations with African leaders, both independent and colonial, reaching out with diplomatic and economic feelers into their continent. Happenings in Hungary and Tibet are unlikely to offset the attraction of Communist support since few Africans have yet a world view and their main concern is with their local imperialism. Those African leaders who have no desire to risk exclusive relations with Russia are naturally inclined to welcome other influences that seem to offset colonial power, and Colonel Nasser's balancing act may seem an attractive example.

A third and rapidly growing external force which gives strength to the nationalists is the massed attack on colonialism by the Communist states and by the ever-increasing number of ex-colonial powers at Lake Success. An analysis of the 83 members of the United Nations explains the order of battle. There are some 25 fairly recently emancipated dependencies, with more to come; 20 South American members who, with a few exceptions, tend to show their anti-colonial hangover in their votes, and 10 Communist states which give solid and automatic support to any anti-colonialist movement. There are 10 other states which for various reasons may feel a pro-dependency or anti-imperial bias. That leaves only 9 states which are likely to take a truly independent attitude and the four older British Commonwealth states. The United States, with the greatest influence, has a somewhat ambivalent attitude, being herself an ex-colonial country, but she has increasingly supported the colonial powers as her North Atlantic Treaty Organization allies. Even so, the five colonial powers fight a losing battle in the international arena. It is true that, apart from Trusteeship matters, the struggle over the non-self-governing territories is for the most part one of words and paper. But these have a cumulative political effect. Above all they provide ideological sustenance of ever-increasing strength for an ever-diminishing number of dependent peoples. And the anti-colonial states can meet away from New York at Bandung or Cairo.

Fourth, and most recent as a stimulus to nationalism, is the activity of African political leaders in entering into contact with each other in Africa, in Europe or in New York. In this way they share experience – how much Dr Nkrumah, the unofficial president of this club, must have to teach the new members! – and generate political energy. These councils encourage the more laggard colonies to aim at levelling themselves up to the stage reached by the advanced, and make it more difficult for moderates to fall below the standards of urgency set by their colleagues.

This attempt at drawing a composite picture of nationalism in British Africa means that the time factor is blurred and that no one territory is exactly portrayed. This demands some correction. The description of motive forces, for example, is more true of the later than the earlier stirrings of nationalism. Over the whole area of colonialism the pace has been quickening. India, by contrast with Africa, had a period of intervention and dependence that can be reckoned in centuries. Her nationalist movement was some fifty years in maturing, and her peoples' internal sources of strength and confidence meant that they had far less need for extraneous moral support which, in any case, only appeared in any strength, mainly from the United States, shortly before the attainment of independence. Egypt more slowly, the Sudan, the Gold Coast and Nigeria more quickly, have moved first along the course for freedom in Africa. Egypt, hardly to be called an African dependency, stood alone in her ancient history as a nation. Among the others the Gold Coast had most cultural unity: the Sudan had experienced from the early nineteenth century an arbitrary political union imposed by Egypt, but neither Ghana nor the Sudan, until very recent years, showed much promise of nationhood. Nigeria, taken as a whole, might have been regarded as a hopeless non-starter in the race. All three, but especially the two latter territories, carried a large proportion of primitive tribes hardly reached by Western economic and political influences. The Sudanese, however, had the unique advantage of the Condominium. This enabled their leaders, supported by the sophisticated dark Arabs of the three cities at the junction of the Niles, and of the Gezira, to win their freedom quickly and easily by playing off Britain and Egypt.

All these three territories needed, and could find, more external support than had the Asian dependencies. All had partial sources of internal confidence greater than anything possessed by eastern and central African peoples. The northern Sudanese belonged to a great world religion and spoke the Arab language: the Gold Coast people, especially in the Colony, had long contact with Europe and a widely diffused Western education, while they shared with Ashanti both historic chieftainships and a prosperity based on cocoa. In Nigeria difficulties have been greater. The northerners were Moslem, but they were partly cut off from the world of Islam by a desert north and a pagan south. Their impressive political structure, reorganized and developed by the British, acted as a stabilizing and conservative force allergic to democratic nationalism. The Yoruba chieftainships, almost as sophisticated, with their civic development, as those of the Gold Coast, though not as wealthy, might have outrun their rivals to the freedom stakes if they had not been enclosed within a larger whole, the three parts of which have had harder work to come to terms with each other than with Britain. It is interesting, and a confirmation of the view expressed here about the major part played by the sense of inferiority as a motive force, that, while the Hausa and Yoruba peoples, with their long-established city-states, carefully recognized by the British, had little cause to feel this sense, it was the most primitive of the three main Nigerian groups, the Ibo and kindred peoples of the south-east, who played the lead in the agitation for self-government. Through his Press Dr Azikiwe ceaselessly spread the idea that the Nigerian peoples were enslaved and must follow him in the fight for freedom. This was his bludgeon, but he also made great play with darts of ridicule, raining these continually upon the government, from the governors downwards, in order to destroy the Africans' sense of respect for the authorities they had so long obeyed. Among a numerous people who had no chiefs and no political unity outside the kinship group, he built himself up as a leader and saviour so that the women would drink the pools in which he had trodden.

THE PSYCHOLOGY OF AFRICAN NATIONALISM [1960]

Thus the peoples of these three African territories, each enclosing very contrasting elements of the advanced and the primitive, helped by increasing external encouragement, and by a quick response from Britain, were led forward by their intelligentsia to achieve their purpose in a far shorter period of agitation than the Asian countries whose just preceding emancipation had, indeed, helped by precedent to advance their own.

The three mainland territories under British rule in eastern Africa have not yet attained their independence. Possessing even less of the internal material for nationhood than the Asian and West African states, and with a shorter experience of European contact and government, their leaders are forced to rely much more upon the increasing external support. They have also a greater wealth of precedent, some of it now from Negro Africa while even the sprawling Belgian Congo awakened from political somnolence. Furthermore, in the political climate of the world today, the remaining colonial peoples feel, or can be made to feel, even more acutely than their predecessors the stigma of their political subjection. These must be the reasons for the rapidity with which movements for independence have swept across the East African territories. This is especially striking in Tanganyika and Kenya since their arbitrary boundaries enclose scanty, ill-distributed peoples, showing great contrasts of culture and way of life, and inadequately linked by communications.

Uganda is more compact, and has been the scene of a rare attempt by a British governor to take the initiative in the creation of national unity and self-government. The failure so far, as already stated, has been due to the existence of one leading tribal group which distorts the usual pattern of colonial emancipation the other parts are trying to follow. The Baganda ruler and traditional leaders are torn between the desire to separate from the rest of the territory and the desire to dominate it, and the peoples of the other provinces are thwarted in their desire, which is also that of the British Government, to work for a united, self-governing and democratic Uganda.

By contrast Tanganyika, with its African population awakened to the first stirrings of political interest in a period that can be calculated in months rather than years, seems to be passing with ease and speed to the goal of majority rule and independence. At least one reason lies in the fact that Tanganyika, as a trust territory, is wide open to the influence of the United Nations, and once an African leader could evoke and represent the response of the people to this relationship, the end foreseen in the trust was in sight. In an impressive constitutional debate in the legislature on 19 March last year, the European and Asian representatives, quickly accepting the inevitable, vied with each other in their readiness to throw away the briefly held protection of parity of racial representation, and to line up behind the young African leader, Julius Nyerere, in his demand for democracy and self-government. His striking moderation may be due in part to character, but the ease with which, after a brief and able organization of support, he has reached the threshold of power, has relieved him from much temptation to extremism. The daunting nature of the task of making a nation out of Tanganyika and building an economy that can support and advance that nation may well incline him to cling to all the assets and all the allies he can find.

Kenya offers almost too many points of relevance to our scheme for us to examine them all. Of all African colonies it was, perhaps, the least well qualified to become a nation-state. Its characteristics were the exceptional isolation of the interior; a small population concentrated in a few widely separated parts of the large area; no political organization above the clan; and a coast with a history of its own under Arab influence. The Kenya of today has been created by British administration, by an arterial railway, and by the British settlers who have farmed the almost uninhabited highlands, and by the Asian craftsmen and traders. The Africans played the part of the unskilled labour force. Now they are learning skills, and Africans' agricultural production, with the first beginnings of their trade and industry, is playing a large and growing part in the economy. The Africans were stirred early into political consciousness by observing the struggle of the settlers to obtain full 'self-government' from Britain. They felt a growing bitterness as they realized their own poverty and inferiority beside the apparently wealthy colonists, and contrasted their crowded reserves with the spacious European farms. Kenyatta, returning from many years of living in England, showed an almost mesmeric power in mobilizing the discontent of his Kikuyu tribesmen against government and settler. The tragic madness of the Mau Mau was the sequel to all this excitement.

The movement which has followed this has, so far, been purely political. Two able young men, Mr Mboya and Dr Kiano, the first educated at Ruskin College, Oxford, and the other at an American University, have taken the lead in trying to build up a national movement. Nairobi is necessarily its centre. In its spreading locations the consciousness of discontent welds the tribes and is reinforced by the

THE PSYCHOLOGY OF AFRICAN NATIONALISM [1960]

tension over housing and employment, which fail to keep pace with the inflow from the districts. Faced by the entrenched settler position and the government's hesitation to surrender it to majority rule, the leaders here, more than anywhere else, seek compensating strength abroad. Mr Mboya has travelled and lectured in Britain, Asia and America. He presided at the All-African Peoples' Conference at Accra in December 1958. As president of the Kenya Trade Union Congress he draws help and advice from the International Confederation of Free Trade Unions and from Transport House. (He has not, it may be noted, so far used the Kenya trade unions for direct political action.) His problem will be to decide between a policy of moderation which could win the confidence of all races, or one of seeking quick results by trying to fuse tribalism with the strong emotion that each African feels, or can be helped to feel, at his political, social and economic subordination to the immigrant races.

In Central Africa, taken as a whole, the indigenous population was even more scanty and ill distributed than that of British East Africa. Nyasaland, though more populous than the Rhodesias, had been ravaged by the Arab slave trade and by the inter-tribal wars it fostered. Under British rule a large proportion of its manhood was spending its energies scattered abroad as migrant labour. Education in the protectorate, well begun by the Scottish missions in the 1870s, had stopped short of the higher levels, and there were hardly any of the all-important returned graduates to give a lead. The sparse population of Northern Rhodesia had been dominated by the influence of the settlers and the mines. The apparent African political backwardness of these two protectorates was, presumably, one reason why the governments concerned thought it possible to incorporate these territories in a federation dominated by the European colonists of Southern Rhodesia. But the very discussions that accompanied its inception woke the northern Africans to their being diverted, as they saw it, from the straight Colonial Office road to self-government into a by-road which, in their words, would lead them into slavery to the European settlers. Unable, the Devlin Report tells us, to produce an adequate leader within Nyasaland, and aware now of the example of other colonies, the local nationalists invited the long absent Dr Banda, then in Ghana, to return and lead them, with the expressed intention of building him up as the 'political messiah' as this 'would cause great excitement, and should precipitate almost a revolution in political thought'. The importation was certainly effective, and is one more example of the speed

[1960]

with which the almost universal, latent, anti-government and anti-European feeling can be called into expression and action.

Thus the conditions of Africa today act as a forcing house for the remaining dependencies. Since the British Government has made it clear that Tanganyika and Uganda have full scope to grow into self-government, the heat of pan-African and anti-colonialist feeling will increasingly be turned upon Kenya and, even more, upon Central Africa. There it will be concentrated especially upon the European minorities, who are now regarded by Africans as the main, if not the only reason, why the people in these territories are denied the same destiny as the rest of British Africa and, indeed, of kindred tribes just across an artificial border. The point will be driven home by the hesitation of France, because of the numerous *colons*, to grant Algeria the freedom so generously and dramatically given by De Gaulle to the rest of French Africa. South Africa is, of course, an even nearer warning to Negro Africans, and the extreme polarization between the rapidly growing freedom of tropical Africans and the increasing repression in the Union, even if it is unlikely to produce much immediate effect upon the resolute Nationalists of that state, heightens tension throughout the continent.

The pot of racial controversy will be kept boiling by all the external influences we have reviewed, and the programme of African events for 1960, which includes the emancipation of Nigeria and of Somalia, the Kenya constitutional conference and the dispatch of the rather unwieldy commission which is to debate the Central African Federation, will add their quota to the restlessness.

We have been looking at African nationalism mainly from the African side. The other side of the picture would be found in the character of the colonial governments and of the unofficial Europeans, settlers or businessmen, under whose control or influence that nationalism has been moulded and against whose policies it is now solidifying its form. This is outside our scope. But one thing remains to be said. An endeavour has been made to deal objectively with a subject that is highly controversial and which arouses deep feelings upon both sides amongst those who live in Africa or who are concerned with it. Let me then, in conclusion, offer my own opinion. African nationalism arises as the inevitable result of the forces working in our world and, indeed, in our own nation. To oppose it is to oppose these forces. The alternative is to endeavour to guide and assist it, a difficult task indeed. It may assist a right mental approach to remember that it is through no fault of the

Africans, or, except to a marginal degree, of their European rulers, that this universal passion has reached Africans when these are so unready to give it constructive expression, and when it threatens the interests and achievements of European colonists. The desire to find relief from, and compensation for, a sense of inferiority is one that the psychologists identify in greater or less degree, in every human being: it is reflected in the behaviour of groups, including almost all the nations of the world. It is the burden of the Africans that their history has bred in them this sense to a pathological degree, and it is the burden of the Western powers that they must pay for their century or more of domination over most of the rest of the world by being the object against which their former political or economic subjects must lever themselves up into the desired equality. The bond of humiliation extends outside the colonial people and links them psychologically with all who have had reason to hate or to fear the superiority of the so-called imperialist powers. Britain, for all her respect for native society and care for the masses, may suffer more at this stage than France which offered her African subjects, especially in the persons of Westernized individuals, more equality of both social and political status.

Since at least the time of the Renaissance mankind has had to endure the excesses of nationalism which today threaten humanity itself, and some nations are already experimenting in the limitation of sovereignty. Yet it is difficult to see how Africans or other formerly dependent peoples can find the dignity and self-expression they need, with the experience of civic life and of economic development, except by following the rest of the world through the stage of nationhood. In political terms, which have been outlined here as realistically as possible, African nationalism inevitably leads to a struggle for power. We have, in fact, been witnessing a series of rebellions, but this reality has been veiled because of the growing readiness on the part of the colonial rulers to attempt by concessions to ensure that the rebellions shall be peaceful. It is, however, much to expect of young national leaders, whose impatience is encouraged from so many quarters, to conduct their movement at the permitted pace and strictly within the rules of law, the law of their rulers.

It would surely help our understanding of these movements if we could always remember that, though on the surface they are political, at a deeper level they are psychological and only psychological treatment will satisfy them. It is for this reason that even the attainment of independence does not complete the cure. British Africa's resources for nation-building, for immediately successful independence and, above all, for democracy, are very deficient. True, much of tribal society was democratic in spirit. But this spirit, essentially tribal, has to be made inter-tribal by the sudden extension of the sense of social obligation. This need and the demands of unity and self-respect may serve to increase the tendency of the new nations, even when independent, to continue to exploit the negative impulse of anti-imperialism. This tendency is still present in some measure in the New Asian states. The Western nations, if they want to complete the emancipations which, voluntarily and involuntarily, they have set in motion, will have to go on paying the penalty of their former domination in patient understanding, in unrequited aid, largely through international channels, and in such gestures of respect between equals as the British Sovereign has recently paid to Dr Nkrumah in entertaining him at Balmoral. Altruism has, indeed, become the best policy. But something warmer than mere calculation will be needed to secure success, the realization that the achievement of African freedom is, or at least can be, a spiritual as well as a political gain.

The conviction of those who have lately become conscious that they are in subjection and that dignity and self-realization can be gained only, and immediately, in full political freedom, clashes against the opposite conviction, held by Europeans in the 'mixed' states. They believe that such freedom would bring disorder and poverty to all concerned, and therefore that African nationalism must be defeated, curbed or diverted – for the defenders are less united in their aims than the attackers. But whatever policy is devised to deal with an issue which is imminent and has no close precedent, it should be founded upon a reasoned measurement of the content of African nationalism in its various contexts and its growing strength.

Staffing the Transfer of Power

Letter to *The Times* 9 April 1960

Sir, – Events in East and Central Africa foreshadow rapid advances there towards majority rule, which the Union's crisis may well accelerate. But as one set of problems ends another will begin. Having just returned from visits to British West and East Africa I would emphasize two lessons which the experience of political advance on one side of the continent may have for the other.

The States created by Britain in East Africa enclose peoples even less ready than those of West Africa to become nations – their isolation longer; their populations scantier; their resources poorer; their education and political experience less advanced; their tribal and ethnic divisions more unbridged. For these very reasons external enterprise plays a far larger part. Take Kenya, the nodal region. The very recent structure of civilization might collapse, if left inadequately supported during the coming transition. I would support Mr Marrian's reasoned plea in his letter today that much more than the sum now under discussion will be needed, not to finance a settler exodus but for the general land settlement and development which could retain confidence and achieve a marriage between European and African agriculture, so long at odds. Immigrant enterprise in Tanganyika and Uganda might also need temporary support. The external element could thus be sustained through the remaining years of British control and so allow the new African Ministers time to appreciate its contribution and practise responsible interracial co-operation. During this period, since African needs are almost illimitable, international aid and private investment from all friendly Powers should be vigorously attracted.

Secondly, East Africa's staff shortage being far greater, our Overseas Service requires much more support than that given in West Africa or the Sudan. In the past few weeks I have seen our agents, from Governors downwards, attempting the almost impossible task of achieving with the sanction of force all but forbidden, the orderly canalization of the tumultuous flood of African political assertion. And this at a time when their own careers are threatened with extinction or continuance under changed and obscure conditions and uncertain tenure. Since wrangling on this issue poisons the delicate period of transition, Britain should supply the compensation and inducement pay which new African governments may be unable or unwilling to provide. We have not only here a debt of honour but a solid interest in generating viable African States and willing members of the Commonwealth.

These purposes make two demands. One is a much better articulation in Whitehall between the Colonial and Commonwealth phases. The other is money. Here I endorse Mr Francis's letter today. Britain cannot cheaply disengage herself from the large obligations she undertook so confidently some sixty years ago. Labour and Liberal parties especially, who have built up political pressure for African self-government, should now teach their followers to accept the obligations and sacrifices demanded by the resultant situation. Otherwise the way to nationhood in East and Central Africa, especially for the minority groups, European, Asian, Arab and even African, may be along a *via dolorosa* of poverty and disorder.

Yours faithfully

Kenya: the Decisive Years

The Listener 12 May 1960

I have returned from what has become my annual visit to East Africa, and from Kenya I was able to bring back the impression that the recent constitutional conference at Lancaster House was the most important event in the history of the territory since it was annexed by Britain at the end of the last century.

I have been visiting Kenya with increasing frequency since 1930, so, looking back from this watershed of 1960, I can trace nearly half of the events from personal experience. Through my friendship and collaboration with Lord Lugard my impressions go back even further – even to the time, seventy years ago, when he walked up from Mombasa to Uganda and took four months to do it. Then came the annexation; the building of the railway, the coming of the British settlers (members of my own family were among the earliest of these), their prolonged attempt to gain political control, and Britain's growing realization of the intractability of the relations between Europeans, Asians and Africans. This resulted in the long sequence of commissions, committees and White Papers which crowd my bookshelves. Later came the awakening of political consciousness among Africans; their representation on the Legislative Council; the Mau Mau rebellion; and, finally, Lancaster House. What happened there becomes all the more startling when one remembers that for almost the whole period the European colonists hoped to turn Kenya into a Southern Rhodesia, and that round about 1930 they nearly succeeded.

For now the road ahead is going to lead in a very different direction. It will take us, I am sure – and soon – to African majority rule. This proposed Macleod constitution marks an important advance in the

Africans' share of government. For they will probably get a good deal more than half the Legislature and, in the Executive, not counting officials, four Ministers against three Europeans and one Asian. True, the minorities will have rather greater representation than their numbers warrant, and also a Bill of Rights and other safeguards. But overshadowing these provisions is the assumption that this constitution is only a temporary stage on the way to full African control. While I was in Kenya I had some opportunity to consider the reactions of the several racial groups to this new state of affairs.

First, the settlers. For them Lancaster House was a place of disaster. They have split between those who have forced themselves to accept harsh realities – and here I was deeply impressed by the courageous lead in realism given by Mr Blundell and his supporters – and those who cannot bring themselves to do so. For the settlers face a future of complete uncertainty. History has dealt hardly with them. Originally they took advantage of a wonderful opportunity. Here were these cool fertile uplands, almost – but not quite – uninhabited, crying out to be productively used by man, while at home the British Government was eager for such immigrants to produce a revenue and to make the long haul of the railway to Uganda pay its way. True, there was an African population, but it seemed then very scanty and primitive, and at that period, too, European colonization was regarded as the best agency of civilization for 'the natives'.

I have visited many European farms, mostly modest bungalows, set in Kenya's marvellous flowers. I have seen the crops; fruit of many different kinds; wheat; maize; the dark regiments of coffee; the light green of tea; the fine herds of Guernseys, Friesians and the rest; all of them the result of long experiment and of costly fights with disease and drought. The settlers do not only cultivate the country of their adoption; they love it. It is indeed a country to love. There can be few more glorious drives in the world than the one that runs down from the Uganda border to Nairobi – rolling downs, patched with dark forests; sudden ravines so high that there is one climate at the top and another at the bottom; great lakes, embroidered with pink flamingos; splendid mountains standing alone, like the snow-bearing Kenya itself, or in ranges – and always the immense blue distances. And then, on the very edges of cultivation, there is the exciting promise of wild life, a gazelle sprinting across the road or an incredibly tall giraffe gazing at you from above the tree-tops. No wonder the settlers and their Kenya-born families find it hard to believe that their lives and fortunes are soon to

[1960]

pass under the control of the Africans, whom they have known as simple tribesmen, or as their rather amateur labour, coveting, and now, perhaps, even claiming their farms.

Of course, the European population of 65,000 is not made up entirely of farmers. But indirectly a high proportion of Europeans are dependent upon European farming. And the farmers have dominated the politics of the country. They are the first true Kenya nationalists.

The second group, the Asians, slender and handsome, seem to fill the towns. They run the shops and the offices and some big businesses. One can see their clubs, schools, sports grounds, temples, mosques; their women enliven the streets with the coloured silks of their saris. But the Asians are not so politically strong as their numbers, some 200,000, might seem to warrant. And they tend to be regarded as interlopers – though in fact there were Asians on the coast long before the Europeans came. They are mostly small traders and craftsmen, and as such they seem to stand right across the immediate advance of the Africans. I have known leading Asians who were fine and generous citizens, but they have not been able to play as prominent a part as the British settlers. These, after all, had the British Government behind them in London. And then the Asians are split among themselves – Pakistanis and Indians, Moslems and Hindus, and the few but very important Christian Goans. Like the British settlers, they are all the innocent victims of a historical process they could not have foreseen and they are deeply worried to see, in the small share allotted to them in the new constitution, an alarming index of their present weakness.

Finally there are the Africans whose 6,000,000 now threaten to engulf all the other groups. Upon them now lies – or soon will lie – the main responsibility for the future of Kenya. Even if there were no immigrant group, the tribes who happened to be included in this haphazard slice of Africa would not offer a very promising foundation for nationhood. Their contact with the outer world has been brief as compared, for instance, with that of west African peoples. They have only recently been able to produce their first, untried generation of leaders, mostly educated in the West. And between these men and the masses there is no relatively large, sophisticated, semi-educated class of clerks, traders, mechanics and the rest that one finds on the west coast. Secondly, the Africans are very unevenly and patchily distributed over the surface of the country. Thus their two main blocks of population are round Lake Victoria and on the lovely wooded and watered hills of the Central Province, with the European Highlands between them. Thirdly, they are divided not only by tribe – and tribes that have no political unity – but also by race, into Bantu, Nilotic and half-Hamite. These divisions can be bridged by the handful of educated leaders at the top. But between the masses there remain real cleavages not only of language and custom but of way of life, since most of the half-Hamites are pastoral people, while the Bantu are primarily agriculturists.

Physical division, tribal division, and educational immaturity: here are three weighty handicaps for the new, inexperienced leaders. Yet next year, if not earlier, they must appeal to the even more inexperienced voters in a first general election. Common political ideas can hardly yet exist among them, but common emotions do; and these are the electoral raw material out of which policy and unity have to be made. Unfortunately such emotions tend to be all negative – anti-colonialism, anti-European, anti-settler, anti-Asian – coupled, inevitably, with an immense desire to gain quickly the good things of life, money, land, education, senior posts, rapid promotion.

I know some of the leaders, and I was able, the other day, to talk with them while they were considering whether to accept some ministerial positions in the Government now, or to hold aloof for a while. I found their attitude was extremely interesting. Negroes have been told for so long that they are backward that, in very natural reaction, they will not now themselves admit that they suffer from *any* handicaps. They therefore shrug off the need for some apprenticeship in ministerial responsibility. They have so worked up their followers' thirst for immediate *uhuru* that they might well become the victims of their own agitation. For as they begin to handle the hard realities of public life, they will need to urge upon their supporters those very compromises and delays which they have taught them to reject: if they do, they will risk their own political lives; if they do not, they will risk the life of Kenya. Fortunately our latest news is of some courageous African rebukes for extremists.

Rich countries can stand shocks. But Kenya is not rich. It may look big on the map; but, apart from the coastal strip, its peoples are crowded into the high rainfall area, that is only about a quarter of the whole. Here the cultivators may be 400 to the square mile, while south, east, and still more to the north are vast steppes where the pastoral people following their gaunt beasts from one water-hole to another are only two or possibly four to the square mile. Could this poor country, this brittle economy, stand having the large immigrant sector which is built into it roughly cut down or torn right out? Its total revenue is little over £30,000,000, and until recently almost the whole of the exports were the products of European farms. Even today they grow about half of the domestic agricultural production. And could this inexperienced country bear to lose the political experience and professional skill which the immigrants have injected into almost every aspect of its life?

What then? Have we, as many of the settler leaders and their friends over here tell us, made a dreadful mistake in committing this precarious colony so suddenly into inexperienced African hands? The question makes us face two hard truths. The first is that the climate of our world has changed from that of the 1920s and 1930s when our countrymen so confidently developed their little colony in the very heart of black and quiescent Africa. It is a world in which Britain is relatively weaker and poorer, one which is now almost 100 per cent hostile to the domination of white over black, a world in which African nations are asserting their influence. Two of them, Ethiopia and the Sudan, are right on Kenya's borders. Two others, Uganda and Tanganyika, her other neighbours, have been promised freedom soon. Kenya's African leaders have plugged in to all these electric forces round them, drawing a power from them which they could not have generated in an insulated colony. Mau Mau showed that even a rebellion within one tribe, and so repulsive a movement that it could not attract much external sympathy, would have ruined the colony but for British forces and also some £25,000,000 of British aid. The settlers on the isolated farms and the Christian and loyal Kikuyu bravely endured this murderous nightmare. But could they do it again? Could any British Government allow them to take a risk so costly to them and to us?

The second hard fact is that, not the Kenya problem itself, but the acute form in which it presents itself today, is partly due to mistakes in the past. In these both the settlers and the British Government share. From the 1920s onwards voices were not wanting to warn against Kenya's land and labour policies. Official attention, almost up to the Second World War, was concentrated far too much upon settler interests and problems. Take one example: it is not many years since the prohibition was lifted upon the Africans growing coffee. Now their neat little terraced coffee plantations decorate the wooded hills of both Kikuyu and Kamba. Production has risen dramatically and Africans have even won prizes for the best coffee in the Colony. So they can say, with some justice, that if this kind of development had begun rather sooner, the economy would have been more healthy because more balanced. Again, with greater foresight, fifteen – even ten – years ago, much more could have been done to train Africans for responsibility in politics and in administration. And on the political side it was the prolonged struggle of the settlers to gain control that kept the Colony restless, and which gave the Africans both a lesson in agitation and also a deep fear of the claims of the settler.

African memories, deeply rooted in their land, are long, and unfortunately they have some reason to look back in anger. They seem to find their only escape from the long stigma of racial inferiority in unqualified self-assertion. If the few moderate and experienced Africans attempt to co-operate with the Government, those who cannot argue with them in rational terms may use the cruel weapon of intimidation. Its use is terribly rife in Africa today, and while I was in Kenya there were already signs of its revival in the Kikuyu districts. Africans have no monopoly in cruelty, but there has been little in their experience to teach them respect for human life.

In Kenya, between the evils of going too fast or going too slow, the first evil has been chosen. Can we find any factors to mitigate this evil? It is surely to the good that the spirits of some millions of people should be released from a sense of inferiority and given hope of stretching out their arms and lifting up their heads in the attempt to build something by themselves and for themselves. However badly they may do it at first, they will at least have *begun* their inescapable process. For once they become conscious of their deep need for self-assertion, the control of the British Government, though I believe that it has been essential hitherto in Africa, ceases to be beneficial, and in time may even become injurious to both sides. At this stage the one purpose must be to transfer power with the largest possible measure of goodwill.

The next few years, while Britain still retains the ultimate control, will be decisive. The Africans will need political guidance and financial support to keep the ship steady to face the still rougher waters of independence ahead. But this must be supplied with the utmost tact. Only in this way can we save the Africans from imperilling their own future by quickly throwing the minorities overboard, with all the wealth and skill they represent. The mood of revolt *will* pass: self-assertion will find *some* satiety. And there will be steadying influences other than those of Britain at work; there will be those, we may hope, of the Commonwealth club, and of other nations and international agencies whose confidence the Africans will have both to win and to keep. There will be intricate and hazardous problems over which they will need advice and help: Zanzibar claims on the coast; Somali claims on the northern frontier; the need for East African unity. These and other unavoidable problems may force the new African leaders to develop the necessary qualities of statemanship. For responsibility can be a good, if rough, schoolmaster, and at Lancaster House Mr Macleod had the courage and strength to open the door through which the Africans can now go forward to the greatest of all responsibilities – independence.

Federation in Central Africa on the Defensive

The Listener 9 June 1960

1960: certainly the Africans' year, with independence movements finding fulfilment over wide areas. Yet these meet a check in five regions where they run into another kind of independence, that of rooted European settlement – South Africa, where the first weak African challenge has been beaten down for the moment; Portugal's colonies, held in firm and covert grip; Algeria, where a bloody stalemate drags on; Kenya, though, as this year has shown, the colonists have not been strong enough to hold out; and central Africa. Here, in the Federation, the issue hangs in the balance. When it comes before a conference later this year, Britain's judgement may well be decisive.

The British citizen will find some guidance in a new book, *A New Deal in Central Africa*. Three students of politics have written most of it: Colin Leys of Balliol College; Professor Cranford Pratt, a Canadian; and Dr Bernard Chidzero, a Rhodesian African, with a MacGill doctorate and now working in my own Nuffield College at Oxford, and fourthly, an American economist, Professor Barber, who also studied his subject from Nuffield. None of these writers pursued his research only under the dreaming spires: they all extended them to Africa itself.

This complicated region is four times the size of the United Kingdom. It contains three territories, the European-dominated colony of Southern Rhodesia, all but independent before Federation; the Protectorate of Northern Rhodesia with its rich copper-mines; still further north, the other Protectorate, the small, beautiful Nyasaland – Africa's Scotland – which exports some of its overcrowded African population to the two more developed states. Thus we have three territorial governments, all different in shape, two still partly under the Colonial Office, a third dominated by white colonists, and also a Federal Government; and a population of between 7,000,000 and 8,000,000 Africans and about 300,000 Europeans – about twenty-five to one.

The book first analyses the Federation's record; how the Africans' first constitutional safeguards were whittled down; how the complicated franchises and methods of representation, especially in Southern Rhodesia and on the Federal plane, ensure a very limited minority representation for the African majority and give them little hope of ever correcting the balance. The vague promise of racial 'partnership' has produced only meagre results, though enough to distinguish it definitely from apartheid. The writers then measure the growth of police forces and of security measures to contain the increasing African discontent which led up to the tragic emergency in Nyasaland. It is therefore with surprise that one reaches their main conclusion, that, for a transitional period, there should be at least an equal number of African and European voters on the roll. How, in the complicated racial distribution of central Africa, could this difficult equilibrium be introduced or maintained? Did the authors shrink from prescribing the severe surgical operation to which their own grave diagnosis pointed? Could a temporary course of electoral parity achieve a cure? I commend their well-marshalled evidence and also their advice that the British presence in the Protectorate should be firmly maintained. But I cannot agree with their main conclusion. Before I offer my own I would like to put the Federation in its wider setting.

Its success must surely be judged by its purposes. There were two parties to the 1953 settlement, the British Government and the local colonists – especially those of Southern Rhodesia. (I call them colonists merely to distinguish them from the Africans and the temporary official and other residents.) By 1953 they were beginning to feel themselves a very small minority in a very big Africa, squeezed between opposing pressures from south and north. From the south, the Union's Nationalist Party was pushing its apartheid policy to dangerous extremes and also, a more intimate threat, throwing overboard the remaining British influences and steering towards a republic. The colonists had voted against incorporation with their large uncongenial neighbour in 1923 and still had no mind for it in 1953.

From the north the colonists were feeling a very different pressure, following what they regarded as Britain's weak surrenders to African nationalism. If this process engulfed the two northern Protectorates, the Southern Rhodesian colonists might have to make a desperate choice between surrender either to African or to Afrikaner nationalism. There was one way out – to throw the three territories together and make a large state under civilized, that is white, control.

Why did British governments, Labour and then Conservative, entertain this plan? If, they calculated, Southern Rhodesia were dragged into the Union's orbit, then Northern Rhodesia, with its many Afrikaner miners, would almost certainly go the same way and Nyasaland might follow. British influence might thus be edged out of all southern Africa. There was the more altruistic fear that the Protectorate Africans might lose the impartial British administration with its open end towards African self-government. And so a bargain, partly unspoken, was struck between Britain and the colonists. The colonists should have their federation if they would treat the Africans increasingly as partners. The Protectorates would retain their Protectorate status. Two different purposes and two conflicting loyalties were thus built into the Federation: purposes, because most British opinion wanted the maximum of African advance and most colonist opinion wanted a great deal less than that; loyalties, because the Protectorate Africans and their officials still, as Sir Roy Welensky complains, look over their shoulders to Whitehall. For Britain has written into the preamble – and this is our pledge and the Africans' sheet-anchor – that the Protectorates shall 'enjoy separate governments for so long as their respective peoples so desire'. But in the silent tug-of-war between British and colonist opinion the colonists have been inching their way to victory.

Of course they have. They were the stronger party. They were on the spot. Britain was far away, her ministers distracted and undecided. I have met Lord Malvern, Sir Roy Welensky, Sir Edgar Whitehead and others. They are not the tyrannical ogres painted by some of their critics, but men who have inherited a dangerous position in a dangerous continent. They rest their case first on history. It is only some sixty years ago that the pioneers came to one of the least civilized parts of Africa; marked out boundaries; imposed peace on warring tribes; built railways, roads and cities; brought modern agriculture and industry. They have now built the mighty Kariba dam. All this they have done themselves, following where Cecil Rhodes led, coming up from the south, and owing little to Britain except their blood. Nor was their work all material. They brought British ideas – parliamentary government, the rule of law, the mercy of twentieth-century medicine. As well as mines and factories they have built churches, theatres, schools, and, with Britain's help, a university. In all this, they claim, the Africans have had their share. Life in the bush, with its little huts, its scratchy cultivation, its witchcraft, still goes on. But millions of Africans have now been apprenticed to civilization. They earn good money, good housing and amenities in the mines and elsewhere.

In this economic argument lay the main case for federation, and here the colonists claim its greatest justification. Has it not given poor Nyasaland £4,000,000 extra revenue a year? True. But two Oxford economists, Hazlewood and Henderson, in an important new study,[1] have probed the Federation's economics to show that their case is not 100 per cent valid. The rate of growth must not be seen in isolation from that before 1953 or that of other territories since 1953. And how far has the economy been managed to favour Southern Rhodesia? What has Nyasaland lost in tariffs on imports used by Africans to offset her revenue gain? The case may well go in favour of the Federation, but perhaps not so far as the loud assumptions. And as Hazlewood and Henderson insist, far too little serious analysis has gone into this vital economic aspect.

Even so, the colonists' case is strong. Especially when put to you *in situ*, with the skyscrapers of Salisbury rising like a great cliff, the charming European villas spreading round them into the great African emptiness, the giant activity of the copper mines, and the pylons marching through the virgin bush. All this was willed by the few thousand Europeans, built by them, and is maintained by them. The Africans supplied the unskilled labour, but there is hardly an African in the region who can yet contribute anything to this kind of development except as a semi-skilled assistant on a European installation. The colonists offer to share their civilization progressively with the Africans. But, they say, majority rule would mean the end of civilization. They stand by their Founder's aphorism: 'Equal rights for all civilized men', and *they* will define civilization. It is easy enough for Britain to walk out of her African colonies. Her officials can pack their bags and haul down the Union Jack. But for the colonists Africa is home. They have nowhere else to go and they mean to stay.

Now, the other side of the case. I have spoken of a bargain between two sides, Britain and the colonists. But why not between three? Because in 1953 the 7,000,000 Africans had not the political experience to express their opposition as a third party. When it was first canvassed I publicly opposed federation as ultimately unworkable because unjust.

[1] *Nyasaland: The Economics of Federation*, 1960.

Britain had a treaty only with the Barotse tribe. But to rule a people for sixty or seventy years is surely to develop a moral contract with them not to hand them over to another government against their will. They certainly feel this. Nyasaland Africans would say to me almost with tears: 'Why have you thrown us away? What have we done – were we not loyal to Britain? Now you have destroyed our loyalty.'

Why do the Africans reject federation? Nationalism? They are not yet a nation, but 7,000,000 individuals who have come to feel – or can quickly be made to feel – their subjection as a personal and increasing indignity for which the freedom and dignity of self-government is the only relief. Since 1953 the winds of change have blown the sparks into flames which burst out in Nyasaland. And the wind continues to rise. The Belgian Congo and Tanganyika, their nearest neighbours, have just been promised independence, neighbours whose boundaries in some parts actually divide their tribes. How convince Africans that some members of the same tribe are fit for freedom and the others unfit?

How should an open-minded British citizen approach this problem? His political principles – 1832 and all that – will instruct him that it is not right for minorities to rule majorities; though practical common sense may persuade him that African unreadiness demands a moratorium on democratic principles – at least for a period. But, on purely hard practical grounds, can federation, as at present constructed, hope to succeed in extending this moratorium indefinitely?

I must now state my own belief – and it is not easy to say this – that it cannot. We have been warned, on the highest of all authority, that no man should begin to build a tower which he is not able to finish. To the colonists even to doubt they will command success must seem treacherous or cowardly. And we British, nourished in peaceful compromise at home, can hardly bring ourselves to admit that abroad we have often been forced to give to violence what we have long refused to persuasion. Must we again wait until it is too late, or almost too late? Remember the American colonies, Ireland, India, Palestine, Kenya, and then pause upon contemporary Cyprus. Hateful to face this record? But it is no secret from the Africans. Not long ago I was in Africa urging a group of dissident leaders – not in central Africa – on no account to resort to unconstitutional or violent means. 'But', they retorted, 'that is just what we want now – a nice little bit of bloodshed and then Britain will send a Commission of Inquiry and we shall get all we want!' Certainly violence is not always spontaneous. It may be the work of a small minority. But is there a majority *against* it? The colonists complain of intimidation.

True! It is widespread in Africa and often brutal. Africans resort to it because they dare not allow their one great advantage, the solidarity of their numbers, to be broken by the subtraction of groups or individuals. Again, the colonists' gradualist plans – how dearly we should all like to believe them possible! – depend upon attaching the rising African élite one by one to their minority. The Africans reject and persecute the 'co-operators' because this process means skimming off their still scanty leadership as it comes to the surface.

Violence is repellent to us. But when Sir Roy Welensky so often asserts that Africans are primitive, inexperienced and the rest, the temptation is to reply with the expressive current query 'So what?' Such as they are he must deal with them, and so must we. And is there not a sense in which Africans are innocent? What they are today is largely what we have made them by our unavoidably sudden and shattering intrusion into their tribal isolation.

And is not Britain's attitude to their problems another of the conditions within which the colonists must find their solution? For, in defence of Britain, her surrenders to violence were due less to military incapacity than to the realization that prolonged subversion must spring from deep-seated political causes. And to such promptings Britain grows more, not less, responsive. The Devlin Report, even the more recent Southworth Commission, reveal the growing sensitivity of Britain's conscience. As John Plamenatz has said in his recent book *On Alien Rule and Self-Government*, when the rulers begin to doubt the moral validity of their rule and the subjects absorb this new doubt, the game is up – though he uses more academic words than these! And – more inescapable conditions – behind Britain stands a multi-racial Commonwealth, just seen in action for the first time; and an Africa on the edge of widespread liberation; and behind Africa a world which, for reasons honest and rather less than honest, condemns the rule of Europe over coloured races.

Put baldly, then, could the colonists in their policy of Federal independence and European domination go it alone? They might do so for a long time in Southern Rhodesia, which in any case Britain no longer controls. But if the attempt to enforce the Federation upon the northern Africans is going to lead to prolonged strife, more police, increasing repression and then most probably end in failure and bitterness, would it not be the lesser evil to begin to come to terms now with the Africans' protonationalism, raw and emotional as it is?

I believe, then, that the African leaders – and there are some I know

[1960] COLONIAL SEQUENCE 1949 TO 1969

and respect – should be taken into full and equal consultation at the coming conference with no possibilities barred, the Protectorates offered a phased advance to majority rule, and then, if they demand secession, this must be granted: but on the understanding, which I believe they might accept, that, following secession, they would of their own volition enter into a looser association, planned to give them as many as possible of the economic and other benefits of federation. (The Central African Council which preceded federation died of inanition or strangulation largely because its parents were more interested in bringing Federation to birth.) If it were possible the copper mines should be put under a consortium of the companies and the new common authority to preserve efficiency and to continue the use of the taxation of the mines for the benefit of the whole region, or perhaps of a union of the two Protectorates.

It is only upon some such lines, I believe, that some peace and progress may be insured for Central Africa, not easily but with time and with trouble. The dismantling of federation would be a bitter blow to the colonist's hopes, but it would rejoice the hearts and release the energies and skill of the great majority of the African millions from frustrating political and economic controls. Out of the ruins of an enforced Federation a new and free association of the territories and the races might be slowly built. In this the Europeans would still have an immense part to play. They might even have a larger and a longer part than to play in any scheme built upon the present Federation.

Problems for the Somali Republic

The Times 4 July 1960

Mogadishu was not equipped to deal with a sudden influx of visitors from all over the world, still less for the dispatch of reports by the world's journalists. One of them was kind enough to take this article, written on a night of wild and noisy rejoicing, to Nairobi by plane, and dispatch it from there in order to reach Printing House Square in time.

The new Republic of Somalia has come to birth in this pleasant little city of Mogadishu. Good fairies – and some perhaps not quite so good –

have come from nearly all nations of the world for this interesting event. The new state can boast three godparents – Britain, the United Nations and Italy. The birth was in fact one of Siamese twins, Italian Somalia and British Somaliland, but in this case none of those attending the affair, with one possible exception, wants to see them disjoined.

The young provisional Government of the new nation, discreetly and efficiently helped by the Italians, gave a splendid welcome to its guests. A luxury hotel has been run up in some three months out of prefabricated parts sent out from Italy at a cost, it is said, of much more than £1 million, and a fleet of cars was brought in, driven by smart uniformed drivers, to rush guests from one function to another.

The main welcome was in the overwhelming pleasure and courtesy of the Somalis in receiving their guests. Surely one of the most handsome races in the world, with their aquiline features and incredibly slim hips, they are brimming over with joy and good fellowship, and their women, even more handsome than the men, have come out well into the open to express their sense of joy.

One volley of fire against dissidents unfortunately marred the proceedings. The young state is coming to life in a dangerous part of a dangerous world, and even before it faces outwards it has its own internal problems. It suffers less than some new or forthcoming African states from those deep divisions of culture, language, or religion which seem to deny the possibility of their nationhood. There is no mistaking a Somali anywhere in the world, but though there is this unity of language, customs and religion, this encircles a strong internal sectionalism.

The diplomatists who fly in and out of Mogadishu to be entertained by the young ministers and permanent secretaries in their well-cut lounge suits and in the setting of the excellent public buildings of the capital will have little idea of the real Somalia, which stretches away to the north and west. To fly right over this is to see something very close to desert flecked with grey-green bush and the ghost of grass with hardly a road, a modern installation or a house that is not a hut. Worse still, for all the veining of the surface with watercourses, none of these, except the two rivers of the former Italian Somalia, carries permanent water. The writer, here as the guest of the new government, once lived in the first European house built in Hargeisa, trekked among the Somalis along the unexplored Ethiopian border, and took the impress of the hard life of searching for water and grazing for their camels and sheep which has given a fierce belligerency to the clan unit.

The urge of the new African state is, inevitably perhaps, towards centralization from the capital. But Mogadishu will not find it easy to impose its will, however beneficent, upon these strong nomadic units. The new political parties, for all their modern-sounding names, are still closely linked to tribal realities. And, for all the efforts of both the administering Powers, local government as the basis of a modern state does not easily take root among a shifting population, for the character and the customs of nomads are as tough as their spare, sinewy bodies.

Another problem, though not on so deep a level, lies in the sudden union of two colonial systems, the British and the Italian. It is true that, because of the conservatism of the pastoralist, foreign influences have bitten less deep than with settled and more prosperous African populations. And Italian Somalia had a period of British military administration. Yet the new rulers have to co-ordinate two different systems of rule, with the concepts and methods which govern them. They have to harmonize two legal systems and two adopted languages and at the same time decide how to employ their own unwritten tongue in public life.

Of all the internal problems, poverty is the most intractable. The population is small. The 500,000 'British' Somalis are uniting with the 1,250,000 of the 'Italian' zone. Both territories have had to rely heavily on grants-in-aid from the colonial powers amounting for most of the colonial period to about half their revenues. British Somaliland's total revenue in 1958 to 1959 was £1,653,000 and 41 per cent of this was provided from Britain, without counting Colonial Development and Welfare grants. Italian figures of the same kind can be roughly doubled. Both godparents have come forward with gifts in money and kind to tide over the infant state for the immediate future, but the long-term prospect remains alarming. Independence is never a cheap experiment. It arouses expectations of social betterment that few apprentice politicians dare refuse. Yet the Somalis confidently look to the world, and especially to their old protectors, to help them, and if their human need deserves help it should rightly come from the West.

The Horn of Africa may seem a barren triangle, but it is a land surface of great strategic importance. Two threats of trouble hang over it. One is the very natural Somali irredentism. The innocent looking white star of the new flag which decorates the streets of Mogadishu today has five points. Two represent Somaliland and Somalia, but the other three point in dangerous directions, towards the million or more Somalis who live in northern Kenya, in French Somaliland and in the Ethiopian Ogaden. This last is the most immediately dangerous because the Somalis refuse to recognize the line drawn by treaty which not only divides Somali from Somali but which must annually be crossed by a large proportion of former 'British' Somalis in search of essential seasonal water and grazing. It would be madness for the new Somalia to challenge Ethiopia or even to try to assert its strength by building expensively from the nucleus of armed strength left by the 'British' Somali Scouts and the 'Italian' police force.

What is needed, and needed immediately, is a large effort by the Western Powers, in co-operation with Ethiopia and Somalia, to work by modern methods of hydrology and conservation of pasture to solve the stubborn and dangerous poverty of the pastoralists. If this effort is not made there are plenty of neighbours near and far who could play a dangerous hand in this sensitive area.

In face of problems and poverty it is wonderful to see the rapture of the Somalis as they face the unknown. They have shown the usual passionate desire to cut short the brief months of probation. As one watches their joy, and is indeed irresistibly drawn into it, the thought arises how we in Britain, for all our constitutional liberalism and all our experience, still underestimated the passion for equality and for freedom from alien rule. There is respect and even affection here for Britain but less perhaps for what we have done for Somaliland than for our readiness to cease doing it. This people, high spirited, gifted, exposed to almost every danger, makes a confident demand not only for our continuing economic help but for the most practical and human expressions of our friendship and understanding.

A Prospect of Nigeria

The Listener 20 October 1960

For the second time in one year, 'Africa's year', I found myself the guest of an African government celebrating its independence. The uninhibited rejoicing of the vast crowds on Lagos racecourse as the Union Jack was run down and the handsome Nigerian flag run up could not drown the seemingly inappropriate fears with which I watched this substitution. Though I referred to these in the article the occasion seemed to demand that they should, at such a moment, be mentioned with restraint and hope.

I have recently returned from attending the independence celebrations in Nigeria. I can still feel their warmth: not the humid physical heat of

Lagos, but my warmth of gratitude for such splendid hospitality and the warmth of the Nigerians' recognition – their frank, generous recognition – of the part Britain has played in making their country. On all sides I heard the determination that Nigeria should remain united, and peaceful, and so take a leading place – perhaps *the* leading place – in Africa.

This preoccupation with unity is fundamental. For we all know that here, as in the rest of Negro Africa, the existing states were created only some sixty or seventy years ago by the European powers drawing boundaries round great blocks of Africa and enclosing sometimes hundreds of diverse and independent tribes. Nigeria's boundary was not finally drawn until 1903. It was put under one administration by Lugard only in 1914. The result is a state four times the size of the United Kingdom, holding some 35,000,000 people, seven times more than Ghana. And it is attempting to retain this unity in independence just when another large block of Africa has failed in the same attempt and is in an agony of dissolution. Indeed the Congo hung in the back of our minds like a skeleton at the Nigerian feast.

In Nigeria's own prospect lie elements of strength and weakness, deeply intertwined, causes for hope and for doubts. Reason for hope lies in the material out of which Nigeria was made. West Africa was far less isolated from the world than most of the continent south of the Sahara. Nigeria was open at both ends. Upon the north influences flowed down, a little languidly perhaps, from the more active civilizations beyond the Sahara. Islam penetrated slowly during the Middle Ages. And much later the south coast was reached by the ocean-going ships of Europe's age of exploration. True, they traded first in slaves, but they did not, like the Arabs in the east, have to ravage the country for their slaves, since there was ready supply on the coast. So the first Europeans to penetrate found in the north the large, red clay cities of the Hausa–Fulani peoples, spreading round the mosques and the labyrinthine palaces of their emirs, with lettered and learned men, lawcourts, a system of taxation and a network of trade routes reaching far beyond the future Nigeria. South, in Yoruba country, they found, still earlier, extensive walled cities, a people with a widespread, intricate pagan culture and, as in the north, weavers, dyers, metal-workers and other craftsmen. Elsewhere hill and forest had sheltered a more poor and primitive way of life, above all among the large Ibo and Ibibio groups of the south-east, peoples without cities and with little organization above the clan. Yet archaeologists and historians are finding

A PROSPECT OF NIGERIA [1960]

every year in Nigeria more evidence of cultural links which cross tribal and regional boundaries, representing a widespread complex of some of the most remarkable, beautiful and ancient sculptures in Africa. One of the most striking sights during the independence celebrations was the stream of Lagos people – 20,000 or more a day – men, market women and toddlers, suddenly queuing up at the museum to see these evidences of their art and their unity. Certainly Britain found here no waste of barbarism but a land of peoples, divided, various, and at many levels of culture, but with areas of considerable homogeneity and advanced political structure.

Nigeria's next advantage lies in forty-six years of unified government under Britain. But the matter is not as simple as it sounds. Britain let loose in Nigeria two contradictory influences, those lying at the very heart of her own historical experience: autocracy and liberty. Britain has perhaps shown that a democracy can rule an empire, but also that it cannot rule it consistently. I believe it may be just this inconsistency which saved her from the kind of immediate, all-embracing grasp, the stifling control, which could have been broken only by a violent upheaval.

I can only explain this historically. Britain introduced the concepts of liberty and democracy by starting, as soon as she annexed Lagos, a legislative council which was certain to be regarded as an embryo parliament. She also introduced British law and law courts to Lagos. This sent coastal Africans hurrying early to England to master the legal heritage of their masters, including their civil liberties, while the new schools taught English history, and with it ideas of nationalism, and democracy and unity. On the other hand, as she went on to annex the immense hinterland, British control was – perhaps at first it had to be – purely authoritarian. But how did her autocratic governors, especially Lugard, use their powers? To create local governments, carefully constructed to fit the mosaic of existing native societies. And these range all the way from a great emirate like Kano, with large revenues and powers of life and death over tens of thousands, down to little councils of elders for shy, naked, pagan groups. The system of indirect rule was like a steel grid with slots of various shapes and sizes holding the hundreds of native societies (now called Native Administrations), peaceful, secure, even efficient, but separate. But the grid could not continue to be entirely effective. The peace and the new communications, the rapidly increasing wealth, Christianity, education, clerical work for the British Government, wage labour on roads and mines – all these resulted in increasing mobility and in numbers spilling out of their tribal slots. There was an ever-growing company of secondary school and university men, especially in the coastal towns. They began to demand not indirect rule and local government but an increasing share in a central government; not division but unity; not tribalism but nationalism; not subordination but control.

It is largely due to the very anomalies of British rule that Nigerian nationalism found its voice. The pressure began between the wars. It was voluntarily throttled down during the last war, to burst out with renewed strength after the peace. There was – let us admit it – some bitter conflict, though only of words, while Britain hesitated, appalled by the size of the change demanded. But our hesitation was brief, and the Nigerian leaders have shown a remarkable patience and flexibility during the decade of commissions, conferences and constitutional experiments which led up to the present constitution and independence.

This constitution starts with two great advantages. It has not been imposed from Britain but has been hammered out over several years by the Nigerians themselves. Secondly – and I think this is one reason why independence has been so smoothly and amicably achieved – there has already been a very large transfer of power under the present Governor-General not only in the Regions but at the centre.

The fact remains that the constitution itself is a forced marriage between diversity and unity. The diversity rests in the three regions. The Western Region, with Lagos detached as the federal capital, holds nearly 7,000,000, two-thirds of which are Yoruba. The Eastern Region has 8,000,000, and again two-thirds belong to the dominant tribe, the Ibo. The Northern Region is disproportionate – three times as large as the others put together, and holds 18,000,000, more than half of Nigeria's total population. Here again the dominant group, more religious than tribal, that of the Moslems, is roughly two-thirds of the whole. These regions each have their own regional governments, with Houses of Assembly and Houses of Chiefs.

To hold together these diverse and uneven parts the Federal government has been given strong powers: foreign policy and defence, major communications, external trade, a complex but powerful control over revenue, the ultimate command over the police – the result of a long controversy – and the power to obtain external loans. Nigerians hope that this last will be an important link. For Nigeria is one of the poorest countries in Africa.

This is the *form* of the constitution, but without a motive power to make it work it would be like a motor car without petrol. The motive power was artificially supplied before by Britain from outside. Now it must be supplied from inside, by the Nigerians. Like other African peoples suddenly presented with a democratic constitution and universal franchise – only the Northern women being left out – they have had to construct political parties to activate the links between leaders and electorate. Dr Azikiwe started in good time with his National Council of Nigeria and the Cameroons; Chief Awolowo followed with the Yoruba Action Group; and then came the Northern People's Congress. But it would be too much to expect the new voters to act as individuals on ideological grounds. In fact the parties are based mainly – not entirely – upon the three dominant regional groups. In so far as each region shows dissident votes they are cast less for another party than as an ethnic protest against the dominant group by minority tribes. Federal unity, therefore, is balanced somewhat precariously upon a tripod of the three regional parties with north and east in coalition and west providing the necessary opposition. At present it is almost as though no one dared to breathe lest the tripod should shift and topple.

Beneath this difficult restraint regional differences are great. I believe that the Ibo are the main force for unity. They need unity. As the poorest region – though perhaps their recent strike of mineral oil will change that – they have had to pour out of their overcrowded forests to seek work all over the other regions. Again, having no great history, no impressive chiefs or cities, they need to find their pride, their fulfilment, in the new Nigeria itself. Able, individualistic, hard-working, democratic, they could be the unifying leaven, and Dr Azikiwe could properly express, as Governor-General, not only the independence but also the unity for which he has worked so long.

What a difference in the west! Here are the Yoruba with their large cities, their long traditions of urbanization; their rich intricate pagan culture; their early contact with Europe, its Christianity and education; their superior wealth; their almost bourgeois society. They tend to be self-sufficient, their leaders more concentrated upon building themselves up – indeed building themselves *in* – as a self-sufficient and well administered welfare state. The only danger for the Action Group is that some Yoruba townspeople are now so sophisticated that they are beginning to vote, as electors should, by conviction, for the opposition party.

Turn to the north, to princedoms with centuries of authoritarian rule behind them, and a conservative, apparently docile, Moslem peasantry.

[1960]

When you see one of their emirs ride out from his palace attended by his bodyguard and richly robed officials upon some great Moslem festival, and watch the delight of the crowds in their great man, you do not wonder that the Prime Minister of the north comes from the royal and holy lineage of Sokoto, or that he prefers his Regional office to that of Federal Prime Minister. Could this pageant of high authority disintegrate? Could this north ever bow peacefully to a non-Moslem majority? The emirs have certainly made some concessions to modernity in recent years. And their great overall majority depends upon their holding within their party the so-called middle-belt, their southern fringe of mixed pagan tribes who long ago welcomed the Christian and Western educational influences the Moslems disdained. Now the proud northerners suddenly find themselves at a disadvantage with the once despised pagan south and their leaders are desperately building up Western education and ruthlessly weeding out the Southerners who have for so long supplied their lack of trained men. The other parties *could* filch away the allegiance of the northern pagans. The Action Group has had some success in this direction. Unfortunately for southern political agents, to stir up simple tribesmen against their age-old masters comes close to incitement to revolt, and this evokes police action.

The future lies in the gradual dissolution of the tribal and regional solids into a true fluid Nigerian electorate. The constitution does its best in a chapter of Fundamental Rights with a list of civil rights which out-Diceys Dicey. The whole constitution seeks to enshrine the British democratic pattern. But our minds turn to Pakistan, to the Sudan, to the 'guided democracy' of Ghana, to portents in Ceylon. We must remember that these new governments are responding to pressures which no copybook constitution can meet. In Britain we had in sequence across the centuries political and cultural unity, then strong central monarchical government, then widespread economic prosperity, and then universal education, and finally complete democracy. (I do not forget that I did not get a vote until some years after I had both my majority and my degree.) The Africans are having these things just exactly the other way round, and all in some sixty years. But in Nigeria the democratic colours are on the mast, the tripartite balance seems for the moment to forbid dictatorship and the habits of political co-operation and compromise may thus have time to grow.

Perhaps the greatest motive for unity and moderation is the Nigerians' desire to take their place in the world. They enter the African stage like some chief actor for whom the world audience has been impatiently waiting while the minor characters played their parts. There is so much tragedy today in Africa – north, centre and south – so much tension in the east – that we look eagerly to Nigeria to use her strength for sanity and moderation. Here, for external and internal affairs, we come to one of Nigeria's greatest assets – her Prime Minister, Sir Abubakar Tafawa Balewa. I have known him for some time and I have just heard his fine, full-throated, independence speeches. He has the *gravitas* of a great man with the double strength of his religion and his own integrity. Yet it will not be easy for him to fuse the diverse impulses of Nigeria and so write this new name in bold characters in the world's news. The N.C.N.C. may well cry 'Forward!' while the N.P.C. cries 'Back!' The Moslem north may look north and east to the world of Islam while the south may want to experiment in contacts with the Communists – or Israel! Even so, as his speech at the United Nations shows, he will do his best to make Nigerian policy honest and moderate.

We can no longer influence that policy. We must stand aside, not even presuming upon the goodwill built up by the hundreds of our men and women who served Nigeria in the past, not trying to pull even the Commonwealth bond too tightly. Nigerians, like other newly independent peoples, want to go out into the world and judge themselves between men and nations. Yet they need our help – though not ours alone – if it is given in the spirit of equality. And above all they will welcome our help in the sphere of education. For the English language will be a growing bond since it seems that between the diverse regions it must remain the *lingua franca* and the official language for Nigeria. The report of the recent powerful Ashby Education Commission – a joint Nigerian-American-British achievement – sets a staggering programme of educational advance for the next twenty years if Nigeria is to man the technical and administrative services which the now dwindling British staff has begun. There would be no greater service with which Britain could crown all her past efforts than by giving generously, in men, women and money, to the educational services by which alone these African peoples will be able to make of Nigeria not only a name but a nation.

1961

White Minorities in Africa

Letter to *The Times* 15 March 1961

Sir, – In terms of current politics, with a Cabinet, an Opposition, and most of his own party in his support, Mr Macleod needs no additional defence. But I believe that history, over which Lord Salisbury should cast a retrospective eye, will also be on his side. Africa – as your Colonial Correspondent's brilliant series of articles show – by its long isolation and sudden penetration has played some cruel tricks upon its own peoples and is now dealing out harsh treatment to its European and Asian colonists. These built their slender predominance in the tropical belt upon the vast foundation of native ignorance and disunity. Now, in these 'mixed' areas, and partly as a result of their own constructive work, that foundation is heaving into resentful movement, one which has behind it Britain's own political principles and the support of almost the whole of a world suddenly concentrating its attention upon Africa.

The colonists might be less embittered, though not less endangered, if they could be assured that their own errors or selfishness, which have been less, perhaps, than those of any similarly dominant caste, can have had no more than a marginal effect in arousing opposition. The reason for their danger is that to the Africans, moved by the hunger for human dignity and facing the immense task of creating states out of arbitrary tribal maps, they have become obstructive or irrelevant. Unless, of course they can accept the hazardous reversal of becoming minorities under prentice African Governments.

The colonists' predicament should indeed evoke not only the understanding and sympathy of Britain but also our practical help, difficult though the constructive application of help may prove. But no sympathy can do much to soften the hard reality that in 1961 small immigrant minorities can no longer hope to dominate large African majorities except, as in the Union, by increasing resort to methods which must drain 'white civilization' of its moral claim to leadership.

This reality, in spite of many warnings from impartial observers, British governments have been culpably slow to face, thus preserving the illusion of a settler's paradise. Sooner or later, therefore, a British Colonial Secretary had to put our policy suddenly into reverse.

Mr Macleod has had the courage to undertake this difficult and ungrateful operation. He may prove to have been just in time in Kenya. Central Africa is more difficult. Here the very attempt of the Europeans, by means of federation, to entrench their position against both African nationalism and imperial control has awakened the first and so brought the other into play. There may be a case in the pivotal state of Northern Rhodesia for a brief phased and educational plan for transferring power, as Professor Harlow has suggested, if this is still attainable. But any weakening of ministerial and parliamentary support for Mr Macleod, in face of the attack led by Lord Salisbury, could result only in a postponement of the inevitable settlement with African nationalism. This delay would ultimately fail to salvage the colonists' position and might also lessen Britain's capacity to assist in the subsequent development of Central Africa or of other parts of this exacting continent.

Yours faithfully

Portuguese Africa: The Achilles Heel

Letter to *The Times* 10 May 1961

Sir, – Your article today, 'Achilles' Heel', draws grave attention to the Angola situation. But it does not sufficiently emphasize the wider aspects of these disorders. The critics and enemies of 'the West' have an interest in regarding Western 'colonialism' as one manifestation, and Portugal's membership of NATO and her long alliance with Britain make it difficult for Britain to disclaim all interest in the crisis. It has even been said that Portuguese forces are dropping on African villages napalm which is 'Made in Britain'. We may hope this will be denied.

Britain and her NATO allies should, as their first urgent step, warn the Portuguese Government against continuing the excesses of which her troops are widely reported to be guilty. It is true that those external leaders who, it seems, have instigated the Bacongo rebels to indulge in wholesale murder of helpless white colonists bear the gravest responsibility, and that fellow-colonists and soldiers who see such horrors or hear of them are under severe temptation to indulge in wholesale reprisals. But, as Britain learnt in Kenya, it is the test of a civilized government, and the only hope of future good relations with the Africans, that the instinct for revenge that is likely to strike the innocent with the guilty should be restrained and order restored, difficult though this may be in wild country, with discipline and due forms of law.

The standards of humanity in our world are sagging under the load of accumulated atrocities and our Government should do all that lies in its power to use its influence with our ally in the course of restraint. We may hope, too, that in this Roman Catholic country, the hierarchy from the Pope downwards will use their influence in the same direction. We have already heard of the courageous sacrifice made by one priest.

But the problem of Angola is more than a matter of immediate restraint. What is to be its future in a continent in which the greater part is self-governing and is pressing hard upon the Portuguese colonial position?

The Congo fell into chaos because the Belgians, for all their excellent work upon the economic and educational substructure, had not achieved the training of Africans for the higher responsibilities of self-government. But the Portuguese dictatorship recognizes no duty to train its African subjects for a self-government it denies to its own people. From the days of the anti-slavery movement until today it has been in the dock for its treatment of African labour. Are we to stand by and do nothing while the people of Angola, and perhaps, later, of Mozambique, stirred by external precept and example, either drift into a chaos far worse than that of the Congo or else are held in the immobility of a repression which must increase the tensions between white and black men in Africa and white and black states in the west?

This is a situation upon which Britain and her allies, above all the United States, have powerful influences which they can direct. We must hope that these governments have been able to pierce the Portuguese curtain of secrecy and that, estimating the dangers that are opening up, have already through their representatives now in Oslo, begun to make a remedial use of that influence.

Yours faithfully

Northern Rhodesia's Right to Secede

Letter to *The Times* 17 August 1961

Sir, – It is tragic for the Northern Rhodesian Africans that their crisis should have arisen while Britain's attention is divided between holidays and the Berlin problem. It was inevitable, when Africans saw that the British Government still calculated that European pressure was more effective than theirs, that they should try to demonstrate the contrary.

The Government can hardly claim that it is acting upon any principle. Are Northern Rhodesians any more politically inexperienced than Tanganyikans whom we have almost caressed into independence? Why should Northern Rhodesia be treated differently from Nyasaland? Must its people be forced to use the same tragic methods as those by which Nyasaland Africans forced us to reverse our policy? If so, just how much blood must be shed to produce the same result?

If the industrial character of Northern Rhodesia is given as a reason for the present policy it can be answered that Africans know the value of the copper mines to themselves and would therefore co-operate with the companies and they also know how their organization could be used to undermine production, if not, indeed, to sabotage the mines.

The determination of Sir Roy Welensky and his party to maintain European control over the Rhodesias is perfectly natural, as natural as was that of the Kenya settlers to maintain their former predominance. Upon what principle has the government taken the painful decision to reject the Europeans' demand for Kenya and to accept it for Northern Rhodesia?

European colonists, enclosed in the fears and dangers of a changing Africa, tend to ascribe such views as those in this letter to an unnatural prejudice against their own 'kith and kin'. But they are based upon such serious study of the total situation of Central Africa as lies behind the dozen or so books that have been published on this region in the last three years.

It is possible that the Northern Rhodesian Africans might be cowed for a few years more by repressive measures. But it is impossible to believe that they will ever willingly accept the complex and tricky constitution now proposed when almost the whole of the rest of Africa is independent and is able to give them support both locally and internationally. A longer view of their own best interests should persuade the colonists to agree with their own more realistic members and with the local church leaders that the wisest policy is to give the Africans real responsibility before the moderate Kaunda is pushed aside by more ruthless leadership.

Responsibility alone can cure the rising anger of the Africans against their subordination and bring out their constructive and generous qualities. The Federation as constituted was morally out of date before it was enacted, and in supporting Sir Roy Welensky the Government is fighting a losing battle against the African majority in Rhodesia, against all independent African states, against the great preponderance of world opinion and a very large section of their own countrymen.

By admitting their mistake they might inaugurate a period which, difficult though it must be in view of African inexperience, would at least be constructive and not merely negative. They might even, at the forthcoming conference, save the Federation by shifting it on to a new basis of freely willed African participation.

Yours faithfully

1962

Yesterday's Rulers: Introduction

This is the introduction I wrote for a book on the British Colonial Service by Professor Robert Heussler. It was published by the Oxford University Press and, in the United States, by the Syracuse University Press, in 1963.

An immense literature has been written about British colonial policy and administration and surprisingly little about the men who expressed policy in administration. There are, of course, many studies of individual pro-consuls: it is as a service that they have been given inadequate attention. We have general studies by Sir Charles Jeffries and Sir Alan Burns, two men who have the knowledge which comes from long and direct responsibility in this sphere.[1] The special characteristics of Professor Heussler's present work are detachment, thoroughness and selectivity. All these require some explanation.

The detachment is neither from a vast distance, nor from superior eminence: it results from both his nationality and his experience. Professor Heussler has qualities of heart as well as head which have enabled him to enter with imaginative understanding into the more human and idealistic aspects of colonialism without being drawn away from his usefully external viewpoint. For myself I have found it a stimulating if sometimes uncomfortable experience to follow the probing light thrown by this American mind as it passes over a subject much of which has been left by us British in the shadow of the unquestioned.

About the thoroughness there is more to say. Those of us for whom the Colonial Service filled a large part in our lives must be grateful not only for the comment but also for the lively and detailed picture upon which it is based. For this is not one of the hundreds of academic theses

---

[1] C. Jeffries, *The Colonial Empire and Its Civil Service*, Cambridge, Cambridge University Press, 1938; Sir A. Burns, *Colonial Civil Servant*, London, Allen and Unwin, 1949.

[1962] COLONIAL SEQUENCE 1949 TO 1969

composed in studies and libraries out of the relevant records and then loosened up for publication. The essential work on the records is there, but few students of foreign institutions have been able to spend so much time out in the field of their studies. In Professor Heussler's case this field covered almost the whole of Europe's dependencies and ex-dependencies, some of which he visited not once but many times. It was from the skies as a U.S. Army Air Force pilot that he began to view the world and to make contacts with his British opposite numbers. Work for an oil company posted him to China and Hong Kong and this was followed by assignments in aerial photography in parts of the West Indies, nearly all of tropical Africa, the Arab States and the Mediterranean, and all of ex-British Asia. In 1959 Professor Heussler came to England and to Oxford as a Fulbright scholar, determined to study the British Colonial Service whose work he had so often encountered in his travels. In Britain he interviewed large numbers of Colonial Office officials, active and retired, academic workers in Commonwealth affairs, and other informants. Everywhere, I know, he made a great impression by his understanding, both deep and wide, of their problems and by his seriousness of purpose. As a result he was everywhere given the maximum of information and access to the records. In 1960, as an associate director of a Ford Foundation survey to determine the possibility of attaching American graduates to colonial governments for training, he took time off to revisit much of tropical Africa – I saw him at work in Tanganyika – and South-east Asia, and he reached Borneo and Fiji. He estimates that in the course of these travels he interviewed 150 British colonial civil servants and perhaps another fifty non-British. It would, indeed, be difficult to imagine an approach which so fully combined the documentary, the human and the [geographical sides of a large aspect of modern government.

Professor Heussler was faced with many intricacies and obscurities in his extensive study. But he was helped by one great simplification. He might have expected that, as is usual in the history of British institutions, the policy behind the formation of the Colonial Service would have to be disentangled from the activities of a succession of ministers and officials, expressing the subconscious standards and the unspoken purposes of their class and nation. But he found something very exceptional in the British record. Not only had one man directed the recruitment of the Service for the entire twenty-five years under review, but he had done so according to clear principles and by means of a sustained and brilliant administrative campaign. This man was Major Sir Ralph

'YESTERDAY'S RULERS': INTRODUCTION   [1962]

Furse, K.C.M.G., D.S.O., M.A., Hon. D.C.L., Oxford – unusual and significant combination of titles! – and he has confessed that he owes his success less to Eton, Balliol and Oxford than to his early training as a cavalry officer. For by a fortunate coincidence the present study has been preceded by the vividly personal recollections of this official. These should certainly be read alongside Professor Heussler's book, since much of this is a description and commentary upon Furse's life work.[1]

I must confess here that in commenting upon the subject of this book I cannot claim complete detachment. As the pages which follow may suggest, both Sir Ralph and Sir Douglas Veale, the former Registrar of Oxford University and another main actor in these events, were my admired friends and colleagues, and I was involved both in helping to plan the courses for the Service in Oxford and in teaching these courses in colonial history and administration.

Turning now to Professor Heussler's selectivity, he has cut a section out of a very large field by imposing upon himself four limitations. Firstly, he has selected the quarter-century following 1920 for his period, covering the years when the Colonial Service grew to its brief maturity both in size and in clarity of vocation. Secondly, he has confined his attention mainly to the administrative cadre of a service which was rapidly extending its ancillary social and technical branches. Thirdly, he has concentrated his attention upon the aspects of recruitment and training, though with a clear sense of the wider horizons to which these aspects pointed. Fourthly, among the three universities which were centres for training – Oxford, Cambridge and London – he has concentrated upon the records of the first in its relations with the Colonial Office.

To some it might seem at first sight that the second and third of these limits have unduly narrowed the subject. But if no understanding of the British colonial empire would be possible without a study of the men who were the distant and scattered agents of their country's policy, it follows that the administrators must demand first attention because they were for many years almost the only agents and remained the dominant branch of the Service until the later years brought their ever-widening concept of the scope of government. Such a service does not come into existence by any autonomous process similar to natural growth. Recruits have to be attracted, assayed, appointed, stationed,

[1] *Aucuparius: Recollections of a Recruiting Officer*, London, Oxford University Press, 1962.

promoted and, later, perhaps retrained and transferred. All these intricate operations should be carried out under the direction of some guiding principles. They will certainly reflect the governing *mores* of the society within which they are conducted. Professor Heussler's concentration upon the two first processes of recruitment and training is justified since, although by the intelligent administration of administrators the best use can be made of given human material, there are limits to what can be done to change and develop the material itself.

We are confronted in this book by a major theme, one that was bound to strike forcibly upon an American mind but which, until recent years, was largely taken for granted in Britain, especially in civil service and professional circles. There was the determined and largely successful effort of Furse to make the administrative branch of the Colonial Service what the writer calls an élitist corps. Today a majority both of Americans and of British will almost certainly regard this as a serious criticism of the Service. When I look back over the thirty years during which I have been involved in teaching for the Colonial Service and also in studying its work overseas, I realize now that I took this aspect for granted. It needed this book and Furse's own recollections to reveal its significance and also the single-minded tenacity with which Furse pursued his aim.

Those who criticize this policy should re-examine their own reasons. They should measure the speed with which education has spread in Britain and with it the assertion of social and political equality and observe that it has been a natural, perhaps a necessary, part of this assertion to condemn the concepts of a 'ruling class' and a 'public school type'. They should reconstruct both the conditions of the early inter-war years and the different ideas then prevailing and study the character of the need which Furse was trying to meet. His Service needed a steady recruitment of men who combined a high, though not necessarily the highest, intellectual standard with the desire and the stamina to face an adventurous life in strange, distant and sometimes dangerous conditions. An unusual combination of qualities was needed – courage with adaptability; firmness with sympathy; enterprise with reliability; obedience with authority. In lonely stations, far from the restraints of European public opinion and supported by no lavish remuneration, the officer must remain dignified and incorruptible. Moreover, with whatever margin of individual qualities, the members of this increasing corps must share the same standards of conduct and manners sufficiently to allow them to understand one another. They must act, when dispersed over wide and testing regions, upon similar principles and in pursuit of the same almost unspoken purposes. Officers of the Colonial Service needed a pride in their Service, derived from an almost indivisible devotion to their own country and to the people they felt they were serving. The book describes how by recruitment and training this need was largely met in what was, in the years concerned, the most obvious and reliable way. This was from the public schools and the two ancient universities from which most of the boys from these schools proceeded. For it was in the confident, athletic and privileged – but not too privileged – class that the necessary combination of qualities could most often be found.

There is one special point I would add from my own experience of the work of training. Although the Colonial Office, as Professor Heussler shows, was in a sense the employer of the university in this work, there was never to my knowledge even the suspicion of interference with the freedom of those engaged in teaching. I was myself engaged in the most controversial of our subjects, colonial administration. I was, and was known to be, critical of some aspects of our colonial policy, especially in areas of white settlement. I used the opportunity, even after the difficult challenge of African nationalism had begun, to discuss these difficult issues. As far as I know neither I nor any of my colleagues who may have used their freedom in this way ever received official criticism or caution. If such criticism ever emanated from a colonial government it was smothered in the Colonial Office before it ever reached us. I think that, in general, the influence of the university teachers would often have tended to question rather than confirm accepted ideas of colonial policy. It is a tribute to the liberalism of the Colonial Office, and its respect for the British tradition of academic freedom, that this remained possible until the end, in places the somewhat difficult end, of its rule. It is, perhaps, also a tribute to the officers that they did not resent this doubtless sometimes rather unrealistic handling of their life's work. Certainly they never seemed to me to belong to a uniform type. If the second courses sometimes contained men whose conformist minds had become further rusted through the exercise of power and the effects of isolation, I can remember few classes which were not enlivened by others with open and questioning minds.

It will already be clear that from the starting point of recruitment this study leads on to wider considerations of the British social structure. In the background, moreover, lies the whole question of imperialism, now called colonialism, upon which world opinion, stimulated by the sudden awakening of African political consciousness, has so vigorously reversed an acceptance as old as the historical record. The past is now seen in the highly coloured light of the new political emotions of our time and it is not possible at present to find any agreed standards by which to judge the record of past, and passing, colonial rule. It is much too soon to judge how far the emancipated peoples will consciously or unconsciously use the colonial foundations for their new political erections and, if they do use them, how serviceable they will prove. This is not to say that no preliminary attempts can yet be made to weigh the mistakes and the achievements of colonialism. In Western countries students of this subject are right not to reserve all judgement. They analyse and record and in the process devise at least provisional standards by which to weigh both the intentions and the achievements of the men of their own age. In making his record, Professor Heussler is thorough and lively: as a judge he has the necessary moderation and personal and national detachment. Dealing with an often obscure but central part of the whole subject of colonial rule, this book is likely to remain one of the most convincing parts of the evidence in a controversy which much of world opinion has turned into a prosecution.

1963

Foreword to *Mau Mau Detainee*[1]

This book, published by the Oxford University Press in 1963, and later as a paperback arose from an unexpected visit to my home by Mr Kariuki, still showing the marks of injuries received in detention. He was introduced to me by Mr John Nottingham, an administrative officer who later settled in Kenya and founded the firm 'East Africa Publishing House'. We gave Mr Kariuki some help in producing and publishing his story. When not long after I attended the independence celebrations in Kenya as the guest of President Kenyatta, Mr Kariuki met me in a Mercedes car and has since flourished as possessor of a farm in the former 'White Highlands', as a racehorse owner and as a junior minister in the present 1969 government.

I must begin by saying that Mr Kariuki, the author of this book, has agreed that I should be free to write what I wish in this Foreword. This was for him a considerable act of trust; it follows, of course, that he has no responsibility for what I write.

This book must have a deeply disturbing effect upon those British readers who believe its story. Those, especially in Kenya, who regard it as untrue or greatly exaggerated may deplore its publication. Yet I believe that it is right that it should be published. It records the experiences of a young Kikuyu who was detained from 1953 to 1960 as an activist in the Mau Mau movement in Kenya and who describes his periodical ill-treatment while in detention. But it also reveals what passed in his mind during this experience and there can be little doubt that, in greater or lesser degree, his attitude is shared with thousands of other Kikuyu who, as the so-called 'hard core' of Mau Mau, are likely to play a very active part in the future Kenya. It is also probable that his story will arouse sympathy and understanding among Africans in general and in much of the non-African world. For us British, whether in Britain or

[1] J. Kariuki, *Mau Mau Detainee*, Oxford University Press, 1963.

[1963]   COLONIAL SEQUENCE 1949 TO 1969

in Kenya, who were shocked by the character of the Mau Mau outbreak, to know all may not be to forgive all but it is still important to *know*, and few who read this book are likely to close it with quite the same views of Mau Mau, or, perhaps, of Africa in general, as those with which they opened it.

The effect of Mr Kariuki's book must depend upon the extent to which it commands belief. For myself I believe that he has given a substantially true account of his own experiences. I say 'substantially' because he could not be expected to take a panoramic view of a total situation in which, beginning as little more than a schoolboy, he occupied one small and inevitably isolated part. I will return to this point in a moment. In judging the question of credibility I have had the advantage of meeting him. I had no predisposition to like a 'hard-core' ex-Mau Mau detainee, yet I quickly felt a liking for him. This was because he made an impression not only, as could be expected, of resolution, but also of modesty, friendliness, balance and humour. More surprising, he revealed a healing desire for reconciliation with those Europeans or Africans who had ill-treated him. The result of our meeting was that I decided I ought to do what lay in my power to facilitate the writing and publication of his story.

My personal impression is not enough to authenticate this record. Others will make their own decision. Most will be able to judge only from the internal evidence of this book, but others will have external evidence of the background of events. If those with intimate knowledge of this recent history can produce evidence to refute this account, either in whole or in part, that would be one important result of this publication. But we must remember that there is published evidence that some of the authorities concerned *were* guilty of acts of negligence, harshness and cruelty in dealing with the Mau Mau outbreak. In the early years of the Emergency some incidents of the torture of prisoners came to light. When I was in Kenya in 1953 I heard stories of harsh measures and I made my own protest to the Governor. The death of eleven 'hard-core' prisoners at Hola Camp at the hands of African warders in 1959 shocked British opinion and led to a searching inquiry into the incident. It also led to a more general Committee of Inquiry which found some evidence, not only of inefficiency and neglect in the detention camps, but also of violent methods being used against prisoners, abuses which were generally, but not always, committed by African warders. A list of the relevant official reports follows this Foreword.

FOREWORD TO 'MAU MAU DETAINEE' [1963]

A balanced view of the large-scale detentions and of the policy behind the administration of the camps can be attained only in the context of Kenya's years of crisis during the fifties. The Mau Mau movement was in fact a rebellion and, in the main, the rebellion of a single tribal group, that of the Kikuyu, with some kindred and neighbouring groups, the Kamba, Meru and Embu, affected in a varying but lesser degree. This Kikuyu tribe lives in the very heart of the Colony. Its lands reach close to the capital but they also stretch northwards into a large hilly and forested area which proved ideal for guerilla war. The outbreak was utterly unexpected. It almost broke down ordered government and its suppression cost some sixty million pounds and a prolonged military effort with the help of British troops. This was not all. Incitement to kill was directed against Europeans. It was not, however, very effective for, though some of the resultant murders were peculiarly cruel, the number of Europeans killed was surprisingly small, some thirty as against the 1,000 reported to have been massacred in Angola in 1961. But over a wide area for several years Europeans in their isolated farms lived day by day, and especially night by night, in almost hourly fear of the arrival of assassins with their pangas – heavy-bladed agricultural implements – with which victims were slashed to death. The maiming of cattle, a device reminiscent of Irish history, caused the European farmers an indignation far greater than that aroused by the financial loss. Africans, and indeed Kikuyu, suffered far more than Europeans or Asians. As a minority of Kikuyu, especially some of those holding responsible positions, openly supported the Government, something close to civil war developed. It is estimated that 1,700 loyalists were killed and many others were wounded or tortured. At a mission station in the height of the rebellion I saw a little of the courage of the Christians as they carried on with their work in the face of danger, ostracism and death. When the Lari massacre by the Mau Mau of a whole village, men, women and children, occurred, I met a friend, a senior police officer, who an hour before had been at the scene of the events, and he was almost unmanned by what he had just seen. On the other side some 10,000 Africans were killed by the security forces and nearly 90,000 detained before the rebellion was brought to an end.

In the face of terrorism and counter-terrorism as employed in the contemporary world, the would-be humane and impartial onlooker feels a sense of moral helplessness. Such is the power of the modern state that rebellion has become more of a murderous than a military effort, and the most atrocious conflicts have generally been those, of

[1963]

which Algeria is an example on the larger scale, in which a subject race rises against alien colonizers. It was in Algeria that some French authorities seem to have legitimized the use of torture. Our author refers to some of the brutalities committed by Africans but seems to believe, with other African politicians, that their extent has been exaggerated. There is a natural temptation for Africans, in retort, to exaggerate the harshness of repression. It must be left to historians to sift all the evidence when passions have cooled.

I have dwelt upon this aspect because it is necessary to recall to those who read this book what can so easily be forgotten, the pathological atmosphere in Kenya when the events described in it occurred – not only the sense of personal fear in which Europeans and loyalists were living, but fear for the future of white settlement, and fear even for a colony-wide breakdown of order if an initially Kikuyu movement should spread to other tribes. But in addition to these very explicable fears there was something more. The movement was fostered and bound together by secret and graded oaths, and the bestiality of the more advanced of these was so revolting to Europeans, and not only to them, that it seemed to many that those who used such methods ceased to be normal human beings. It appeared that these oaths had extraordinary psychological effects upon many of those who took them. Here again there is no certain evidence as to the prevalence of the more extreme oaths. Our writer who, as he records, took only the first two relatively milder oaths, has hard things to say of the practice of pressing prisoners to confess to their oaths. The danger of such an attempt is obvious but the intention behind the policy was reformist and not punitive. It was an attempt to accelerate release by breaking the spell of the Mau Mau oath and passing men through what was known as the 'pipeline'. This was a progression for the detainees from the more severe to the more lenient camps until they could be detained finally in sight of their home country, and visited by their families, in the hope that this would complete their reformation.

I saw many of these 'hard core' men and women in the camps I visited, and the dark look upon their faces, which seemed to add an extra darkness to the colour of their skin, and their look of settled hatred as they sat about motionless on the ground, evoked something much deeper than normal fear both for them and for those they hated. If they were sometimes treated with brutality by officers at their wits' end in dealing with them, the sincere attempts to apply psychological and other redemptive methods should also be remembered. I recall an in-

FOREWORD TO 'MAU MAU DETAINEE' [1963]

cident in which an Englishwoman who was in 'moral' charge of some of the 'hard core' women, and who had studied their customs and their language, believed she had won a group of them back to a basis of understanding and co-operation and so to the possibility of a release to which they had seemed almost indifferent. As a final proof of trust she handed to them her own very young baby and I caught my breath as they took the small white bundle and passed it around among themselves. But their looks and gestures were the universal ones of motherhood, and before long they were in a lorry *en route* for their home villages.

It should also be remembered, in considering the background of this book, that from the purely practical angle the policy of detention faced the Kenya Government with an almost impossible task. They had to build their camps quickly and with equal haste recruit such hundreds of European staff as they could find, few of whom had any experience of such work. These, in turn, had to rely upon rapidly recruited and raw African warders – 14,000 was the 1954 figure – who were, as a matter of policy, in the early days chosen from non-Kikuyu tribes. Where the officials in charge were faced, perhaps in camps containing many thousands, with the defiance of these 'hard core' prisoners, who, perhaps, just sat still refusing to work or to co-operate in any way, there was always a danger that their spirit might infect the whole vast mass of the detainees. I would assume from his own account that if the writer was called 'hard core', and, indeed, assumed this name himself, it was because of an obstinacy derived from his strong will and not from the spiritual state of mind which the authorities discerned in the advanced oath-takers. He might not agree with me here since 'hard core' became an honourable appellation, and a bond of unity which no ex-detainee would wish to weaken. But the root cause of Mr Kariuki's defiance of the authorities seems to have been his determination to prove that he and his close associates in defiance were not in the grip of some remedial obsession but pursuing logical and irrevocable political aims.

I would therefore suggest that if we accept – and regret – the evidence Mr Kariuki records of his ill-treatment, we should also give weight to the attempts that were made to deal fairly and intelligently with an unprecedented situation. Mr Kariuki himself gives us plenty of evidence of ways in which humanity tempered violence, for example by the alternation of humane with inhumane officials, and by the opportunities for sport and education in some of the camps. Most important, perhaps, was his confidence that in Britain, and even in Kenya, there were standards of law, justice and humanity to which he could appeal, and to which he *did* appeal successfully, though to do so needed all his courage and skill.

More widely than the issue of humanity, Mr Kariuki's story will be taken as a condemnation of British colonialism as exhibited in Kenya. In this issue the outbreak should be seen in its wider historical dimensions. For neither Mr Kariuki nor his Mau Mau comrades on the one side, nor the officials and settlers who struggled with them on the other, were responsible for the situation which suddenly forced them into such destructive antagonism. The first of the long series of events which led up to the Mau Mau rebellion occurred not, indeed, when Britain annexed East Africa in 1895 – for the record shows how her other 'all black' African dependencies have developed in the main by orderly process into independence – but when the first white settler began to farm in the largely empty highlands. For white settlement meant confronting the tribes which patchily inhabited this then nameless block of Africa with an alien tribe of utterly different culture, one which, for all its small numbers, was powerful in its civilization, wealth and unity, and therefore in its capacity to dominate. This group was determined to take over from Britain the control of the country as other European colonists had done in almost every part of the world where they settled in new lands among the native peoples. It was only through the most strenuous efforts by opponents in Britain of this policy that settler 'self-government' was denied and imperial control retained. But the Africans could not continue to remain ignorant of the significance for them of this long and public conflict over the destiny of their territory. Nor could they be sure that their fear that the European settlers would gain control over the government was no longer valid. For reasons which have been given the Kikuyu were the tribe most deeply affected and the Mau Mau movement was the sudden culmination of their gradual political awakening.

The movement had three aspects: sociological, economic and political. Sociologically it was the assertion of a tribe, perhaps Kenya's most able and ambitious tribe, against the dominating presence of a European colony. Its members had seen the erection upon their borders of a powerful and attractive civilization which undermined their own society while it seemed to deny their access to the new one except as its servants. Economically, as under ordered government the Kikuyu rapidly increased both in numbers and in agricultural skill and ambition, they felt that their own beautiful reserve of hills, woods and streams was inadequate to their needs, and they looked enviously at the nearby European farms upon which many of them went out to work –

FOREWORD TO 'MAU MAU DETAINEE' [1963]

among them the author's family. The Kikuyu had lost only a small proportion of land to European settlement. But a loss which was spatially unimportant was, in the circumstances, psychologically oppressive. Moreover, by occupying empty land the settlers barred Kikuyu expansion. The Africans were too much dominated by the land issue to recognize that European development had created many new opportunities for employment. This is not surprising. The provisions of a welfare state for a changing society were hardly yet envisaged and Africans were faced with overcrowding and unemployment in the towns and the need for farmland to support the children, the women and the aged.

Finally, the tribe, largely through Mr Kenyatta's leadership, had awakened to the idea that their discontents could be cured by political action. They had for long watched European and Asian political activities and had learned much from the observation. They were ceasing by the late forties to be interested in the gradualist policy of the Government. This was one of advancing their political education partly through increasing control of their own local government and partly by minority representatives in the Colony's legislature. By the late forties they were, perhaps, beginning to be moved less by the fear of the settlers achieving political control than by the determination to achieve this for themselves and win the place for the majority which, as they now knew, the rules of democracy accorded them. Their sense of increasing oppression was more psychological than reasoned: as with other revolutions they were advancing in education and economic well-being but the pace was too slow and the presence of an alien community, which regarded them as inferior, had become intolerable to many of the educated Africans. The emancipation of the Sudan, of Ghana and of neighbouring and economically backward Somalia, all helped to turn hope into determination. Apart from its other interest, this book reveals the abrupt awakening of a young Kikuyu to the political facts of life and to a world now suddenly realized as one which favoured colonial emancipation.

I must confine myself to this brief reminder of the political background against which the tragic drama of Mau Mau was played out. It would take too long, and perhaps it is too soon, to discuss with confidence any closer allocation of responsibility for these events. There is a sense in which African tribes must be regarded as the innocent parties since it was the Europeans, especially in eastern Africa, who broke in upon their long isolation and took complete control of the situation. In this sense the responsibility for all that has happened since rests upon the Europeans, many of whom went out with the best intentions to build up in the wilderness a projection of their own civilization in the hope that this would benefit both races. But the time comes when the Africans lose their innocence: with Western education and contact with the world they escape the simpler imperatives of tribal life and eat of the knowledge of political good and evil. In this story we can almost watch the young Kariuki partaking of this dangerous knowledge.

With the shattering of reliance upon the old tribalism and the dwindling sense of trust and confidence in British rule, a new allegiance had to be built up and attached to the new African leaders, an all-inclusive devotion which could sublimate the tribe and even be attached as far as possible to this strange new entity, the nation. This nation has still to be created, both as an idea and an institution, to fill the areas roughed out in the scramble for Africa. It is because of this that the Africans' political consciousness tends to spring directly from the tribe to the race. For it is as Negroes, as black men, that they feel they have been subordinated and despised. Yet, and this is their present dilemma, it is through their claim to self-government as nations that Africans must make their first effective demand upon their rulers and the world for recognition. The Mau Mau movement, however, failed to extend beyond the Kikuyu and those groups closely linked with them. As a collection of clans with no pre-existing political unity, the Kikuyu needed an outstanding leadership to arouse in them a sense even of tribal unity and to direct their confused discontents into a political movement. In this record, we can see reflected in Mr Kariuki's mind the ready and passionate response to Mr Kenyatta's leadership. We can see at the same time the growth both of a wider sense of race and a realization of the need for a Kenya nationalism.

Africans, victims of historical developments the pace of which has almost outrun the comprehension and control of their rational command, are almost obliged to account the strains they experience not to history, still less to themselves, but to the evil will of other men, of colonial rulers and, above all, colonial settlers. It may be long before they will distinguish the services and disservices which both have brought to Africa. Yet can we British, most concerned with the experience of making and so hastily unmaking an empire, be sure that we ourselves as yet understand the forces that have suddenly surged up to break the level surface of our rule?

It is important for us to make a rational attempt to understand these forces. They have broken in upon our preconceived policy for Kenya

FOREWORD TO 'MAU MAU DETAINEE' [1963]

and radically changed its timing if not, indeed, its substance. The underlying cause of all Britain's difficulties in east and southern Africa arose from our conviction, for which we had much evidence, that the peoples of these dependencies, in contrast with the West Africans, were mostly too poor and retarded to advance quickly towards self-government. But it seems that the Kikuyu were torn between the action of two powerful forces, of alien power holding them back while a passionate desire to escape this control urged them forward. With their own society in increasing disintegration, the Kikuyu felt impelled towards insurgence. It has been one costly to themselves, to the other inhabitants of Kenya, and to the British taxpayer, but – the hard fact must be faced – it has roused all concerned with Kenya to accept the need for a rapid advance to majority rule. Some of us may still believe that it would have been better for the Kenya Africans themselves if their independence could have come more gradually, and therefore that their education could have been more advanced, before the heavy responsibilities of nationhood had been undertaken. For they are a people still deeply divided tribally and all too ill-prepared for modern government, whether democratic or not. But Mr Kariuki and his friends can hardly be expected to agree with such a view and to them the impetus given by Mau Mau to their political emancipation must seem to be its justification.

I am aware that this book will not always be read for what it is, the exceptional evidence of one African prisoner, but will be used as evidence against Britain's record in general and will provide valuable propaganda material for our critics and enemies. This is always the penalty of the healthy publicity of our democracy. But, if the British can be accused about Mr Kariuki's treatment, they can ask who judges them and by what standards. The world has probably never seen, in relation to its population, such a high percentage of the imprisoned as in the middle years of this century. Perhaps it has never seen such deliberate and wholesale destruction of our race. But there are surely degrees of guilt between on the one side the calculated and sustained wrongs carried out generally with the maximum secrecy, according to the plans, and indeed the principles, of rulers, and on the other side the random cruelties, unsanctioned by the ruling power, committed by its agents during a few years of exceptional fear and crisis. It can be said for Britain that at least since the abolition of slavery, her people have struggled, admittedly with varying success, to maintain a standard of humanity in their empire. How far the harsh measures used were ordered, or at least condoned, by the colonial authorities, and how far they were the excesses of lower ranks in the scattered detention camps, is a question I cannot answer and it may be difficult ever to find a detailed and exact reply. There is always a difficulty, one which has often recurred in Britain's colonial history, for critics by the fireside or on the padded benches of Westminster, even when they have been able exactly to ascertain the facts, to assess correctly the degree of guilt on the part of their agents caught up in sudden danger on the frontier. But the channels of communication seldom remain completely blocked for long. In the case of the Mau Mau rebellion there was a series of inquiries into allegations of ill-treatment, including a general investigation into the whole system of detention. There was a most interesting report by a medical officer skilled in psychiatry and with experience of Kenya. There were visits by inquiring Members of Parliament, including some especially vigorous members of the Labour Opposition. There were numerous questions in Parliament. The Hola Camp incident of 1959 gave rise not only to two exhaustive reports but also to many questions in Parliament and a Labour motion demanding an inquiry was debated.[1] The camps were also open to visiting missions from the International Red Cross.

This story reinforces the conclusion that it is always advisable for those outside prison to hear the voice of those who are inside. The political prisoner above all may suffer from being condemned, but much more, perhaps, from being forgotten. We may hope that various measures developed by Britain by which the rights of prisoners are protected will be maintained throughout the Commonwealth, including those new African states which already have their political prisoners. The Christians, above all, whose faith is traced back to a prisoner who was unjustly tried for a political offence, flogged, and tortured to death, should be especially sensitive in this matter. Those who make use of the story in this book to condemn Britain may justly be asked whether they are qualified by their own laws and customs to do so. The minimum here should be their own signature and implementation of the Declaration of Human Rights and their guarantee of the right of entry into their courts of international jurists and of the International Red Cross into their prison camps.

Mr Kariuki might have passed in and out of the detention camps as one of an undifferentiated mass. He might have had his spirit broken. He might have developed a bitter, settled enmity towards the white man. He might have died from the effects of his imprisonment or been

[1] *Parliamentary Debates*, 16 June 1959, V. 607. 248-384.

hanged along with the hundreds convicted after trial under the special Emergency laws. I hope that other readers will, like me, be glad, both for his own sake and for what we may learn from his story, that this prisoner, however much on some matters we may disagree with him, survived with unbroken spirit and integrity to write this African *De Profundis*.

What Place now for Kenya Settlers?

The Times 20 February 1963

This and the following entry show that even one who believed that the settlers' political and economic primacy must be ended and that Africans must be given control over their own country, could at the eleventh hour have doubts about the future of this complex state and economy. It will be remarked that I was especially mistaken about the use to which the lately released Mr Kenyatta would put his leadership. I can only claim that many well-informed Europeans and some Africans shared my fears at that time.

Liquidating an empire has been proving a more difficult and expensive operation than acquiring one. Today Kenya presents perhaps our most hazardous and expensive disengagement. The hazards are to all its peoples; but with independence well in sight the European settlers make the most urgent demand upon Britain's understanding and help.

For 60 years they built up their political power and their 'White Highlands'. Aiming at 'self-government', they almost succeeded in making an equatorial Southern Rhodesia out of Kenya. Had they done so their position today would be even more dangerous to themselves and damaging to Kenya than it actually is. But now, abruptly deprived of political power and landed security, they present Britain with an economic, political and moral problem which must be solved before independence.

Economically, the settlers' danger affects the whole territory. Kenya's wealth is almost wholly agricultural and the rainfall allows intensive production upon only about one-fifth of the country, some 41,600 square miles. African tribes cluster thickly upon 34,000 of these; Europeans occupy the rest, most of which they found almost uninhabited and agriculturally virgin. In 60 years these latest migrants, by costly trial and error, have tamed their tropical uplands and mastered its varying soils, its human, animal and vegetable diseases. By 1960 they produced 80 per cent of Kenya's agricultural exports, worth £38 millions, and disbursed £10 millions in wages.

The White Highlands have now become the 'Scheduled Areas', open to all races. The settlement plans, being both complex and evolutionary, almost defy summary treatment. Moreover their three aims are difficult to harmonize. These are first to relieve African political pressure and land-hunger, secondly to sustain Kenya's productivity, and thirdly, and very residually, to offer some market for settlers' land. The total cost for purchase and development is estimated at nearly £30 millions, more than two-thirds to come from British loans and grants, and about £4 millions from the World Bank and the West German Government.

The Settlement Board, now a Ministry, began early in 1961 by demarcating certain blocks, each chosen to eliminate what are known as 'sore thumbs', that is, land long and bitterly claimed as their own by various African groups. Then an array of experts co-operated in an immense operation, first to select, survey, value, purchase and subdivide the farms; then to plan the agricultural and economic potential of the plots, prepare the land, provide for water, access and village centres; and finally appoint staff for future administrative and technical guidance.

Plans have ranged from the so-called 'high density' schemes on good mixed farming land, where Africans, especially Kikuyu, have now been settled on plots averaging about 20 acres, to 'low density' schemes, involving plots about double that size or more for which applicants must provide some of the initial capital. Another scheme, still insufficiently financed, is for 'assisted owners' or 'yeoman farmers' of any race to buy farms anywhere they are offered in the Scheduled Areas.

The economic problem for the colony, with its now precarious budget, is whether this combined fragmentation and Africanization of European farms will reduce total productivity – the key word. Because of the wide variation in the quality of the European lands and of the crops proper to them, there has to be a corresponding variation in the sizes of the plots within each scheme. This is because the criterion is always what x acres will produce after allowing for repayment, over a given term of years, of the costs of purchase, preparation of the land, etc. High density schemes are planned to provide family subsistence plus £25 cash income a year. For low density schemes, on good land, this last figure should average £100.

Can productivity be maintained? It has been estimated that on similar good land a square mile of European farming produces annually £4,150, against £1,180 from African farming. Even a new settlement of selected Kikuyu can reveal a sad contrast between the best plots, with grade cows and poultry, thriving vegetables and flowers, and the weedy maize and impoverished beasts on some other plots. And this is in spite of skilled guidance which, with the run-down of the British staff, may not be maintained at the present level. True, good African farming is becoming better, and African staff will in time replace European. But, at best, a dangerous interval faces Kenya's economy.

What of the economic prospect for the European who sees his farm thus alienated and partitioned? He is not forced to sell. But with the whole European future in jeopardy he, at least, can realize his assets. Should he refuse, he may be left on an island among African farmers, afraid of trespass, theft and cattle or plant disease. A few Europeans have used their purchase money to buy new farms deeper in the settled area in the hope of finding sanctuary. But for how long?

It is here that politics come in. All farmers, indeed most Europeans, are asking, 'Can we – dare we – stay?' Their land, their livelihood, their children's education and future are at stake. The new constitution will, in effect, depose and disfranchise them. What sort of government will the Africans give them?

Each Monday they read the weekend speeches of politicians in the fierce pre-electoral, tribalistic struggle for the votes of an inexperienced electorate. History has left a long-accumulated resentment against the settler. Hunger for land and political assertion lay at the heart of Mau Mau; they are smouldering again in the Land Freedom Army of the Rift Valley among the spill-over from the crowded Kikuyu districts and the unemployed, turned off as farmers emigrate or retrench. Will a sense of justice, respect for a Bill of Rights embodied in the new constitution, or even economic realism, prevent the new rulers from sacrificing the most obvious scapegoats who are also the most profitable victims?

Will security be maintained? And medical services? Some settlers have given their answer already – by going. Others have such a fierce love for Kenya that they will stay at any risk. Between these, on the rack, are the undecided majority. Only the large planters of sisal, coffee and tea can feel protected for the present by the scale, the cost and the great economic importance of their enterprises.

What of the moral problem? A sequence of British governments supported white settlement up to the very moment of abandonment in 1960. The soldier-settlers at the end of the last war were encouraged to commit their all to Kenya. To quote only one of a long sequence of pledges – 'Her Majesty's Government', said Mr Lennox (now Lord) Boyd in 1954, 'are not likely to encourage people to come to Kenya if they intend to betray them or their predecessors'. The argument is not that the Government should have resisted the advance towards African self-government, though it should surely have been quicker to foresee it; it is that Britain, having promoted, indeed guaranteed, a colony which has built up for Kenya an immense asset of wealth and knowledge, should not now leave its members tied in anxiety and possible danger to the wasting asset of their farms.

Is the Government's purpose, in effect, to make the settlers pay the price of preserving public confidence, economic and political, for as long as their waning strength allows? Or is it to save the £130 millions which, it is estimated, would underwrite the settlers' land-value? It is such thoughts which lead many settlers to say that if they are able to go, it will never be to return to a mother-country as cold to them in heart as it is in climate.

It should be remembered that among the settlers are many, perhaps some 400 or more, of the old and infirm, some alone on their decaying farms or in suburban houses which are their only wealth, some in institutions supported by Government pensions and subscriptions. So far the British Government have provided funds for only some 65 of these. To help such people to find new homes, preferably in a warm climate, will be no cheap or easy task, but their care is surely Britain's responsibility.

The settler problem should not, of course, be drawn in disproportionate size upon the total Kenya picture. Our major task in Kenya is to help the seven million Africans to create an orderly and prosperous state. But we have this lesser and inescapable responsibility, which cannot be unloaded upon the Africans. This is to give our own people the help which history makes obligatory so that now, while Britain is still in control, they can make their free choice whether to commit themselves to the future of Kenya or to take their departure with dignity and economic security.

Kenya in Travail

The Listener 21 March 1963

I have recently returned from a visit to East Africa. I found Uganda and Tanganyika with problems enough. But they were regions of calm and hope in contrast with Kenya. Here is a colony hurrying towards independence and no one seems to know when and how it will be achieved or what will happen afterwards. Ask six people in leading political or administrative positions what they foresee and each one will give a different answer. It would seem as though Kenya's people were sitting in a boat just about to shoot two lots of rapids. The first, 'internal self-government', seems less dangerous than the second, independence. The boat may get through safely, though, even if it does, some of its occupants may get thrown out or injured in the process, or it may get completely smashed up. At the moment there is a captain in the boat, Mr Malcolm MacDonald, and he has a crew, the colonial administration, but it is arranged for these to jump ashore just as the second rapids are reached. And now, at this penultimate moment, the largest group of the passengers have been engaged in a quarrel and may at any moment come to blows.

The rift between the Africans is the main – though by no means the only – danger which Kenya faces. It is a mistake to blame them. The reasons for their disunity lie deep in geography and history. A physical map of Kenya shows a limited block of high well-watered land projecting from the eastern shore of Lake Victoria and ending a little beyond Kenya mountain and Nairobi; sweeping round the other three sides of it is a vast area of low, dry land. In human terms, before the Europeans came, this map represented a concentration of agricultural tribes clustered on the higher, greener land, and shifting pastoral groups thinly dispersed over the other four-fifths. Here was one more episode in the world's long rivalry between the sedentary and the nomad, between Cain and Abel, the man with the hoe and the man with the herd. The basic cleavage in way of life is further deepened by differences in customs, political organization and language between the two main groups and even within each group there are further tribal divisions. The agriculturalists are in the majority but in pre-European days they lived in fear of the dominant pastoral people, above all of the warlike Masai, who swept round the highlands, raiding the borders of the sedentary tribes as they went.

Upon this old tribal pattern towards the end of the last century the

[1963]

British came to superimpose their own pattern. They largely reversed the fortunes of the two groups. They did not – perhaps in the time they could not – do much to change the way of life of the pastoral tribes. Most of those still remain aloof, picturesque and proud, brought to order but still occasionally indulging in a little cattle raiding. The new influences tended to concentrate upon the accessible, populous agricultural fraction of the country. Here the missionaries, the officials, the European settlers, made their deepest impress. Deepest of all was the effect upon the 1,000,000 Kikuyu who crowd the beautiful green, hilly country which leads up towards their beloved Kenya mountain with its head of snow. They are intelligent, ambitious people. They swarmed out of their hills to work on the farms of Europeans, and in their houses and towns. Nairobi was at their door. It seemed rich, exciting, yet they felt shut out on account of their poverty and ignorance from any real possession of all the good new things it offered. Watching and fearing the settlers, hungry for more land, they became more and more politically conscious. It is the Kikuyu, with some kindred groups, and the industrious Luo, who form the bulk of the Kenya African National Union, Kanu: a party, not surprisingly, anxious for centralized government, since they see Kenya as their oyster.

The more outlying, mainly pastoral tribes now find their former situation reversed. They are now the endangered ones. They fear the educational superiority of the Kikuyu, their ambition and land hunger. Mau Mau is a horrible and recent memory. Though the bulk of the Kikuyu have been helped by the government to find a new agricultural prosperity in their own districts, the landless and unemployed Kikuyu are again busy with secret oathing ceremonies in the name of the Land Freedom Army. No wonder that fear of the Kikuyu is a dominant motive in binding together the remaining, more peripheral and pastoral groups. They have organized a rival party, the Kenya African Democratic Union – Kadu. In a desperate attempt to defend themselves and their lands from a centralized government that would almost inevitably be dominated by the Kikuyu, at Lancaster House Kadu made decentralization and regionalism the fundamental conditions of their agreement to any political advance.

Kadu *have* their regionalism, delineated by an impartial commission and closely based upon local demands. They have thus entrenched just that element which the Royal Commission Report of 1955 condemned as Kenya's greatest handicap, tribalism.[1] This small country, small at

[1] See p. 122 ff. above for a discussion of this Report.

least in its population, its cultivatable surface, its revenues, its minerals, its resources of skill of all kinds, is now to be cut up into something perilously near federation. Yet month by month tribal feeling has grown and it sees the regions less as administrative units than as tribal strongholds. One of the older leaders of Kadu, a minister in the government, threatened to take arms if his region is not given a certain town in the present European area for its 'capital'. The Masai have been openly sharpening their great double-bladed spears in the fiery hope of winning back more than has been allotted to them of the grazing areas they lost long ago.

The position is thus contradictory. Kadu is moderate but conservative and somewhat unrealistic. Kanu seems to represent education and progress – but in the Kikuyu lies a terrifying capacity for atavism if they should feel themselves thwarted. The new constitution has been painfully hammered out between British experts and officials in consultation with party leaders, and has just been finalized by Mr Sandys. It not only parcels out power between the centre and regions but ties up and seals down the parcels against any possible theft or damage – or tries to! The question which hangs over Kenya is whether Kanu, if it wins, or even if it loses, the first election, will respect the string and sealing wax, the bonds upon its powers. Everything depends upon the character, the moderation, of two or three dozen leading Africans. It is said that in council, alongside their European official and unofficial colleagues, the dozen African ministers of the present coalition have often worked together constructively as, indeed, they seem to have done with Mr Sandys. But when they go out to the hustings they attack each other without restraint. The Kanu leaders also heap criticism and even threats and insults upon the Governor, the leading officials, the settlers. True, this war of words has at least so far proved a substitute for a war of spears and pangas. And we must remember that men inexperienced in politics are appealing to even more inexperienced crowds. The inflammatory anti-European orator of yesterday is today the friendly rational minister who tells you in his office that he, and indeed all of them, must give the crowds what they want. Which is the real man?

Kanu leaders often seem divided and contradictory. Mr Mboya admits that both parties are pledged to regionalism, but Mr Odinga declares that once in power they will sweep away this 'silly' system. One day wholesale nationalization is threatened: almost at once it is denied. The settlers are told that they are welcome to stay: the next day that as they stole their lands, these can be commandeered. Even the intelligent

[1963]

Mr Mboya can assert that the settlers are behind the Land Freedom Army! For all his great international reputation, Mr Kenyatta must be an embarrassment to his party: he is becoming a man they cannot do without but can hardly do with. He is so much more the Kikuyu, and the older Kikuyu, than the national leader he is billed to become. His speeches are often contradictory, sometimes with a disturbing double significance. After asking a Kanu rally to stand for two minutes' silence 'in memory of those who died in our cause', he goes on to say that there should be no bitterness against those who 'tortured the Africans', no hatred for Europeans and Asians. Let them join Kanu! 'We only want to see those who have sucked our blood and ruled us come and join hands with us and work with us' – an invitation slightly reminiscent of that in the old nursery rhyme, ' "Will you walk into my parlour?" said the spider to the fly'.

What of the settlers? The 3,000-odd farmers who have been the political spearhead of the 60,000 Europeans? It seems strange that we can discuss Kenya for so long with hardly a reference to them. Their struggle for what they called 'self-government' on the Southern Rhodesian model and for control of their beloved White Highlands – two mutually supporting aims – has dominated almost the whole of Kenya's history. Yet in a matter of months they have lost all political power, and all security in their land. From having predominant representation in the Legislative Council they will be virtually disenfranchised under the new constitution. Some of their highlands are already being carved up for African settlement and there can be no absolute security for what remains. Even those who opposed their ambitions, who warned them of their dangers, must sympathize with such a sudden, shattering reversal of fortune. Moreover, the settlers can blame a succession of British governments for having fostered their emigration, and the present British Government for encouraging white settlement right up to 1960. They can surely claim that today Britain owes them at least compensation and protection.

Will any settlers stay? Some have already gone: many more are likely to go, to South Africa, Australia, perhaps to South America and other warm countries and under governments against which they have no bitter sense of betrayal. Many stay because they cannot afford to go. They fear, not unreasonably, for their security, for their children's education, for the maintenance of medical and other services. But there are people, not only farmers, who have become, as it were, Africanized; who were born in Kenya or who have been there so long that they cannot imagine themselves living anywhere else. I have been to Kenya often enough to enter into this devotion towards this extraordinary land with its sun-drenched highlands, its startling contrasts of plains, mountains, lakes and almost unimaginable rifts; with its flowers of every kind, tropical and temperate, all the year round; its thrill of sharing the land with great animals, still free; its sense of space and freedom; with an excitement in the air even if it is often laced with fear and uncertainty Those who feel like this will stay and gamble with the future. For in spite of fears, in spite of Mau Mau, they care not only for Africa but for the Africans, in all the variety of their tribes and customs, with their faults, their progress, their possibilities, their laughter. They have friends among them, men perhaps who have worked with them for twenty or thirty years, and they believe that the two races need each other. And even if many Europeans go, once things settle down others will come, business men and tourists of many nationalities. For, to Europeans, Kenya is likely to remain the most attractive country in tropical Africa.

The Europeans are not the only minority in Kenya. The Asians, at some 175,000, outnumber them. They, too, like the Europeans, occupy a special economic and social position. Unlike the Europeans, they are divided into many groups, not only Indians and Pakistanis, nor even Moslems and Hindus, but sub-divisions of each group, some of them tightly integrated socially and economically. This makes it difficult for them to co-operate in the defence, even the assertion, of their common interest. They have played a vital part in Kenya's development, pushing retail trade out into the tribal areas through their little shops, their *dukas*, run on a shoe-string; plying their ancient trades as craftsmen of all kinds; filling the growing demand for clerical skills while Africans were starting on the three Rs. Now the rising Africans begin to look jealously upon them, asserting that they bar the way to their advancement, resenting their tight social seclusion and their still remaining bonds with Asia. It is clear that they will try to stay, will try to placate African nationalism, will suffer perhaps, but will endure. A buoyant economy might float them, but if the economic tide should continue to recede many of them may be stranded in poverty if not in danger. As yet the recession is still far from being desperate.

There are other minorities. The narrow strip of fertile land at the coast turned its back on the dry interior and looked out to the Indian Ocean. Across this many centuries ago the monsoons brought the Arab dhows and Islam, and linked the coast with Arabia and Zanzibar. The mixed Arabicized Swahili people, and the coastal African tribes, feel somewhat detached from the rest of Kenya. They live in a more languorous atmosphere, and are more friendly with the Asians and the Europeans. These last come to plant sisal or to holiday in the little tropical Bognors, to bathe and catch giant fish in the brilliant sea. Most of the coastal peoples cling rather nervously to the promise of regionalism. Mr Sandys has confirmed that promise and seems to have brought the historic claims of Zanzibar to suzerainty over the coast to an amicable conclusion. But on the northern frontier a far from restful minority threatens Kenya's peace. The lean Somalis pasture their flocks in a corner of the semi-desert region of northern Kenya and demand its cession. We have now heard from Mr Sandys that the Somalis' demand has been refused. If the arbitrary frontiers drawn by Europeans in Africa are not to be sacred there is, it seems to me, an irrefutable case for rectifying this one. But the Kenya Africans, who demand self-determination for themselves, will not even listen to the Somali case.

Perhaps we can now see the full extent of Kenya's danger, that of intemperate politics at work upon a population, deeply segmented by race, colour, culture and tribe and with a most vulnerable economy. Kenya's Europeans and Asians have played a large part in building up Kenya's wealth, which is narrowly based upon the agricultural productive capacity of a small part of the country. Some of the agricultural tribes are increasingly good farmers; they grow excellent tea and coffee and breed grade cattle. Under skilled control and guidance they could in time make up for the lost productivity of the settlers. But will that guidance, which is still largely European guidance, be retained? Much more gradually the Africans could replace Asian clerks and traders and mechanics. But no educational programme, however 'crashing', could meet all the needs of Kenya for higher administrative, managerial and technical skills in the next six to ten years. An intensive survey by Mr Guy Hunter and the American Professor Harbison discloses that of the 67,000 men in East Africa holding the highest category of top posts of every kind, 54,000 were Europeans and Asian. And for Kenya alone this proportion of some five-sixths is certainly higher. Apart from the reliance on non-African skills, Kenya depends heavily upon British help to balance the budget. The Kikuyu adventure of Mau Mau cost at least £60,000,000, largely supplied by Britain. Anything like such another outbreak of disorder, one involving more than a single tribe, could have a shattering effect upon the future of the country. It could also damage the hope of federation with the other two East African states which are now linked with Kenya in a common market with many common services.

It seems unbelievable that a people on the edge of their longed-for independence, and faced with a clear choice between political moderation and success on the one side, and political intemperance with something very near disaster on the other, will not make the right choice. There are many thousands of intelligent and realistic Africans in Kenya. Not long ago I talked to an audience of such men, mostly Kikuyu, teachers, clerks, officials, and I was deeply impressed by their moderation and good sense. But the political leaders, driven to create political power out of the votes of an inexperienced tribal electorate, appeal to it over the heads of the moderate minority. The British staff, from the Governor downwards, on the very eve of their departure, are doing all in their power to help the politicians to train their own successors, and to finalize the constitution. I know this: I have lately seen them working long hours in their Nairobi offices or tribal districts.

Mr Sandys has just returned from putting the finishing touches to the new ship of state. The rapids of internal self-government are now only a few weeks away. British power will still be in the background to steady the ship before the plunge into full independence. After that, success will depend entirely upon the African leaders. We must hope and pray that they will rise to the test, and that old tribalism will be swallowed up by new nationalism.

Britain and Africa in 1963

The Listener 4 April 1963

Africa today refuses to be ignored. It continues to demand an amount of space in our newspapers which might seem disproportionate. Asia is about seven times more populous, yet it was making little showing until the Indo-Chinese war and the Malaysian crisis. As for South America, the third continent, which makes demands upon the Western world, President Kennedy has just warned us that 'it is the most critical area in the world today'. Yet in our press coverage South America hardly appears.

But in spite, or even because, of the publicity Africa is now getting, I am not sure that its image grows more attractive. One reason for disenchantment may lie in the sort of news that has lately been coming out of Africa. The Congo was certainly not our responsibility. But the almost continuous report of confusion, tribal fighting, murders, even cannibalism, over such a large block of the continent may have evoked a sense of revulsion against Africa and Africans as a whole. Even outside the Congo, the news of assassinations, actual or attempted, executions, disorder, religious persecution, corruption and other evils has had a disenchanting effect. Here we see one of the dangers of our age, that good news is no news, that the press, especially the cheaper press, reports the angry not the sober speech and feeds its readers with the exceptional, the violent and, especially, the bloody. It has no space in which to explain the underlying reasons for such aberrations. And yet, if we could fully understand the immense and testing difficulties which have faced the new African governments as they have erupted into independence, we might marvel not how much, but how little, disorder and bloodshed has occurred. We might draw some comparisons in Africa's favour with the South American record and with that of some of the Arab states.

It seems especially important that we in Britain should develop a balanced view of contemporary Africa. While we are losing some of our old sources of power and influence this continent offers great opportunities for action and service of a kind appropriate to the modern world. We are indeed doing a great deal in Africa, but it is now one of the conditions of serving this continent that the work must be done quietly, dispensed through many channels, educational, scientific, cultural and economic, without advertisement or expectation of thanks. Even our own public may not realize the extent of the commitment.

It seems that there are three main obstacles to our understanding of Africa, and here I am thinking in the main of Commonwealth Africa. One of these is this continuing expression of anti-colonialism; the second is the apparent African rejection of democracy; the third is the dangerous and seemingly insoluble conflict between white and black in southern Africa.

Consider first this continuing anti-colonialism. Its scope and bitterness have, in fact, greatly decreased in the last year or so. Yet it continues. Dr Nyerere in a recent speech gave warning about having 'a fixation against imperialism', and told Africans to be on guard equally against communism and capitalism. He also hurled fiery darts, some of which were meant to strike the British and the Americans who are doing so much to support his very poor state. Dr Azikiwe, Governor-General of Nigeria, could say only last year that Africa, 'the cradle of civilization', was plunged into an era of degradation 'by a most ruthless form of oppression ranging from slavery to colonialism' – a typically vague, all-inclusive form of African denunciation. Even the missionaries do not escape. In January this year in Nairobi, at a Christian conference, the significant Kikuyu saying, 'there is no difference between a white man and a missionary', was quoted, and Christianity was said to be an integral part of colonialism. At a conference last year in Ethiopia the Uganda delegates told the 'colonialist' members to go back and start civilizing themselves.

The key to these attitudes lies in the African version of nationalism. It draws its main energy from the determination to force the rest of the world to reverse that attitude to the Negro which it has shown almost throughout history wherever that race has been in contact with others. As this attitude is still deeply entrenched today, this dangerous sense of humiliation is likely to be with us for a long time to come. Both science and experience of the educated African seem to show that the Negro is potentially the equal of other races. It is the long isolation of the race which accounts for the poverty and ignorance by Western standards of the vast majority, and so for the correlation in the world's view of the striking physical character of the Negro with cultural inferiority. Even in one of the Communist states which had held out to Africa the promise that there at least they would escape from racial prejudice, West African students have lately been called 'jungle people' and 'black monkeys', beaten up by the crowd, and arrested by the police.

Africans would be less than human if they did not fight back against this world attitude now that they have at last become fully aware of it. I am old enough to recall the days when the desire of most of those Africans who suddenly saw African life with our eyes was to grow out of it, and into ours, as quickly as possible. I well remember the horror expressed by some westernized parents of a girl who wanted to marry the son of a chief, a man who might have to follow tribal customs. 'What – after all the efforts we have made to grow out of all that savagery – to see our daughter sink back into it!' When, in spite of the strenuous education and other efforts of the aspiring minority, Africans were still not accepted as equals, the mood changed. They would now extort the respect which, it seemed, would never be freely given. Thus nationalism, or Africanism, was born, a resolve to force the unwilling world to give Africans social equality through political independence. As the struggle goes on, new mental horizons appear one after another. The claim 'we are capable of becoming just like you' developed, especially in the West Indies and French Africa, into 'we can create something different, unique, of our own'. This evolved into the African personality, which is still in the making. Were Negroes to be regarded as inferior? Let them retort, be it so! In the words of a West Indian poet:

> Mercy for our omniscient naïve conquerors,
> Hooray for those who never invented anything.
> Hooray for those who never conquered anything.

Was black a colour to be despised? Then blackness must be exalted. 'Our God is black. For in his image we were made,' so sang one African poet. The President of Senegal, himself a poet, wrote:

> Woman nude, woman black,
> clad in your colour which is life,
> your beauty strikes me to the heart
> as lightning strikes the eagle.

Yet the writer married a golden-haired French woman. The conflict is indeed fiercest in those who have taken most from the West, from the white man, and who have to struggle against one half of themselves.

Last December, at an international conference of historians in Ghana, a still further advance was proclaimed. As Dr Roland Oliver explained in a Third Programme talk,[1] the African historians, with the help of non-African scholars, claimed that they had a worthy past as well as a future. This past had long been ignored or misinterpreted as savage or meaningless, but it was now being unveiled as a heritage of value, unique, a source of pride. It would be the racial and continental foundation for the building of the future African civilization after the interruption, the aberration, of the colonial regime. This is the psychology we have to try to understand, to help if we can.

The British make better politicians than psychologists, and it may be that we shall find it easier to understand the African rejection of democracy than their rejection of humility. Here we have been lacking both in insight and in foresight. The colonial governments drew their great authority along an invisible cable originating in London. When the Union Jack was run down, this current was simultaneously switched off. Something had to take its place, and quickly. How could the necessary power be generated in a newly devised parliament which had no associations or mystique for the masses? Perhaps we thought – here I quote –

---

[1] Printed in *The Listener* of 7 February 1963.

'that the utmost which the discontented colonialists could do was to disturb authority. We never dreamt they could of themselves supply it, knowing in general what an operose business it is to establish a government absolutely new.' Thus Burke, on the American colonies. What is new out of Africa is that our former subjects have built the state round the party, that same party which had aroused political consciousness and harnessed it to victory under its leadership. Here is the new dynamo from which ideas and energy circulated down to the remotest tribal extremities and back again. The other day in Tanganyika I was able to see how policy is decided within the monolithic Tanu and ratified in the legislature. There is, of course, only one party. 'Was I', Dr Nyerere exclaimed incredulously, 'to create an opposition to myself?'

The first need for Africans is, therefore, to re-create for themselves the unity and order imposed by external authority and now suddenly removed. It sometimes seems as though the only way to impose authority over large African tribal populations is by the dictatorial methods followed, with surprising similarity, by governments conducted by both black Africans and white South Africans – suspension of the rule of law; arbitrary arrests; control of the press; suppression of trade unionism; the expulsion of critics and disapproving bishops. The difference, of course – and it is fundamental – is that where black rules black there is not only the satisfaction of racial pride, but infinitely more hope of growth into unity and liberty than where white stands in increasingly desperate defence of racial minority power over black. After all, the Bishop has returned to Ghana! But the black Africans' divergences from democracy certainly embarrass us in Britain, not to speak of the rest of the democratic Commonwealth: we find it is unrealistic to condemn and yet improper to condone.

The danger to Africa of the one-party state lies in the immense eminence and perquisites of power in relation to the surrounding poverty. The leadership may be tempted to entrench its position, to allow no mechanism for change such as the growing secondary élite of officials, graduates, businessmen and urban and industrial workers, will certainly demand. There is no substitute for an electorate and yet in most of Africa, in anything like the British or American sense, there is no such thing.

One form of escape from the weakness and poverty of the individual states can be seen in the Pan-African movement. There is obvious good sense in this early effort to grasp at peace and practical co-operation on the continental scale. But in political, as in physical building, stages of construction can hardly be skipped. As Ghana and Guinea have discovered, it is easier to make a gesture than a federation. The total of Pan-Africa cannot at least at first, be stronger than the sum of its parts. Any of these parts at the level below optimistic diplomacy and oratory show deep fissures within themselves. They also show large potential divisions between each other. As the need for anti-colonialism slackens, co-operation may weaken between Arab and Negro Africans. The Sudanese and Hausa Moslems have cultures founded on a world religion and political institutions which give them a sense of pride and confidence often lacking further south. The autobiography of Northern Nigeria's Premier, with its serene and temperate attitude towards British rule, contrasts with the bitterness and uncertainty of some other published revelations. And, divisively across the great middle of Africa, lies the Congo in its sprawling helplessness, its poverty and disorder, its immense dependence on external aid. Yet one great bond remains – the bitterness of the independent African states about the continuing control of the southern quarter of their continent by the white man.

This is, indeed, the third factor which, it seems to me, daunts and repels so many observers of Africa, the seemingly irreconcilable conflict between white colony and coloured majority. I believe that at one time all, or nearly all, of us had hoped that the African majorities in settled areas would grow gradually, peacefully, into partnership with the ruling European as they gained the European level of education and prosperity. They would climb, perhaps, rung by rung up the ladder of a qualified franchise. We had not expected the world to break in upon Africa with far more revolutionary and immediate ideas of political emancipation and frighten the white minorities into the reaction of fear. But the uncompromising, the passionate nature of that Africanism which I have tried to describe will have nothing of gradualism. It claims universal, adult suffrage as the gateway to immediate domination; it rejects the elaborate mathematical franchises invented to check and filter African advance.

This situation confronts us British in Central Africa. In Kenya, the European settlers were too few, too localized, to make a stand or to advance an irrefutable claim upon British support. Their disappearance may for a time damage, but it will not ruin, the agricultural Kenya state with its 8,000,000 Africans. But in Southern Rhodesia the danger is not only the numerical one, with 250,000 whites confronting only some 3,000,000 Africans. It is that these whites, and not the British Government, have been the creators, the rulers and maintainers, of a highly complex industrial state, with its large cities, mines and factories. This state could not tomorrow be successfully taken over by Africans who have only a few dozen men of high skill or managerial experience. Nor will the Europeans bring themselves to accept the idea of being suddenly put under African rule. Yet with each refusal, with the hardening of European political opposition to all compromise, the possibilities of African moderation and compromise diminish. Much more is now at stake than even the salvaging of the economic links of the broken Federation, no less than the future existence of the Europeans in Southern Rhodesia. No wonder the British Government shrank so long from the decision, and the public turns away from the costly responsibilities which almost any decision must impose upon this country. And beyond Southern Rhodesia looms South Africa, with almost the same problem but upon a far greater and more obdurate scale. Here African terrorism is now ready to punish any African co-operation with a Government just beginning to play with ideas of compromise. Not Britain's responsibility, it will be said! No, but it is impossible to forget that nearly half the Europeans there were British; that our three High Commission territories are hostages in South Africa; that South Africa's affairs, like those of Portugal's territories, are regarded by all Africans as their own.

I must frankly admit that I do not see even the outline of a peaceful and economically viable solution of these southern problems. My plea is that they should be seen and studied with the other two aspects I have discussed as indissoluble parts of the total African situation. I do not believe that we shall be able to maintain an attitude of cool neutrality towards them. We have played too large a hand in the making of the continent to effect a total disengagement now. The key to understanding lies in the African passion to build a new African Africa out of their dismantling of the old, founded as it was upon the deep, perhaps in some measure, the unavoidable, humiliations, imposed upon their race. The road leading to such an Africa looks obscure and dangerous. But our ideas and policies should be framed in the realization that, until that distant goal is reached, Africa will continue both to torment itself and to trouble the rest of the world.

1964

Africa—Continent of Disillusion?

This is the one piece of writing for which I cannot find the place of publication. I reproduce it, however, as revealing the atmosphere of 1964.

Africa, as seen from this country, does not present a very cheerful picture. The episodic news in the papers, on radio or television is often disturbing, sometimes startling or even horrible. Call up in your mind the map of Africa. Imagine a line drawn down its simple pear-like shape from north to south, say from Tripoli to Capetown. East of this line lies the half – or a little more – with which Britain in the past has had most to do. Run your eye down from north to south. Egypt – not surprisingly, perhaps – broadcasting continuous anti-British propaganda. The Sudan, expelling missionaries wholesale, while part of its Negro south is in rebellion against the Moslem Arab north. Somalia, relations with Britain cut, waging a kind of border war against Ethiopia and Kenya. Zanzibar, scene of a recent violent revolution on the morrow of independence and still in revolutionary turmoil. The three East African states, lately shocked by military mutinies. The Congo, floundering in disunity and division like some great animal in a swamp and only just kept from sinking by life-lines from the United Nations. The state of Rwanda-Urundi broken into hostile halves, its glorious mountain scenery stained with the blood of wholesale massacres. Portuguese Africa, already wounded by one bloody rebellion and threatened with more. The Central African Federation, just broken up in anger, with Southern Rhodesia's white Government drifting towards a fateful decision like a boat on the edge of her own Victoria Falls. South Africa screwing down the iron lid of apartheid turn by turn upon her African majority, and also hanging ominously over our three little High Commission states which are struggling towards a kind of independence which directly defies South Africa's racial policy. If we take a hurried

AFRICA – CONTINENT OF DISILLUSION? [1964]

look at the two main ex-British dependencies west of our imaginary line we see Ghana angrily taking the final steps to dictatorship. And what of Nigeria, which seemed to be Africa's giant not only in numbers but in sound strength? A sudden flash of light, from – of all things – a census return, has revealed cracks in the threefold foundations of the Federation.

It is not surprising that the realist group in this country are saying to what may be called their liberal or idealist opposites: 'We told you so!' And the idealists find no easy retort. The main lines of British policy towards Africa will hardly be diverted by this mood of disillusion but it could affect the spirit in which we offer help and helpers. And Africans are very quick to detect signs of disapproval and to denounce what they regard as distorted news and views. It seems, therefore, that we should try to look below the surface for the deeper African trends which explain the surface events, especially, of course, for the former British dependencies, though these can no longer be seen in isolation from the rest of Africa. Which of the many disturbing signs trouble us most? One is the rejection of so much of our own traditions of democracy and liberty which we thought we had communicated to Africa. The second is the continuing denunciation of neo-colonialists and imperialists of which Britain must obviously be the chief.

I must begin by repeating the view, of which I am more than ever convinced, that our disappointment springs from our failure to recognize that African racialism, called into being to confront white domination, is the main constituent of what we call African nationalism. Unless we can appreciate the strength and the depth of this attitude we shall not be able to deal successfully with the claims Africa still makes upon us.

Consider first the so-called flight from democracy. Have we measured the immensity of the leap Africans have made in a few decades from their isolation, poverty, tribal disunity and artificial frontiers, into independent statehood? How was it done? Mr Mboya has given the fullest and frankest answer in his book *Freedom and After*. In the later fifties in Kenya, Mboya and his colleagues, inspired by the example of Ghana, set themselves to create speedily an all-Kenya movement. The prize was great. For Kenya, independence – and quickly! For themselves, the leaders, a sudden promotion from racial subordination, frustration and poverty into supreme power, wealth and international status.

What was the technique? Not, as with most national movements, an appeal to past greatness, for there had been no nation, only tribal disunity. The basic appeal was that the black man should be freed from the white man's rule. There had to be, Mr Mboya writes, 'a simplification of the struggle into certain slogans and into one distinct idea which everyone can understand without arguing about the details of policy or of governmental programme after Independence'. The instrument for creating a sense of unity was the mass rally, with a father figure aloft bearing a striking insignia and frequently repeating some simple slogan which the crowd could roar back. Mr Mboya explains that these rallies could achieve four purposes. Firstly, create a united revolutionary spirit; secondly, wipe away acquiescence in the colonial government; thirdly, destroy the gradualist influence of the older African generation and those associated with the Government and, fourthly, show the colonial power the strength and unity of the independence movement. There was good psychology in all this. Through these great rallies the leaders quickly aroused in the crowds their latent sense of revolt against their individual subordination to the white man and intensified it by the well-known political technique of maximizing group emotion at the expense of reason. This is vividly suggested by the picture on the cover of Mr Mboya's book showing the faces of part of the vast crowd cheering him. The method was successful. No British governor was likely to follow a policy which might end in having to send police or military to disperse such crowds.

I am not condemning this technique which was, of course, widely employed elsewhere in Africa. The leaders were responding to strong revolutionary forces at work in the world of which their movements were only one result. But for what was – by historical analogies – such instantaneous success, there is a bill to be paid. Both the outgoing and the new state have to pay but the new state pays most. It is said that midnight in the stadium ushers in the birthday of a new nation. But nations are not born, they are made, and made by long years of common experience, by danger, conflict, discipline, failure and success. We should have known this. Perhaps we did. The African leaders begin to learn it on the morrow of an independence to which there was, by the mid-century, no alternative.

The African Studies Association of the United Kingdom

THE PRESIDENT'S INAUGURAL ADDRESS SEPTEMBER 1964
Special issue of *African Affairs*

This new body was founded in 1964 and I was given the great honour of being the first president and so gave the inaugural address at its first meeting at Birmingham University in September 1964.

I must begin on behalf of the Council by welcoming you all for having responded to their efforts by joining this new Association and by attending our first Conference.

There will be later occasions for expressing our gratitude to the University of Birmingham. But I cannot stand here without thanking the Vice-Chancellor for paying us the compliment of attending our first meeting. As one of his colleagues on the Inter-University Council, I have reason to know how deeply and energetically, in spite of his immense range of other duties, he has concerned himself with Africa and especially with African universities.

I must make it clear at once that I have not been given this presidential eminence as a recognition of arduous work upon the foundation of our new body. The first pioneering construction was the work of Professor Roland Oliver, the Vice-President, and Dr Allott, the Treasurer. The most arduous work, that of General Secretary, of compiling the *Bulletin* and of organizing this Conference, fell to Professor John Fage. I fear that this triple task must have been especially hard to perform when he was at the same time settling into his new Chair and inaugurating the important new Centre of West African Studies at Birmingham, which must be of especial interest to our new Association.

When I asked myself why I had been given the honour of election as the first president, it was at once obvious that the main qualification was that of physical seniority. Such a precedence is, of course, very proper in our African context. The instruction followed very naturally that I should try to survey the progress of African studies as they had been reflected in the experience of my own life. I am thus offered the privilege of age to be reminiscent, while I must resist the vice of age to be merely garrulous.

[1964]   COLONIAL SEQUENCE 1949 TO 1969

As I look round this hall I see there are a few elders of my age-grade – some *wazee* shall I call them? – with whom I have had some association from time to time. They will be able to correct or augment my own impressions, either in public or private. But it may be that I have some chronological advantages over them. The first is that I went to Africa when just out of my teens. The second, an advantage gained merely by association, is that members of my family were in Africa, in its remoter parts, from the very beginning of this century. And perhaps I may count it as a third form of association that, through my friendship and co-operation with Lord Lugard, I was helped in vivid fashion to conjure up the Africa of the eighties and to hear him talk of his friend Sir John Kirk, fellow-explorer with Livingstone in the fifties.

I need to vaunt these purely accidental advantages because as an Africanist my qualifications are confined to a narrow strip of the study of history and government. Any parallel reminiscence about the development of anthropological studies would start earlier and be fuller. Still longer, more crowded and complex, would be a survey of the physical sciences, indeed of any one of them, as directed from Britain upon the exotic and sometimes pathological conditions of tropical Africa. Perhaps some future Presidents will attempt such personal surveys. From my restricted position, and from a rather 'Oxford-centric' viewpoint, I want to look back over the growth of African studies. From this I will go on to consider a development with which I have been closely associated for many years and which must be of close and increasing relevance to our new Association – that of the new universities in tropical Africa.

In glancing back over the progress of African studies as they affected me I shall restrict myself to tropical and, indeed, to British Africa, and this for the usual reasons of convenience and brevity and – in my case – lack of knowledge.

The first phase in the world's knowledge of Africa stretches back into the dark abyss of African time with no certain beginning. The shadow of obscurity which hid most of the vast interior from the sight of the world also veiled it from the inhabitants themselves outside the small region which each group could know by sight, by hearsay, or by the myths dimly enshrining past migrations. This is surely true of most of the inner regions of middle Africa. We have known that in the western bulge and along the maritime and inland borders of the central tropical, mainly Negro, block, there were regions and civilizations in contact with the outside world. In recent years some of the younger generation

THE AFRICAN STUDIES ASSOCIATION OF THE U.K. [1964]

belonging to several disciplines – I see a number of them here – have been co-operating to reveal the degree to which influences of many kinds penetrated with more or less strength into the interior. Thus, over those parts of 'darkest Africa' which for long seemed to remain obscure, a new light – still rather patchy, rather grey – is playing. The archaeologists, linguists and the new breed of ethno-historians have been working, with the patience and attention to detail which their co-operative researches require, piecing together the external records of those who circumnavigated the continent, or occupied the coast, with the internal evidence of tribal movements, mythologies, ethnic characters and artefacts. We are all watching in the hope that they will be able to intensify and to widen the beam they are deploying. Alas! for myself and the few others of my generation, in the twenties and thirties this light had not yet begun to shine. Away from the western bulge and a very few lucent regions in the middle and the east, tropical Africa remained dark, if not quite 'darkest'. We shall all watch as the light of investigation is played back with increasing strength, though I expect with unavoidable patchiness, until it loses itself in the real and absolute darkness of a past which it cannot illuminate, except where the spade turns up the bones of primitive man or of his predecessors.

The second phase of African studies is based mainly upon the records of those Europeans who first penetrated the interior at the end of the eighteenth and in the nineteenth centuries. There can be no one in this hall who has not enjoyed these records, so revealing of our grandfathers as well as of the regions they opened to the knowledge of the world. Here I can be autobiographical again, as I was drawn into extensive reading of these impressively bound and dramatically illustrated volumes in the search for passages for an anthology. Owing to pressure of work by day I generally kept this lighter labour for the night, and, living in a flat, had to suppress gusts of midnight laughter at some of the revelations of the exploring ego. The English material is immense, and on the whole the quality of the observation and the writing is very high. There were certainly Victorian giants in those days, not only in the physical energy which carried them across deserts and through forests and swamps, walking over miles which some of them could count in thousands, but also in the energy of their minds, as they encountered and described strange men, strange beasts, insects, plants and the varied extravagancies of the climate.

We all have our favourite explorers. I admit a weakness, in spite of all his faults, for James Bruce. Any Africanist who has not read him and has to endure a long illness – but one not too mentally incapacitating – will find the time pass more quickly if he takes these six volumes for his bedside reading. And what a procession followed this eighteenth-century adventurer! Think, among others, of Burton, Denham, Barth (not British but in British employment) and Livingstone, a strong agent of change as well as a recorder! But most of the explorers were like those who go out at night holding a torch, more or less bright and steady, cutting a swathe of light in the immediate line of their march. Only a few stayed long enough to irradiate a wider circle.

The missionaries, who in general followed the explorers (though like Livingstone they could double the parts), were generally too busy evangelizing, teaching, nursing, building and dying of malaria to make full use of their opportunities for our subsequent advantage. Yet their first recordings of language and custom offer much foundation material to our fraternity. So does their correspondence, and one of our Vice-Presidents, Professor Oliver, has made good use of it.

A third phase in the intellectual discovery of Africa came with the acts of annexation. The soldiers and administrators, following up the explorers and missionaries, began, in the rudimentary form imposed by the conditions of their advance, that flow of official reporting which, in the 65 to 70 years of British rule which they inaugurated, was to reach the vast and not always very readable or enlightening mass of literature in which is embedded the record of our rule. But of the first generation of annexers or rulers it can surely be said of them, as of the explorers, that there were some giants in those days whose lives are part of African history – Gordon, Rhodes, Goldie, Kitchener and, much more self-explanatory, Cromer, Lugard, Johnston, 'Little Johnston', as the not very sizeable Lugard always used to call him.

It is difficult to put dates to the period which may be called that of administrative reporting. Much of the less accessible parts of the newly demarcated territories were hardly reached, still less grasped and studied, District Commissioner fashion, before the First World War. Though the first necessities of control, of development, and of health, demanded some pioneering scientific study, it is safe to say that it was not until the post-war dislocation had been mastered that the study of Africa entered into a new phase, at once wider and deeper and less purely official than anything that had been – or that could have been – attempted earlier.

These inter-war years are the fourth period of African studies, one within the experience of some of us here. The phase of establishing law and order, of laying down the first foundations of the new states on exiguous revenues or minimal grants-in-aid, was over. More officials and, in places, more settlers, meant deeper and widening studies of the African environment. Development was now the keyword, and development had to be built upon knowledge. At last our universities began to take the colonial empire, and especially Africa, seriously and no longer as, in the main, a region to supply exotic diseases and plants for a few specialists, along with witch-doctors and divine kings for the anthropologists.

Here I can return to my orders to be reminiscent. The new attitude certainly affected my own position. But not at first. I managed to fulfil an early dream by going out to Somaliland. The last Mad Mullah campaign had just finished. The Mullah had escaped across the frontier into Ethiopian Somaliland. The country was still much disturbed, but I was allowed to go on a trek with my brother-in-law, who had fought in the campaign, along and over the Ethiopian border. Here I found all and more than childish dreams had promised – long days on camel or pony; camp-fires at night to keep off the lions; wild-looking but beautiful tribesmen who had never before seen a white man and did not seem much interested when they did; and, best of all, perhaps, the word 'unexplored' printed across our very reticent map. It may be that this call of the wild played an initial, perhaps a half-conscious, part in attracting some of you to Africa, at least to the Africa of yesterday. Though I was on the edge of an academic career, there was no one to tell me how to use my knowledge, such as it was, of the nature and the problems of Somaliland. There was no routine of the D.Phil. in those days. So, needing an outlet for my deeply felt impressions, I wrote a novel – now, perhaps happily, out of print.

After that I had to wait some eight years before I was able to find a respectable academic opportunity to specialize upon Africa. The opportunity came partly because of the increasingly serious British interest in the continent, mainly in the British dependencies. Among many reasons for this, the foundation of the League of Nations Mandates system played its part. So did the growing controversies over Kenya. It would be impossible in a few moments even to generalize about the vast growth of old interests and activities and the birth of new ones by the thirties. The Colonial Office grew in range and size – its committees proliferated, bringing officials and British experts of many kinds into council together. If the universities were now starters, they had been pretty slow off the mark. True, anthropology was well-founded here and there, but little had been done to analyse the problems of social change, of the effects of modern government, still less of economics and finance, which cried out for study in swiftly changing Africa.

In these social studies stimulus came much more from men of action than from men of learning. The International Institute of African Languages and Cultures was, on the British side – and the main impulse was from Britain – the construction firstly of Lord Lugard; secondly of the quiet, subtle, tireless ecclesiastical statesman, Dr Oldham; and thirdly of the ebullient and charming Switzer, Sir Hans Vischer, originally one of Lugard's men, his first education officer in Northern Nigeria. Both these were Lugard's intimate and life-long friends. These three played the major part in launching and sustaining the Institute – Lugard and Vischer for some twenty years.

The Institute certainly enters into my own experience, as I know it does for some of you here; above all for Professor Forde, who has taken over the main burden of its administration from Lugard's day. For myself, I was first a beneficiary of the Institute and later a member of its Council. As a holder of one of the Rockefeller Travelling Fellowships for research in Africa, I was instructed to join that distinguished seminar conducted by Professor Malinowski at the London School of Economics. (I see here in Dr Richards one of my fellow-students and had hoped that I might see at least one other. There was, indeed, an upsurge of femininity into African studies at this time – Audrey Richards, Lucy Mair, Margaret Green, Margaret Read, Monica Hunter, Hilda Kuper.) There, as the only student of history and colonial government, I had to endure being the butt of the master. I was generally sinking out of my depth in the dark swamps of anthropology, and, when I did come to the surface, I was generally struck back into submergence.

It was the men of action again who were responsible for the next big advance, the Hailey *Survey*. Lugard and Oldham were again among the chief movers: with them was Philip Kerr (later Lord Lothian) and, behind him, General Smuts, who had reproached the colonial powers for not studying the Africa they were ruling – and changing. As a friend of Lugard I was a marginal member at some of the meetings of the sponsoring group. We met at Lothian's place, Blickling Hall. There were Reginald Coupland, Julian Huxley and others. Eating out of gold plate, with Holbeins and Van Dycks softly lighted on the walls behind us, we planned the massive verbal attack upon Africa south of the Sahara. I remember walking round the lake with Lothian while he argued, among other things, that all the troubles of Africa were due to the arrival there of the Protestant white woman. The upshot of all the discussions was the translation of another man of action, Indian action, into the field of African research, over which he was to reign, intellectual governor-general of Negro Africa, for nearly thirty years. He still lives to receive the letter of allegiance which we are sending him from this conference.

The Hailey *Surveys* were in a sense a one-man achievement because of the dominance of one mind over all that was done. But many others were drawn in to support and extend the master-mind. The outcome of all this was not only the massive *Surveys*, but the promotion of colonial research – and colonial meant at least three-quarters African – as a major duty of the Government in alliance with the academic world. The main break with past imperial policy regarding colonial finance came in 1940, with the £5,000,000 a year granted for ten years, and the £500,000 for research, an open-ended grant. There followed the establishment of the Colonial Research Committee which spawned a number of specialist committees, advancing at last boldly into the social sphere. I need say little here of all this fecund proliferation. Many, both present or absent members of our new Association, worked upon one or other of those committees or gained support for themselves or their students from the Colonial Research Fellowships which they promoted. It would be ridiculous if I were to be reminiscent here of my own contacts with this burgeoning of African studies in the new official sunlight. Mrs Chilver, the sibyl who officiated over the bureaucratic arcana from which all these far-flung sociological activities drew their inspiration – and their cash – is sitting here amongst us. In the first decade of 'C.D. & W.' research, some £7½ millions were spent, more than half in Africa, while the greedy physical sciences had to see 9 per cent of this spent on social and economic research. The fertilizing stream even, at last, reached history, financing that large composite *History of East Africa* upon which some of us here have been – indeed, still are – at work. The anonymity of officialdom prevents us from defining how much is owed to Mrs Chilver, but those of us who were caught up on the C.D. & W. research organization know what it meant to deal with an official, herself a student, who both understood and cared about what we were trying to do.

There were supporting influences at work in this period to foster serious study of African problems. One, I think, was the development of indirect rule. Lugard himself had not only instituted his comprehensive system in Northern Nigeria: he had defined it in detail and had afterwards expounded it in his writings. The concept had great influence in the inter-war period and for long – perhaps for too long – afterwards. But, from our present angle, we should note that the system demanded new knowledge and attitudes from the officers of the Colonial Service. They had to study their African subjects as never before and, ideally, study also the changes which their societies were undergoing.

This need was one reason for the deepening and lengthening of the training of the Colonial Service, especially of the administrative branch, at London, Cambridge and Oxford and so to a very practical demand upon the teaching and writing of Africanists. Another man of action, Sir Ralph Furse, soldier and official, was for many years the impelling influence acting as broker between the needs of the colonies for a new kind of service education and its supply from the universities. To be reminiscent again, it is an interesting comment on the shortage of students in the field of government that for a short time I had to lecture to the Colonial Service Courses both in Cambridge and Oxford. I remember it well because of the astonishing difference in the atmosphere of the two places which had already affected the two sets of officers – Oxford so hyper-sophisticated and blasé, Cambridge so young and keen and so polite that they even laughed at the jokes which were received in silence at Oxford. Another point about this period was brought to my mind by a passage in Mr Newlyn's interesting paper asking for specialized workers in the field of underdeveloped states. Some of us were worried at Oxford by the lack of any economic training for the Colonial Service, which was blindly handling societies dissolving under our economic pressures. We managed to get a chair of Colonial Economics founded. I remember the scorn with which the idea of this specialism was treated by economists. The title was changed. But it ured Professor Frankel to Oxford.

Thus the inter-war years, what I have called the fourth period of African studies, saw the first planned attempt to investigate the social and political aspects of tropical Africa. From my individual standpoint this was my time of opportunity, with generous provision from more than one source for travel in Africa, with a special post created by my own university and, on the eve of the Second War, a new postgraduate college with provision for planned research in the colonial field. Again, from my own limited viewpoint, the period had seen the publication of three major works, Lugard's *Dual Mandate*, Hailey's *An African Survey* and, in between, Raymond Buell's massive two-volume study *The*

THE AFRICAN STUDIES ASSOCIATION OF THE U.K. [1964]

Native Problem in Africa, a lone American reconnaissance in depth of a continent which was one day to attract a mass invasion of American scholars.

We have reached a point in this very selective and necessarily rather egocentric survey when we have to abandon the division by time for that of division by space. African studies in the inter-war years have grown in unbroken sequence and with increasing width and depth in the succeeding years. The war itself was hardly a check, as the need to serve and so to study the colonial peoples was seen as part of the total struggle. The big change conceived during the war and carried out afterwards was the development of academic studies *in* Africa, for Africa and by Africans, in other words, the foundation of the African universities. Of course the new universities do not study only their own continent, but they do study that, and many, if not most subjects in their courses are studied with a difference because they are followed in Africa by Africans. Here is a rapid and dramatic development in which all of us must be involved, in one way or another, as teachers, writers, examiners, visitors and in many other ways.

It may be that in spite of this involvement you may not have followed the stages by which this new growth came about. Here I can return to my commission to recount these developments from the standpoint of personal experience. There were, as you know, by the time of World War II, a number of advisory committees at the Colonial Office. They represented a medium by which the Office brought the colonies into touch with expert opinion in this country. I think this was good for the colonies: it was certainly good for Britain, as it brought scores, in the long run hundreds, of academic and other persons of knowledge and influence into constructive relationship with the colonies and their problems. I heard the opinion in the Office that more good ideas were thus generated than the scanty services in Africa could ever begin to carry out.

I was on the Colonial Education Advisory Committee between the wars, a committee which had owed its inception, and certainly its early effectiveness, very largely to the familiar trinity, Lugard, Oldham and Vischer. During the war, largely owing to the almost brutal insistence of a certain Professor H. J. Channon (who afterwards disappeared from this particular scene), we set up a sub-committee to review the situation with regard to higher education in the colonies. On this body we at once made a startling discovery – that in the whole colonial empire there were only four universities.

Firstly, there was the old University of Malta which had been founded in 1592 and owed nothing to Britain for its past or for its later rather somnolent existence. Secondly, there was the new University of Jerusalem for which, again, Britain could claim no credit. Thirdly, the University of Ceylon, founded in 1921. But Ceylon was clearly on the verge of independence and would need little help in the future. Fourthly, there was the University of Hong Kong – founded in the teeth of local and British opposition by the African bush-whacker, Lugard, during his interlude in that island.

You will see that of these universities three catered for very small, very untypical populations, while for the whole of Africa there was no university in any British colony; nothing, indeed, existed between Egypt and South Africa. True, there were beginnings, bits and pieces of post-secondary and professional education. There was medicine in Khartoum and plans had been discussed for development towards a university at Makerere.

Our little sub-committee, which sometimes had to descend to cellars in air raids, could do little more than report this situation to the main committee, which in turn begat the Asquith Commission. A number of important academic figures were drafted on to this. We worked very hard and produced our report in 1945. In this document African needs took the first place. I expect that all of you will have read this report, and I will remind you of only two main features. One was the high standard set for the degrees, which were to be London University degrees tailored to meet the needs of each region under what was called 'special relationship'. The second feature, another imposition of our own standards – there was no African on the Commission – was in trying to entrench academic freedom in the form of independent university government.

Were we wrong, especially as regards the standard? Already the tendency in some ex-colonial States is to widen the gateways and lower the fences, as well as to challenge the British ideal of academic freedom. The issue is much the same as that of the Westminster model of government. There are two answers. Firstly, especially at that date, we could give only what we ourselves possessed and valued. Secondly, the Africans – the few who then had an opinion on the subject – would have been angry at being offered something 'made for Africa' and which we regarded as second best, if that.

The Asquith Commission gave rise to two other bodies. A commission was sent to West Africa, interesting in that it provoked the first

THE AFRICAN STUDIES ASSOCIATION OF THE U.K. [1964]

really effective expression of African opinion in this context. The Gold Coast demanded a university of its own, built on the excellent foundations of Achimota, rather than see Nigeria as the only locus for a full university. The West Indies Committee, which consisted of Sir James Irvine, Sir Raymond Priestly and myself, *did* consider the alternative of a larger low-level institution. We were, indeed, confronted with one when we were invited to visit the University of Puerto Rico and saw the many hundreds of Iberian-looking students studying everything from philosophy and English literature to home-crafts and hair-dressing. Were we shaken? No! Should we have been? Perhaps. But the two West Indians who had joined our Committee out there never weakened, and one became Principal and the other Registrar of the new University in Jamaica. Certainly Sir Alexander Carr-Saunders, who for many years played a – if not the – leading part in promoting the new universities, has never wavered about the rightness of the Asquith Commission policy and I heard him re-affirm this the other day. I might add that to him, as well as to Lord Hailey, this Conference has sent a message of respectful greeting.

You may wonder whether even personal experience was reason enough for leading you on from African studies to African universities. Whether or not they *ought* to be closely connected, the truth is that in this very practical world they certainly are. Most, if not all of you must have been aware that the existence of these new institutions in Africa, with the traffic of many kinds which goes on between them and our own institutions, has greatly affected us practically, intellectually and psychologically. For one thing – and this takes us back to the initials C.D. & W. and C.S.S.R.C., not to speak of Mrs Chilver – beside each of the first new universities was founded an institute for research, mainly social research. To these, with the fine gesture of precedence they represented, all the universities, all the Africans and all of us owe a debt. For, as Dr Richards could tell us if she would, it was no easy task to plan, to build, to staff, to organize research and to steer without collision a course between the College Council, the Colonial Government, the research staff, and the stream of academic visitors requiring advice, encouragement, literature, accommodation and probably camp equipment, transport and medical care as well.

The African colonies are now independent states, the colleges are universities. Yet the Inter-University Council to which the Asquith Commission gave birth still provides them with aid and advice of many kinds. It is still the main administrative link between these universities

[1964] COLONIAL SEQUENCE 1949 TO 1969

and our own. It might therefore be useful if I said a few words about this working contact which plays an important part in linking our African studies with those being pursued in Africa itself. What I say can qualify as reminiscence, as I have been on the Council since its inception and for many years on its Executive Committee.

The Council meets quarterly. It consists of two representatives from London, one from each of the other British universities, and some co-opted members. The Executive meets monthly. Alongside it is the Colonial University Grants Committee, which sanctions the financial provisions for projects which the Executive Committee passes on academic grounds. An amazingly small staff works to carry out the decisions, and performs an immense variety of services of liaison, of advice, and the arranging year by year of appointments committees for hundreds of applicants for scores of overseas posts. Through this machinery Britain has spent more than £14,000,000, largely on capital grants for buildings.

Alongside this administrative structure, and in close association, London University has played an indispensable part as academic foster mother to these infant places of learning. There has been a close and flexible relationship over the contents and conduct of examinations, the problems of staffing, and co-operation over higher degrees.

As I look back upon all this constructive work, it is easy for me to praise the famous academic men who have played the major parts, and to commend what seems to me one of the best services Britain has ever given to the colonial peoples. It is easy because it must be obvious that my part was inevitably a very minor one, since the need for the new institutions was for advice from those of high authority and long experience in academic administration. My own part was mainly the supply of political comment, and also of contact with Makerere, as a member for some years of its Council. In this critical world enthusiastic praise tends to be out of fashion, but I must express here the admiration with which I have watched these busy men – and one woman, the late indefatigable Dame Lilian Penson – devoting their limited margin of time and strength to this work. These persons, nearly all heads of their universities or of important departments, have attended meetings, flown all over the world, planned and sited new colleges, drawn up constitutions, vetted building plans, and searched Britain for suitable overseas Vice-Chancellors and professors. Much of this work, moreover, was achieved during the first post-war years, when heavy problems of revival and reconstruction faced them at home. Now, again, there is still much to be done just when the university authorities, and above all our new Chairman, Sir John Fulton, are faced with the large tasks of a revolutionary advance in university education in Britain. An unexpected testimony to this work has come from outside the Commonwealth. The Sudan (where a university has been built up with British help on the foundations of Gordon College), Ethiopia, Libya, Jordan, Saudi Arabia and Liberia have all come to the Inter-University Council for help and advice in developing their higher education.

You might well ask me at this point to define exactly the relationship of all this development with African studies in Britain. Some of the links are obvious and are represented in the careers of many of you who are here. The provision of academic centres in Africa has allowed our own scholars to go to Africa, not only to teach, but also to pursue their own research. The other side is, of course, the enormously enlarged opportunity for African students to begin making their contribution to the knowledge of their continent. Of course, in neither case, are studies *in* Africa necessarily studies *of* Africa. On the other hand, in addition to the immense new growth of studies of every aspect of the continent, and especially tropical Africa (the region to which I have been mainly referring in this talk), the very fact of pursuing non-African studies *in* Africa for Africans must in many cases mean that they are studied with a difference. For Africans, their passionate interest in creating the vision of a new Africa, both for themselves and for the world, may deepen this environmental colour for some time to come. But then they would say that African social studies conducted by Europeans in Europe also had their own special colour.

You will see that without finding a clear dividing line we have strayed over into the latest, the current phase of African studies. How suddenly the stream has broadened out from the trickle that some of us can remember! How fast it is flowing! And in some parts – dare I suggest? – the depth is not great, especially in the sphere of politics. Are there any features of the position today which can be described? Here again, even if I had not been so ordered, I can speak only from my own special experience.

The first feature today is surely that the near-monopoly British students had in the extensive part of Africa under British rule is ending. The United States, almost at a bound, has come in beside us. This sudden and powerful invasion should be given our almost unqualified welcome. 'Almost' – because much of the literary ephemera comes from across the Atlantic, though we certainly contribute our share. But this audience needs no reminder of the strong and growing centres of African studies in America or of the generous hospitality offered to ourselves or the large financial help to studies in this country. Two things have especially come my way: one is the high quality of most of the American advanced students I meet working at Oxford in this field. The other is the strong reinforcement provided from America in the development of the African universities. I must say a few words on this last subject.

In about the last decade – and increasingly in the last five years – the Americans have been coming in alongside us to help the new universities. I say 'alongside', for this is the important word. We, after all, had founded and fostered these institutions very much on the British pattern and they were closely linked with our own universities. On the Inter-University Council there was naturally some doubt as to whether the sudden entry of Americans, furnished with great reserves of energy, idealism, numbers and money, would prove a competing or even disruptive influence. For one thing American universities work under far less central guidance and have less unity than our own. These fears have, on the whole, proved groundless. Thanks to the statesmanlike attitude of some of the leading Americans in this venture, and to the untiring alertness of our own representatives, and especially of our former Chairman, Sir Charles Morris, there has been close and constant partnership, even to the extent of mixed commissions and joint reports and plans. A liaison committee was formed and, with our own members ready to fly to America at short notice, the contact has been active and continuous. Of course there has been some entry of American ideas. But then some of their experience is very appropriate, and can be applied as an injection or a supplement. Some of the Americans have been critical of the high standards laid down by the Asquith Commission. The Inter-University Council, not without its doubters, has come some way to meet American ideas. But then some of these are in tune with the growing African needs and demands. It is possible to believe that it was right to start with the highest standards and, while maintaining these where established, to experiment with new, and more flexible, more comprehensive forms, where the need for these was clear.

What about ourselves in all this development? First, as teachers, what demands is Africa going to make upon us and our oncoming graduates in the present phase? In spite of the production of African graduates, in spite of the African desire to break free from colonialist leading strings, the demand is going to remain heavy. You may have read the report of the UNESCO Conference on the future of African universities held at Tananarive in the autumn of 1962. There, in a conference dominated by Africans, it was reckoned that during the next nineteen years there would be a need for at least 5,000 expatriate staff in the English-language universities. Against this need we must note the figure for 1964 of 730 United Kingdom staff in Africa. Let us set this position beside that of African students in this country, since most of us tend to take an interest in these students as an extension of our interest in their continent. In 1963-4, studying in British Universities, there were 2,527 Africans from what we might call Inter-University Council universities, while in all of these there were only just over 11,000 students. In 1962-3 there were in Britain over 704 graduate students from Africa.

These are all parts of the academic jigsaw which we have to fit together to get our total picture of African needs in relation to Britain. Perhaps another figure from East Africa may bring home to us the full meaning of Africa's needs. Mr Guy Hunter has recently carried out a man-power survey of East Africa, which shows that in 1962, in a population of some 26 millions, there were less than 2,000 Africans of graduate or comparable standard. Many, many thousands more are needed if the East African territories are to become the prospering modern States to which their leaders aspire. And what of Malawi and Zambia, even worse off than East Africa?

How is this great demand to be met? It is recognized that in the Africa of the future it will not be possible, for reasons upon both sides, to make many permanent or even very long-term British appointments. Provision must be upon a short-term basis or by secondment. The need is regarded by all the university and Government authorities concerned as so vital that, in the face of Britain's own enhanced demand, every effort is being made to answer the need by devices which will meet all the natural fears and hesitations of possible candidates. It is realized that neither exhortation nor the moral approval of the authorities is enough. The Inter-University Council has devised a number of measures which should meet most needs and fears of those contemplating a spell abroad. In case these are not sufficiently known, I will list them. Firstly, the provision of extra financial help to meet special costs, such as the expenses of moving or fares for children. Secondly, there is an interview fund to allow short-listed candidates to come to Britain for an interview when a return to this country is desired. Thirdly, re-settlement fellowships to give those returning after a period of three years or more a year in which to settle back and pick up their subjects. Fourthly, there are arrangements of several kinds to assist staff overseas with their research, partly by special grants, partly by a service in microfilm material. Fifthly, there are so-called prestige fellowships – grants on a generous scale to induce eminent authorities to offer their erudition for a spell to an overseas university. This traffic is so important, both for them and for us, that I could not resist saying this much on the inducements for academic adventure and discovery. I speak of a changing and growing situation, but the latest information and advice are always to be had from the overworked but devoted staff of the Inter-University Council.

Some of you may be thinking that this Association was founded to advance African studies – not African students. Well, the two are close together – even though they are not the same. I can imagine you thinking that, by the whole-hearted pursuit of your own subject, you might be doing that continent a greater service than by busying yourself with some of the activities to which I have referred – or even struggling to make yourself aware of them.

This is part of the real problem of our time, of our dangerous and demanding world which we can see through the library window or hear knocking on the study door. Each of us has to decide how far to divide our own small allotment of time between our research and the environment in which it is set. The tropical African environment is even more restless than most, as its peoples, in their links with us, are at once bound and repelled, while they turn eagerly towards all those new competing influences which the policy of non-alignment attracts.

It may be that conditions in Africa will grow worse in the coming years before political stability and some measure of economic satisfaction can be reached. If so, in the racial atmosphere which instability breeds, Africans may find it difficult to make those contributions to the understanding of themselves, their own environment, or the world, which both assist and express maturity. The need for external services and studies, offered in the true academic spirit, will grow rather than diminish. One function of this Association – and we on the Council have every intention of limiting its functions to the most modest useful degree – will be to take stock of the situation outside our own disciplines, to meet people whose names we know only on the cover of books, to be kept aware of what other peoples are doing in a field which is no longer a British or a European monopoly. Especially, perhaps, the Association could help us to accept what Africans are doing and attempting, and to make them feel that, with us, they belong to a fraternity seeking the truth, and not to one of academic nationalists working in a spirit of cultural or racial self-satisfaction or aggression.

To conclude autobiographically, it seems a long trek from the days of Africa's attraction to my teenage romanticism all the way to this platform. I do very greatly value the honour conferred upon me by my peers in making me the first President of this new African Studies Association of Britain. I hope, and expect, that this body will perform a useful function in promoting contacts across the barriers of disciplines, space, age and race, and thus achieve what must be our main purpose, to advance knowledge of this vast, clamant, but still little known continent.

Arthur Creech Jones, 1891–1964

A TRIBUTE AT HIS FUNERAL SERVICE, 28 OCTOBER 1964

Mrs Creech Jones has given me the honour, and the sad responsibility, of trying to express what so many of us feel about her husband, Arthur Creech Jones, whose body lies before us.

This is not the occasion for a formal obituary – last Saturday's *Times* gave us that in brief. Nor for an oration or a eulogy. It is a moment of quiet when we want to get behind the biographical facts and figures and let our minds rest for a few moments upon the quality of his life, his special gifts both to his country and in the private world of friendship. What I say must be incomplete. He set his hand to so many different tasks with so many different groups. I knew him only in the later half of his life, when we had much to do with each other in the sphere of colonial affairs. He was also my friend.

He was, of course, a party man, utterly sure of the rightness of that party in its principles and its policies. But it was evidence both of the political maturity and unity of our country, and also of his own character, that he could work constructively with men of all parties, or of none. His character had no cutting edge that could wound political opponents: none of that wholly personal ambition which repels even while it succeeds.

I think that the inner spring of all his actions was the desire to share. He had not come up by any soft way himself, but this had not made him hard. He was versatile in enjoyment, but he wanted to share the advantages and pleasures he had won. Not only with his friends – certainly with them – but with everyone. This may sound a large claim. But it is truth.

He loved to walk in the country – so he helped to found the Youth Hostels Association. He loved foreign travel – I have seen him indulging in that love in France and Italy – so he organized the Workers Travel Association. He had a devotion for mountains – so he achieved the Access to Mountains Act. And when he began to look across the seas at our colonial subjects he wanted them to share in what had been won in this country in welfare, in education, in legal and political rights.

In the thirties it was no easy task for an already busy opposition back-bencher to extend his care to our many and diverse colonies. Yet he achieved this. He developed a far-flung network of contacts with individuals overseas – all he did led him quickly to the individual – and these kept him informed, and asked his help, when they believed themselves wronged. He once told me that colonial affairs were too dispersed, too numerous and exotic for any Colonial Secretary to master. The great merit of the parliamentary question was that on the subject of the question at least, with its possible supplementaries, the minister had to make himself informed. As a ceaseless questioner he must, therefore, have done much to educate his predecessors in office.

His arduous self-imposed task for the colonial peoples had a wider significance. The first self-appointed colonial leaders were beginning to raise their heads – sometimes their fists – above the quiescent masses. It was no small thing for them to find a man in the imperial parliament to voice their protests and defend their legal rights. His work, and that of the one or two others who stood with him, must have helped to soften the bitter edge of colonial assertion which – though no one could then foresee this – was to gain so rapidly in strength, and which might have roughly cut the colonial bond instead of untying it in mutual consent.

In his office as Secretary of State he showed himself as no party theorist. At his desk, and by travel, he quickly learned the full meaning – by Western standards – of colonial ignorance, of colonial poverty, of the need for education for self-government, not only in the school and the university, but also on the farm, in local councils and in trade unions.

His term of office may not stand out in the record in the brilliant colours of success. But the colonial empire was no longer the material out of which political success could be made. Power had begun to leak.

ARTHUR CREECH JONES, 1891–1964 [1964]

There was an increasing amount of quiet constructive work to be done but there were also hazardous concessions to be made. For some of his supporters his pace seemed too measured, his policy too bi-partisan. He certainly did not believe it to be his duty to force socialism upon the dependencies. His opponents respected his devotion and integrity but they sometimes took advantage in Parliament of his weakness as a controversialist. He was always reasonable but sometimes at too great length, forgetting, perhaps, that most men prefer to be convinced rather than informed.

But this is not the time either to list or to weigh his achievements as Colonial Secretary. In so far as possible we are now trying to think of the man behind the work. In his case this approach is possible. For as whether in Ceylon, Africa or the West Indies, he met colonial leaders, it was his humanity, his simplicity, his generosity, even his humility, in trying to serve them which gave them a new experience of empire as he expressed it, a new hope of humane and sensible response to their turbulent and often confused desires.

His tenure was certainly costly to himself. If it is a virtue in a minister, as it may be in a surgeon or a judge, to forget his day's work as he unlatches his own front door, our friend often missed the benefit of that anodyne. I remember how bitterly he suffered through the tragic confusion over Palestine, over the Gold Coast murders, wherever, indeed, life and death were in the scales he had to use. And long after he had left office, he was sometimes anxious and perplexed at the shape of things in some of the states he had helped to emancipate, at the rejection of much he had helped to give in the belief that it was the best this country had to offer.

There might be doubts of his capacity as a parliamentarian. There could be none of his work as head of the Colonial Office. In the twilight region of departmental organization he was an initiator, helping to adjust a historic Office for its changing functions. His power to remain always more the man than the minister – and the kind of man he was – affected all who worked with him. I believe that, when he finally left, he said a personal good-bye to every member of the Office, from the highest to the lowest. The ambience of his personality reached even the wide dispersion of the Colonial Service. Among the many good things he began, he founded the Service journal, *Corona*, and in or out of office he never missed the annual Corona dinner when he could meet the Service. One of its members said to me only yesterday 'We were mostly Tories by nature and office. But we knew that Creech Jones was utterly sincere and honest – that he had faith in us and our work and would never let us down.'

Turning to his later, indeed his last years, we should not forget the courage and cheerfulness with which he met disappointment, some ingratitude, physical suffering and growing political eclipse. He set himself to humbler, though valuable tasks, helping others often in projects he had himself initiated.

So much for the public man. There is little that need be said of the private friend – the subject is so simple and complete.

His friendship, which would grow out of common purposes and actions, never failed. He was utterly constant – and his wife with him. No trouble was too great: the long, perfectly handwritten letters; the journey undertaken at any cost of precious time; the vital official paper sent just when needed by the recipient; the all-too-generous present chosen with perceptive genius. His was a friendship – it is only now possible to realize this – that could without any conscious effort make its recipients better people and better citizens.

I have a last word to say. This is a humanist ceremony. There was one thing, to my great sorrow, I could not share with my friend – my Christian faith. But I could not end these words without confessing it. I believe that the souls of the righteous are in the hands of God. I know that this was a righteous man. I am very sure that this is not the end.

1965

Britain's Role in a World of Racial Challenge

The Listener 3 June 1965

This was a talk in a series entitled 'Thinking aloud about Africa'. It appears that I felt able to write little on the morrow of the almost complete emancipation of Africa, but had now begun to adjust my mind to the prospect of a largely independent continent.

Last week we took a panoramic view of ex-British Africa. We saw it in almost volcanic action as it erupted into independence – eleven new states in seven years. In contrast to this dramatic political landscape I want to come back now to this country, looking at the same events as seen from these shores; trying to assess what we have done or left undone and what tasks still remain.

The anti-colonial case is that Europe's annexation was an almost unmitigated misfortune for Africa – that it broke in upon some pre-European golden age, that even before their annexation the present states were free nations. To defend our record we seem forced to depreciate the Africans. Yet even if we allow for the standards of Victorian explorers and their tendency to dramatize, we are still left with convincing evidence of an equatorial region in which, for the most part, the tribes lived in extreme poverty, often naked, and lacking any permanent buildings. They knew neither the wheel nor the plough and their other tools for living were few and inadequate. They were illiterate, fragmented into vast numbers of independent and often warring groups. They waged no very successful war against Africa's natural enemies to man – the diseases, wild animals, insects, droughts and floods. I do not speak here only from the records: I began my travels in Africa forty years ago and saw for myself the tribal fragmentation and, by our standards, the almost unbelievable poverty.

Admittedly these conditions were not universal. Early explorers found in Benin an impressive state with an almost Louis Quatorze court ritual, large pagan cities in Yoruba country and large Moslem cities in Hausaland, with all the arts – including the political arts – which go with city life. In the time of our William the Conqueror a king in the western Sudan could put 200,000 men in the field and give audiences surrounded with splendidly dressed princes and pages and guarded by dogs with collars of silver and gold. A thirteenth-century king from this region visited Cairo en route for Mecca and brought so much gold with him that he caused a currency crisis in the city. Archaeologists working in an almost virgin field are finding figures and pottery of refined art which are pushing their dates back even before the Christian era. Yet the poverty of by far the greater part of middle Africa was real. Arab colonization on Africa's eastern coast failed to penetrate inland more than a few miles from the sea.

These issues are not academic. The attitude to the Negro race is partly based on the general view, however vague, that the Negro comes from a wild and primitive continent which needed the rough intrusion of the white man to bring it into the twentieth century. Two ideas might help to square this circle. First, we need a longer time-scale of history and prehistory that takes us outside our complacent, almost suburban, Western snobbishness. In the millions of years which it took man to become man as we know him, it was only yesterday that he began to create his civilization and for by far the greater part of that period we western Europeans remained savages. Secondly, let us remind ourselves that the scientists have ruled that there are no inherent differences in the mental equipment of the different races and so in their potentialities. But potential equality in terms of civilization as we define it is, of course, something very different from actual equality.

I suggest that it was only the intrusion of Europe which caused the full awakening of the latent potentialities of Africa, the dark sleeping beauty, even though the intrusion was a rape rather than a kiss. How otherwise could our former dependencies have been brought so quickly, so peacefully, into constructive contact with the world? There was then no international machinery for the task. The alternative was uncontrolled, haphazard exploitation – already begun here and there – by any masterless men, white, brown or black, possessed of some of the new instruments of power, above all the rifle.

The achievements must be measured against the difficulties. Occupation was very slow because of the shortage of staff, of roads, and of knowledge. Then the world to which Africa now belonged was hit by war and by slump and again by war. Revenues had to be built up, officials trained, famines and tribal wars checked, tribal laws and language studied. Each African country was different. What then were the achievements? First, settled boundaries within which states could be built up out of tribes. Some of the boundaries were badly drawn but they have at least allowed Africans to make a quick start to nationhood. Significantly, nearly all the new governments have joined in an agreement to respect them. Secondly, the colonial rulers, just because they had annexed, were willing to invest the capital needed to build up an infra-structure of road, rail, government buildings, and the rest. The British staff increased in numbers and in experience. Health, education, agriculture, veterinary problems were studied and services developed, and local government adapted to the needs and traditions of the tribes. Production, trade, and revenue figures soared. New ideas of freedom, of law, of individual opportunity were introduced.

Behind the massive output of reports lay the intimate reality of the colonial task, the officials trekking in the bush, talking to people along the roads, on their shambas, dealing with chiefs, courts and councils, teaching how to build bridges, roads and dams, to grow more and better crops, and terrace hillsides against erosion. Or, on the negative side, teaching how not to raid the next tribe's cattle, how not to kill twins or reputed witches, how not to take bribes or put a hand in the local treasury safe.

What standard between the real and the ideal can we apply to the work of thousands of men working for more than half a century in Africa? If it was bad, who would have done it better? Had not Britain some qualifications for the job – long prior experience in many parts of the world, a large supply of manpower from the public schools of a reasonable educational standard, honest and humane, with a sense of discipline and service, a desire for adventure and an outdoor life? Not, perhaps, the total spectrum of human virtues, but a fair proportion. We had a society with a long humanitarian tradition, and a lively political life in which at least any major colonial scandal would be discussed.

An African, if he could have endured the argument so far, would have broken in with the reproach – 'What did you do to prepare us for self-government? Look at our lack of men trained for politics, administration, or technical service!' The answer is that the British had not annexed Africa with the single purpose of disannexing it at the earliest possible moment. The assumption born of our own national and imperial experience that the goal of all political evolution was self-government was extended only hesitantly to Africa. For the speed of advance caught us by surprise, especially in east and central Africa. We had emancipated the Asian dependencies in the late forties. We then concentrated most of our attention upon Africa. There was a general sense that it needed everything we could give it, including self-government – but not yet! With the welfare state a new theme arose in policy. Lord Hailey, the Nestor imported from India to Africa, expressed it by saying that it was no use when the African was asking for bread to give him the vote. But another text states that man cannot live by bread alone. Something else held us back, harder to define. The service, deeply interested in its African task, developed a momentum of its own. It seems that something like this happened in the Indian Civil Service. The work became so enthralling, so much a matter of professional pride, that administration became almost an end in itself. The thought of diluting the service with raw native talent, still more of allowing politicians to impair the fine administrative structure, was distasteful, rather like asking a government to help the opposition to replace it.

I think that history may give Dr Nkrumah the credit of having broken the spell of African acquiescence in Britain's leisurely constitutional programme. Returning from America, he acted as the vigorous assistant to the established opposition party, the United Gold Coast Convention. There was a moment of tension in 1948 due largely to the shortage of imported goods, high prices, and therefore antagonism against the foreign firms. At this moment some ex-service men decided to march, against instructions, to the Governor's house to present their grievances. This led to the police firing and killing one man. The incident sparked off riots in Accra and some other towns. The British Government, according to form, appointed a commission of inquiry. Its radical report, as I happen to know from talks with him at the time, startled the Colonial Secretary and forced his hand. An all-African committee of intelligentsia under an African judge was set up. It drafted a new and moderate constitution. But Nkrumah had read the lesson of the riots. He saw what could be done by bypassing the minority of the educated, and rather Anglicized minority. He appealed directly to the masses through a new party under his own dynamic leadership, the Convention People's Party. He organized this widely through the country, addressed mass meetings, appealing successfully to the trade unions, the market women, the young half-educated and the dissatisfied. Even so it took nine years from the date of the riots to the proclamation of independence in 1957. Nkrumah's success and his uncompromising methods sent an electric shock through the continent. Then came his calling of all African leaders to Accra on the morrow of independence to inspire them to do likewise.

Ought we not to have understood the meaning of this? We thought of Ghana as an exceptional African state, small, advanced, prosperous, united. We were thinking in terms of the politics of democracy and gradualism, of separate African states, each different. We believed that West Africa was several generations in front of the east and central African states. And some of these had the added problem of the white colonists. On this reckoning we needed time for the essential work of preparation; we had not realized that we were dealing with a continent, with a race, which could be stirred in a moment with the hope not of working towards this or that constitution but of throwing off the white man's control as quickly as Ghana – tomorrow – today!

Early in 1960 something happened to shatter our gradualism. The change was proclaimed to the world by Mr Macmillan in – of all places – South Africa. At the end of a tour of 20,000 miles through Africa, he told the parliament there that 'the most striking of all the impressions I have formed is of the strength of this African national consciousness. The wind of change is blowing through the continent.'

This was the public avowal. But just when and why had the minds of British Ministers changed? We shall not know exactly until the cabinet archives are opened. And that, on present rules, will not be until the year 2010. But we can piece together the events which produced this cumulative effect. There was Mau Mau ending with the ghastly Hola incident. Then the return to Nyasaland of Nkrumah's friend, Dr Banda, the subsequent 1959 riots there and the shootings. From the time of Abel the cry of blood from the ground has been the strongest of all appeals to man as well as to God. So the Devlin Committee was sent to report upon these incidents. It said the Africans demanded 'above all else self-government for the black people in Nyasaland such as they have seen happening in other parts of Africa' ... 'Nothing matters but political freedom' ... 'poverty is better than slavery, and than being a second-class citizen'. In Nyasaland and all eastern Africa the intelligentsia, the African middle class, was scanty, but this appeal could be made to the masses. Had Britain now enough strength and status to play a strong delaying hand? Could she shoot again in face of world opinion and, indeed, of British opinion? She had lately tried shooting in another part of Africa with disastrous effects to her pride and prestige – at Suez. If she could not shoot – what then? The Africans now had already guessed the answer. Gradualism was out. For the eastern and central African states there was to be no time for further preparation, no stages of advance. A few quick strides in the early sixties and – independence, *now*!

The white settlers whom British governments had encouraged up to the eleventh hour took the brunt of the reversal of policy. One of them, Sir Michael Blundell, has written a deeply instructive and moving book *So Rough a Wind*. His quotation is from Shakespeare's *Henry IV*:

> We shall be winnowed with so rough a wind
> That even our corn shall seem as light as chaff
> And good and bad find no partition.

He is right. Only history will be able to look at the settlers' brief record and winnow the corn from the chaff.

Blundell was among the first to feel the shock of Britain's changed policy. At the 1960 Lancaster House conference he at once sniffed the atmosphere of surrender. He was arguing with the new Colonial Secretary when a telegram was handed to Mr McLeod, who said: 'Look at this. This is a message to say that the Belgians are giving the Congo independence in June this year – 1960. Do you know what this means? We are going to be the last in the colonial sphere instead of the first.'

There are still Europeans not only in central Africa but here who take a dark view of the new Africa and believe the surrender need never have been made. If the Gold Coast riots – so this argument runs – had been treated to a whiff of grapeshot, the wind of change could then have been harnessed to a steadily controlled pressure. This would have resulted in better prepared African states and would have retained the contribution of the white settlers. But I cannot believe that any firefighting apparatus could have stopped the wind blowing the sparks from Ghana over the east and centre of Africa, all the same combustible material. Britain's power in Africa rested not on force, which was negligible, but on consent. The consent gone, only one way was open.

No, the mistake was surely not to have seen what was coming, not to have used the few years that remained to carry out a crash programme of Africanization. This would have left the Africans a little, if only a little, better prepared for independence. The abruptness of the emancipation also struck the settlers what may prove to be a fatal blow. The British Government was giving the Kenya settlers promises of support, then of multi-racial half-way houses, to within a year or two of the end.

BRITAIN'S ROLE IN A WORLD OF RACIAL CHALLENGE [1965]

In central Africa British ministers ignored the most earnest expert advice and set up in 1953 the white-dominated Federation. Its very erection awakened the African majority into political consciousness and protest. Two years ago, in face of growing African antagonism, a Conservative government destroyed its own construction, a government which actually contained some of the ministers who had set it up.

The period of colonial power is over. Our ex-colonies are independent states. We have gone a long way towards making a successful readjustment to this new situation. Yet I believe that we carry over into our post-colonial period one characteristic which could prove a liability: our attitude to race. Some people may think that in these talks I have overstressed the racial factor in the African assertion. It was not, of course, the only agent of change. But we cannot deny that the growing sense of unity in Negro Africa as a whole is based upon race. Further, the Africans have found themselves part not only of an even wider Negro group but of other races with which they share one common feature – a skin that is not white, a skin regarded as a mark of inferiority by the whites – or by enough of them to make the indignity felt. The whites, though a minority in the world, and their empires largely lost, still have most of the wealth, the weapons, the scientific knowledge, and a confident tradition of command. So, in response, the isolated racial resentment of African, Arab, or Asian spreads first over a state, then a continent, and then seeps over from one continent to the next until it reaches right across the world.

This is a picture which confronts us almost daily in our newspapers. Britain should be able to take a lead among white nations in inter-racial tolerance. But do we? Unfortunately we share with other peoples of northern Europe a deeply defensive and superior sense of our race. For most of the colonial period our administrators, sometimes alone in control of thousands of Africans, not unnaturally felt some sense of racial superiority. They could hardly make any equal contact across the barriers of numbers, language, and custom. But pride in our own culture had another side, respect for that of others. We did not force assimilation. But as more Western-educated Africans emerged, we may have been too slow to recognize and welcome them. More serious was the position where settlers established a ruling, or would-be ruling, minority. They were driven to try to prove in theory as well as in practice that the black man is not only different but deeply and permanently inferior to the white.

The French have been in some ways more successful than ourselves in their African relationship. It seemed to me in my travels in French territories that their administration was not only less efficient but less humane than ours towards the tribal masses. But those who took advantage of the very thorough, very French education offered to them could rise into a full social equality, and even participate in French political life. The leading example of the contact, the poet-politician Leopold Senghor, President of Senegal, traces the French success to the philosophy of their revolution which enshrined the potential unity and equality of mankind. There was also something human and earthy about the French grasp of Africa as contrasted with something fastidious and cold about much of our own. Even justice, even altruism, can be cold. An Indian writer has referred to the label on imported tinned meat, 'not touched by the human hand'. 'That', he adds, 'is how we felt about British administration!' In French colonies the deep link of sex was open and unashamed. A French colonial governor thought nothing of asking me to camp in half a house the other half of which was occupied by a polygamous French official and his four African 'wives'. (My well-trained Nigerian servant was shocked and insisted upon sleeping across the doorway.) The Negro writers of French Africa are now theorizing about their debt to France. Negritude, the new expression of the Negro mind, is something indefinable, changing and growing as Negroes converse with other Africans, with West Indians, with American Negroes, with Frenchmen and anyone who will join in the conversation. Negritude, says Senghor, is the fruit of the French Revolution through action and reaction. As Sartre has said, Africans have taken the intellectual weapons of the colonizer and turned them against him.

In a striking passage Colin Legum has described the new black intellectual lying comfortably in the embrace of French charms, then breaking violently away to explore the womb of his own past and so rediscover his own roots, his own identity. Under British influence with its so-called 'indirect' approach, with our sense of the difference rather than the unity of cultures, Africans could keep at least some of their own tribal institutions proudly alive. The Western-educated African returning from abroad is torn between his new need to exalt the African past and his fear of its divisive influence. The greatest French gifts were cultural, mainly directed to the few. Our great contribution was in the sphere of politics and administration, directed to the many. Certainly the offspring of the coming marriage in West Africa between Franco-Negro and Anglo-Negro culture and experience should be interesting.

That is for the future. For the present we in Britain should face our deep-seated sense of racial superiority. The problem is no longer comfortably overseas. It is here, on our doorstep. With little foresight we have allowed hundreds of thousands of West Indians to enter this crowded country without making any plans to house them and initiate them into our society. The growing contacts between all Negroes means that our treatment of these West Indians affects our relations with all black groups. And, scattered among our towns, observing, often suffering themselves, are thousands of Africans, workers as well as students.

The black people among us represent a race which has suffered oppression beyond any measurement and some of it at our hands. West Indians know this. They were bred from this oppression. Africans have been more concerned with recent than with ancient injuries. But they are beginning to study their own history. They will read how the slaves sold by Africans to English merchants on the Guinea coast were examined, sorted out into lots, priced according to age, sex, and physical condition, and branded with the purchaser's mark, branded with hot rons. And how instructions were issued from England by big-business slave-merchants to their local agent on the west coast: 'You are to mark them on the right breast R.A.C.E., and the children of them at three years of age'. R.A.C.E. meant 'Royal Africa Company of England'. After their sorting, branding and the storing in cavernous go-downs, came their deadly voyage to the plantations of the Western world, packed prone and chained in the ships.

That is history. But what can it still mean to be a Negro? The body of the Negro civil rights worker who was recently murdered with two white men in Mississippi was found to have been beaten with chains until every bone was broken. The men accused of the murder are now out on bail. The actions of Dr Luther King, the hopeless attempt of the Black Moslems to contract out of a society which degrades them, the writings of James Baldwin – all these have lately opened their minds and ours to what men can suffer for the offence of being black. As the Negroes feel a growing unity they tend to fasten upon all white men, all us Western allies, a common guilt. We know that racial conflict is by no means confined to Western white and African black. The African has met with racial prejudice in Russia and in India. Africa has it own cruel racial massacres in Rwanda and the Sudan, and the bloody elimination of Arabs and Asians in Zanzibar. But these are local. Africans suffer throughout history and throughout the world because their distinctive features and colour are still associated with the poverty and strangeness of their continent. The gap of culture between most

Africans and most white men is still wide, and it is the Western-educated Africans who see it and suffer for it. The end of this discrimination will not come easily. It may not come this millennium. It will be undermined less by negative than by positive means. By far the most important of these is the hope aroused by the liberation of Africa itself; a continent – or nearly all a continent – released from white rule. Already, in spite of mistakes and deep problems, there is a new hope and pride among Africans. Their leaders are following the West Indian Negroes in handling man's supreme and critical tasks of government and leadership. In spite of mistakes and delays, yes, in spite even of our racial exclusiveness, Britain did more then than any other nation, more than is yet understood or acknowledged, to bring Africans forward to self-government and to lay the foundations upon which they are now building their states.

Conservatives' Responsibility for Rhodesia

Letter to *The Times* 20 December 1965

Sir, – The Conservatives should think very hard before they vote to undermine Mr Wilson's position in dealing with Rhodesia. Their party and some of their present leaders have a large responsibility for the present crisis.

It was they who, in effect, put the Rhodesian whites in control of Central Africa, overriding the passionate opposition of the Africans of the two northern states, much missionary opinion especially in Nyasaland, and the most earnest advice of many who had studied this region. Working closely with Lord Malvern and then Sir Roy Welensky, they increased federal power in an Africa of quickly growing independence.

When Africans resorted to the only argument which seemed left to them, violence, the Conservatives were forced rapidly to dismantle the Federation.

A Conservative attack upon Mr Wilson cannot now halt the policy of sanctions; it can only weaken it. The longer Mr Smith, encouraged by British division, can hold out the more chance there is of bloodshed. The killing of white Rhodesians, above all at British hands, would send a wave of emotion through this country which could undermine any consistent policy.

CONSERVATIVES' RESPONSIBILITY FOR RHODESIA [1965]

On the Rhodesian side, such a tragedy would result in closer, if still unofficial, co-operation with South Africa, with all this portends for the rest of Africa and for the precarious independence of the High Commission Territories.

We must ask for how long would it be possible, in order to preserve the rule of one-sixteenth of the population, to contain along the Zambezi the pressure of all independent Africa to the north?

South Africa could prolong their rule, but only for a time. Is that what we want? The white Rhodesians, like other minorities, through little or no fault of their own, have been cut off by the tide of history. That tide, in their case, is made up of Western democratic principle, of racial feeling, of national interests and Communist ideology. This tide, which brings together some of the strongest forces in the contemporary world, is something more than can be permanently held back.

Yours faithfully

1966

The Rhodesian Crisis: the Background

International Affairs January 1966

In the last few weeks the Rhodesian crisis has covered an immense area of print in Hansard and in the newspapers, and it is an issue which is likely to deepen in intensity and to widen in extent. It would be impossible to deal with its day-to-day manifestations in an article which will not appear in print until the rush of events has flowed far beyond the point reached as I write this article. Yet the issue takes place within a framework of history and of present conditions which must in large measure govern its course. It may therefore be useful to look up from the daily succession of events and remind ourselves of the wider and older setting in which they occur.

Since it is Mr Smith who has thrown down the glove, the issue must turn largely upon the character and strength of his movement. We should first consider from what experiences he and his people draw their strong and defiant sense of autonomy. A glance at her short history reminds us that Rhodesia is a colony in a sense that has no close parallel with any other British dependency since the settlements in North America. The country was the creation of men who trekked into this region at the end of the last century at the bidding of that most autonomous of men, the coarse visionary, Cecil Rhodes. This mobile colossus, shouldering aside imperial control, strode from the Cape, over the Dutch Transvaal, across the Limpopo and the Zambesi, reached out a helping hand to the British presence in Nyasaland and strained his gaze towards Cairo. The pioneers who answered his call in their ox-waggons wrote the first chapter of a history which, on its smaller scale, was as adventurous and bloody as the Americans' winning of the West or as the advance into Africa of the Dutch voortrekkers whose trek, indeed, they were over-riding and extending. There followed the Matabele war, the Matabele rebellion – with more than 100 whites murdered on their new holdings – and the Mashona rising, all evoking repressions which the Africans have certainly not forgotten. This rough annexation is not recalled as a charge against the contemporary white Rhodesians. What valid judgement can we pass today? We must not forget that by the nineties the alternative for the tribes was not some sub-tropical Arcadia, not even the old freedom, that of the militant Matabele to ravage their neighbours and of the Mashona to be ravaged. The alternative to Rhodes's take-over was the ungoverned exploitation of freebooters or the alternative yoke of Boers, Portuguese or Germans.

The strong theme of colonists' autonomy was carried on from that date, only some seventy years ago, when the colony was founded. While nominally under British sovereignty, the settlers were ruled by Rhodes's Chartered Company. They gained their unofficial majority on the Legislative Council in 1920, to the envy of the Kenya settlers, and at once demanded responsible government. Two years later they gained complete political freedom from the Company and voted, with little encouragement from Britain, to remain independent rather than to become a fifth province of South Africa. (It is of interest to note that in the referendum 8,774 votes were for independence while just on 6,000 wished to join the Union.) Northern Rhodesia was put under Colonial Office rule. During the 30 years between this event and the federation the white Rhodesians grew in numbers and in independence of spirit. British authority was minimal in internal affairs. Its most important manifestation was the reservation for imperial assent of bills affecting native interests. This feeble device, employed partly to meet humanitarian demands, had already shown itself of little use in New Zealand and in Natal. In Rhodesia this veto was never once used, not even over the Lands Apportionment Acts of 1936 and 1941 which allotted some 50,000 square miles to 2,630,000 Africans and 75,000 square miles, mostly the better land, to 215,000 Europeans. Whether some control was exercised in London before legislation came to the Council we shall not know until the archives are opened. But the very existence of this curb, however nominal, chafed the increasingly independent spirit of the white Rhodesians as, by their own efforts, they grew in numbers and wealth.

This spirit, to be understood, has to be encountered in its own setting. It does not help understanding to repeat that the white Rhodesians represent in number only the population of a medium-sized British town. Rather, they constitute a micro-nation. The newly arrived clerk or hairdresser from Britain quickly absorbs a spirit of independence which looks back to the founding fathers, some of whom have lived on into this decade. The newcomer soon revels in the intoxicating sense of freedom from the old restraints, in the immense vistas, in the brilliant sunlight, in good pay and housing, and in the hope, in this land-locked region, of achieving one of those swimming pools which wink in the sunshine from all over the Salisbury suburbs when these are seen from the air. The observer from Britain will also discern in Rhodesians a strong sense of enhanced personality, of status, which is quickly bred in a white group surrounded by another numerous race which serves them, a race so black, so unintelligible to most white men that these soon come to see its members as not only different but inferior. The white man's status and way of life is built upon the technically 'unskilled' service in the house, the factory or on the farm, of this other race so that any change in its status seems to be a direct threat to his own. It is men, and their wives, haunted at the back of their minds by this fear, who make up a large proportion of the electorate from which Mr Smith draws his support. To oppose, within Rhodesia, this pervasive atmosphere demands rare qualities, foresight, a sense of justice and humanity, and an independent and courageous mind. It is seldom the latest arrival from equalitarian Britain who shows this courage; the outstanding men have mostly been from the families of earlier settlement, sometimes of missionary origin.

The Rhodesian sense of autonomy was in part a reflection of Britain's own political detachment from the Colony. It needed no protection, no deliberate fostering of trade: it offered no bases: its natives were quiescent. There was, however, one strand in Britain's composite colonial policy which did in time begin to affect Rhodesia. This was the humanitarian strand. The impulse had reached its height during the long campaign against slavery: it maintained its strength for a time after abolition in 1833 and then declined in face of the issues, far more complex than slavery, involved in the government of native races. Certainly there seems to have been only very limited humanitarian attention paid to Rhodesia in the first quarter of this century. An exceptional figure in the thirties was the devoted missionary, Arthur Shearley Cripps, who worked hard to defend African rights, especially in land. From him a stream of letters came to me, as to others, in the thirties about the wrongs done to Africans. He wrote some verses, one picturing Rhodes sent to purgatory:

> Like a fecund vine to sprawl
> On the width of Sion's wall
> In penitence imperial.[1]

[1] A. S. Cripps, *African Verses*, 1939, p. 80.

But, on the whole, it might be said that the humanitarian fire burned rather low in this century until it flared up again when the end of the First World War released, in conflict, the forces of national cupidity and of a universal idealism.

The new humane influences, radiating in the main from people who were not personally involved in the stark issues of black-white relations, reached Africa with complex effects. The mandates system offered new ideas and a new, if still weak, sense of international accountability. British impetus to develop Africa entailed developing Africans. The new techniques of indirect rule could be used in all-black territories to build upwards from the still strong tribal foundations. Later, in settled countries, they could be used as a dividing wall. Self-government for Africans was sometimes mentioned, but as a misty and far-away conception. Yet in West Africa the people were increasingly open to new influences from many quarters, including Negro America, and news of some interesting precedents was beginning to drift across the ocean from India. In southern Africa it was still possible to ignore these portents. General Smuts, lecturing at Oxford in 1929, could talk of Africans as a child-race utterly dependent upon the white man for guidance. Claiming to be the part-author of Article 22 of the League of Nations Charter, he interpreted it as meaning that the sacred trust for peoples not yet able to stand by themselves meant that their progress was to be in accordance with their own institutions. Whites in East and Central Africa should turn to the Union for inspiration in their native administration. Yet some people were beginning to look ahead. I was startled when, in Salisbury in 1930, a very senior native affairs official confessed that he saw no hope for black or white in his country unless all the blacks could be moved north of the Zambesi.

During the twenties, however, the humanitarian spirit, rooted ultimately in the belief in human equality, had begun to affect East Africa, due largely to the initiative of churchmen, especially of Dr J. H. Oldham, and also of Norman Leys, whose uncompromising book, *Kenya*, was published in 1924. The passivity there of the British Government, in face of the settler thrust for the same 'self-government' as had been taken by Southern Rhodesia, was challenged, as were the fundamentals of the settler position, with its demands upon African land and labour. The Hilton Young Commission, of which Oldham was a member, reported in 1929 in terms of a new and informed idealism about African rights. It also visited Central Africa and though it reported against a federation of east and centre, Southern Rhodesia was made aware of the new spirit at work. Even so, the British Government came very near to selling the political pass in Kenya to the settlers through the efforts of the Colonial Secretary, Mr L. C. S. Amery and Sir Edward Grigg, Governor of Kenya. The Labour government of 1929 made a quick left-about turn and issued what the colonists called the two 'Black Papers'.[1] Although these dealt with East Africa they laid down general propositions about the rights of African populations to share ultimately in the government of the country, as well as strong directions about their rights as regarded land and labour. They caused great shock and anger among many Europeans in the Rhodesias. It was natural that the possibility of combining the two territories in a defensive autonomy against the intrusion of such dangerous ideas was discussed. At no time since the Roman Empire, and in no place in the British Empire from North America through South Africa and Australia to New Zealand, has the frontiersman not resented restraint from the imperial centre. The white leaders in the Rhodesias did not like the changing atmosphere to the north of them or the zephyrs from the west, the first stirring of the breeze that was one day to blow up into the famous wind of change.

In 1939 the Bledisloe Commission considered the relations between the states in Central Africa and decided that the differences in native policy between Southern Rhodesia and the Colonial Office dependency of Northern Rhodesia were too great to allow of immediate amalgamation.[2] A Central Africa Council was therefore set up as a compromise. But fears of Colonial Office native policy, combined with the great growth of the copper industry in Northern Rhodesia, made closer union increasingly desirable to the white leaders – both for negative and positive reasons. Sir Godfrey Huggins (now Lord Malvern) and Sir Roy Welensky worked ceaselessly for amalgamation of the Rhodesias or, failing that, federation. They made no secret of their determination to secure complete white domination and to expel the mischievous interference of British cranks and idealists. Both are men of forthright, bluff manner, never making any secret of their views, and it is impossible, even in the most intense disagreement with their aims, not to feel the force and charm of their personalities. These qualities certainly made them

---

[1] *Memorandum on Native Policy in East Africa*, Cmd. 3573, London, H.M.S.O., 1930, and *Statement of the Conclusions as regards Close Union in East Africa*, Cmd. 3574, London, H.M.S.O., 1930.

[2] *Rhodesia-Nyasaland Royal Commission Report*, Cmd. 5949, London, H.M.S.O., 1939.

welcome, in their strange hybrid status, as members of Commonwealth Prime Ministers' Conferences.

They won their Federation in 1953 with Nyasaland thrown in. Governments and parties never apologize for their past mistakes. Office holders change, current problems crowd out those of the past. Yet, in studying the Rhodesian crisis of today, it is impossible not to ask how those in charge of Britain in 1953 could ever have imagined that federation could succeed. Ranged against it were students of African affairs, missionaries, churchmen, especially in Scotland with its deep concern for Livingstone's Nyasaland, and all the Central Africans who could find any way of voicing their passionate dissent. Some of these last came to England to lobby Parliament and public opinion against the fate they so much dreaded. In my file of African letters of this period is an early one written from London, NW6, and dated 1949, protesting against the handing over of the Africans of Nyasaland to the southern settlers 'like sheep'. In 1921 it had been quite easy, the writer said, to hand over the Southern Rhodesian Africans. But in Nyasaland 'it will not be so easy this time'. The letter was from Dr Hastings Banda. In face of all the importunities and warnings, the Conservative cabinet persisted in their course. The question must arise in this, and in some other recent overseas issues, as to how governments come to their decisions. It certainly does not appear that they check their political purposes with serious or expert investigation of the facts or the trends of such complex and distant problems. It should have been quite clear in 1952–3 which way the tide of African development was beginning to flow, and that no breakwater run up along the southern boundary of Tanganyika – a Trust Territory – could keep that tide out of Central Africa. It was not as though the central Africans were asking for self-government. They were not ready for that. They were asking only that the road leading to the goal of self-government, which existed in all Colonial Office dependencies, should not be closed to them by putting them, in effect, under an all but independent white colony.

The Africans and their supporters proved only too right in their fears. Even apart from the question of native policy, a political structure in which five governments were expected to keep in step, and in which two territories were responsible to London and two, in effect, to the local white settlers, was hardly likely to interlock very smoothly. Inevitably it put the northern governors, and especially the one in Northern Rhodesia, in an impossible position, while the Colonial Service officials, with their expatriate status and principles, became objects almost of hatred among European Rhodesians striving to create a local patriotism. The protagonists of the Africans had been granted, as a concession which was most unpopular with many of the Europeans, an African Affairs Board as a check upon discriminating legislation. When, however, its members protested against the Federal Franchise legislation of 1958, the Board was overruled in London; its missionary members resigned and it became otiose.

In the previous year the British Government did a deal with Welensky – the expression is not too strong – even before the coming 1960 review of the working of the Federation, by which they promised never to exercise their right to legislate for the Federation except at the Federal government's request. They also promised that all civil services, federal and territorial, should eventually be locally based, thus threatening a safeguard deeply valued by the Africans. Thirdly, our Government accepted that the 1960 Conference, which was to be a free discussion of the future of federation, could agree upon constitutional advances, including a programme for the attainment of independences, a pretty authoritative hint of how the review was meant to go.

It has been necessary to recount these events because they lie close behind the grave situation which faces us today. They at once confirmed the colonists' hopes and turned African leaders to desperation. The very next year after the signing of this Convention the Africans acted against the Federation in the only way they felt open to them, by violence. Dr Banda returned to Nyasaland, and the disturbances began which were the beginning of the end for the Federation. A strong, independent Commission of Inquiry under Sir Patrick (now Lord) Devlin told the British Government what it should certainly have known, that opposition to the Federation was 'deeply rooted and almost universally held', and they condemned some of the methods used in the suppression of disorder. Reports such as this,[1] offering the views of intelligent and detached minds upon heated and distant issues, have played an important part in our colonial history, and notably in Ghana. This was no exception. Another Commission, with large, balanced membership and a broad instruction to report upon the Federation, produced so doubtful a judgement on the Federation and its future that it led the way to its dissolution in 1963.[2]

[1] *Report of the Nyasaland Commission of Inquiry*, Cmnd. 814, London, H.M.S.O., 1959, p. 22.
[2] *Report of the Advisory Commission on the Review of the Constitution of Rhodesia and Nyasaland*, Cmnd. 1148, London, H.M.S.O., 1960.

To understand the effect of these events upon Sir Roy Welensky and the colonists who had pinned all their hopes upon the building of a great British self-governing dominion in Central Africa, one more liberal in its native policy than that of South Africa but still one which would close to Africans the doors kept open in Colonial Office areas, it is necessary to read Welensky's passionate and outspoken book, *Four Thousand Days*.[1] Here is his bitter attack upon a succession of ministers who worked so whole-heartedly with him to advance his Federation and then suddenly, and in his view cravenly, surrendered to African violence and destroyed their joint creation. His pages sizzle with anger.

This chapter of recent history must be remembered if we are to understand the mind of Mr Smith and his supporters. Their scorn for Britain's surrender, as they see it, to African violence is linked with their reading of the total African scene as viewed from Salisbury and Bulawayo. To them this view is at once repellent and alarming. Algeria is perhaps too unique and too far away to be seen as an example of the doom awaiting white minorities. It is the disorders, the rejection of democracy and the violent speeches of many African leaders which disgust, and to some extent alarm, many Rhodesian Europeans. They find it almost unbelievable that Britain could grant independence to such backward countries which at once, in their view, jettison their constitutions and attack their benefactors, while in Rhodesia civilized Europeans are denied that last instalment of an independence which they have for so long shown themselves worthy of exercising. Of all the negative lessons they draw from the stormy prospect to the north, none has been more horrifying than the events in the Congo. If to us the atrocities perpetrated in that country were almost unbearable to read, how much more dreadful they must have been to white people, themselves minorities in the heart of Negro Africa, who watched these bloody events from a place not so many miles away and who saw some of the refugees from the terror arriving in their country.

These, then, are some of the events, and the ideas about them, that have helped to create that white Rhodesian opinion with which we are now in conflict. The same dark view of independent Africa is, of course, held in the Union. It is no answer to belittle either the facts or the fears they arouse. The comment, which can hardly be too often repeated, is that Africans and all concerned with the continent are suffering from the physical and historical conditions which kept the greater part of the

[1] London, Collins, 1964.

interior almost completely secluded from the rest of the world. Their isolation was followed little more than half a century ago by a penetration from Europe, so sudden, so powerful that it resulted in almost total domination of the thousands of tribes by the colonial Powers. Not many years ago it was widely believed in Britain that this domination would last as far ahead as we could see, and that it would be under strong, if humane and progressive, tutelage that Africa would very gradually be brought to civilization and self-government. We have learned, but only in the last ten or fifteen years, that we were wrong. We helped the first generation of Africans who have become our equals in education and, in some measure, in experience: now it is only they whom their peoples will follow. We see Africa as presenting perhaps the greatest human problem in the world, one that we can help the 250 millions of its inhabitants to solve only by assisting their own efforts to achieve stability and prosperity. For once the leaders had learned how to arouse the latent hatred of the masses at being ruled by another race, and had taught them to seek a new self-respect through freedom, both humanity and self-interest prompted the ruling powers to abdicate. Although we knew that we had been taken by surprise, with our tasks of education and development hardly begun, yet we made a brave public assumption that all had happened according to plan. Europe's abdication left the settled minorities in Algeria, Kenya, Central Africa and elsewhere face to face with a new Africa resolved to bring the whole continent under native rule. In this situation the Rhodesian colonists are naturally interested less in historical and sociological assessments than in self-preservation. It must seem to them almost as though we had allied ourselves with the Africans to destroy them as a community. We must make the attempt to understand their almost desperate resolution to survive. But we must also try to clarify our own involvement in this hazardous decision.

It has been the misfortune of Mr Wilson and his Cabinet, like their predecessors of 1928, to handle an African situation which was not of their making, and which was indeed allowed to develop in spite of their opposition. The need today is for firm, clear action, and it is dangerous, even perhaps for the white Rhodesians, that the grave responsibility should be carried by a government as insecurely placed as that of Mr Wilson. It is clear that the Opposition, with a sector prepared to raise three cheers for Mr Smith, is divided, but the hope must be that, in spite of deep domestic differences, their present degree of bi-partisan agreement will continue and so make possible consistent national action.

Britain's colonial policy has seldom been wholly partisan, and many Conservatives, or persons who might be regarded as potential Conservatives, have supported, and even, in Africa, directed, a wholehearted policy of African advancement, political as well as economic. Even allowing for this, there is clearly a greater sense of affiliation between the settler leaders of Rhodesia and many Conservatives. Some of these, and this is no reproach, have investments or even more solid interests in Rhodesian farms or industry. The squirearchical tradition, lingering in the party, may prompt them to regard Africans as a 'peasantry' requiring guidance, kindness and justice, rather than freedom. The Labour Party, and especially its more dogmatic members, draw upon different traditions. In its novitiate the young party was inclined towards a revulsion from the guilt of ruling an empire. But, with growing knowledge and responsibility, there was a change towards a policy of actively preparing subject peoples for self-government. Some shared with Conservatives the hope that they would have a long period for their many-sided tasks of education. Even so there were real party differences. Many Labour Party members had a fellow feeling for the under-dogs, and some suspicion towards the public school service which administered them, still more towards the settlers as rulers and landlords. The Party's commitment against Mr Smith may therefore be stronger than that of many Conservatives who may – who should – feel some responsibility for his recoil from an inconstant Britain.

Both parties make their ritual claim to have the support of the electorate in their somewhat different attitudes to the Rhodesian problem. What would a referendum reveal? Many who feel strongly about coloured immigration may speculate whether they would like to be suddenly put under the rule of a coloured majority, one far less assimilated than their new neighbours. They may have friends or relations who have been in Africa, or write from there, and who are in support of all that Mr Smith stands for. But it is likely that there would be much honest uncertainty, and so a tendency for opinion to wait upon events.

Policy towards Mr Smith must depend in part upon a calculation of what he is likely to do with his independence. The white Rhodesians were ready, in their anxiety to win their federation, to go a long way towards meeting British pressures for a more liberal deal for Africans. Rhodesia's native policy has for long been more liberal than that of South Africa. True, many of the African workers suffer the hardships of low wages, barrack accommodation and separation from their tribal homes, while domestic servants are obliged, because of the physical separation of residence, to go long distances to their work. But some of the African locations have excellent housing, including superior homes for the more highly paid workers. There are also several important mitigations of the South African system. A federal and residential university, founded in partnership with Britain, brings both races to the campus and, most happily, our Government is still continuing its support. African members, however late in the day by Colonial Office and even Federal standards, are at last allowed to sit in the Rhodesian legislature. There have been official relaxations, difficult to enforce, of the colour-bar in public places. In lower levels of education and in agricultural extension work for Africans, Rhodesia has for long had much to teach some northern colonies. But not the hope of freedom.

In this article I have concentrated mainly upon the recent historical background to the issue which confronts us. But there are some general conditions which govern almost any choice of current policy which may be worth considering.

First, if through indiscriminate action on our part, the conflict drags on for a long period, there are several factors which may gravely complicate the solution. Mr Smith must himself be driven to more extreme and autocratic methods which his electorate, in their anger and anxiety, may be ready to support. Unemployment added to a political tension, which may be increased by external propaganda or intervention, could make the Africans very difficult to handle. Although the Rhodesian state is powerful and experienced in controlling its Africans, severe measures may not be able to keep pace with the growth of discontent and will further discredit the régime in the eyes of Africa and the world. All the experience of South Africa suggests that white minorities do not grow more liberal as Africans grow more politically competitive.

The second possibility, that Mr Smith will make terms in the very near future, will also have its problems, especially for Britain. If the Europeans confront this country, with little attrition of numbers or confidence, it will not be easy to enforce the minimum of reforms which are acceptable to Britain. We should have, to a large extent, to work with and through them. The main difficulty would be with the Africans. They will have been taught by the events of the preceding months to expect large reforms. Will they be content with the gradual enlargement of the franchise which has been offered to the Europeans as a moderate solution which they could reasonably accept? Certainly the African states will not accept this gradualism, and thus neither the internal nor the external troubles will decrease. So far our experience has been that

Africans move straight from subordination to mastery. Co-operation on the level is not easy for them or their white colleagues for reasons bound up with the total African situation. And the Rhodesian Africans, with their divided parties, have no wise, single, experienced leadership to lead them towards co-operation.

A third possibility is that, either as a result of internal upheaval or, more likely, following a very long period of economic siege, Rhodesia collapses entirely in disorder and bankruptcy. Britain would then have to go in with both hands to keep order and help to rebuild prosperity. This would be an immense and difficult task. If we planned to stay until it was possible to hand over to an effective mixed white–black government, this might take a very long time. The cost to Britain financially and in other ways could be very heavy. It is difficult to accept the views of Sir Edgar Whitehead, the former Rhodesian Prime Minister, when he advocates a Union with Rhodesian representation at Westminster. It is impossible to imagine British political circles accepting this. The possibility was very seriously considered for Malta. But the history of the Irish vote hung over the issue. In the close struggle between the parties, the presence of external members, representing only distant interests yet able, perhaps, to sway with their votes the vital issues of this country, is unthinkable. Clearly, if Rhodesia does stand out to the edge of ruin, Britain will have to supply help in cash, in kind and in staff, and face heavy financial and administrative commitment. It is well that we should be mentally prepared for such a demand.

These possibilities assume that we have a free hand to deal unilaterally with Rhodesia, that is with the Rhodesian whites, for nothing is more misleading than to follow the usage of Mr Smith and of many Conservatives in speaking of Rhodesia as if to describe a nation rather than a ruling and racial minority. But of course this is no simple confrontation between Mr Wilson and Mr Smith and their governments. We have it on the highest authority that a ruler entering into conflict with another generally sits down first and calculates whether the odds are in his favour. Did Mr Wilson make this calculation? A quarter of a million whites ruling four million Africans on the southern border of Africa's independent and hostile 200 millions or more would not at first sight appear to represent a formidable proposition. But the Colony is amazingly well placed for defence. Inaccessible by sea, she is more than half encircled on the east by two states now under white minority rule, Mozambique and South Africa. To the west stretches Bechuanaland, dry, bare, poor in men and resources, on the verge of a precarious independence and too weak to dispute the passage through its western edge of the railway which can feed Mr Smith's state with vital necessities from South Africa. Northward lies Zambia, Mr Smith's hostage, to which he can pass on some of the pains and penalties Britain is inflicting upon him, while we can only reach Zambia across 2,000 difficult miles by air from a base in Tanzania, a country which has broken off diplomatic relations with us. In all this distant and, to us, largely defiant region neither Britain nor Zambia have any forces which could begin to challenge those on guard in Rhodesia.

Behind Rhodesia stands South Africa, with the riches and military power which so far only Europeans have been able to create in black Africa. The Nationalist government knows that Mr Smith's cause is its own, and that the Rhodesian crisis could be a curtain-raiser for its own much more distant drama. The South African press reflects the passionate and partisan interest of the white population. So far, however, the Prime Minister has shown remarkable restraint: it seems clear he will not lightly risk overt diplomatic involvement. He can without risk, almost unobserved, offer the white Rhodesians the massive support of a rich neighbour. Strangely it has been the United Party which has been most vociferous, greeting the news of Mr Smith's declaration of independence at the party conference with cheers. It seems that the event may accelerate the movement of the bulk of English-speaking South Africans further away from any lingering attachment to Britain and British liberalism and towards a closer sense of association with their Afrikaner fellow-citizens.

So much for Mr Smith's safe or supporting west, south and east. What has he to fear, and Britain to gain, from the opposition towards him of all the continent to the north? There is vigorous action now amongst the African states, and it may be clear before this article appears what form it is to take. But here, also, there is a background which is worth consideration. It may be that some of the angry states, especially those outside the Commonwealth, may have little knowledge of Rhodesia, or may imagine that Mr Smith is a rebel in an active sense and has overturned a local British government. But such misconception would not be important. The intensity and the unity of the African states in their condemnation, which is almost more of Britain than of Mr Smith, derives from the racial content of the issue which touches all Africans in the deepest part of their natures. To the more extreme it may even be tempting to try to force Britain to spill the blood of her own race in defence of theirs. The issue is also one which can be expected to create a valuable degree of pan-African unity and can be presented to the masses, at least in the towns, as an exciting and unifying gesture of their leaders. President Nyerere has almost brought the issue to the stage of government by mass meeting by asking the huge Dar-es-Salaam crowd whether they wished him to break relations with Britain. The relative moderation of the Prime Ministers of Nigeria and Kenya, each of whom has a strength of a different kind, is the more impressive by contrast. It must, however, be admitted that there is some truth in the African belief that we care too much for people of our own blood to bear to see them physically hurt or killed, while it is only on principle that we stand by the Africans, an anonymous mass into whose longings and humiliations we cannot enter except by an effort of imagination. This bond of nationhood between ourselves and the white Rhodesians is something that Africans can hardly yet understand. Their deep experience is of the tribe and the race: they have still to make the inhabitants of colonies into nations.

It is the racial unity of Africa, suddenly intensified by the Rhodesian crisis, which strains a Commonwealth which aims to bind nations and transcend race. It is too soon to say whether in its present form and numbers it will survive the crisis. There are some who believe that the real bonds which foster co-operation within our ex-empire may be weakened rather than strengthened by shrouding them in a rather indefinable association developed in a different historical context. But it is certainly not for Britain to act or to utter in such a way as to end a relationship, which, with time and patience, might meet new needs of African states as they grow out of the rather belligerent racial attachments which are natural at the present stage of their continent.

Two final questions must be in our minds as we consider the repugnant task to which we are committed. Firstly, what are our chances of success? The answer depends partly upon realistic but still hardly calculable statistics of trade and transport, but also, in part, upon more imponderable factors. We must now reckon with the resolution of a white Rhodesian society more determined and united than we had expected, and we must also measure our own difficulties in fighting with one hand behind our back and with no lethal weapon in the other. The United States is busy elsewhere, and Africa is not a continent of main concern to her government. Western Europe is likely to be correct rather than actively co-operative. The majority in the distant United Nations may be vocal but this will be more in our condemnation than in our support. To a large extent we are committed to handling this conflict alone. Success must therefore depend upon the degree of unity and vigour with which we act and this in turn must depend upon the answer to a second question: 'Is our policy politically and morally right?'

The answer will be derived from our political principles, and from our reading of the direction in which our world is moving. The dangers of division as all its peoples are forced into increasing contiguity are the theme of nearly all serious students of its affairs. No division is deeper and more pervasive than that of race. If Britain has any moral contribution to make to this situation, if our granting of independence to our former colonies was due as much to our principles as to their pressures, then we must ensure that the four million silenced Africans of Rhodesia shall not be denied the freedom for self-development with which nearly all their fellow-Africans are experimenting.

Whether the Commonwealth survives or not, one of the greatest exercises open to Britain in place of vanished imperial power is to help in meeting the immense needs of Africa. Admittedly the new African states are not easy to help. Not even the wise 1965 African Reith Lecturer felt able to admit the vast service which the West, and especially Britain, both by accident and design, have given to Africa. But we shall long have to pay the price for the unavoidably absolute strength of our mastery. It is legitimate to believe, though never to assert, that we still have something more to offer than even technical and financial aid. In working with Africa we shall be using a great store of experience and exercising practical and spiritual capacities which might otherwise atrophy. But we may find it difficult to continue to give this service unless we are able to make, and to make in time, a just and firm settlement of the Rhodesian crisis.

The Nigerian Crisis and After

The Listener 23 January 1966

When I heard the news of the political murders in Nigeria I seemed to realize in a sickening moment of foresight all the forces of disunion and conflict they might release. I was moved to ask the B.B.C. if I could speak about them and, at short notice, the distinguished Cambridge historian, Sir J. Thompson, gave up to me the period assigned to his own talk.

The news of the political murders in Nigeria comes as a deep shock. Sir Abubakar Tafawa Balewa – described by the new military government in Lagos as 'this great son of Nigeria' – has been struck down and was buried today in Bauchi, the town of his birth. The shock is all the greater because in a disordered continent Nigeria seemed by its size and stability to be a bulwark of democracy. Add to this that the two Moslem leaders, Sir Ahmadu Bello and Sir Abubakar himself, whatever may now be charged against them, were men of large achievement and men with whom our own ministers had worked for many years. It would be an insult to Africans to make a calm acceptance of murder as their natural way of changing governments.

But this evening I don't want to dwell upon these latest events. I want to look behind the stop-press news to the seeds of the present crisis which have been sown over the last one hundred years and more.

I first went to Nigeria some thirty-five years ago and travelled over most of its large surface making a study of its government. I returned to Britain to write my book and worked closely with Lord Lugard, whose own career from the nineties onward had been so largely bound up with this region. After the war I went again to Nigeria, got to know its leaders there and in England, and was their guest at the independence celebrations in 1960.

I have a vivid sense of the differences between the three main regions of Nigeria, which later developments, communications, buildings and European customs have tended to mask, especially in the towns, and it is these differences which are the key to the latest events.

The Yoruba of the south-west were the first people to take the full impact of Britain: our slave-trading gave way to anti-slave-trading, to Christian missions and finally to the annexation of Lagos in 1861 – Lagos, already a Yoruba city and one which still has its Oba or king. We found the Yoruba a highly sophisticated people, grouped within city states, each different – and often at war. These burly, cheerful people lived in their large family compounds in the city and outside lay their farmlands in open country, patched with light forest. Vigorous city life went on under our rule. I used to talk to the old city fathers – old slave-traders. They welcomed British rule. Their sons sought law degrees in Britain. Their great city of Ibadan was the natural site for Nigeria's first university.

North from Yoruba-land – I have to simplify the political map – over the Niger, you pass through the so-called Middle Belt, a kind of political no man's land between north and south, where the early nineteenth-century thrust of the Moslem Fulani petered out. Further north the land becomes drier, more open to the horses, cattle and camels– the Hausa states. Here are grouped round famous cities, holy Sokoto, Kano with its great market famous for centuries, and other walled cities. Red mud palaces, mosques, robed and turbanned horsemen, huge markets, elaborate state governments – a structure Lugard was able to purge of its worse abuses and use for his famous system of indirect rule. The confidence and pride of the Emirs could meet ours on equal terms. Reforms were possible but even with the coming of roads and railways, schools, hospitals, a great trade in ground-nuts, deep change was more difficult. The later story of the too-slowly changing north drawn into union with the fast-changing south can be read in the autobiography of the murdered premier, Sir Ahmadu Bello, the Sardauna.

He admits to pride – I quote – 'in the trust God has given me to lift up our people from their primitive conditions into the . . . happiness of contentment . . . I know that I am only an instrument carrying out God's will and pleasure. A new future lies ahead into which I go trusting in God's eternal mercy.'[1] We now know what that future was to be.

The Sardauna never even went to Lagos until 1949 when he was thirty-nine. His comment is very significant: 'The whole place was alien to our ideas and we found the members for the other regions might well belong to another world as far as we were concerned.' So, when the Federation came, he chose to stay in the north as Premier and let another man of great ability, a commoner, go to Lagos as Federal Prime Minister. This was Sir Abubakar Tafawa Balewa, the ex-schoolmaster who presided so impressively at the recent Commonwealth Conference at Lagos, a matter of days before his disappearance. He was a man who impressed

[1] Ahmadu Bello, *My Life*, 1962, p. 238.

everyone – certainly all Europeans – very upright in his flowing robes, the voice deep and melodious; the mind seemingly honest and confident.

When you turn southwards from the dry flat north and pass again through the pagans of the Middle Belt, the forest grows round you and you come into the heart of the eastern region. Here the picture is dominated by the crowded Ibo. The Ibo were largely protected from the enslaving Moslems by their forests, deadly to horses and cattle. They were sheltered, too, for a time from those external influences which played so strongly upon the coastal Yoruba. To the Ibo the forest was a dividing as well as an isolating influence and these eastern groups by western standards were small, poor and backward. They had little to show of material civilization, no large chiefs or political units, but extended family groups. But they were not slow in coming forward when at last the outer world did effectively penetrate their forest. Indeed, the Ibo dramatically refute the old idea that primitive conditions make primitive men. When opportunity and education were added to the stimulus of poverty and intense individualism, the Ibo and some kindred groups leapt into activity. Soon they were pouring along the forest tracks on bicycles with great loads of palm kernels, the ready natural wealth of the trees surrounding them. They gave one a sense of riotous thrust and vigour: the crowds of market women, uninhibited, shouting, clutching, seemed almost as if they were out to lynch you rather than welcome you. Soon they were pouring out of their crowded forests into the other regions, taking jobs, any jobs, doing them well, hanging together and becoming anything but popular in the west and north.

Here, then, in rapid outline, are Nigeria's three main regions and peoples.

Was Britain right to bring these contrasting people and regions into one state? If we had kept them apart we should have been accused of Balkanizing. The two coastal southern states started colonial life in separation but it seemed obvious in 1906, as control and communications increased, to bring them together. The north, which had not been formally annexed by Britain until 1900, looked different and it *was* different. But it settled down to production for export: railways were planned to reinforce the rather inconstant Niger, and it seemed obvious to join this impressive land-locked protectorate with its coastal outlet. Lugard was sent to do it. It was an immense task of administrative conjunction; and it could not be a true union in spite of attempts to spread the northern system of indirect rule. In the old empire vastly different, even potentially hostile people could be held together not indeed in amity but in co-operation, guaranteed by British power. Danger always came as political stirrings aroused fears of closer contacts.

In Nigeria political consciousness grew slowly, first in Lagos and the southern towns, with their lawyers, doctors, clerks, clubs, newspapers, religious synods and contacts along the coasts and with Britain and America. In the forties the pace quickened. An Ibo, Ben Azikiwe, arose, a political genius, a man with seemingly all the talents. He went, with little schooling, to America and came back loaded with academic, literary and athletic honours. He awakened political energy among his own Ibo and beyond and turned it against the colonial government.

His party, N.C.N.C. (National Council of Nigeria and the Cameroons) aimed to cover all Nigeria, both on democratic principle and because Nigeria was the Ibo's oyster. The sophisticated Yoruba were more interested in their own region. Their party, the Action Group, under Awolowo, reflected this attitude. The northerners remained aloof, but were beginning to realize that for all their pride, they were woefully unskilled in modern techniques. They had the humiliating need to import hordes of hated southerners to do the clerical and technical jobs.

Self-government and federation were hammered out by the Nigerian leaders in prolonged conferences with British ministers and governors during the fifties; it was a leisurely and laborious process compared with the later abrupt emancipations on the other side of Africa. The northerners dragged their feet. Yet in 1960, just three years after Ghana was born, the independent Federation *was* launched thanks to the energy and tact of Sir James Robertson, the last Governor-General. It started life under a strange coalition of the northern party and the N.C.N.C. with Sir Abubakar as Prime Minister and 'Zik' as Governor-General, later President. Yet the three parties remained largely regional, the northern leaders bitterly resolved to hold their position against the south.

I must abbreviate the intricate sequel. The Yoruba Action Group, under Awolowo, became increasingly unhappy in their minority position. In 1963 this man, who seemed to me so sane, so moderate, so soaked in English law and literature, was condemned to prison on a charge of attempting a violent short-cut to power. So was his colleague, Enaharo, the famous fugitive offender. A northern-supported politician became western premier, Akintola, another victim with wife and son of the recent assassinations.

Tension rapidly increased and became feverish as new census returns revealed a northern population greater than that of the other regions combined. This meant that, even in combination, the southern regions would, in their view, always be the prisoners of the north. When the fixed date of the 1964 election came many of the southerners, especially in the eastern region, boycotted it. The northern party, in alliance with Akintola's splinter group, sailed home, not without some strong-arm methods. So the year ended in grave crisis. Dr Azikiwe was torn between his constitutional duty as President to call upon Sir Abubakar to form the new government and the pull of his Ibo tribe, his eastern region and the party *he* had created. After several days of dangerous tension he bowed to his moderate and judicial advisers and turned a deaf ear to the demands of his old supporters. Today, as he waits in his hotel in Dorking, he must be wondering if the Ibo have forgiven him. A compromise was patched up over the elections. But a second crisis arose over the purely regional elections of last October in the west. The N.C.N.C. joined with its old foes, the Action Group, against the northern party which was still allied with Akintola's western breakaway group. Akintola, thus backed, won the election, but by force and fraud so extensive as to have made the election a mockery. There was widespread anger in the south, especially among the Ibo. Here, it seems, the fuse must have been lit which led on to the assassinations. We may ask why the upright Prime Minister, Sir Abubakar, allowed this perversion of electoral law and order. The only possible answer would seem to be that as the Sardauna had remained head of the northern party, and had kept all control in his own hands, the Prime Minister was isolated in Lagos and he may not have had the power to intervene. It might be said 'He could have resigned'. True. But this was Lagos not Westminster.

The savage retribution inflicted by Ibo army officers upon the two northern leaders and their southern ally brings out the fragility of constitutions which are managed by tribes and regions rather than by citizens of a nation. How are we to assess what has happened? Perhaps by asking why Mr Heath does not arrange for the assassination of Mr Wilson. After all, there are plenty of Conservatives among army officers who might well add Messrs Brown, Callaghan and Crossman to their list. I don't say this lightly. The answer to the contrast can be found only by re-examining our own history, pausing perhaps a moment at Charles I's execution, but going a long way further back in search of our emancipation from the tribe.

There are hundreds, even thousands, of educated West Africans who live both in our world and their own trying to make them one. They will have suffered today over this event and most of all at any contemptuous conclusions that Africans are incapable of democracy. They have proved themselves, but below them are millions of ex-tribesmen who are not yet an electorate, who have expected more immediate benefits from independence than it could possibly give. Moreover, new African ministers are always open to accusations of luxury and corruption, regarded as occupational diseases of their trade. They may be so; on the other hand what seems to be luxuries to the African peasant may represent the necessities of the new international ministerial life; large cars, air travel, hotel suites and the rest. And, as our Walpole discovered, corruption may be that degree of patronage which keeps a still immature party and parliament working smoothly. Major Nzugwa and his fellow assassins who strike down such ministers should remember that assassination is a weapon that can ricochet, especially when used for political or, worse, tribal motives. For it is significant that all the military names in the news are Ibo, that fifty other officers are reported to have been murdered, and that the head of no *Ibo* politician has rolled.

Obviously – and understandably – this event will make it still easier for Africa's white minorities to draw up their case against independent Africa and against Britain for her part in promoting that independence. They can muster impressive facts about the order reigning in southern Africa and even more impressive figures of its production and trade as against the dramatic poverty of black Africa. There is an answer, one that I find myself forced to repeat, one that demands a longer setting in time than theirs. I refer to the trick which geography and history have played upon Africa and upon those who have lately been in charge of it; the virtual isolation of so much of the tropical African interior from direct contact with the outer world. This left the thousands of fluid tribes at the mercy of each other and of a capricious, often hostile environment, more jailor than nurse. Tropical Africa's real history is only just beginning.

These governing facts give us the answer to Mr Smith and those who support him. If he remains in power with all Africa to the north working upon his own Africans he will be forced, like the Afrikaners, to resort to more and more restrictions in defence of the white garrison. This is the way backward, the way of sterility. The way forward is the way of life, of tumultuous, liberated African life. It is a life we can no longer control; we need not, we certainly cannot, commend all its manifestations. But we can try to understand what this bewildered

Africa is experiencing, what it is that moves demonstrating students and murdering subalterns. Above all, we must continue the help, the widespread and varied help, we are already giving. For we have to live close alongside this Africa. It is not going to be run by Voerword or Mr Smith. I know Africans who feel a deep bond with Britain and a hope for future contact which they could never publicly admit. We must not let this violence in Nigeria weaken our resolve to help, but join with Nigerians in mourning the death of its first Prime Minister. The B.B.C. correspondent, John Osman, in a radio report from Lagos earlier this evening told us that his taxi-driver had said as they heard of the death of Sir Abubakar, 'It's sad: he was a good man.' Indeed, he was a good man. But only in independent Africa could he have shown how good he was, risen to his full stature.

I cannot end this talk without expressing the hope that people here, and especially the generous young, will not lose faith in independent Africa or Britain's work in creating that independence. Southern Africa may look materially impressive but its people never shouted with joy round a flag as they grasped this precious, dangerous thing called independence. And in the south no African could hope to grow to the stature of command and achievement of this man we are mourning this evening.

Rhodesia: a Search for Fundamentals

The Listener June 16 1966

The Rhodesian question! What is the answer? What result would we get if we could have a referendum upon it in this country? Two confident minorities at each extreme and a vast majority of 'Don't knows' in the middle? Yet we cannot plead that we do not have enough information about the problem.

One of the really important documents is obviously the 143-page *Blue Book* which gives us a summary of the discussion – confrontation would be a better word – between Mr Smith and the British Prime Ministers and Commonwealth Secretaries. It must be one of the strangest British reports of top-level negotiations ever produced. It covers the period November 1963 to November 1965, and in it you see our Ministers, and especially Mr Wilson – for he has made this problem so very much his own – going on and on, and often it seems round and round, while Mr Smith seems to remain almost woodenly impervious to every argument. Yet the report tells us little about the more fundamental differences between Rhodesia and Britain – the historical origins of the dispute and the wider issues and principles behind it. We need to clear our minds, for the hour of decision cannot be much longer delayed.

First, let us look at the Rhodesians' history. It is stamped deeply and recently upon these people: they are like coins fresh from the mint. And when I say Rhodesians here, I am referring to the white minority which cannot be called a nation. There are people still alive in Rhodesia who can remember its beginning some seventy-five years ago.

The colony's history begins with Lobengula: so does its controversy. His tribe barred the way northwards. His Matabele regiments were trained on the Zulu pattern, armed with assagais, the great spears which they had to wash in blood before they were allowed to marry. In the 1880s white adventurers and concession hunters were beginning to pester Lobengula, and they have left behind many descriptions of this six-foot-four, twenty-stone, Rider Haggard kind of Chief, who received his European visitors in his kraal – naked except for a sporran of leopard skins. His tribe exercised a reign of terror over their neighbours, especially over the Mashona, the other tribe which was to be enclosed within the future Rhodesia. The raiding parties killed off the men and old women and they took the young women and the cattle.

This tribe stood right across the path of white expansion. It naturally got a very bad press from the pioneers. Yet some white men, even missionaries, did see good elements in Lobengula. He dealt fairly with the white intruders who plagued him, and protected them from his angry soldiers. And he foresaw how it must all end. 'Did you', he asked a missionary, 'ever see a chameleon catch a fly?' The stealthy approach, the immobility, the renewed advance, the final dart. 'England is the chameleon and I am that fly.'

And so it happened. Rhodes's agent got a concession out of the king; a pioneer white column went up from the Cape with their horses and ox-wagons; conflict with the Matabele broke out, the pioneers won – but not without loss. Later there followed rebellion. The warriors crept up to the new, isolated farmsteads and speared the Europeans, 240 in all. I need not say they were revenged. And so Rhodesians look back not only to an epic and heroic beginning; they also claim to possess the perfect title-deeds that come from having replaced a bloody tyranny with their peace and order, and saved the poor Mashonas as well. And, of course, if they remember these events, so do the Africans.

RHODESIA: A SEARCH FOR FUNDAMENTALS [1966]

Was Rhodes really a big man or were his achievements big only spatially and not morally? They were certainly big in space. From his political base in the Cape, and his economic base in the Kimberley diamond mines, he took a great step north past the Boer republics to beat Boers, Germans and Portuguese in the race for central Africa and win it for what he called 'the British race'. 'God', he said, 'is manifestly fashioning the English-speaking race as the chosen instrument by which he will bring in a state of society based on justice, liberty, and peace.' He was always a little bit hazy about God but he was clear that he was God's instrument in Africa and beyond.

I have recalled Rhodes because Rhodesia was his creation and he set his stamp upon it. There is truth for his colony in the famous inscription on his memorial:

The immense and brooding spirit still shall quicken and control,
Living he was the land and dead his soul shall be its soul.

There is also a less mystical reason for remembering him and thinking of his spirit standing behind Mr Smith's chair at the conference table. It is that his devotion to the British race was not at all the same as devotion to the British government. Britain had little hand in the foundation of Rhodesia – and Rhodes played down what little it had. *His* agent got the all-important concession from Lobengula: *his* colonists went out not from Britain but the Cape: *he* interposed the South Africa Company between Britain and the Colony: *he* went unarmed and almost alone into the Matopo hills to make peace with the rebellious Matabele. *His* colonists, he said, were much better able to manage their own affairs than a government 7,000 miles away. And *he* gave Rhodesia from the very first a somewhat different slant to their native policy from that of the Afrikaners. 'I do not believe' – and these are important words – 'that they are different from ourselves.' This may sound little enough today, but then it was much, and it divided Rhodesian native policy just a little from that of the Afrikaners, a difference which is evident today.

The colony maintained its virtual autonomy. It was first administered under Rhodes's Company for many years. But in 1907 the colonists gained an unofficial white majority in the legislature, something the envious Kenya settlers never gained. In 1923 the Company's power was removed. Northern Rhodesia, then a mainly native state, was put directly under the Colonial Office, while Southern Rhodesia was formally annexed to the Crown, but only formally for it was still left self-governing in internal affairs and the colonists still did what they wished with its land and labour. No wonder that one historian entitles this chapter of Rhodesia's history as that of 'Averted eyes' – the eyes of Britain.

Why were they so long averted? Britain had not always been so neglectful of native interests. In the 1830s the humanitarians, who were fresh from their victories over slavery and the slave trade, turned their attention to the frontiers of empire where their countrymen were everywhere advancing at the expense of the natives. And they laid down that no representative body composed of settlers ought to control native affairs, since, they said, 'the legislature was virtually a party'. And this is the principle which, after 130 years, Mr Wilson is trying to revive. This is not easy since the graph of liberal concern with native interests has been running so low for so long.

However, it never quite fell to zero. One device used by Britain was the retention of control over native policy when all other internal powers had been given away. But this attempt at remote selective control was very largely ineffective. It broke down in New Zealand and again in South Africa. We cannot know its full record in Rhodesia until the official archives are opened, but it does not *seem* to have had much influence upon native policy. A Rhodesian Prime Minister once showed me – most improperly – a bundle of his correspondence under this heading with our Colonial Secretary. It dealt mainly with the Land Apportionment Act by which the settlers took some half of the total land, and it did not appear to me that much good had come of the exchange of correspondence with London upon that subject.

Meanwhile Britain herself was dealing with the millions of tropical Africans in her own dependencies. In many places her officials worked out the principles of indirect rule, that of developing Africans gradually through their own chiefs and their tribal institutions towards more modern forms of local government. But as the inter-war years went on, we began to see that the new influences that we had ourselves brought were undermining tribalism, that it represented a parallel line with Western rule, a lower line, and that the two would never meet. The Europeans who had settled in Africa also saw the new forces as a danger, but mainly to themselves, and began, rather late in the day, to try to get their Africans back on to their lower parallel line, to revive the shattered tribalism which their impact had destroyed more completely than had our colonial rule. Hence Mr Smith's insistence that it is not the political leaders – who are now in restriction – who should speak for his Africans, but the chiefs and the elders, who tend to be conservative men and who are dependent on the government for their pay. The Europeans of southern Africa maintain that it is the British who have abandoned the true principles in face of African nationalist violence.

True, Britain *has* changed, but only to meet changing Africa. In the 1920s Rhodesians began to observe a little cloud, no larger than a man's hand – a black man's hand – which began to appear in East Africa. Britain was beginning to have doubts as to whether the Kenya whites could be promoted to the kind of 'self-government' the Rhodesian whites won so very easily in 1923. The missionaries and humanitarians were encouraged to take the warpath again. Added to that, a Labour government came in, and in 1930 issued two White Papers – 'black papers' the Rhodesians called them. These talked about native interests being paramount and the impossibility of Britain transferring power over politically immature Africans to local Europeans – just what Britain had done in Southern Rhodesia.

The Rhodesians were alarmed. Where did they belong, in a dangerously changing Africa – north or south, or all alone? In 1923 they had voted in a referendum against joining South Africa, where Afrikanerdom was stirring into new life. Yet to Rhodesians looking northward the land was not bright. It was getting politically black. The idea of going in with East Africa therefore faded. But what of nearby Nyasaland and Northern Rhodesia? In 1939 the Bledisloe Commission was sent out to inquire into the possibility of linking them with Rhodesia. But it turned down the idea, at least for the moment, because – a disturbing reason for the southern whites – the native policies of the two northern Colonial Office territories were incompatible with those of Rhodesia. All the Rhodesians got was a co-ordinating council for central Africa.

Why, then, we may ask, did they succeed in getting their Central African Federation in 1953? Why, indeed, asked some of us who had studied the region? The Africans of Northern Rhodesia and Nyasaland were even more opposed to it than they had been in 1939 – and labour migration meant that they knew Southern Rhodesia very well and preferred Colonial Office rule. Although, under the new constitution, power was parcelled out, it was the southern whites who were really the dominant force. I must say I found the Federation in 1958 a tense, unhappy place. Business was booming, as the whites had prophesied, and many useful practical things had been done for the Africans. Britain had helped to found an inter-racial university. But no less than five governments were concerned in the Federation – the British, the

Federal, and the three regional governments – and they were all more or less at odds, with their clashing traditions and responsibilities. The explosion came in Nyasaland in 1959. A strong commission under Lord Devlin was sent out. Its report showed considerable understanding of the rioters and their cause and was critical of their severe handling by the authorities. This report was really the beginning of the end for the Federation, which was wound up with much bitterness and re-crimination in 1963.

The southern white leaders felt, with some justice, that they had been led up the garden path, the path to the promised land of a great central African state in which their race would be dominant for more years than it would be politic to say. The imperial factor which, on Rhodes's example, had for so long been kept out of Southern Rhodesia had, it seemed, come back to wreck the hopes of the colonists. As the Federation broke up, the southern whites drew up their 1961 constitution and at last accepted some Africans into their legislature. They did it in the confident hope – indeed they claimed it was a clear understanding with Britain – that this would be a qualification for their own complete independence. But no! The white Rhodesians have now found that they still cannot have their independence from Britain, unless they accept Mr Wilson's principles. The first of these is 'unimpeded progress towards majority rule', and another demands guarantees against retrogression from this rule *after* independence.

So much for history, the brief eventful history of Rhodes's colony. Now let us turn to the present. What are these people like, these Europeans, with whom we are now at odds, mostly of our stock, living between the Limpopo and Zambesi rivers? They have been made, they are being made, not only by history, also by environment – that of a spacious land, drenched with sun, a little removed from the pressures of a dangerous world. They enjoy good food, good housing, good sport; they are freed from drudgery by the service of a more numerous subject race, whose presence seems to enhance their own sense of individual power and worth. They are proud of the wealth in farming, mining, and in manufactures which they have built up in the wilderness, and they believe they have done their duty, and more, for the Africans, reaching across the gulf they feel between the two races.

I think it is hard for anyone who has not lived in Africa to understand the unspoken attitude to 'the native', the rejection of a full common citizenship in any forseeable time with the Africans who are in truth so different in so many ways, and yet are not so different as they seem, above all, in their capacity to advance. The visting European feels the immense force of this atmosphere. Indeed, the most newly arrived immigrants from Britain tend to be the most extreme in their attitude to the Africans. Some of the older established Rhodesian families, often the most liberal, reckon this as another account against Britain. If the visiting Briton goes on to South Africa he must mark the difference between the implacable apartheid of the south and the Rhodesian adherence to Rhodes's principle 'equal rights for all civilized men' – however long they may take to become civilized. 'However long'? The southern whites have been watching, with a horror not untinged with fear, the behaviour of independent Africa during the last five years. Their condemnation of Britain for what they regard as her cowardly surrender to the first African demands for independence became more intense with each item of disorder or cruelty. We must try to measure this anger and fear. If these African events trouble *us*, how much more those who live in the same continent where, one after another, the names of new states come so disturbingly or tragically into the news. Above all the Congo! Remember that the fighting in Katanga in 1961 was on Rhodesia's very doorstep. They saw the terrified white women and children fleeing to them for safety with tales of what they had suffered from Africans and even from some United Nations troops.

There *is* an answer. But it is not the easy one of some doctrinaire liberals who have the colonists' colour prejudice in reverse. Certainly I could never lightly argue away these African events. My work has been too closely concerned with some of these new states. Some of my closest African friends were Baganda, and I do not yet know their fate. No, the first answer lies in trying to understand the formidable, the almost insurmountable, difficulties with which Africans have been confronted by a unique history for which none of them was responsible. I find myself repeatedly forced to emphasize this history – the seclusion of Africa, above all central and eastern tropical Africa, from the rest of the world, its poverty, its difficult natural environment, its division into innumerable tribes and clans of all kinds and sizes, within which Africans developed institutions and experiences which were almost utterly irrelevant to the new world which European annexation has so abruptly super-imposed upon them. The ruling powers had hardly begun their work of bringing Africa into the mainstream of Western civilization when the Second World War, and all the subsequent changes it released, brought their power to an end. Then why, say the Rhodesians, did Britain set the example of relinquishing control at almost the first demand, the first sparks of disorder? Because we held these colonies so lightly, because – let us confess it – the world had changed and we had neither the power nor the will to enforce their subjection. That is why Britain so quickly freed Africa.

But why, on their side, were Africans so precipitate and uncompromising? The reply, one which Africans are hardly likely to make – at least in this age – lies in what I have just said of the problem with which geography and history have confronted Africa. Perhaps we were too optimistic about independence. What should we have expected of these collections of tribes thrown together within arbitrary colonial frontiers? Their tribal life may have been virile and effective in its context but it was no preparation for running a large modern state and economy. When we measure all these difficulties, does the African record look so bad? Who can judge such an immense and obscure case? We have little enough evidence in our newspapers of all that *is* satisfactory and normal in independent Africa: this does not make news. And if we start reckoning up violence, there is enough that is comparable or worse, even in Europe's recent history, above all in the German and the Russian record. How long ago is it that most people in Britain thought it right to shoot the Irish into submission and execute them when captured? In the contemporary world our glance can fall upon Iraquis crushing Kurds; Egyptian planes bombing Yemenis; Indians' dealing with Nagas and Mizos; Indonesian massacres of thousands of Chinese and Communists; while Vietnam presents such a complex of horrors that the mind shrinks from regarding it. No, alas! Africa's lapses are not unique.

The southern white case against Africans is clear enough. Far less obvious are the purposes for which all Africans were struggling and which in part they have won. They have, of course, the universal reasons why people seek independence. But in addition they want to escape from that crushing mark of inferiority which the world, in varying degree, continues to brand upon the black skin. They are escaping it to some extent in the West Indies and in West Africa – especially perhaps in ex-French West Africa. The agonizing struggle still goes on in the United States. But the southern Africans are being subjected to an intolerable contrast between *their* subjection and the African freedom just across the frontier. Many of the Africans may be unaware of the contrast, may accept a subordination which has some material advantages. No opinion poll has been applied to them! But there is impressive evidence that as southern Africans reach a full appreciation of their status, they find it intolerable. Sometimes we get a glimpse into their feelings. Africans who, as migrant labour, knew Southern Rhodesia well, told the Bledisloe Commission: 'They do not look upon a black man as a person. They just treat them as dogs. I am a person, not a dog.' Again: 'They do not speak to you properly. They get hold of you and push you about. It is not pleasant.' An observant missionary wrote that in his tribal life an African is a self-respecting person, but if you kill that self-respect, he loses his head entirely.

Certainly in the last few decades the white Rhodesians have done much in social services, in agriculture, primary schools, housing, and the rest. But can this be enough? Nearly all Africans are poor, but the Rhodesian poor have to live alongside the desirable, unattainable wealth of a ruling race whom they must serve.

Mr Smith and his party offer the Africans a gradualist advance but they demand that only they must judge the pace. Can we be sure that, as Africans assert themselves, white Rhodesians will not show the same hardening of attitude and action which has marked South Africa? Today South Africa pretends to have racial separation – apartheid – but they build their wealth increasingly on the labours of the African majority. Every voice of criticism, every gesture for freedom is met with ruthless repression or even with life imprisonment. The English-speaking South Africans have themselves gone all the way from the liberalism of the old Cape Colony to compromise with Afrikaner policy. The United Party Congress meeting greeted Rhodesia's U.D.I. with cheers. In Rhodesia, too, there has been in the last years a movement away from the greater liberalism of earlier Prime Ministers, from Todd and Whitehead, by way of Winston Field to Mr Smith; and behind Mr Smith, we are told, stands an even more extreme caucus which would disown him if he showed signs of moderation.

And if the Europeans would find it difficult to *cede* power gradually, are the Africans likely to *accept* power gradually? True, the Rhodesian Africans have on the whole shown quite unusual quiescence. We must wonder how deep-seated is this patience when we remember that Europeans have nearly always been wrong in estimating Africans' political sentiment, in measuring the full strength of their passionate rejection of their racial status. And ceaseless external stimulus will be applied to the Rhodesian Africans. Their shared racial feeling binds all Africans and African states together and gives them a political strength which compensates for their poverty, their inexperience, their divisions, and their military weakness. The indignation of independent Africa about Rhodesia is real, but it is also the perfect racial cause for the expression of their feelings and for the fostering of their unity. The very depth of Africans' racial feeling, combined with their inexperience, makes it difficult for them to accept any half-way house between the bottom and the top. This was shown in the record of nearly all African states in the achievement of their independence. The leaders, who had naturally employed the political dynamisms of racial assertion, found that, even if they wished, they could not control its activity so as to co-operate with the Colonial powers in that gradual, educational transfer of power upon which these rulers had counted; it had to be independence, complete independence now! It is this 'all-or-nothing' response of Africans to their former subordination that drives the southern African whites to an all-or-nothing response. It also makes Rhodesians doubt the possibility of gradualism. The passionate decision of Mr Kaunda to risk cutting away his Zambia from its economic Siamese twin of Rhodesia, in obedience to his racial principles, is one indication of the African state of mind.

Mr Wilson's aims may therefore be very hard to achieve. If the gradual transfer of power to Africans should prove impossible, what should Britain do? Has the Government, having abjured force, the economic *power* to achieve its policy? Well, that is a technical question outside the competence of the ordinary citizen. Has Britain sufficient *interest* in pursuing this policy to the end? On one side our trade and investment in wealthy southern Africa may be at stake; on the other our relations with the poverty and the potentialities of the rest of Africa and, also, with a Commonwealth that might yet confound its critics by surviving.

And what of the moral issues in pushing Mr Wilson's policy to the end – if we can, for in Africa we are trying to ride the storm. On one side of the balance we have to set the loss for the white Rhodesians. This would be, above all, the loss of their political power. Doubtless many would leave Rhodesia. But many would stay, for they would be needed to meet the demands of a highly sophisticated economy. Others, like many Kenya settlers, would stay for love of the land and for the adventure of helping independent Africa. On the other side of the scales must be weighed the start in freedom for 4,000,000 black Rhodesians, who cannot even begin to grow to their full stature except through the opportunities and the dangers of responsibility.

I have tried to put this profoundly difficult issue fairly, but I expect that my own decision, painfully achieved, will be clear.

Preserving the Records of Empire

Letter to *The Times* 4 August 1966

Sir, – So after three hundred years – by rather generous reckoning – the Colonial Office has passed away, or is *in extremis*. It is unlikely to get a very favourable obituary from a world in which anti-colonialism is an essential springboard for young nationalism and tends even in Britain to be an ingredient of the anti-establishment mood.

The phase will pass and historians, ex-colonials among them, will assess the record of the Office judicially. They will remark that from the time when Sir James Stephen gave it a humanitarian bias some one hundred and twenty years ago the Office has generally used the exceptional initiative inherent in its task in this tradition.

The records of the department are safe. Not so those of the Colonial Service which was its agency among millions of people in some forty dependencies where personality, from that of the governor to that of the assistant D.C. in the bush, decided the nature of Britain's contact with the colonial peoples. The intimate, human side of this immense range of contacts is contained in the private letters, diaries and other unpublished writings of many hundreds of ex-colonial service officials.

In the present climate of opinion, many retired men or their widows or heirs may think, not without bitterness, that these records are hardly worth preserving. Yet one day they could be of value both here and in the ex-colonies as essential and very human documents.

For some years in Oxford we have been collecting this material. With help from several Foundations we have been able to support a small staff, who seek out, secure and process the heterogeneous material into the Bodleian Library. In a few years the search will reach its natural end but until then we still need help to support our small staff in their race with time to preserve the human side of our colonial record.

Documents should be sent to Mr J. Tawney, Oxford University Colonial Records Project, Institute of Commonwealth Studies, Oxford.

Yours faithfully

In Defence of the Commonwealth

Letter to *The Times* 8 September 1966

Sir, – Last night in *Panorama* the B.B.C. staff seemed to slant their questions upon the Commonwealth as if to evoke depreciatory opinions.

Is this part of the often undiscriminating recoil from long established institutions and concepts? If so, let us observe that the Commonwealth today is more new than old, more potential than existent.

The potentiality lies in the strong, extending growth of relationships between Britain and the associated states. A list of these contacts, even in shortest form, could hardly be compressed into this or the adjoining column. Hardly an important public activity in Britain does not have vital Commonwealth links, formal or informal – the churches, parliament, universities, law, medicine, the press, broadcasting, trade unions, agriculture, industrial training, scouting – these are only a few names from a long list. In addition there are the intricate and diffused economic relationships and the supple diplomatic co-operation. True, the whole world is drawing together and all these links would not snap with the Commonwealth bond, but the easy, elastic and personal nature of the contact would be lost.

The impoverishment would not be all on one side. For many years, and with many states, Britain in a material sense may be the giver. This may be one reason for some of the recoil from the relationship, especially as regards Africa, because of the smallness, poverty, or political troubles of some of the states. Are we to meet their physical impoverishment with our moral impoverishment? Despite our immediate economic maladjustments, we are by contrast incomparably richer and can spend on our betting, gambling, and overseas holidays a sum which reduces our grants in aid – much of it tied – to the size of a little small change.

Moreover, these new African states result from the power we took over their peoples and lands. We made the states but not the men who rule them and these have a just claim upon our understanding as well as our aid. If they make the difficult gesture of commonwealth fraternity, should we refuse it? It is surely a great opportunity to be in at the political start of a new continent, or the greater part of it, and to bring non-African members of the Commonwealth into closer relation with it. This is not an alternative to 'going into Europe'. The Common Market is already busy in Africa and as Europe ceases to be at sixes and sevens, we might all go in together in a planned co-operation.

Finally, as Professor Oliver pointed out in his letter of September 3, the Commonwealth, and above all its African members, are testing Britain today on the world issue of race. The Rhodesian issue is our most immediate test. We have to show the coloured, especially the African, members of the Commonwealth that if we ask to solve this issue in our own way it is one that will lead at no very distant date to that release of suppressed African personality and energy that we have helped to achieve in so many other states on the continent.

Yours faithfully

Conservatives' Attitude to Central Africa

Letter to *The Times* 18 October 1966

One of the main arguments used in defence of continuing white minority rule in Rhodesia was that it was a haven of peace in a continent where African rule meant disorder and bloodshed. This always seemed to me the facile opinion of those who had neither studied the exceptional history of Africa before and after subjugation nor viewed the picture, the total picture, of contemporary enfranchisement. It seemed to me especially distressing that the leading Conservatives who had held the post of Colonial Secretary could speak to their party conference in words which showed lack of historical sense and of understanding of Africa's unique experience in the last seventy years and which could also cause deep offence to the new African members of the Commonwealth. Mr Sandys made a reasoned reply in a letter published in The Times *on 20 October. But his concluding assumption that Mr Smith could be relied upon to observe agreements has still to be proved. I, on my part, was too optimistic about the prospects of success for the Labour government's policy.*

Sir, – You report Mr Maudling as saying at the Conservative conference yesterday that Rhodesians see to the north 'a sea of chaos and carnage', while Mr Sandys is said to have thought it enough to remark that Conservatives do not want Rhodesia to go the way of Ghana, Nigeria, and Zanzibar. These seem strange statements from ex-Ministers who played their part in the de-colonization of Africa.

They better than most should have been able to assess the strength and nature of the forces of African assertion – I do not call it nationalism – and of those other forces at work in the world which made it expedient for Britain to yield to that assertion. They should know that the causes of these events lay deep in the strange situation which had kept so much of tropical Africa out of the main currents of world development and then exposed it to them so suddenly and so lately. No leaders have ever been faced with more difficult problems than those who have been trying during the last ten years to convert arbitrary regions of tribal Africa into states and nations.

We must watch mistakes and atrocities with distress – not forgetting that, as in Zanzibar and the Sudan, we are not without some responsibility for them – but can we say that these have been so much worse than those committed by mature and Western nations? Our press, moreover, tends to leave what is normal in the shadow and picks out in its searchlight incidents of conflict and bloodshed. As concerns British-administered Africa, except for the southern Sudan, the picture has been one not of general carnage but of incidents which are islands in a sea of calm. As for Ghana, its return to normality has been exemplary.

Upon what grounds, then, are we to deny or to defer indefinitely the political advance of Rhodesian Africans?

Our study of black-white relations throughout the world must persuade us that no entrenched white minority will voluntarily lead an African majority, in any reasonable period, to an enfranchisement which must destroy its own social and economic mastery. How would Conservatives, without the threat of sanctions, hope to persuade Mr Smith's government to accept the defined obligations and afterwards – even more difficult – hold him to their fulfilment?

Judging by the booing of moderate views at the Conference there are Conservatives who believe that the Rhodesian majority should be denied the opportunities and risks of political freedom which have been given to all other Africans north of the Limpopo and even to some fragile ones south of it. There are very grave hazards whichever course we pursue but at least that chosen by the Government will be not the denial but the consummation of all our imperial precedents.

                    Yours faithfully

Dr Adams and the University of Central Africa

Letter to *The Times* 29 October 1966

Sir, – Defamation and possibly deprivation of office by student vote is a new and unfortunate precedent in this country. I do not claim knowledge of every phase of Dr Walter Adams's career, especially in the latest months, but I will state what I do know.

As a member of the Inter-University Council for Higher Education Overseas from its beginning in 1946, and of its executive committee, I was able to assess Dr Adams's contribution to its work. We began with two war-stricken universities and a few post-secondary colleges. By the time he left there were nine flourishing universities of international standing with 10,000 students. Those with experience of committees staffed by busy public men – and our first chairman was in St Andrews – will know how much depends upon the devotion, wisdom and initiative of the secretary.

Dr Adams showed immense courage in leaving Britain to undertake the creation of a multi-racial University in Central Africa, the difficulties of which he was so well qualified to assess and which I was able to measure myself upon visiting him in Salisbury.

By 1964 it was possible for the University Review Commission to report that 'the growth of the University has been spectacular and has more than justified the faith and vision' of those who founded it to serve all races. But even Dr Adams could not have foreseen how the whole constitutional and territorial structure within which the university had been built was to crumble under his feet and the already tense racial relations be fanned to white heat. Yet, under almost intolerable pressures and financial uncertainties, the University has survived.

I am aware that in his report of April this year Dr Birley had some criticisms to make of the University administration and of over-centralization by the Principal. I cannot comment upon this. I write of what I know and this is enough to have won for Dr Adams an honoured place in the record of one of Britain's greatest services to the peoples of the Commonwealth since the last war.

Yours faithfully

1967

Rejected Africans

June 1967

This was the heading given by The Listener *to a review of two books,* Not yet Uhuru, *the biography of Oginga Odinga, Heineman, and* Desecration of my Kingdom *by the Kabaka of Buganda.*

Among the immense flow of books upon Africa the most basic documents for future historians will probably be those by African political leaders, even though few of these provide the whole truth, or even nothing but the truth. The two books reviewed here illustrate the fascinating political variety of the continent. One is by a king, scion of a long and famous dynasty and ruler of one of Africa's most advanced peoples. The other is by a self-advanced member of a tribe whose multicellular state and physical nakedness led European pioneers to regard them, by contrast, as very primitive. The king and the commoner are thus wholly different as types: what they share is the position of rejection from which they now write.

Consider first the commoner. Almost from the moment when the missionaries brought English education to the remote Luo on the eastern margin of Lake Victoria, Oginga Odinga was in opposition to the European power which had broken in upon the unrecorded millennia of tribal life. The book records his increasingly effective attack, through personal assertion and later through political organization, upon every facet of colonial rule. It is common knowledge that, increasingly from the twenties, Kenya was to Britain a place of conflict between expediency and justice, between white settler interests and those of the African majority. There is new evidence here to show the stages by which, through organized opposition, the weak became the strong and eventually won their independence. Odinga's pages burn with his indignation against the wickedness of all the white men concerned in the story, with the partial exception of that famous and splendid schoolmaster, Carey Francis. Odinga had the single-mindedness which is the necessary equipment of the revolutionary but which is less appropriate in the post-revolutionary phase. He therefore drew apart from his African colleagues and even from the revered Kenyatta whose freedom he had helped to win. Kenyatta increasingly disapproved of the writer's uncompromising anti-colonialist policies and his very remunerative relations with Communist governments.

What Odinga's strong, narrow shaft of light reveals may be the truth, but how much lies outside it! – the long struggle of missionaries and humanitarians for African rights; the immense advantages brought to Africans, alongside the injustices, by British rule and even by settler contact and example, political and agricultural. We are told how much, not how little, land the Kikuyu lost; we are not given those aspects of Mau Mau which aroused such revulsion among other races and even other tribes. At the end the concentrated vision of the writer, now rejected by his political colleagues, sees only the faults and not the relative stability and prosperity of independent Kenya. Even so, in the hands of the informed reader, this book, written at white heat by an individualist and lavishly illustrated by pictures portraying his political activities, if an essential document.

The story of the ex-King of Buganda, who is also the ex-President of Uganda, offers an almost complete contrast. It is economical both in style and length, and the humorous detachment with which he can view his own position is rare, above all among royalties, and recalls our own Charles II. In brief sketches we see him at school, an undergraduate at Cambridge, and an officer in the Grenadier Guards. Back in Africa he assumes his throne and dispassionately analyses his colonial governors. Then comes the spectre for Buganda of federation and the more immediate fear of an independence in which monarchical and wealthy Buganda will be linked by the new dangerous bond of democracy with northern tribes as innocent of central organization and all that goes with it as Odinga's Luo in Kenya. It is from this irreconcilability that the Kabaka's exile results. But the setting of Buganda kingdom in tribal Uganda is never explained nor is the resultant rift between the Nilotic Prime Minister and Bantu Buganda, which culminated in the ruthless attack on the palace with which the book begins. One cannot end this comment without complimenting the publisher upon the production of the book, the royal purple of the binding and the effective portrait of the Kabaka on the jacket.

[1967]

Both stories reveal in personal terms the variety of problems which Africans face in making states out of tribes. Not only Africans but their British rulers. The reader may sadly wonder whether, if our officials had possessed the insight into African human nature, and into African problems as seen by Africans, which these books belatedly provide, our policy, not wholly mistaken, might not have been better prepared to meet the crisis of independence.

The Many Faces of African Socialism

Forum World Features 28 October 1967

'Socialism' is a chameleon of a word, changing colour according to its setting. In the Oxford Dictionary, we find that socialism is 'a principle that individual freedom should be completely subordinated to the interests of the community'. The Russians and the Chinese would follow Oxford here. But most Western minds would boggle at the word 'completely' and would regard socialism as a principle which can be progressively applied in order to achieve increasing equality as between persons and classes. Historically the aim in the West has been to achieve through social democracy the welfare state which political democracy failed to achieve. In Britain the Labour Party presses forward, but still with moderation, along this path, while the Conservatives, by no means static, advance, in their turn, at a more measured pace. How far Britain can be called a socialist state may be in question, but it is quite certain that she is democratic, with every citizen free, within the law, to play a full civic part and to organize and vote freely as a member of his party. Britain can claim, like her immediate neighbours, to be a social democracy with a mixed economy in which the state and private enterprise play their parts but with a shift towards more state control.

It was necessary to say this much of Britain, not only to avoid false simplification but also because a number of African states were nurtured by Britain and are still closely associated with it economically and as members of the Commonwealth. Yet Africans, exulting in their release from colonial rule, want to claim the utmost measure of freedom and originality in developing their new states and to create something distinctively both African and socialist. There are many common features between the numerous new states of tropical Africa, and especially within the two main groups of ex-French and ex-British colonies, but even in each group there are interesting differences. We can see this even if we confine our attention mainly to three states on the eastern side of Africa: Kenya, Tanzania and Zambia.

Like most African states, these three claim to be socialist and also make a common assertion that African socialism is unique in that it is derived directly from tribal life. Socialism is therefore, they claim, in the blood; it is not something to be sought and painfully developed, still less borrowed. Thus, the Sessional Paper put out by the Kenya government in April 1965 asserted that African socialism can and must draw upon African traditions. It is claimed that two of these, political democracy and mutual social responsibility, form the basis for African socialism: in African society political rights did not derive from wealth or status. Mr Tom Mboya said this African family spirit must extend to the nation as a whole.

In somewhat different terms the religious idealist, President Kaunda, applied the same idea to Zambia. In his published letters to the Rev. Colin Morris, he claims that the tribe was a mutual, accepting and inclusive community and that these three precious characteristics could be carried over into the modern multi-tribal state. 'The extended family system constitutes a social security scheme – following the natural pattern of personal relationships rather than being the responsibility of an institution.'

President Nyerere of Tanzania has carried the idea of the tribal basis of the new state even further. The theme runs through the numerous speeches and pamphlets by which he tries to mould his state and people. Traditionally, he says, African society was a socialist society and 'we intend to adopt the same attitude in the new circumstances of a nation-state which is increasingly using modern techniques of economic production'. In September this year, he repeated this theme at length, stressing the mutual respect, the equality, the communal property and the obligation upon all to work, which governed tribal society.

How, we may ask, can these Arcadian qualities be carried into the complex modern world? To begin with, however admirable the conduct of life within the tribe, outside it tribal enmity and conflict were the rule and the boundaries drawn by colonial annexation included numerous, very distinct and often mutually hostile tribes. The new leaders have met this basic danger in several ways. To begin with they have undermined the power of the chiefs as the agents of disunity. They have tried to bring over into the post-independence period the emotional unity of the independence movement with, of course, the prolongation of their own leadership. But the degree of unity achieved in that struggle arose to meet a relatively simple issue and one which was based upon common *racial* rather than national assertion against the white rulers. This unity is not so easily extended to deal with the many complex problems of the post-independence era. The leaders therefore try to embrace the whole population and smother tribalism in a one-party state.

President Nyerere seems, at least for the present, to have succeeded in this aim. His tribes are mostly small and scattered widely round the arid centre of the country and he has the great asset of a common African language, Swahili. His party T.A.N.U. (Tanzania African National Union) is vigorously organized down to the grass-roots and he has hit upon the idea of giving some reality to elections by allowing choice between two party members in each constituency. In Zambia the scrupulous President hesitates to obliterate by force the small rival party but he hopes to see it voted out of existence in the next election. Meanwhile he inveighs against tribalism and calls for unity. Kenya has had what now turns out to be the immense political advantage of a prolonged struggle with European settlers to gain power and also the unquestioned leadership of Mr Kenyatta, the President. So far he has been able, by his immense prestige, to bring a number of very diverse and once warring tribes into unity. There are two parties, but one is now weak and threatened though it might well re-assert itself when the aged President is no more. We should also note, in this matter of one-party unity, that the nascent trade unions have been firmly disciplined in all three states.

These three eastern states have been fortunate in the degree of unity they have retained. By contrast, in Uganda we see what can happen when a large and advanced tribe threatens to dominate the whole. It was crushed by the army. Further afield, we can see Nigeria stained by massacre and civil war as one major tribe comes into conflict with its neighbours.

The three states of Eastern Africa, in trying to establish their African socialism, face other difficulties. One of these is that their poverty makes it difficult to extend the social services, and, above all, education, as widely as their socialist principles demand. Furthermore they are not working in an African vacuum. For all their assertion of their unique African character, they still carry the heritage of colonial rule, not all of which they could jettison at independence. Fortunately that rule, however authoritarian, had by necessity some of the aspects of state socialism. More serious, because of their poverty they are heavily dependent upon external investment and because of their lack of expertise in the skills of the modern world they need many experts from outside. Aid, investment and staff come mainly from the Western world. In this matter the situation in each of these countries is somewhat different.

Zambia, with its small population of some four millions, is heavily dependent upon the great copper mines. When, therefore, the President issued his 'blueprint for socialism' in April this year, he could promise co-operative development for agriculture and vigilance against capitalist tendencies. But the manifesto goes on to recognize that the dominant mining development should remain in private hands, that is the giant hands of private companies, dependent upon Anglo-American capital and largely run by white managers and experts.

Kenya has been obliged to make a similar compromise with realities, represented here by the long domination of white settlers and Asian businessmen and technicians who have built up elements of a free enterprise economy too deeply founded and, indeed, too prosperous to be wholly dismantled. Kenya, indeed, is booming, and the blueprint for socialism, while it finds scope for action in social services and a partial re-distribution of land to Africans, stops far short of thoroughgoing socialist consistency. Indeed, Mr Oginga Odinga, who leads his small opposition party and is suspected of very close relations with Communist agencies, protests that Kenya has neither socialism nor true independence.

Only Tanzania, under its idealistic President, has been able to approach the socialist ideal. In his Arusha declaration, which became official T.A.N.U. policy early in 1967, President Nyerere abruptly nationalized the foreign-owned banks, commercial houses, insurance firms and other foreign companies. By his independent policy he has deliberately offended two of his chief givers of aid, the United States and West Germany, and has broken relations with Britain over Rhodesia, and accepted Chinese help and helpers. He admits that his devotion to African socialism and his independent attitude towards the wealthy Western powers has lost him much investment, but he asserts that if traditional African socialism is to survive it must be based mainly on a better agricultural and social life for *all* the people and not on large foreign-supported industrial enterprises. Further, he has tackled with severe measures another of the almost unavoidable dangers to African socialism, the emergence of a political and official class living at a strikingly higher level than the masses, a danger run by Kenya and one cause of the deep disillusionment of Nigerians. His ministers are forbidden to have two cars or two houses and demonstrating university students were sent home to work on the land as a discipline.

What of the future? Russia and China, in competition, offer Africa their own kind of socialism. But they have come late upon the scene and Russian experts have found it difficult to adapt their theories of the class war to Africa's equalitarian peasant societies. But African socialism is as new as African independence and it would be politic as well as moral for Africa's Western helpers to help rather than hinder her peoples in their attempts to build up unique systems of government to meet the uniquely difficult problems of their continent.

1968

Broadcast Addressed to Colonel Emeka Ojukwu

I made this broadcast on 7 September 1968, when I was in Nigeria at the invitation of the Federal Government. I spoke entirely upon my own initiative, with no censorship. At that time it seemed that the Federal armies were about to make a successful attack upon the shrinking Biafran refuge. I had just been behind the lines on the northern and southern fronts and it seemed that nothing could save the besieged millions from the final horrors of war and starvation. The appeal, like those of other foreign sympathizers with their plight, produced no result; and shortly afterwards the injection by air of new arms into Biafra changed for a time the whole balance of operations. I realized afterwards, and stated in The Times, *that, in face of the Biafran attitude, I should have used the expression 'enter into negotiations' rather than surrender. This talk was printed in the Nigerian press.*

This is Margery Perham speaking.

I am speaking to you, Emeka Ojukwu, and to the Ibo people with you.

You know – for you have written to me – how many Ibo friends I have and how I have tried to put the Ibo case in Britain for many months. I know that many wrongs have been committed both against your people and by your people since this conflict began. But it is no time to speak of these things now when your Biafra is being surrounded by Federal troops, and it cannot be long before you and your people will have to face defeat.

If you try to fight to the end, many thousands of lives which Nigeria cannot spare will be sacrificed, both on your side and on the Federal side. More than this, if you insist upon holding out to the end, then thousands, perhaps millions, of women and children may die, or be wounded, or have their health fatally destroyed by hunger and hardship. And those people who have come from Britain and elsewhere to help you – doctors, nurses and others – they too might be killed or wounded. It is feeling for your people, and especially the innocent women and children, which has so deeply stirred the sympathy of people in Europe and America who have seen their suffering on television. The world which is watching would condemn you if they now believed that you were using your leadership to prolong a hopeless struggle at their expense: there would be not only sorrow, but indignation against you.

You might say that I have been put up by the Federal Government to make this appeal. It is not so. I think I am too well known in Britain and by many of your own people for it to be thought that I would act or speak in any other way than upon my own judgement and initiative and as a Christian. I cannot speak for the Federal Government. I can only say that from what I have seen and heard, not only in Lagos but in visits to other parts, the East and the North, I do not believe that your people would be in danger of massacre or revenge. You must know, even if your people do not, that an immense effort is now being made to prepare the way back for your people into life in Nigeria.

I therefore beg you not to take upon yourself the terrible responsibility of refusing to surrender and of fighting to the end.

The Nigerian War

The Times 12 September 1968

I wrote this article which was headed by The Times *'Why Biafran leaders should surrender' on the day I returned from Nigeria. Much has happened since the date of this article, especially the change in the fortunes of war, but neither the basic facts nor my own general approach to this tragic issue have changed.*

The Nigerian situation is complex and obscure as well as tragic, and anyone who presumes to speak about it must provide some credentials. As the war takes the terrible form of the siege of a whole people, emotion rises higher and the Ibo and their friends in Britain feel an anguish that tends to master reason. My own position is that of a student of African affairs, but one who cannot claim to have the cool detachment with which, by some academic standards, I ought to observe the present conflict.

THE NIGERIAN WAR [1968]

What are my credentials? I first went to Nigeria in 1931 when I spent a year there and wrote a book on its administration. I have kept in touch with it ever since. I was a guest at the independence celebrations and saw the joy and hope of the crowds as the new flag of independent Nigeria was run up. I was the friend and biographer of Lord Lugard, who in 1912 created the present Nigeria out of the three main tribal areas, Hausa North, Yoruba West and Ibo East.

I had every political and sentimental reason to want this potentially great African state, with something over 60 million inhabitants, to advance in unity and wealth. But it is one thing for a variety of tribes (and there are many more in Nigeria beside the three main groups) to live together in peace and co-operation when they were all held within the seemingly unassailable framework of an external power, and quite another for them to hold together when that power departs.

Like others I watched with dismay the tragic sequence of party bitterness and the political assassinations of 1966. In the disorders which followed it was certainly the Ibo who suffered most, though the statistics of massacres differ wildly. It was not surprising that the Ibo military governor, Ojukwu, began to call his people back from the other regions, or that the sense of rejection after the massacres should have led on to the idea of secession.

Secession is a wicked word among African leaders for the obvious reason that as nearly every African state began as an area marked out by European pioneers in Africa and by diplomatists in Europe they could all begin to shake and fall apart if tribal prejudice were allowed free will. But the situation can arise when secession is a lesser evil than the enforced enclosure of a quasi-rebellious tribe.

This is what the Ibo felt. Nigeria had been their oyster. Propelled by the crowded poverty of their own region and attracted by opportunities which their vigorous initiative qualified them to take they overflowed into the other regions. They occupied a place not unlike that of the Jews in eastern Europe or the Asians in East Africa. Such people are seldom popular, however much they galvanize an economy. To add to their unpopularity it was Ibo officers who murdered the prime minister, the premiers of the northern and western regions, and many of their non-Ibo fellow officers. So the Ibo exodus went into reverse and they crowded back into their tribal area with a sense of bitter injustice; and step by step moved towards the idea of secession.

Politically they seemed to have a case. Numerically the Eastern Province, as it was then, enclosed some 12 million people (there is no valid census in Nigeria) and was numerically and economically superior to many independent African states. But when the non-Ibo segments to the south wavered in their support and, with the advent of the Federal army, went over to the Federal side, Biafra became a questionable proposition. It has lost its access to the sea, its major harbour of Port Harcourt and its potentially booming oil wells. The Federal army slowly increased in numbers and efficiency, powerfully aided by its British Saladin armoured cars and mortar artillery. Biafra began to shrink on the map.

How should we, the British, observers of this tragic little war, assess the situation today? We know the Biafran case. For many months a great mass of Ibo documentation has piled up in my study. I think I can measure their passionate revulsion from the Federation. I admire the Ibo and have many friends among them. I believed that in the face of their suffering and their apparent rejection, the abstraction of the former Eastern Province offered a viable state. But with the excision from Biafra of the invaluable southern region and with the encircling grip of the Federal army, the end now seems certain. Should the Biafrans' friends encourage them in their determination to fight to the last and die, men, women and children, by war, starvation and disease? Must we not think also of those splendid people from the outside world, nurses, doctors and missionaries, who have gone in or stayed in to help them? Is it not better for the Biafrans to live not to fight but to work and flourish another day?

The Biafrans' reply was simple and to them unanswerable. It was, and is, that surrender means total destruction – and here the emotional word genocide comes into use. Of course, with these new makeshift African states there is material for their dark pessimism. The recent history of Nigeria has been a bloody one. Some of my Ibo friends have brought me letters from home telling in convincing form of the massacre of civilians down to mere boys killed in their homes in front of their mothers. There can be no doubt that there have been counter-atrocities: the statistics of massacres are seldom either complete or convincing in a population still hyphenated by tribes; real unity is still only in the making and it is mostly to be found in the top levels of the civil services and the intelligentsia. Religion is also a barrier but a less effective one among the tolerant Africans than most other peoples. Certainly the Federal army is not a Moslem force attacking the very Christian Ibo: it is a very mixed force coming from the relatively neutral middle belt.

The Federal government is struggling to rebuild unity. As yet we cannot be sure that they will be able to hold this vast country together, but it would seem that such influence as the ex-colonizers still have should be used to serve the ideal rather than indulge in easy condemnation of the weaknesses of the real. Are we, especially those of us who have felt the force of the Ibo cause, to join with them now in what seems a hopeless and suicidal cause? Are we to fall in with President de Gaulle, who is adapting to Africa somewhat the same policy which he applied towards Canada? French policy was to fragment their west African empire, a policy which certainly made easier the maintenance of French influence through economic and even military support.

Yet the policy of our own Government has been less than candid. It has supplied the mortars and Saladin armoured cars which are said to represent only 15 per cent in monetary value of the arms supplied from outside, but which have been far more effective than the expensive Russian Migs and Ilyushin aircraft. We may hope that this whole business of our trade in arms will in the near future be reconsidered.

The issue now may well be the survival of the Ibo, and for myself I found it difficult to join them in their apparent deathwish. It was with this terrible issue in mind that I went to Nigeria to try to find out if there could be a less fatal conclusion. Of course, in a country at war I had to make use of Federal facilities. But Nigerian officialdom is neither very close knit nor is it efficient in subterfuge and cover-work. Also I had many old friends and contacts. My main purpose was to test the possibility, ridiculed in Biafra, that the Nigerian Government did not plan their destruction. I found to my surprise that many thousands of Ibos were living safely at various levels in Lagos; some, though not many, holding senior posts in the Government. One, a permanent secretary at one of the Ministries, gave a large party at his home for me, attended by many senior officials. In addition, I found that a considerable department was being constituted, headed by senior Ibo officials, to devise plans for the reincorporation of Ibos in the reconquered areas.

Flying to other parts of the country I saw the beginnings of administration in the reconquered areas with Ibo officials in charge. I saw markets reopened with Ibos starting again to trade alongside the Hausa and Federal soldiers, and Ibo women strolling peaceably about the market. Making a test demand to inspect a large structure near the road, I found it full of Ibo women complete with beds, busily cooking for their reasonably healthy children. It was a transit camp from which they could be dispersed to their homes. In more than one place I found a scheme in operation to list and protect abandoned Ibo houses and to retain for their original owners any rents paid by other occupiers. All this is patchy and makeshift, but it is a very long way from genocide.

I do not doubt that this civil restorative work is incomplete and still less that the Federal soldiery, raw recruits with the barest training and with little knowledge of the Geneva conventions, may lose their control in fighting or even afterwards. But the senior men, civil and military, are now well aware of the dangers. Colonel Adekunle, the so-called 'Black Scorpion', famous for his ferocity, of which I felt the lash when he came from the capture of Aba to see me at his military headquarters, can also be ferocious in the maintenance of discipline, as his recent public execution of an offending officer demonstrated. In a three-hour talk with General Gowon I was impressed by the sincerity of this very Christian soldier, especially in his decision to win back the Ibos by moderation following victory.

The second man in the military Government with whom I discussed these issues was Hassan Katsina, who had risked his life to save the situation during the Kano massacre when his company mutinied to attack the Ibo.

I have quoted only a fraction of the evidence which leads me to question whether Ojukwu's insistence that surrender equals genocide is altogether valid. I do not understand why to advocate surrender rather than to dedicate some millions of people to death by war and starvation should be regarded as a disgraceful proposal. Even if such were their desire, the Federal authorities could not easily get away with a policy of brutal repression. The affairs of Nigeria are not being transacted in a corner: journalists and practical philanthropists of many nations throng the hotels and visit the battlefields.

The Federal Government, as a sensitive and sovereign entity, has shown some measure of patience and co-operation over the mercy flights. Humanity calls for the end of this monstrous siege and the friends of Nigeria should bring their influence to bear upon both sides to work out a compromise. It was in this spirit that, entirely upon my own initiative and using my own words, I broadcast from Lagos an appeal to Ojukwu to surrender.

Nigeria needs the Ibos; even more the Ibos need Nigeria.

The War in Nigeria

The Listener 19 September 1968

I have included this talk as it enabled me to expand upon the points I had made in The Times *article and to add further material.*

It was on 22 January 1966 that I came to Broadcasting House to speak about the assassinations of the Prime Minister of Nigeria, of the Premiers of the northern and eastern regions and of many officers of the army. I spoke almost at a moment's notice and it was under the deep sense of shock which these murders had evoked. I remember that while I was in the studio working on my script, I saw on the television screen the Ibo officer who had just murdered the Premier of the north – and I had known that Premier – still holding his gun and proud of what he had done. As I looked I felt a sense of horror, caused by something even deeper than the immediate tragedy. I seemed as in a flash to see a vista of all the great and terrible consequences which might result from these murders, with their perpetrators honestly believing them as something that would open the way to a new and better political life for Nigeria.

They were wrong. The blood of political assassination seldom, if ever, nourishes healthy political growth. Confusion, suspicion and then fragmentation were the results. As I speak here the Ibo leader, Colonel Ojukwu, and his five or six million Ibo are concentrated within a narrowing portion of their former region. We have all felt a deep, indeed, a passionate anxiety about their danger. The impact of television has brought the facts of suffering and of starvation, and especially among the women and children, right into the homes of probably the majority of people of this country. They have seen such terrible things as the shooting of an unarmed Ibo and then the execution of the killer. Such a projection of the atrocities of war and suffering is surely something quite new in history. I tested it for myself the day before I went out to Nigeria. I had to go to a number of departments in a large store and in each one as I went I mentioned to the assistants that I was just off to Nigeria. The response was immediate – almost dramatic. They knew only too well what was going on in that African country. And yet it is hard for any of us – even for those of us who have studied Nigeria and worked in it – to get a really full and fair picture of the background to the immediate events.

For myself, I thought I knew enough of the issue to venture to write about it as I did, on and off for many months, mainly in letters to *The Times*. I have a very large number of Ibo friends and I had been seeing many of those who are in this country. I had invited leading Ibo who were visiting Britain to meet people in Oxford and I had studied the really immense volume of literature in which the Ibo have put their case. But there were two points which seemed to stand out. One was the question as to whether Britain ought to supply arms to one side in such a tragic civil war. Did this policy really give us the influence our government kept claiming for it and if so what use have we made of that influence? These are still, in my view, very open questions.

The other point which I put forward was that if the Federal government could not offer a secure and a viable existence for the Ibo within the Nigerian state then this people had a legitimate case for opting out of that state. Secession is, not surprisingly, a dirty word in African political circles, and for very obvious reasons. But it must be remembered that the previous boundaries were all made without African consent and imposed upon the tribes by Western powers. If therefore circumstances develop which make the association of widely contrasting groups intolerable to one or the other side, may not even secession be the lesser of two evils?

It did begin to appear that this stage had been reached when, under Ojukwu's leadership, the Ibo embarked upon the secessionist state of Biafra. There was the basic reason of the very wide difference between the Ibo way of life, and that of the other major tribes in Nigeria. This difference had seemed to matter less when all the tribes were held together within the overarching structure of the British government. But with independence, with the full tribal competition for power and economic advance, certain deep rivalries began to appear. The Ibo are a very vigorous, very democratically inclined people; they are thirsty for education, they must have hundreds of D.Phils, and they are, for the most part, Christians, very largely Roman Catholics. They were eager to break out of their rather poor and restricted environment and to use the whole of Nigeria as their sphere of opportunity. Up in the north the Ibo settled in the towns of the Moslem Hausa; these are proud people with a long history and a developed civilization. But they were cut off partly by their inland position and partly by their own conservatism from the modern forces which had been so very eagerly absorbed by the poorer, the more egalitarian Ibo. The Yoruba too had their old and developed civilization. They, like the Hausa, were grouped in large city states; they were pagans until they began to absorb both Islam and Christianity. They were men with famous chiefs, and developed trade and local industries. The Ibo had little or nothing of these things.

Here, in this main threefold division, lay the powder that some unhappy event could ignite. And it came from the bitter political and tribal antagonism which developed between the three main Nigerian groups. It was this tension which led to the assassination in 1966 by Ibo officers of their Hausa Prime Minister, Abubakar Tafawa Balewa, the Hausa Premier of the north and the Yoruba Premier of the west. And in addition to this we must remember the Ibo officers also murdered a number of their fellow officers of other tribes on the same night.

It is necessary I think to recall this tragic event in order to show how the inter-tribal tension in the country grew more intense. The assumption of power after the murders by the most senior soldier, the Ibo Ironsi, only deepened the hostilities. He tried to impose a more unitary system of government upon the country and in doing this he simply roused the fears of the other elements that there was going to be more Ibo domination. For this reason, and also in revenge for the earlier military assassinations, he too was murdered by non-Ibo soldiers. Events had thus moved by ominous steps to the series of massacres in 1966 which have still further darkened the first decade of Nigeria's history as an independent nation. In these troubles there can be no doubt that the worst, though by no means the only, sufferers were the Ibo living scattered about in the northern towns. Claims were made by the Ibo that 30,000 of them were killed. On the other side the figure is given as 3,000. Well, it is doubtful if any accurate figure will ever be agreed. The already crowded Ibo country was now swelled by tens of thousands of the refugees, coming down from the north, bringing their wounded with them and their stories of the terrible events through which they had passed.

The rest can be briefly told. After the failure of a determined effort to make peace and unity the Eastern Ibo segment under the leadership of the soldier, Colonel Ojukwu, drew further apart until at last it reached the extreme of complete secession. Meanwhile another soldier, General Gowon, had become head of state. He is a member of a small tribe, he is a Christian, and yet, as he counts as a northerner, it was hoped he would straddle the regional and tribal divisions. And in addition to this he was known as a man of the highest character, moderate and magnanimous. And he at once began efforts at conciliation. But the war went on.

And the war still goes on, with the Ibo confined now into a smaller and smaller area, in desperate need of food and medical care, which heroic people of many nations are trying to supply, often at terrible cost to themselves. But this does not pretend to be an up-to-the-minute report on the war. And I am sure that many want to try to see it as rationally as is possible and to probe into the reasons for the tragedy. Speaking for myself, I had seen the strength of Biafra's case – I had reluctantly conceded that here, perhaps, was a situation which secession might cure. The Ibo seemed convinced that there was no future for them in Nigeria. They even asserted that wholesale massacre was all they could expect if they surrendered. I therefore felt that I must go out for myself and for the first time see the other side, the Federal side, and learn all I could of policies and of intentions there.

So I went. I was given freedom to do what I wanted, to see whom I wished. And this wasn't difficult. Indeed the central government is manned by men of too many different tribes and regions to have developed any close autocratic control of officials and politicians; or indeed of enquiring visitors. I met anyone I wanted. I flew about the country to other centres and I was able to gain some estimate of how the present Nigerian Government is handling the conduct of the war and the plans for peace. The fact that I knew the country and many of the personalities made access all the easier and the quicker.

It seemed to me that a new spirit was being bred, an acceptance of the reason why the united Nigeria had failed and a new vision of how it could be re-established on new and better lines. There can be no doubt, of course, that the murders by the Ibo military officers had caused a passionate resentment. This was especially true of their murder of their fellow-officers and comrades. Some of those who survived that night of the revolvers in 1966 told me some terrible stories of what they had seen and of how they had escaped. But I think that this mood of anger and desire for revenge seems to have passed, at least in responsible circles to which I had some access. The war, however, is being pursued with increasing energy; less I think for vengeance than as the way towards peace and unity. It must be remembered that war on this scale is really a new experience for Nigerians and that the assassinations had a very destructive effect on the unity and efficiency of the officer class, and, indeed, of the army as a whole.

General Gowon has called in the political leaders of other tribes to advise his military government. He has a civilian consultative council of notables to advise him. The main danger to Nigeria, as he and his advisers saw it, seemed to lie in the existence of the three main tribal blocks, northern, western and eastern. But Ironsi's plan of a high measure of centralization had failed as a cure for this perilous tripartite imbalance. The new plan has been the division of Nigeria into twelve states – with a question mark hanging over the proposed Ibo state. Nigeria of course has so many tribes that most of these states are made up of a number of tribal units.

The boundary allotted to the Ibo state is a denial of their claim to what, under British rule, was the old Eastern Province, a region running right down from the Ibo north to include a number of smaller groups living near the coast. These peoples have now been split off to make two smaller states, South-Central State and the Rivers' State. Now by this excision Biafra is reduced in numbers, it is limited to the Ibo tribes and it is cut off both from the coast and the harbours of Port Harcourt and Calabar. Above all, the Ibo lose the highly promising oil wells in the south. It is indeed doubtful now whether Biafra in its truncated form could be a really viable unit, especially if it had to exist within a resentful Nigeria.

I flew down to see something of this area. It is tragic to see the devastation of the old and historic town of Calabar where fierce fighting took place, and certainly terrible things were done, probably by both sides. I attended the first meeting of the new State Council with the military governor sitting as president, and was asked to address it. I saw the energy and satisfaction of the people at embarking upon this new structure of government. I paid my respects to the monument to Mary Slessor, that heroic woman who in the mid-nineteenth century did so much to Christianize the local people and whose memory is so much respected in Calabar.

I visited other regions. Above all I was allowed to go into the areas recaptured from the Ibo and see the beginning of something like civil government there. This was really the crucial test; for it became clear that the Ibo fears of massacre as the sequel to surrender were very much mistaken. Attempts were being made – I saw them – to sort out refugees, and to send them back to their homes. Ibo officials were being put in charge. And in Lagos a department manned by senior Ibo officials is now being built up. It is meant to deal with the whole problem of reincorporating the Ibo again into the Nigerian state and society. In Lagos itself I found thousands of Ibo still working unmolested, even holding senior posts in the Civil Service.

But, it might be argued, it is one thing for the Central Government to have rational plans. How far can the old hatreds, the sequel of all the bitter conflicts of the past, be exorcised from the people in general? And even if the civil Government is struggling towards a new, and more efficient rule in which tribalism may be controlled, what can be promised for the army? No visitor, even with prior knowledge of the country, can be in a position to make promises on this matter. The new army is made up of hastily gathered recruits, briefly trained and brought to battle. There are – there can be – no strong traditions of soldierly conduct and restraint and Africans tend to work up an immense excitement in battle.

I can do no more than state that the military commanders I met convinced me that they were fully aware of this danger and that they are doing all they can to guard against it. It must also be remembered that not only Lagos but the military fronts are almost literally thronged with witnesses from all over the world, above all the energetic young men of the press with their cameras and tape recorders. The Government is highly responsive to this inquisition. I had long talks with General Gowon and with the other military commanders and with many of the leading figures in politics and in administration. True, there is undoubtedly much resentment at the demand of the humanitarian agencies to overfly Nigerian air space. It is felt rather as a hangover from colonialism. But even this has been accepted and it must be admitted that General Gowon has gone a very long way in accepting plans for the supply of food to the besieged, more perhaps than in any other instance in military history.

But nothing can minimize the tragedy which is being enacted before the eyes of the world. The picture – and, through television, it really *is* a picture – of millions of men, and above all of women and children, being hemmed inside a contracted area and suffering from disease and starvation has evoked a magnificent response in practical action. It may be hoped that the story of the courage of those who have stayed in Biafra or have flown in landing upon the perilous so-called air fields to serve these people, will be fully recorded for the benefit of history.

But is it enough to show even courage? Have we not to ask whether this resolute refusal to surrender is a justifiable policy? It is not for us to decide. But world opinion, and above all I think opinion in Britain, the nation to which Nigerians still look as their oldest and best friend, should surely use all the influence we possess to bring this unspeakable suffering to an end. For myself I cannot believe that those whose first care is for the future of the Ibo can want to encourage them in a resistance which seems now to be beyond the hope of success. No one can guarantee a future for Nigeria – this vast area, this conglomerate of sixty million people divided into many tribes. We can only watch the leaders groping their way towards greater unity and greater justice and give them what understanding and help lies in our power.

The Nigerian Civil War

Letter to *The Times* 21 September 1968

This was written in reply to a moving letter from a leading Nigerian, indeed African, writer, Mr Chinua Achebe, which was published on 19 September.

Sir, – I could have no more effective critic than Mr Chinua Achebe, (19 September), whose writings are to me the deepest revelation of African experience in this age of revolution for his people, and I felt honoured to attend the party called to bid him farewell upon his courageous decision to commit himself to Biafra.

But he does an injustice not only to me but to his own better perceptions in saying that the Biafran cause means no more to me than a vast pile of documentation in my study. I have had more contact with Ibos, students and others, than with any other Nigerians. Since hostilities began I have been in frequent contact with them. I arranged a meeting in Oxford for Sir Louis Mbanefo and his distinguished colleagues, and I recently entertained the delegation of Biafran women. I have been shown terrible letters from Ibos whose relatives have been murdered.

I can fully understand that my offence in Ibo eyes is to have accepted the changing realities of their situation. Following the terrible massacres in the north and the flight of Ibo back to their own region it seemed to me that there might be a case for secession and it seemed wrong for Britain to supply arms to subdue this injured people. In this sense I wrote more than once in these columns. But in the last few weeks it seemed likely that the Federal forces were on the verge of complete victory.

The Biafrans, it appeared, were refusing to make any terms on the grounds that, whatever they did, their complete extermination was intended. But by their action they were insuring that, even against Federal intentions, the tragedy would result, by famine as well as weapons. Could the friends of the Ibo support them in their terrible decision? The answer depended upon whether the Ibo conviction about the Federal attitude was valid. It was to test this that I made my urgent visit to Nigeria.

I do not want to repeat here what I said in my article of 15 September. Even in that I could reproduce only a fraction of the evidence I collected. The self-constituted Federal Military Government is a loose-knit body, composed of many types and tribes, struggling towards a new unity and efficiency. I can only repeat that, although I did hear the case against the Ibos (who, though greatly wronged, are themselves charged with acts of political murder and massacre), there was a wide recognition that if the dissidents were to be won back and the Federation rebuilt on the new basis of 12 states, it must be by a policy of constructive restoration. There was widespread appreciation of the duty to control the troops and recent news shows the need also to control the Egyptian airmen. Fortunately there is a wealth of concern, O.A.U., national, international and humanitarian, playing upon the Federal Government, and it is well represented in Lagos.

In this situation are the friends of the Ibo to support them in flying in the face of the hard realities of the situation as it is today? Many peoples have successfully survived military defeat and the Ibo are among the most able and resilient of any African tribe. I am no military expert but cannot believe that guerrilla war, even with French help, can effect more than a prolongation of death and destruction. The Ibo should not believe that the widespread sympathy with their sufferings is the same as total and practical support of their political cause.

One final and most urgent point. Whatever the political or military events of the next few days, what matters most is the feeding of the millions besieged in their contracting area. The British Government, in concert with others, should act today rather than tomorrow in response to the demand of Lord Brockway's Committee for Peace in Nigeria. Nothing less than a massive operation, by land and air, to rush supplies to the crowded millions of Ibo and their helpers can avert one of the most terrible tragedies of history. The Ibo may seem determined to die: it is surely for us to try to save them even from themselves.

Yours faithfully

1969

Britain's Responsibilities for Nigeria's Troubles

Le Monde 23 January 1969

On 5 December 1968 an article was published in Le Monde *by M. François Debré in which he accused Britain of having, by her policy, fomented the divisions in Nigeria. The argument was so historically unsound that I was asked by the Central Office of Information to write a reply to it. This appeared, in slightly abbreviated form from that printed below, in* Le Monde *on 23 January 1969.*

In his article on Nigeria entitled 'Britain's Former Responsibilities', published in this journal on 5 December, M. François Debré charges Britain with responsibility for Nigeria's present troubles by her deliberate fostering of division. Where did he study his history?

My own credentials are as follows: forty years of contact with Nigeria; a study of its Government published in the thirties; a close friendship with Lord Lugard who first occupied the north and later unified all Nigeria; the inheritance of his papers and the writing of his two-volume biography; visits to the country both before and since independence and as the Government's guest at the independence celebrations. All this experience would be valueless if I were a blind admirer of Britain's record. But all my writings, up to my most recent contributions to *The Times*, show that I have been critical of many aspects of Britain's colonial policy.

I cannot accept M. Debré's thesis that Britain deliberately intensified the main threefold division of Nigeria. I contend that he ignores both the slow, piecemeal way in which Britain occupied the region and the depth of the tribal fissures that were encountered.

Britain tentatively occupied toeholds at different points of the coast when, poacher turned gamekeeper, she tried to stop the slave trade, first from Lagos (1861) and then from the Oil Rivers further east

(1885). In between, up the Niger, she chartered the Royal Niger Company for a brief fourteen years (1886–1900), though M. Debré writes as if the Company was Britain's sole agent. In 1900 Lugard was sent to take over the vast northern region which he did in three years and ruled it for another three. All those separate administrations were run on the minimum of revenue and staff and were not united until Lugard created one Nigeria in 1914 and immediately ran into World War I with its local campaign. A full unified administration could hardly be begun until the thirties when it, in turn, ran into World War II.

If M. Debré really believes that a British colonial Government, making this late start in the unified control of this vast region, had the power to overcome the tribal divisions he must greatly underestimate their depth, based as they were on physical conditions more diverse than any found in temperate Europe. The dry savannah of the north allowed the spread of Islam from North Africa and the individual development of powerful Kanuri and Hausa city-states, strong in their isolation. The Yoruba city states of the south-west differed, as M. Debré rightly says, from the northern emirates, being pagan and less centralized, but they were even more different, as he should have added, in being open, from the mid-nineteenth century, to strong direct contact with European economic and missionary influences which still further differentiated them from the Hausa states. The major group to the east, the Ibo, were also the product of very special physical conditions, those of the rainforest which kept them in isolation and prevented them from developing any unifying social structure above the extended family.

Could Britain, in the brief period of her unified administration, have ironed out the deep differences between the three major groups, not to speak of the 248 minor tribes into which the population is divided?

I agree with M. Debré that in the conservative north British officials could have done more to educate and to modernize; my criticisms are on record. But there were limits to the possible in an immense, isolated region, for a staff which, until the forties, was working with no sense of a terminal date. Did France not have her difficulties in Algeria with an Islam far more open to world influences?

What can M. Debré mean when he says that the 'feeling of belonging to a Nigerian nation was brushed aside'? Or, of the British who had just brought the north out of its centuries of isolation, that we 'cut off the population from all contact with Europe'? Or that Britain 'hindered intellectual development' when she invited advanced Moslem teachers from the Sudan to revive the local faith, established schools and founded a northern university?

Perhaps the most astonishing of M. Debré's strictures is that Britain imposed a foreign political and military occupation on the south by using Hausa and Fulani soldiers there. In the few military expeditions of the early occupation doubtless some northerners were used as soldiers, but they had no political significance and to say that the south was kept under foreign 'British and *northern* occupation' is pure fantasy.

I have admitted that, with a greater sense of urgency, Britain might have somewhat speeded up her northern reforms. But this does not apply to the Yoruba or the Ibo who stretched out both hands to accept the innovations of their rulers. The Ibo, especially, unshackled by any heirarchy, leaped straight from isolated backwardness to vigorous participation in all the new ways of life and in all Nigeria. Led by Dr Azikiwe, they forced the pace politically and, as soon as the British ministers and officials realized that independence must soon be the goal, they set themselves to guide these numerous and divided peoples towards unity within a democratic constitution. They promoted discussions from village and district level, leading up to regional and central conferences in Britain and Nigeria, lasting some ten years. M. Debré should read a book by Mr Kalu Ezera, now in Biafra, an Ibo student of my own Nuffield College, published in 1960 and entitled *Constitutional Developments in Nigeria*. In this he describes in detail the series of conferences and constitutional experiments by which the British, to whom he gives full credit, helped the divided leaders to construct a unified parliamentary system. While recognizing the conservatism of the north, he says that 'since the inception of British rule, however, this feudalistic authoritarianism is gradually giving way to greater individual liberty'.

It is all too clear that the preponderant size of the north and the incompatibility of the Hausa and Ibo ways of life have prevented independent Nigeria from achieving unity. But no colonial Government could, in the brief colonial span, have eliminated these deep ethnic, social and religious differences.

Nor is Nigeria unique, as M. Debré seems to suggest, in its class divisions and corruption, the result of the sudden emergence of political and economic élites in a very poor continent. As for the tragic problem of the Ibo secession, only the issue of the war and the form of the peace will decide whether the Ibo section of the old Eastern Region can become the nation foreseen by M. Debré. I have myself been deeply concerned with their sufferings.

But let us not forget that the rest of Nigeria is now embarking upon the experiment of an eleven-state system, a brave attempt, which only the people themselves could make, to break away from the dangerous triform imbalance of the past, the root cause of all the evils which M. Debré describes.

A Letter to General Gowon

The Spectator 31 January 1969

During my visit to Nigeria I gained a very good impression of the young Head of State, General Gowon. With no responsibility for the troubles that had struck Nigeria he had assumed supreme power over a deeply divided and confused people. He is a Christian and, I believe, a man of moderation and compassion who would do his best to use victory with restraint. But since I was in Nigeria in September 1969 the war has become a stalemate with the increasing danger this means to the Biafrans and to Nigerian unity. The external observer must relate his hopes and offer his advice in accordance with the situation at any given moment. It seemed to me at this date that neither side seemed likely to achieve its aim and that the danger to Nigeria and to the sufferings of the besieged demanded some saving compromise.

My dear General Gowon,

I presume to write this open letter to you because in the three hours we spent discussing your civil war and in our subsequent correspondence you showed yourself so humane and so ready to understand the nature of the concern which I share with so many for the people of Biafra.

When I was in Nigeria in September it seemed as though a Federal victory was imminent and my one great hope was that Colonel Ojukwu should not hold out to the end, one that could mean the further destruction of the people by war and famine, in the belief that your Government was determined to destroy the Ibo, and there was therefore nothing to be gained by the attempt to open negotiations. That phase passed with the unexpected entry of new arms into Biafra and your own problem of extended communications. Now we are told again that the Federal armies are poised for a new advance. If so there are bound to be immense losses on both sides, but especially among the Biafrans, from fighting and from starvation accelerated by the disturbances of warfare. For it would appear that Colonel Ojukwu and his people will struggle to the end.

I wonder if the Nigerian authorities and people can understand the depth of the impact made upon western nations by the television pictures we see of the sufferings of the Biafrans, and especially of the starving and dying children, with their bones almost breaking through their skin and the appeal in their dying eyes. There is no neo-colonialism about the passionate response, the desire to send food to them somehow, anyhow, or about those brave foreigners who are working in Biafra or on the hazardous food planes. It is possible to blame the Biafrans for their refusal to surrender but we have to bear in mind the main motive which explains their obduracy, the belief that they were expelled from Nigeria by hatred and massacre. I know that the full unbiased story of all the tragic events since January 1966 has still to be written. I accept that there have been murders and massacres by both sides. But the largest of the items in this obscure balance sheet is that of the massacres in the north. Now when the Federation is overwhelmingly the stronger side, able to import all the arms it needs, is surely the time for your Government to show the generosity of strength and bring about effective negotiations. I admit that your Government has shown a tolerance of external humanitarian services to your opponents rare in the history of warfare and this emboldens me to ask for still more generosity and restraint.

How could this be shown? It is difficult for a half-informed outsider to answer the question in exact terms. Obviously a cease-fire, and a neutral presence composed in a form acceptable to both sides are necessary elements, accompanied by massive provision of food supplies. Clearly such action is difficult without some agreed basis upon which negotiations could begin. Would it not be possible to offer the Biafrans some interim status as a temporary measure? There would in any case have to be a period during which Biafra was in a special category while the region was restored to normal life and the human and physical damage repaired. During this period the Federal authorities could do much to win over these alienated people by their generous and humane treatment. And the Biafrans could realize the degree to which their future must depend upon fully co-operative relations with the great state of which they are physically and economically a part and in which a large proportion of their own people are living as full citizens.

I realize that this may not be an easy policy to put forward in the Federation. Nigeria has been through a series of crises. The prolonged war has put a strain upon your Government and people and, like all wars, had aroused combative and angry feelings. But on the other side must be reckoned the deep revulsion of all the civilized nations for the horror they see continuing in Biafra, and the harm it does Nigeria's image in the world.

There is another consideration. The world today and in the past is full of examples of the unsatisfactory political results of forcing people by arms into political subjection. The survivors of a Biafra which has been turned largely into a graveyard will never forget their wrongs and will always look back to the tragedy of their enforced suppression. Events such as this not only leave an enduring stain on a nation's history but have injurious practical results. We in Britain have not to look beyond the so-called British Isles to see the long and deep results of the suppression and massacre inflicted upon the southern Irish and even today the embers of that old fire are still glowing in Northern Ireland. Your great federation of peoples, for the future of which I hope and pray, could best win back its rebellious subjects and also gain great honour in the world and for the future by a gesture now of patient and humane reconciliation. All the humane peoples of the world look to you and your Government to show the wisdom of the statesman and the generosity of the strong.

Yours very sincerely

Kenya Revisited

A talk given on the B.B.C. Third Programme 14 August 1969

The version printed here is a little longer than the spoken version as I have re-inserted a few last moment cuts made to fit the talk into its prescribed duration.

I have been visiting Kenya for forty years. I have always found it an exciting country. Physically exciting with its astonishing variety of equatorial scenery. Politically exciting, its history dominated by the long struggle of the white settlers to turn it into another Southern Rhodesia. Their final defeat came only in 1960, and in December 1963, as the President's guest, I saw the new flag of independent Kenya run up amid wild rejoicing.

Since that day Kenya has disappointed many prophets of disaster. It has been a country of prosperity and order, until Mr Mboya's recent murder to which I must refer again. Nairobi greets the visitor with an atmosphere of confidence. It is still a city of flowers: large new buildings are going up; foreigners of many nations in the streets; African men striding with a new confidence; the new, modern African women looking well-dressed and self-reliant. The prosperity – with some qualifications – is genuine. This is not the occasion for reeling off those excellent statistics of which Mr Mboya was a master. Perhaps it is enough to say that the gross national product has risen during the six years of independence from £K306 millions to £K400 millions, and the average growth rate of 6.3 to 6.6 in 1968. Kenya's varied crops – no minerals alas! – have on the whole done well in a difficult world, and an increasing range of industries testifies to the faith of investors.

This has been achieved in spite of the political and economic revolution entailed in the dethronement of the settlers. The end for them came suddenly. Some walked out early, feeling their irreconcilability with an African-ruled Kenya – some broken-hearted at leaving farms that they may have hacked out of virgin bush. The Afrikaners, not surprisingly, were among the first to go. They inspanned their tractors in place of oxen and made the Great Trek in reverse. There was no confiscation, no legally forced sale, but many settlers sold their farms in areas demarcated for sale because they feared to be left in a minority, among the new African farmers.

Perhaps a thousand, more or less, still remain. Many of these mean to stay and have become Kenyan citizens. I visited their farms, admired their plantations of tea – a lovely crop – and viewed their herds of high-grade cattle. They have a great love for Kenya. Some were born there, some are even third generation. They have gardens splendid with flowers and flowering trees, often with staggering views of the Rift valley and with mountains visible a hundred miles away. Add to this cheap and cheerful African labour, often born on the estate, and – most unexpected – friendly new African farmer neighbours. Inside the houses is the furniture they brought from England, the elegant silver and china – some of the urbanity of this life of a vanished England. And yet – and yet – the old wonder how they will face their end in a land increasingly bereft of friends and doctors, and the younger worry about their children's education now that all schools are suddenly open to a new, large, still raw African intake. Meanwhile settlers – even former political leaders – perform many invaluable tasks, especially in matters of agriculture and human culture. Only one of them has got real power in the state: Colonel Bruce Mackenzie, the South African ex-airman, who holds in his strong efficient hands the all-important Ministry of Agriculture.

The more numerous Asians have fared worse. They came in increasing numbers to meet the urgent need for skilled artisans and shopkeepers and, later, many rose into the professional and business class. Few were popular. Socially they lived a life apart, divided even among themselves into religious and social groups. Now the Africans feel that their 9,000 commercial undertakings, mostly small shops, are blocking their way and want to get rid of at least a large number of them – a personal tragedy for the Asians and for us in Britain, too, a problem for these are British citizens.

If British residents decrease, British and other white visitors increase. Tourism indeed is booming. Increasing numbers of Nordics pour in on the cheap all-in tours to fill the excellent hotels, swelter on the radiant beaches, gaze at the panorama of wild life, and enjoy killing the giant fish since killing the giant animals has become too expensive. These exotic pleasures are expected to bring into Kenya £20 millions in the coming year.

So far I have been telling a success story – without referring to the hero, President Kenyatta, the first African to dream, against all the odds, of an independent African-ruled Kenya, the man who, largely upon evidence later proved to be false, was condemned at the outbreak of Mau Mau to seven years of imprisonment, followed by two of detention. After the end of Mau Mau the authorities hesitated to free him. The then Governor refused on the grounds that he was 'the leader to darkness and death'. Yet, when release came at last in 1962, Mr Kenyatta used his immense prestige not only to bridge the rifts between his own tribe, the Kikuyu, and the other tribes which had not joined in the Mau Mau movement, but also between white and black. And he worked closely with the British to bring about a harmonious transfer of power. He made inspiring calls to unity and hard work. He urged his people, if they could not forget, at least to forgive. He is the battle-scarred leader with forty years of struggle to his credit, the true African, who yet knew the West from living for many years in England: the man of letters, author of a famous book exalting his tribe and his race. He is old – Africans still respect age – but vigorous, shrewd and resolute. He is seen as a man who is – almost? – above tribe. Perhaps only he could have led and united the vigorous young leaders who emerged during the later fifties. He lives in the beautiful Nairobi house where I have stayed with a succession of British governors. He never sleeps there – 'too full of colonial ghosts', he says. He goes at night to his beloved Kikuyu farm. He is not in Parliament but is said to keep a hot line tuned in to their debates.

At an estimated seventy-eight, people of all races watch his health with anguished interest. I, too, took stock as we watched the strange spectacle of a football match between his Cabinet ministers and the foreign ambassadors. (The ministers won – 'our man', forgivably, retired hurt!) The President looked fit, moved briskly and I marked the watchful eyes and humorous subtle smile I had seen on the young student in London in the thirties.

But Kenyatta cannot be the only cause of the success – so far – of Kenya's self-government. External stimulations have worked upon the African basis. Many Kenyans have worked – like Mboya's father – on settler estates and farms or in their houses; or have had the dramatic experience of watching – even if resenting – the lively settler politics, following the debates in the Legislative Council, observing the frequent reactions in Britain to Kenya's racial problems, reading the local controversial press, English and African. And profiting for sixty years, as most Africans acknowledge, from the services of good missionaries and from the work of many devoted administrative officers, though Africans are still perhaps in no mood to evaluate this.

Kenya has a Parliament – that's the word they use. It is perhaps the nearest thing to a real parliament in any new African state. (Though Ghana could certainly have won the prize if it had not been wrenched out of its constitutional course by Nkrumah. Such a large impress can the first leaders make on these still plastic states!) Kenya's legislature is a charming, light-hearted, blossom-embowered expression of Westminster, complete with a Tom Tower clock. Its procedure is closely modelled upon that of the House of Commons and a much respected British Speaker has provided both discipline and education with the ardent support of most of the members. Outside its walls the opposition, the Kenya Political Union, under the Luo leader Oginga Odinga, has lately been much harassed by the ruling party, the Kenya African

National Union (K.A.N.U.), though it did manage to win an overwhelming by-election in Odinga's Luo tribal area the other day. Inside Parliament this small opposition criticizes the administration quite freely. But many of the Government back-benchers also sustain a lively attack upon their own ministers. This is reported and discussed in a press which has a large measure of freedom, at least enough to discuss how free it is! This situation contrasts with Kenya's neighbours and, indeed, with most new African states. In the last few weeks the Government back-benchers have actually carried critical motions against their own ministers for voting themselves tax-free gratuities. This is the more healthy since the opposition only numbers about eight and there is news that two of them have just indulged in the common African tendency towards 'carpet crossing'.

The Cabinet contains some very able men – and some very inadequate ones. It is difficult in Africa to have a ministry of all the talents if it has to be a ministry of all the tribes – though here the Kikuyu do predominate. There is much comment both inside and outside Parliament about the so-called ostentation and wealth of the ministers and, indeed, of some of the senior civil servants as well, and especially about their large houses and cars. This is a real and a universal African problem. Senior Africans at home and abroad have to meet foreign representatives on the world's accepted standards of entertainment and social life. They also need good cars to get round their large countries – the popular Mercedes is always singled out for criticism. While the majority of Africans still live in little huts of sticks and mud the contrast is bound to be glaring. And between the two extremes are thousands struggling to escape from the land and primitive poverty – but also the protective family self-help system. They struggle to gain their passport – in Kenya it's the Cambridge School Certificate, which 17,000 took the other day when I was there. Thus armed, they demand jobs which do not exist and housing in the capital which also cannot keep pace with the need. They demand posts held by expatriates whose work may still be quite essential to the economy. A 3 per cent population rise and birth-control only just begun – here is the great problem for Kenya, for Africa and indeed the whole tropical world, and also for the rest of the world which has to deal with its results.

This fierce competition can foster tribal jealousy. No wonder Kenyans speculate anxiously about the presidential succession. The hope must be that the Vice-President, Mr Arap Moi, member of a small pastoral tribe, and known as an honest, moderate man, will succeed.

KENYA REVISITED [1969]

This brings me to Tom Mboya. It is difficult, indeed, to think of Kenya without him. Here indeed is a terrible loss, but not, I believe, of a President, almost certainly not of the immediately next President. It was his strength and his weakness that he was never a tribal man and this both by temperament, and by belonging to a small rather unrepresentative section of the Luo group. He drew his authority first from the trade-union movement and later from a Nairobi constituency. I knew him from Oxford days. We even began to write a book together but he was much too busy to finish it. I saw him again on my recent visit and we talked at length both at his home and in his office. He was not only a great Kenyan but a great African, a man both of his own world and of the international world, calm, resolute, rational, restrained, with a magnificent brain, and not only for the figures that he mastered so well. The Afrikaners and Rhodesians should study such a man and realize what potential ability they are suffocating with their blind, destructive repression.

I am no prophet. I doubt if anyone is very certain what will happen on the death or decline of the President. So the trial of Mboya's murderer – the name given is ominously a Kikuyu one – could be a difficult hurdle. So could the election now promised after being unconstitutionally postponed for two years. Most African Governments dread elections. K.A.N.U. is a composite, not an all-Kikuyu party. But among some forty lesser groups this tribe – estimated at some 2,000,000 – predominates in numbers over the next largest tribe, the Luo. The Kikuyu are, in addition, the best farmers in all Kenya – perhaps in all Africa. Ironically the British Government fostered their agriculture during the Mau Mau as a distraction from rebellion and began the all-important consolidation of scattered holdings. Now the Kikuyu are bursting out of their fertile reserve into the good land of the former European high lands. Among the new settlements I lately visited, the Kikuyu ones stand out – beautiful little mixed farms, good houses, good crops, good cattle. They thrust out into shopkeeping on the heels of the departing Asians, and inevitably provoke jealousy. They have been called the Ibo of Kenya. Their character may be comparable but not their position. For the Ibo are near the border and they wanted to break out of Nigeria. The Kikuyu are right in the middle in and around the capital and they tend to dominate the whole. It is rather the potentially rival tribe, the Luo, who are on the western periphery. The question is – have the Kikuyu learned moderation from their terrible sufferings in the Mau Mau insurrection? If, however, the worst came to the worst – and the worst *can* happen in Africa – the Government has strong weapons so long as these do not split in its hands. The British, from handling Mau Mau, left behind a strong police force. Its General Service Unit – said to be mainly Kikuyu – showed the bite of its teeth outside the Roman Catholic Cathedral at Mboya's funeral. The provincial and district administration, kept directly under the President, has been given ever increasing authority even over the local elected councils. When I visited Provincial and District Commissioners in their offices, the whole setting, the uniforms, the helmets, the air of authority, the courteous self-confidence, took me back to the old British days.

Will Mboya's death provoke tribal reactions? There are some ominous signs. There have been furious parliamentary debates only last week about the bus loads of Africans going to the President's farm. For what? – it is asked – to condole with him over the stones thrown at his car during Mboya's funeral, or for the dreaded Kikuyu oathing which started off Mau Mau? Perhaps it is all to the good that this issue should have been raised in Parliament, and answered by the President.

Kenya has indeed been fortunate in its colonial legacy and especially in the political and agricultural stimulus of the settlers ending in the quick take-over of the country as a going concern with the inspired Malcolm Macdonald to ease the new leaders into the controls. If only tribalism could be leashed the future could be bright.

Yes, it *could* be, in the internal view. But Kenya is not an island. As a member of the East African Economic Community it has built-in advantages which arouse its partners' jealousy. And, in the wider scene, Africans tend to regard Kenya as a too deeply westernized, almost capitalistic state. Eastward President Obote lately announced an intention of moving to the left. Southward, President Nyerere is developing his own interesting brand of socialism but fails to incorporate his Communist off-shore island, Zanzibar. Kenya's northern neighbours, the Sudan and Somalia, are infiltrated with Communist influence, and Christian Ethiopia, with its very large Moslem elements, could be wide open to attack and fissure when the shield drops from the aged Emperor's hands. The Chinese are penetrating eastern Africa as builders of the projected railway line from Dar-es-Salaam to Zambia – the project turned down by Britain and America with, possibly, similar results as over the Aswan Dam. China is pressing on both with economic enterprise and with the training of the guerilla forces gathering against the white south. The Chinese version of Communism could outflank that of

Russia in Africa by being based upon the rural peasantry, and Mao's little red book is circulating widely south of the Kenya frontier. Kenya police pounce upon all who import it or who possess Communist literature and quite heavy sentences are passed on them.

Where will Kenya stand if these developments advance upon what seems their all too possible course? Her leaders, like all Africans, have committed themselves, verbally at least, to the common African front against the southern white laager and this may increasingly turn out to be a commitment to a guerilla partnership with China. Can political forces be kept at different levels inside and outside Kenya's frontiers?

Surely these danger signals are a warning that Kenya's Western friends and business partners, the British above all, should not use their considerable influence to buttress the conservatism of this young state, useful and remunerative though it may seem to be. What is needed in Africa is not the probably vain attempt to stamp out one or other of the main competing ideologies but rather to allow their open dialectic – without that attempted repression of university freedom which I saw in Nairobi. Either course has its dangers. But Kenya should be strong and prosperous enough to risk free debate and so help to bridge the ideological polarization which endangers so much of the world but most of all the politically immature states of Africa.

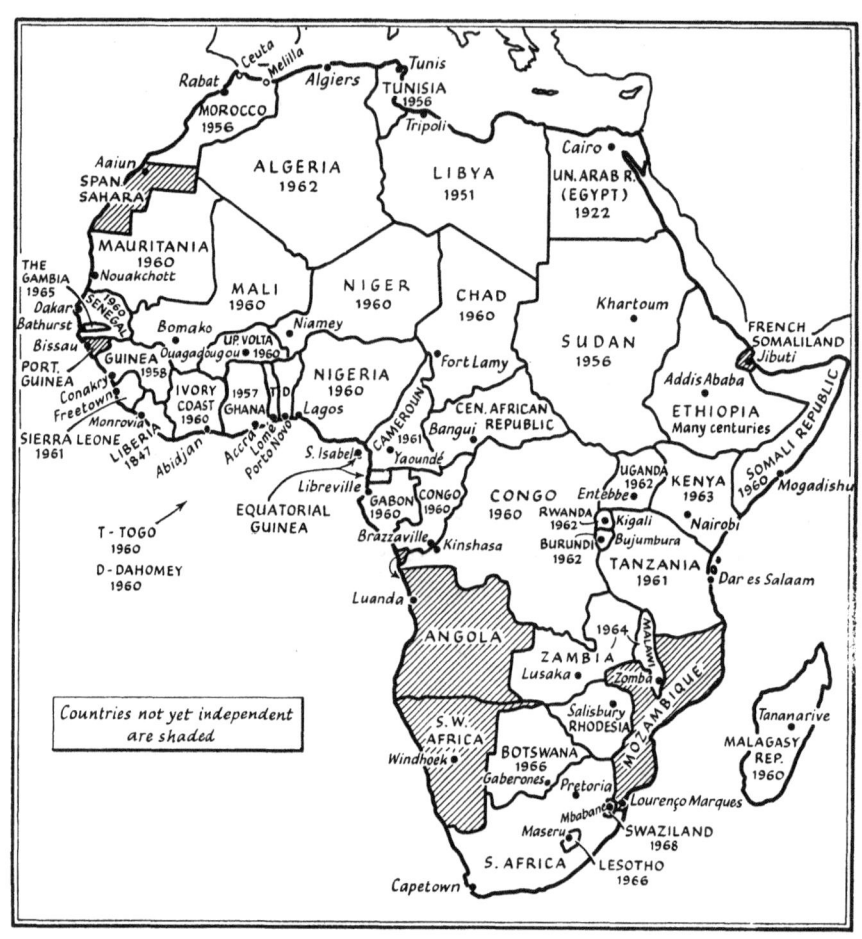

Africa 1969

Index

Abboud, xxvi
Abdel Rahman al Mahdi, Sir, 3, 7
Abdullah Bey Khalil, 10
Aberdares, 109, 111
Abubakar Tafawa Balewa, Sir, 221, 307, 309, 310, 312, 313, 315, 339, 343, 345
Accra, Conferences of 1958, 167, 168, 195, 287
Achebe, Chinua, 349
Achimota, 273
Adams, Dr Walter, 329
Adekunle, Colonel, 342
Aden, 155
Administrative service, *see* Colonial Service
Africa for Africans, An (Cripps), 296
African Affairs Board, 77, 300
African studies: in Britain, 263–79; in United States, 275–6
African Studies Association of the United Kingdom, 263, 264, 278–279
African Survey, An (Hailey), 268–269, 270
African Verses (Cripps), 297
Agriculture: in East Africa, 124–6; in Kenya, 148, 169, 201, 203, 243–5, 357; in Sudan, 6, 41, 91, 123, 192; in Zambia, 335
Ahmadu Bello, Sir, 105, 220, 258, 309, 310, 313, 339, 343, 345
Akintola, 312–13, 339, 343, 345
Algeria, xxvi, xxvii, xxix, xxxi, xxxv, 134, 161, 162, 175, 196, 206, 236, 301, 302, 352
Ali Mirghani, Sayed Sir, 3, 7, 8
All-African Peoples' Conference, *see* Accra

Alport, C. J. M., 81
America, *see* United States of America
Amery, L. C. S., 298
Anglo-Egyptian Condominium (*see also* Sudan), 3, 4, 5, 6, 9, 55, 92, 93, 191
Anglo-Egyptian Treaty of Alliance, xxv, 6–7, 8, 56, 58
Angola, xxviii, 223, 224, 235
Ankrah, General, xxxiv
Apartheid (*see also* South Africa), 14, 44, 144, 150, 171, 207, 260, 321, 323; United Nations' attitude, xxvi, xxx
Arabs: in East Africa, 216, 284, 291; in Kenya, 140, 169, 194, 251; in Nyasaland, 117, 195; in Sudan, 2, 4, 54, 192, 260
Arap Moi, Daniel, 360
Ashanti, 184, 186, 192
Ashby Educational Commission 1960, 221
Asia, 27, 84, 96, 98, 135, 183, 184
Asquith Commission 1945, *see* Higher Education in the Colonies
Aswan Dam, xxvi, xxxii, 362
Attlee, Clement, 8
Aucuparius: Recollections of a Recruiting Officer (Furse,) 229, 230
Australia, 70, 97, 98, 298
Awolowo, Obafemi, xxxi, 103, 104, 106, 131, 219, 312
Azikwe, Dr Nnamdi, 104, 107, 192, 219, 254–5, 312, 313, 353

Baganda, 33, 88–9, 185, 193, 330, 331, 334
Bamangwato, 18, 23

INDEX

Banda, Dr Hastings, xxvii, xxxi, xxxiv, 195, 287, 299, 300

Bandung Conference of Afro-Asian peoples, 115, 154, 167, 191

Barber, Professor, 206

Barotse, 210

Bases, British forces, 179, 296, 306

Basutoland (*see also* High Commission Territories *and* Lesotho), xxiii, xxxiv, 13, 158, 184; population in 1951, 32

Baudouin, King of the Belgians, xxvii

Bechuanaland (*see also* Botswana *and* High Commission Territories), xxxiv, 17–19, 23–6, 144, 306; population in 1951, 32

Beira, 132

Beja, 54

Benson, Mary, 23

Bevan, Aneurin, 139

Bevin, Ernest, 8, 155

Biafra (*see also* Ibo *and* Nigeria): secession, xxi, xxxv, 337, 344, 345, 354–6; Federal civil policy towards, 338, 340–2, 343, 347–8, 350, 354–6

Birley, Dr, 329

'Black Papers', *see* White Papers, 1930

Bledisloe Report, *see* Rhodesia-Nyasaland Royal Commission, 1939

Blue Book, *see* Rhodesian independence

Blundell, Sir Michael, 100, 137, 168, 201, 288

Boers, 294, 295, 317

Botswana, xxxiv

Boyd, Alan Lennox (Lord), xxvi, 102, 159, 168, 169, 246; Lennox Boyd constitution, 102

British South Africa Company, 170, 295, 317

Brockway, Fenner (Lord), 350

Buganda (*see also* Baganda, Kabaka *and* Uganda), xxvi, xxviii, xxxiv, 88–9, 167–8, 176, 331, 334

Burke, Edmund, 189, 257

Burundi, xxix, xxxiv

Cairo, 167, 191, 294

Cambridge University, *see* Universities

Cameroons, xxviii, 144; Southern Cameroons, 103

Canada, 97, 98

Cape Colony, 13, 43, 294, 323

Capricorn Society, 138, 142

Carothers, Dr J. C., 100, 131, 242

Carr-Saunders, Sir Alexander, 273; and his Report, 82, 83

Central African Council, 36, 212, 298, 319

Central African Federation (*see also* Closer Union): attitude of British government, xviii, 42, 158, 159, 171, 172, 195, 207–8, 225, 289, 292, 300–1, 319; attitude of members, xviii, xxv, xxvii, 36–7, 80–2, 88–9, 150–1, 158–60, 170–1, 179–80, 195, 207–10, 211, 223, 225–6, 292, 298, 300, 319, 331; Commissions, xxvii, 180, 196, 211, 300–1; population in 1959, 164; reasons for failure, xviii, xxxii, 69, 78–80, 158, 207–12, 225–6, 289, 298–301

Central African Republic, xxviii, xxxiii

Ceylon, xxv, xxvi, xxvii, xxviii, 97, 98, 220, 272

Chagga, 33

Chamberlain, Joseph, 116, 118

Channon, Professor H. J., 271

Chartered Company, *see* British South Africa Company

Chidzero, Dr Bernard, 206

Chilver, Mrs, 269, 273

China (*see also* Communism), xxv, xxix, xxxii, 27, 95, 118, 322, 332, 335, 336

Christianity (*see also* Missions), 11, 153, 172–9, 224; in Central Africa, 208, 226, 297, 299; in

366

Kenya, 109–10, 147, 204, 235, 255; in Nigeria, 107, 217, 219, 220, 340, 344, 345, 347; in S. Sudan, 9, 11, 76
Churchill, Winston Spencer, xxvi, xxxiii, 2, 11, 42
Civil Service Commission Report 1953, 79
Closer Union of the Dependencies in Eastern and Central Africa; Commission of 1929 (Hilton Young Commission), 298; Rhodesia–Nyasaland Royal Commission of 1939 (Bledisloe Commission), xviii, 42, 298, 319, 323; White Papers of 1930, 298, 319
Cocoa, 103, 192
Coffee, 148, 201, 204, 245, 252
Cohen, Sir Andrew, xvii, 88, 89, 167, 193
Colonial and Commonwealth Secretaries, xxv–xxxv, 168, 223, 298, 315, 327
Colonial Development and Welfare Fund, 214, 269, 273
Colonial Office (*see also* Colonial Policy *and* Colonial Service), 20, 24, 70, 98, 100, 108, 123, 139, 155, 161, 163, 181–2, 228–31, 267, 317, 325; and Central African Federation, xviii, 79, 299, 301, 319; and Creech Jones, 281–2
Colonial Policy, Belgian, xii, xxvii, 38, 175, 210, 288
Colonial Policy, British: on constitutional advance, xiv–xxii, 26–32, 34, 35–7, 39, 93, 136, 158, 167, 171, 176, 189, 211, 272, 285–8; native policy, 18–22, 24–8, 32, 35, 37–8, 68, 78, 80, 93–9, 159–60, 166, 262, 285, 296–8, 318–19, 332
Colonial Policy, French (*see also* Algeria), xii, xx, xxii, xxvi, xxvii, xxviii, xxix, 38, 175, 185, 196, 236, 256, 289–90, 322, 341, 352

Colonial Policy, Portuguese, 38, 206, 223–4
Colonial Policy, Roman, 39, 102, 298
Colonial Research Committee, 269
Colonial Service, British, xv, 71, 96, 121, 227–32, 256, 284–5, 286, 316, 325; in Bechuanaland, 18, 25; in Central Africa, 79, 300; in East Africa, 100, 112–13, 167, 199, 253; in Nigeria, 105, 107, 353; in Sudan, xxiii, 3–5, 40, 45–6, 47–64, 75–6, 84–5, 90–1; courses, 229, 231, 270
Colonial Sequence, 1930–49 (Perham), xii, xviii
Colonial Universities Grants Commission, 274
Colour prejudice, *see* Race Relations
Commissions, *see* Closer Union; (constitutional) Nyasaland Commission of Inquiry 1959 (Devlin), Rhodesia–Nyasaland Advisory Commission 1960 (Monckton) *and* Southworth Commission on Federation 1960; (educational) Ashby Educational Commission 1960 *and* Higher Education in the Colonies 1945 (Asquith) Committee for Peace in Nigeria, 350
Commonwealth, 13, 21, 70, 98–9, 162, 181–2, 307, 326–7; Conference, xxxiii, 98, 299, 310; membership of, xxvi–xxxiv; Relations Office, xxviii, xxxiii, 20, 24, 70, 77, 98
Communism, influence in Africa, xviii, 27, 29, 122, 167, 190, 362–3
Congo, xxvii, xxviii, xxxi, xxxii, xxxv, 216, 223–4, 254, 288, 301, 321
Constitutional Development in Nigeria (Ezera), xvi, 353
Convention People's Party, 286
Copper: in Central Africa, 34, 36, 170, 206, 208, 209, 212, 225, 298, 320, 335; in East Africa, 89

Corfield Report, xxvii
Creech Jones, Arthur, xxv, 279–82
Cripps, Arthur Shearley, 296–7
Culture, in pre-colonial Africa, xiii, 163, 216–17, 256, 283, 284
Cyprus, xxvi, xxvii, xxxi, xxxii, 210

Debré, François, xx, 351–4
De Gasperi, Alcide, 16
De Gaulle, General Charles, xxvii, 162, 196, 341
Democracy, in independent Africa, 254, 256–7, 261
Desecration of my Kingdom (Kabaka), 330, 331
Devlin, Sir Patrick, 300, 320
Devlin Report, *see* Nyasaland Commission of Enquiry 1959
De Vries, Professor Egbert, 173
Dow, Sir Hugh, 123
Dual Mandate in Tropical Africa, The (Lugard), 118, 119, 270
Dutch Reformed Church, 44, 152–3

East Africa (*see also* Closer Union), 163–4, 199, 298; Economic Community, 252–3, 262; High Commission, 36, 163; Institute of Social Research, 124; Royal Commission, 112, 122–8, 138, 140, 248; socialism, 334–5
Education (*see also* Higher Education *and* Universities), 71, 150–4, 188; in Central Africa, 80, 82–3, 195; in Kenya, 135, 140, 168, 252, 358, 360; in Nigeria, 217–18, 221; in Sudan, 5, 57–8, 62, 76, 86, 91, 275; in West Africa, 29, 165–6
Egypt (*see also* Anglo-Egyptian Condominium *and* Treaty): relations with Britain, xxvi, 1–6, 8–9, 10–12, 42, 46, 55–7, 91; relations with Sudan, 58, 73, 75, 84, 92, 191
Elizabeth II, 198
Emirates, 105, 106, 118, 216, 217, 219–20, 310, 352

Enaharo, Chief Anthony, xxxi, 312
Eritrea, xxv, 144
Ethiopia, xxv, xxviii, 156, 362; in Somalia, 16, 154, 155, 213, 214
Exploration, in Africa, 163–5, 263–7, 283–4
Ezera, Dr Kalu, xvi, 353

Fabian Colonial Bureau, 130
Fage, Professor John, 263
Farouk, 55n.
Federation, *see* Central African Federation
Field, Winston, xxx, xxxii, 323
Finance and Economics: British financial policy towards colonies, 108, 140, 147, 199–200, 204; Central Africa, 77, 208–9, 319; East Africa, 122–8, 334–6; Kenya, 147, 203–4, 243–5, 252, 357; Nigeria, 218; South Africa, 77, 306; Uganda, 89; Sanctions policy towards Rhodesia, xxxiv, 292, 305, 306, 328; Colonial Economic Affairs in Oxford, 123, 270
Forde, Professor Cyril Daryll, 268
Foreign Office, British, 9, 20, 40, 41, 45, 91, 155
Four Thousand Days (Welensky), 301
Francis, Carey, 331
Frankel, Professor Sally Herbert, 123, 124, 270
Freedom and After (Mboya), 261
Frontiers, colonial, 183, 185, 252, 285
Fulani, 216, 310, 353
Furse, Major Sir Ralph, 228–9, 230, 270

Gaitskell, Arthur, 123
Gambia, xxxiii
Germany, in tropical Africa, 29, 167, 244, 295, 317, 335
Gezira scheme, 6, 41, 91, 123, 192
Ghana (pre-1957, Gold Coast), xvi, xx, xxvi, xxix, xxx, xxxi,

INDEX

xxxii, xxxiv, 98, 185, 186, 187, 192, 220, 258, 261, 281, 288, 328, 359; constitutional advance, 26, 30, 31–2, 166, 167, 185, 191, 286–7
Gillan, Sir Angus, 51
Gladstone, W. E., 116, 118
Gold Coast, *see* Ghana
Gomani, Chief, 81
Gordon, General Charles George, 2, 66, 266
Gordon College, 5, 11, 58, 62, 275
Gordon-Walker, Patrick, 23, 25, 26
Gowon, General Yakubu, xxi, xxiv, 342, 345–6, 347, 348, 354–6
Graduates' General Congress (*see also* Sudan), 7, 59, 65
Greenwood, Anthony, xxxii–xxxiii
Griffiths, James, xxv
Grigg, Sir Edward, 298
Ground-nut scheme, 124
Guiana (British Guiana), xxv, xxix, xxxi, xxxii, xxxiii

Haggard, Sir H. Rider, 143, 316
Haile Selassie, Emperor, 362
Hailey, Lord, xv, 93, 268–9, 270, 273, 286
Hammarskjöld, Dag, xxviii
Harbison, Professor, 252
Hargeisa, 213
Harlow, Professor Vincent, 181, 223
Hausa, 105, 120, 145, 192, 216, 258, 310, 344–5, 353
Hazlewood, A. D., 209
Henderson, K. D. D., xxiii, 47, 59, 62, 66
Henderson, P. D., 209
Heussler, Professor Robert, 227, 228, 229, 232
High Commission Territories (*see also* Basutoland, Bechuanaland and Swaziland), xxix, xxxiv, 13, 18, 20, 24, 34, 43, 96, 153, 259, 260, 293
Higher Education (*see also* Higher Education in the Colonies, Inter-University Council *and* Universities); Achimota, 273; Central African College, 150–1, Gordon College, 5, 11, 58, 62, 275; Makerere, 63, 135, 150, 272, 274; Royal Technical College, 140, 147, 151; West African colleges, 150, 273, 329
Higher Education in the Colonies, Commission on, 1945 (Asquith), 151, 272–3, 276
Hilton-Young Commission, *see* Closer Union
History of East Africa, 269
Hoare–Laval Pact, 19
Hola detention camp, xxvii, 234, 242, 287
Huddleston, General, 9
Hudson, R. S., 123
Huggins, Sir Godfrey, *see* Lord Malvern
Humanitarians, influence on Colonial policy, 35, 77, 178, 266, 295, 296–7, 318, 319, 325, 331
Hunter, Guy, 252, 277

Ibadan, 103, 104, 107, 310
Ibo: people, 104, 105, 192, 218, 219, 311, 312, 313, 339, 344, 352, 353, 361; assassinations, xxxiii, 309, 312, 313, 314, 315, 339, 343, 345, 346, 350; civil war and its immediate causes, xxxiv, xxxv, 337–56
Imperial British East Africa Company, 117
India, 103, 186, 189, 191, 290, 291, 322
Indian Civil Service, xv, xxiii, 53, 123, 286
Indian Congress, 94
Indirect Rule (*see also* Lugard), xix, 18, 120–1, 127, 186, 290, 297; in Kenya, 112; in Nigeria, 217, 218, 310, 311; in Sudan, 5, 54, 318
Inter-African Labour Conference, 132

INDEX

International Confederation of Free Trade Unions, 132, 167, 168, 195
International Institute of African Languages and Cultures, 268
Inter-University Council for Higher Education Overseas, xii, 82, 150–1, 263, 273–8, 329
Ireland, 93, 210, 235, 305, 322, 356
Ironsi, General, xxxiii, 345, 347
Islam, 156, 183; in Ethiopia, 156, 362; in Kenya, 156; in Nigeria, 216, 218, 219–20, 258, 284, 352; in Somalia, 155; in Sudan, 4, 7, 129, 192, 258
Islamic Review, 156
Italy (*see also* Somalia), 15, 16, 17, 19, 57, 62, 213, 214

Jack, Professor H. A., 123
Jock of the Bushveld (Fitzpatrick), 143

Kabaka of Buganda, xxv, xxvi, xxxiv; autobiography, 330–1; tribal and constitutional positions, xxv, xxvi, xxxi, xxxiv, 88–9, 167–8, 186, 193, 321
Kalahari, 17, 118
Kamba, 235
Kano, 103, 217, 310, 342
Kariba Dam, xxviii, 208
Kariuki, Josiah Mwangi, 233–4, 236–43
Kasavubu, xxxiii
Katanga, xxvii, xxx, 321
Katsina, Hassan, 342
Kaunda, Kenneth, xxxii, 226, 324, 333, 334, 335
Kavirondo plain, 146
Kenya (Leys), 297
Kenya: administration by Britain, xxx, 100, 112–15, 139, 147–8, 199, 235, 239; constitutional advance, xxv, 36, 133, 138–9, 168–9, 203, 239, 248, 288; Emergency 1952–9, xxv, xxvii, xxxii, 100–1, 108–15, 131, 142, 147, 204, 233–43, 252; Land, 108–9, 126–7, 140, 148, 168, 244–5, 357; Land Freedom Army, 245, 248, 250; population in 1951, 32; population in 1959, 124, 164; post-independence, 333, 334, 335, 357, 359–60, 362; relations with neighbours, xvii, 78–9, 140, 206, 252, 260; settlement, xvii, 33, 34, 114, 126–7, 133–7, 140, 163–5, 200–2, 238, 245–6, 250–1, 357–8; tourism, 251, 258; trade unions, 132, 195, 361; tribalism, xxii, 195, 248–9
Kenya African Democratic Union (KADU), xxix, 248–9
Kenya African National Union (KANU), xxix, 248–9
Kenya Political Union, 335, 359
Kenya Question: An African Answer, The (Mboya), 130
Kenya Regiment, 111
Kenyatta, Jomo, xxii, xxv, xxviii, xxxiii, 194, 331, 334, 358–9, 362
Khalifa Abdullahi, 2, 11
Khama, 18, 120
Khama, Seretse, xxxiv, 17, 18, 23, 24, 25
Khama, Tshekedi, 23–4, 25, 120
Khartoum (*see also* Universities), xxxiii, 5, 58, 86
Khatmia, 92
Kiano, Dr Gikonyo, 178, 194
Kidaha Makwaia, Chief, 123–4
Kikuyu (*see also* Kenya), 101, 108–15, 131, 147–8, 194, 204, 233–43, 245, 248, 361–2
King's African Rifles, 111
King, Dr Martin Luther, xxxii, 291
King Solomon's Mines (Haggard), 143, 146
Kisumu, 169
Kitchener, Lord, 2, 3, 266
Kordofan, 52, 54

Labour, migrant, 80, 112, 127, 195, 206, 319

INDEX

Lagos, 217, 218, 309, 310, 341, 347; Conferences, xxv, xxix, xxxiii
Lake Victoria, 33, 125, 146, 202, 247, 330
Lancaster House Conference 1960, 196, 201, 206, 248, 288
Land Apportionment Acts of 1936, 1941, 295, 318
Land Freedom Army, see Kenya
Lari massacre, 235
League of Nations: Charter, 297; Mandates, 118, 267, 297
Lee, Frederick, xxxiii–xxxv
Legislative Councils: Kenya, xxv, 36, 138, 146, 163, 168, 201, 359; Nigeria, 217; S. Rhodesia, 295, 304, 317, 320; Uganda, 163, 168
Legum, Colin, 290
Lesotho, xxxiv
Leys, Colin, 206
Leys, Norman, 297
Libya, 38
Limpopo River, 294, 320, 328
Livingstone, Dr David, 264, 266, 299
Lobengula, 316, 317
Local government, xix, 32, 166, 318; Kenya, Local Government Workers' Union, 132
Longford, Lord, xxxiii
Lothian, Lord, 268–9
Luangwa River, 158
Lugard, Lord: life, 116–21, 145, 200; activities on behalf of the colonies, 178, 268, 271; and indirect rule, 5; in Nigeria, 118, 120–1, 217, 270, 310, 311, 339, 352; in Uganda, 117–18, 145
Lukiko (council in Buganda), 89
Lumpa riots, xxxii
Lumumba, Patrice, xxviii
Luo, 132, 248, 330, 331, 359, 361, 369
Luthuli, Albert, xxviii
Lyttelton, Oliver, xxv–xxvi, 89; Constitution, 146, 149

MacDonald, Sir Malcolm, xxx, 247, 362
MacKenzie, Bruce, 358
MacLeod, Iain, xxvii–xxviii, 206, 222, 223, 288; Constitution, 200, 206
Macmillan, Harold, xxvi, xxvii, 179, 180, 287
Macmillan, Professor W. M., 160
Mad Mullah, 267
Mahdi, the, 2, 3, 11
Mahdia, 92
Mahdism (see also Umma Party), 3, 8, 92
Makerere (see also Universities), 63, 135, 150, 272, 274
Making of the Modern Sudan, The (Henderson), xxiii; Introduction, 47–67
Malan, Dr Daniel François, 13, 31, 156
Malawi (Nyasaland, pre-1964. See also Central African Federation): and Federation, 81–2, 89, 209, 299, 319; and resulting disorders 1959, xxvii, 158, 171, 195, 207, 210, 287, 300, 320; and independence, xxxii, xxxiv
Malaya, xxxi, xxxii, 97, 111, 253
Malinowski, Professor, 268
Malta, xxviii, xxxii, 272, 305
Malvern, Lord, 37, 208, 292, 298–9
Marrian, Peter, 199
Masai, 144, 146, 247, 248
Mashona, 294, 295, 316
Matabele, 170, 294, 295, 316, 317
Mathu, Eliud W., 139
Matopo hills, 317
Maudling, Reginald, xxviii, 180, 327
Mau Mau, see Kenya
Mau Mau Detainee (Kariuki), 233–4, 238–43
Mbanefo, Sir Louis, 349
Mboya, Thomas, Joseph, 130–3, 146, 194–5, 249, 261–2, 361; assassination, xxii, 357, 362
Mekki Effendi Abbas, 59, 62, 65

371

INDEX

Migrant labour, *see* Labour
Minorities, *see* Settlers
Missions: Christian missions in Africa, 266, 323; in Kenya, 109–110, 178, 255, 330; in Nigeria, 352; in Nyasaland and Central Africa, 77, 161, 178, 195, 292, 299; in S. Sudan, 75–6, 260; in Uganda, 178
Mobuto, Joseph Désiré, xxvii, xxxiii
Moda (Sudanese sub-chief), 9
Mogadishu, 212, 213, 214
Mombasa, 169, 200
Monckton Commission, *see* Rhodesia–Nyasaland Advisory Commission 1960
Morocco, xxvi
Morris, Sir Charles, 276
Morris, Rev. Colin, 333
Moslem, *see* Islam
Mount Elgon, 146
Mount Kenya, 108, 109, 111, 147, 149, 201, 247, 248
Mount Kilimanjaro, 144
Mozambique, 224, 305
Multi-racial government, 100, 137, 142, 168
Mussolini, Benito, 16
My Life (Ahmadu Bello), 258, 310

Nahas Pasha, 6
Nairobi (*see also* Universities), 112, 140, 147, 194–5, 248, 357; City Council, 132
Nandi, 146
Napalm, 223
Nasser, Gamal Abdul, xxvi, 190
Natal, 42, 43, 295
National Council of Nigeria and the Cameroons, 104, 219, 221, 312, 313
Nationalism: British government's attitude, 93–6, 115, 171, 177, 178, 180, 199, 280, 'wind of change', 287, 302, 319, 328; in tropical Africa, 137, 162, 176, 179, 182–198, 255, 261–2; in C. Africa, 210, 211; in E. Africa, 207–8; in Kenya, 240, 253; in Nigeria, 218; in S. Africa, 171, 208; in S. Rhodesia, 170, 208; in Sudan, 6–7, 59, 65, 85
Nationalist Party, 31, 162, 170, 207
National Unity Party, 8, 11, 92
Native Policy: in Kenya, 115, 127, 141, 204–5; in S. Africa, xxv, xxvi, xxvii, xxix, xxxi, 13, 14, 20–2, 31, 34, 35, 37, 44, 150–4, 196, 222, 260, 297, 323; in Rhodesia, xviii, xxx, 33, 37, 42, 77, 171, 208, 295, 297, 301, 304, 317, 323, 324
Native Problem in Africa, The (Buell), 270–1
Nazir, 7, 9
Neguib, General Mohammed, xxv, 72, 73
Nehru, Jawaharlal, xxxii, 184
Newbold, Sir Douglas, xxiii, 47–67
New Deal in Central Africa, A (Barber *et al.*), 206
Newlyn, W. T., 270
New Zealand, 42, 70, 97, 98, 295, 298, 318
Ngwato, 18, 23
Nigeria: constitutional advance, xvi, xxi, xxv, xxvi, xxviii, xxxi, 98, 102, 105, 177, 187, 217–18, 312, 353; Federation, 218–19, 220, 312–13, 340–2; federal reorganization, xxxv, 346–8, 350, 354; civil war and its origins, xxxiii–iv, xxxv, 103, 107, 261, 312–14, 334, 336–56
Nigeria, Eastern (*see also* Biafra, Ibo), 104, 216, 218, 311; oil, 219, 340, 347; trade, 211
Nigeria, Northern (*see also* Emirates), 105, 120, 218, 219–20, 284, 310, 311, 352–3; Northern Peoples' Congress, 104, 219, 221, 312; trade, 216, 311
Nigeria, Southern, 106, 166, 353
Nigeria, Western, xxx, xxxi, xxxiii, 103–4, 216–17, 219, 309–10;

Action Group, 103, 104, 106, 219, 220, 312, 313
Nile River (*see also* Gezira), 4, 6, 8, 12, 41, 46, 56, 76, 86, 144
Nkrumah, Dr Kwame, xvi, xx, xxvi, xxx, xxxi, xxxiv, 191, 198, 286–7, 359
North Atlantic Treaty Organization, xxv, 191, 223
Northern Advisory Council, *see* Sudan
Northern Peoples' Congress, *see* Nigeria, Northern
Northern Rhodesia, *see* Zambia
Not Yet Uhuru (Odinga), 330–1
Nuffield College, Oxford, 151, 206, 353
Nyasaland, *see* Malawi
Nyasaland Commission of Inquiry 1959 (Devlin), 195, 211, 287, 300, 320
Nyasaland: The Economics of Federation (Hazlewood *and* Henderson), 209
Nyerere, Julius, 167, 194, 257, 307, 333, 334, 335–6, 362
Nzugwa, Major, 314

Oba, 309
Obote, Milton, xxix, xxxiv, 331, 362
Odinga, Oginga, 249, 330–1, 335, 360
Oil, mineral, 219, 340, 347
Oil Rivers, 347, 351
Ojukwu, Odumegwa Emeka, xxi, 337–8, 339, 342, 343, 344, 345, 354, 355
Oldham, Dr Joseph Houldsworth, 178, 268, 271, 297, 298
Oliver, Professor Roland, 256, 263, 266, 327
Omdurman, 2, 5, 65, 84
On Alien Rule and Self-Government (Plamenatz), 211
Organization for African Unity, xxxi, 350
Osman, John, 315
Oxford University, *see* Universities

Oxford University Colonial Records Project, 325

Palestine, 12, 93, 155, 210, 281
Pan-Africanism, 196, 257–8, 307
Pastoralists: in Kenya, 203, 247–9, 360; in Nigeria, 106; in Somalia, 155, 213, 214, 215, 252
Path to Nigerian Freedom, The (Awolowo), 131
Perham, Margery, bibliography of her works, ii; concerned with colonial studies, xii, 150, 229, 230, 231, 263, 270–4; own links with Kenya, 160, 200, 233, 264, 268, 356–7, 359; with Nigeria, 215, 309; with Somalia, xxiii, 267; with Lugard, 116, 120, 145, 200, 268; with Mboya, 132, 361; with Newbold, 47–8
Plamenatz, John, 211
Pope, the, 224
Port Harcourt, 340, 347
Portugal in tropical Africa (*see also* Colonial Policy), 223–4, 259, 260
Pratt, Professor Cranford, 206
Press, African, attitudes to colonialism: in Sudan, 5, 7, 65, 66, 185; in West Africa, 30, 68, 185, 192
Psychology of Mau Mau, The (Carothers), 100, 131, 242
Public Accounts Committee, 182
Public Records Office, 98

Race relations (*see also* Native policies), 66–72, 99, 165–6, 188–189, 222, 224, 240, 255, 261–2, 284, 289–92, 296–7, 302, 322
Red Cross, in Kenya, 148, 242
Reeves, Bishop Ambrose, xxvii
Renison, Sir Patrick, xxx, 358
Rhodes, Cecil, 57, 170, 172, 208, 209, 266, 294, 295, 296, 316, 317, 320, 321
Rhodesia (pre-1965, Southern Rhodesia; *see also* Central African Federation *and* Native policy): Federation, xxv, xxvii,

Rhodesia—*contd*
80, 159–61, 292, 298–301, 319–320; independence, xxxiii, xxxiv, xxxv, 292–3, 301–8, 315, 323; native policy, xxvii, 161, 304, 323; settler dominance, xxvi, xxix, xxx, xxxii, 161, 170–1, 208–9, 258–9, 294–306, 316–21; population in 1951, 32; population in 1959, 164

Rhodesia–Nyasaland Advisory Commission 1960 (Monckton), 196, 211, 300–1

Rhodesia–Nyasaland Royal Commission 1939 (Bledisloe), xviii, 42, 298, 319, 323

Richards, Dr Audrey, 124, 268, 273

Robertson, Sir James Wilson, 40, 61, 67, 218, 312

Rockefeller Travelling Fellowship, 268

Rome, *see* Colonial Policy

Royal Africa Company, 291

Royal Niger Company, 118, 352

Royal Technical College, 140, 147, 151

Ruanda–Urundi (*see also* Burundi *and* Rwanda), xxviii, 260

Rural Wages Committee, 132

Ruskin College, Oxford, 130, 132, 194

Russia (*see also* Communism), xxvi, xxvii, xxxi, 30, 122, 155, 190, 291, 322, 332, 336, 341

Rwanda, xxix, 291

Sahara, xxvii, 31, 132

Salima, 142

Salisbury (*see also* Universities), 179, 209, 296

Salisbury, Lord, 160, 222, 223

Sanctions, *see* Finance and Economics

Sandys, Duncan, xxix–xxxii, 249, 252, 253, 327

Schweitzer, Dr Albert, 157

Scott, Rev. Michael, 23, 81–2, 156, 157

Seaford, Sir Frederick, 123

Secessionist movements, xx, 339; Biafra, xxi, xxxv, 344, 345; Buganda, xxviii; Katanga, xxvii; N. Rhodesia, 225–6; Nyasaland, xxx; Rhodesia, xxxiii, 82, 294

Self-government, attained in British Africa, xiv–xx, xxv–xxxv

Senghor, Leopold, 256, 290

Serowe, 23, 24

Settlers, 33–5, 69, 161–72, 222–3; in C. Africa, 34, 160–1, 170–1, 208–9, 258–9, 294–302, 316–20, 357–8; in E. Africa, 113–14, 133–7, 201–2, 245–6, 250–2, 357–8

Sforza, Count Carlo, 16

Sharpeville, xxvii

Sidky Pasha, Ismail, 8

Sierra Leone, xxviii, xxxv

Sisal, 245, 252

Slade, Sir Humphrey, xix, 359

Slavery, 38, 119, 296, 318; in E. Africa, 116, 195, 216; W. Africa, 216, 291, 309, 310, 311; abolition, 97, 116, 117, 241, 296, 318

Smith, Ian Douglas, xxxii, xxxiii, xxxiv–xxxv, 292, 294, 296, 301, 302, 303, 304, 305, 306, 314, 315, 317, 318, 323, 327, 328

Smuts, General Jan Christian, 268, 297

Socialism, in East and Central Africa, 332–6, 362

Sokoto, 105, 106, 220, 310

Somalia: external relations, xvii, 149, 155–4, 206, 214–15, 252, 260, 362; unification, xxviii, 15–17, 154–5, 206, 212–15, 239

Somaliland: British and Italian, xxviii, 15–17, 213–14; Ethiopian, 267; French, 214

So Rough A Wind (Blundell), 288

South Africa, Republic of (*see also* Apartheid, *and* Native Policy): native policy, 20–1, 31, 150–4, 162, 259, 260, 323; population

in 1951, 32; relations with African countries, xxxv, 18, 21, 196; relations with Britain, xxviii, 13–14, 19, 34, 42–3, 127, 153, 207; relations with Rhodesia, 37, 170–1, 207, 293, 295, 305, 306; relations with U.N.O., xxx, xxxi, xxxiv
South Nyanza, 132
Southern Rhodesia, *see* Rhodesia
South-West Africa, xxix, xxxiv, 20; population in 1946, 32
Southworth Commission on Federation 1960, 211, 300–1
Stack, Sir Lee, 5, 56
Stephen, Sir James, 325
Strijdom, Hans, 156
Sudan: Anglo-Egyptian agreements, of 1899 (Condominium), 3; 1936, 6; 1946, 8; 1953, 72–3; Defence Force, 91, 128; history, 2–9, 58, 92, 191–2, 284; independent external relations, 57, 86, 362; internal relations, xxi, xxvi, xxxiii, 9, 11, 40, 75–6, 84–5, 93, 129, 260, 291, 328; Northern Advisory Council, 7, 9; progress to independence, xxvi, 5, 7, 9–12, 40–2, 45–67, 72–4, 84–5, 90–2, 192
Sudan Plantations Syndicate, 6, 10
Sudan Question, The (Mekki Abbas), 59
Suez, xxvi, 91, 287
Swahili, 252, 334
Swaziland (*see also* High Commission Territories), 32
Swynnerton Plan, 148
Sykes, Frank, 124

Tanganyika, *see* Tanzania
Tanzania (pre-1961 Tanganyika; *see also* United Nations *and* Zanzibar): constitutional advance, xvii, xxvi, xxix, xxx, xxxii, 158, 163, 166, 167, 193–4, 210; external relations, 140, 306–7, 335, 362; ground-nut scheme, 124; mutiny, xxxii; population in 1951, 32; population in 1959, 164; socialism, 333–4, 335–6
Tanzania African National Union (TANU), 257, 334, 335
Tawney, J. J., 325
Tea, 148, 201, 246, 252, 257
Technical Co-operation, Committee for, in Africa, 132
Times, The, xi, xiii, xviii, 79, 222
Todd, Garfield, xxvi, 323
Toynbee, Professor Arnold, 106
Trade Unions (*see also* International Confederation): in tropical Africa, 257, 334; in Ghana, 286; in Kenya, 132, 195, 361
Transport: in Central Africa, 208, 306, 362; in East Africa, 194, 200, 201; in Sudan, 57
Tribalism (*see also* Indirect Rule *and* Secessionist movements): in Africa, xx–xxi, 27–8, 97, 186–7, 255, 318, 333–4; in East Africa, 124–7; in High Commission Territories, 14, 24; in Kenya, xxii, 115, 140, 248–9; in Nigeria, 102–3, 313–14, 347, 352; in South Africa, 151; in Sudan, 5; in Zambia, 334
Tshombe, Moise, xxx, xxxv
Tunisia, xxvi

Uganda (*see also* Buganda *and* Makerere): constitutional advance, xxix, xxx, xxxi, 88–9, 163, 166, 167–8, 176, 193, 362; disorders, xxxii, xxxiv, 331; external relations, 21, 129, 140; history, 117, 200; population in 1951, 32; population in 1958, 164
Uhuru, 203, 330
Ulster, 78, 356
Umma party (*see also* Mahdism *and* Sudan), 1, 8, 9, 10, 11, 90, 92, 93

United Gold Coast Convention, 286

United Nations Educational, Cultural and Scientific Organization (UNESCO) Conference 1962, 277

United Nations Organization: membership, 190–1; and colonialism, xxix, 12, 20, 30, 38, 44, 95, 153, 167; in Congo, xxvii, xxx–xxxi, xxxii, 260, 321; Somalia, 15–17; South Africa, xxvi, xxix, xxx, xxxiv; Southern Rhodesia, xxx, xxxi, xxxiv, 307; Sudan, 1, 8, 213; Trusteeship, xxxi, 33, 38, 167, 193, 299

United Party, 306, 323

United States of America: as a colony, 44, 210, 257, 294, 298; and colonialism, 30, 38, 69, 167, 190, 191, 307; Central Africa, 335; Egypt, 86; Ethiopia, 154; Somalia, 16, 155; and African studies, 271, 275–6; the Negro in U.S., xxvii, xxxii, xxxiii, 34, 291, 297, 322

Universities: Accra, 273; Ahmadu Bello, 353; Birmingham, 263; Cambridge, xxiii, 229, 270; Ghana, 273; Hong Kong, 118, 272; Ibadan, 107, 273, 310; Khartoum, 58, 86, 91, 272, 275; London, 268, 272, 274; MacGill, 206; Makerere, 63, 135, 150, 272, 274; Nairobi, 140, 363; Oxford, xxiii, 123, 132, 151, 152, 206, 229, 270, 325, 353; Salisbury, xxxiv, 80, 82–3, 150–1, 209, 304, 329; South Africa, 150–4; West Indies, 151, 273; Zambia, 336; academic freedom standards, xix, 82, 151, 231, 272; colonial studies in British universities, 267–8; Colonial University Grants Commission, 274

University Review Commission, 329

Veale, Sir Douglas, 229
Verwoerd, Dr, 306, 315
Vischer, Sir Hans, 268, 271

Wafd, 4, 6
War Council, 101
Welensky, Sir Roy (*see also* Central African Federation), 37, 298–9, 301

West Africa, history and development, 30, 145, 163, 165–6, 189, 202, 313–14

West African Studies Centre 263

West Indies, xxvi, xxix, xxxiv, xxxv, 30, 97, 114, 137, 189, 256; emigration, 291

Whitehead, Sir Edgar, xxvi, xxx, 208, 305, 323

White papers (*see also* Closer Union *and* Commissions), 78, 166, 200, 298

Williams, Ruth, *see* Khama, Seretse
Wilson, Harold, 313; and Rhodesia, xxxiii, xxxiv–xxxv, 292, 302, 305, 315, 318, 320, 324

Winterton, Lord, 44
Workers' Travel Association, 132, 280

World Council of Churches, 21, 172, 179; Conference 1959, 172–9

World War: First, 4, 174, 266, 297, 352; Second, and affect on colonies, xiv–xv, xvi, xviii, 7, 29, 30, 55, 60, 62, 166, 167, 174, 185, 190, 218, 321, 352

Yesterday's Rulers (Heussler), Introduction, 227–32

Yoruba, 103–4, 192, 216–17, 219, 309–10, 312

Zambesi River, 37, 170, 293, 294, 297

Zambia (pre-1964 Northern Rhodesia. *See also* Central African Federation): inclusion in

INDEX

Zambia—*contd*
  Federation, 36–7, 96, 172, 225–6, 319; disorders, xxxii–xxxiii, 225; mines, 34, 36, 212, 225, 298, 335; population in 1951, 32; population in 1959, 164; Rhodesia, 306, 324; Socialism, 333–5

Zanzibar (*see also* Tanzania): constitutional advance, xxix, xxxi, xxxii; external relations, xxxii, 206, 251, 252, 362; revolution, xviii, xx, xxxii, 260, 291

Zimbabwe African Peoples' Party, xxx

Zulu, 31, 43, 61, 184

For Product Safety Concerns and Information please contact our EU
representative GPSR@taylorandfrancis.com
Taylor & Francis Verlag GmbH, Kaufingerstraße 24, 80331 München, Germany

www.ingramcontent.com/pod-product-compliance
Lightning Source LLC
Chambersburg PA
CBHW070749020526
44115CB00032B/1433